BOUNDARIES
AND PASSAGES

THE CIVILIZATION OF

D1145679

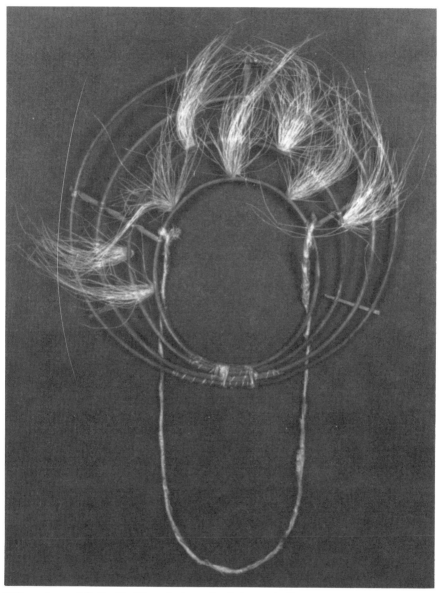

"Woman's mask." In *Yup'ik each hoop is designated* ellanguaq *(pretend universe).*
A. H. Twitchell, 1910; National Museum of the American Indian.

BOUNDARIES
AND PASSAGES

RULE AND RITUAL IN YUP'IK
ESKIMO ORAL TRADITION

BY ANN FIENUP-RIORDAN

UNIVERSITY OF OKLAHOMA PRESS : NORMAN

Other Books by Ann Fienup-Riordan

The Nelson Island Eskimo (Anchorage, 1983)
When Our Bad Season Comes (Anchorage, 1986)
The Yup'ik Eskimos as Described in the Travel Journals and Ethnographic Accounts of John and Edith Kilbuck, 1885–1900 (Kingston, Ont., 1988)
Eskimo Essays: Yup'ik Lives and How We See Them (New Brunswick, N.J., 1990)
The Real People and the Children of Thunder: The Yup'ik Eskimo Encounter with Moravian Missionaries John and Edith Kilbuck (Norman, 1991)

Published with the assistance of the National Endowment for the Humanities, a federal agency which supports the study of such fields as history, philosophy, literature, and language.

Library of Congress Cataloging-in-Publication Data
Fienup-Riordan, Ann.
    Boundaries and passages : rule and ritual in Yup'ik Eskimo oral tradition / by Ann Fienup-Riordan.
        p.   cm. — (The Civilization of the American Indian series ; v. 212)
    Includes bibliographical references (p.   ) and index.
    ISBN 0-8061-2604-3 (hardcover, alk. paper)
    ISBN 0-8061-2646-9 (paperback, alk. paper)
    1. Yupik Eskimos—Legends. 2. Oral tradition—Alaska. 3. Yupik Eskimos—Rites and ceremonies. 4. Yupik Eskimos—Religion and mythology. I. Title. II. Series.
E99.E7F44 1994   93-23220
398.2'089971—dc20   CIP

The paper in this book meets the guidelines for permanence and durability of the Committee on Production Guidelines for Book Longevity of the Council on Library Resources, Inc. ∞

Boundaries and Passages: Rule and Ritual in Yup'ik Eskimo Oral Tradition is Volume 212 in The Civilization of the American Indian Series.

2 3 4 5 6 7 8 9 10

CONTENTS

List of Illustrations   ix
Preface   xiii
Acknowledgments   xvii
Transcription and Translation   xix
Yup'ik Orators   xxiii
1. Metaphors to Live By: The Boy Who Went to Live with the
   Seals and the Girl Who Returned from the Dead   3
2. The Relationship between Humans and Animals   46
3. Clearing the Way: The Entry of Animals into the Human
   World   88
4. Preparing the Path: Becoming a Real Person   143
5. The Reproduction of Life: The Relationship between Men,
   Women, and Animals   159
6. Boundaries and Passages of the Human Body   189
7. Death and the Renewal of Life   211
8. Yup'ik Spatial Orientation: The Ringed Center   251
9. Nakaciuq: The Bladder Festival   266
10. Elriq and Kelek: Living Spirits and the Souls of the Dead   299
11. Kevgiq and Petugtaq: Ambiguity and Renewal   324
12. Following the Universe   355
    References   371
    Index   381

LIST OF ILLUSTRATIONS

"Woman's mask"   *Frontispiece*
Land surrounded by water   *Page* 12
Clouds over Nelson Island   13
Moving through the ice out of Toksook Bay for seal hunting   15
Simeon and Paul John hauling an adult bearded seal onto the ice   16
Frank Woods's family and friends travel out to the tundra   19
Women gutting herring, Toksook Bay, 1981   20
Processing herring on Nelson Island   21
Getting ready for commercial fishing, Toksook Bay, 1981   22
Pulling fishnets during stormy weather   24
Belukha whale alongside boat, 1930s   26
Collecting rye grass in the fall   27
Eskimo angels in a Moravian pageant   31
Collections of a trader about 1900   32
Technology in transition   33
The *qasgiq*, or men's house   36
Sod house   38
Off-loading freight at Toksook Bay, 1981   41
Toksook Bay, spring 1985   43
Paul John dancing at St. Marys Dance Festival, 1987   44
Kuskokwim mask representing the *yua* of a seal   60
Human/fox mask made for a Messenger Feast, Nunivak, 1946   70
Mask representing Amekak *(amikuk)*   81
Hunters at the mouth of the Kuskokwim   89
Cutting blubber from a seal, Tununak, 1933   99
Seal-party distribution, Toksook Bay   100

Seal-party distribution, Chefornak   101
Loading seals, Umkumiut   102
Umkumiut fish camp   109
Storing dried herring in an *issran* (grass basket)   110
Kurt Bell of Hooper Bay modeling a linoleum hunting hat   129
Bentwood hunting hat collected by E. W. Nelson   131
Bering Sea Eskimo visor   132
Qissunaq man wearing bird-skin parka   133
Mask representing a swan that drives white whales to the hunters   135
Vernon John using dance fans with owl-feather "fingers"   136
Men seated on the back bench of the *qasgiq*   148
"Just-married" couple, Bethel, 1930s   170
"Eskimo medicine man"   206
Coastal grave, early 1900s   218
Coastal graveyard, Quinhagak   219
Tununak burial grounds   220
Burial-ground image   221
Another view of Tununak burial grounds   222
Close-up of a burial-ground image   223
Intact grave   224
Kuskokwin grave board and effigy   224
Turn-of-the-century Kuskokwim grave   225
Grave effigy with inset ivory eyes   226
Drawing of a *qasgiq*, after E. W. Nelson (1899)   253
Yup'ik cosmology in cross-section   254
Interior of *qasgiq* at Tununak, still used for dances in the 1970s   256
Kuskokwim mask representing Tomanik, or "Wind Maker"   261
Mask representing *Qaariitaaq* as an androgynous person   274
Wooden mask representing "Walaunuk"   282
Model *qasgiq*, or men's house, with bird and bladder suspended
    from the center   290
Stakes planted at the graveside to call the dead   301
"Eskimo medicine man," Nushagak, 1890s   306
Shaman doll   314–15
Mask representing "Negakfok," the cold-weather spirit   317
Wooden mask representing "Isanuk," the walrus   318
Kuskokwim mask representing young Avanak   319
Masked dancers performing in Qissunaq, 1946   321
Billy Lincoln holding dance wand, St. Marys, 1982   338
Boys dancing at Toksook Bay, 1975   339
Author trying to perform the mouse-food-hunting story dance   341
A comic mask made and worn by Cyril Chanar of Toksook Bay   346
John Milo dressed in woman's *qaspeq*, St. Marys, 1993   349

John Milo and Sebastian Cowboy "getting married,"
St. Marys, 1993   350
"Woman looking into the future" through the *ellanguaq*   357
Martina John, Frances Usugan, and Paul Agimuk dancing
at St. Marys, 1982   363
Young people dancing traditional dances at Stebbins   365
Nelson Island elders and their grandchildren, Toksook Bay, 1977   368–69

MAPS

The Yukon-Kuskokwim Delta region   *Page* 11
Qaluyaaq (Nelson Island), early 1900s   35

PREFACE

This Yup'ik way cannot be told only one way. The aperyarat *[sayings] can only be told in many different ways. . . . If the Yup'ik rules for living were written down, they would be a very big book!*

—*Sam Carter, Quinhagak, May 11, 1989*

THIS BOOK BRINGS together as complete a record of traditional Yup'ik rule and ritual as possible in the late twentieth century. I have tried to highlight recurrent themes, meanings, and metaphors to convey what is unique to the Yup'ik view of the world. The cosmology and ritual cycle of the Yup'ik people are much more sophisticated than most people ever imagined, and I have documented that complexity and creativity the best I know how. Still, I have accomplished only a "partial job." As Marilyn Strathern (1988:xii) reminds us, "Ethnographies are the analytical constructs of scholars; the people they study are not. It is part of the anthropological exercise to acknowledge how much larger is their creativity than any particular analysis can encompass."

Boundaries and Passages addresses the organization of ethnographic detail by the anthropologist and the place of that detail in the lives of the people the anthropologist represents. In "speaking their past" in the 1980s, Yup'ik elders selectively represented themselves for contemporary social and political purposes. They spoke of both their past and their present. Their "oral archive" challenges nonnative listeners to rethink their concept of history as a record of individual action. Though this manuscript is not "event history," it contributes to Yup'ik history by detailing contemporary elders' recollections of the elaborate system of rules that guided the actions of their parents and parents' parents around the turn of the century. They told me repeatedly, "You *kass'at* [white people] always want to know about the things we do, but it is the rules that are important."

My work with Yup'ik Eskimos in western Alaska began in 1974. At first I spent my time watching, and I wrote down what I saw (Fienup-Riordan 1983). I focused on ceremonial exchanges—especially the exuberant seal party, or Uqiquq, and the midwinter exchange dance, or Kevgiruaq—and the cycling of

xiii

names, gifts, and persons that these events elaborated and embraced. I asked many questions and got few direct answers. Although I made a dozen tape recordings, I was more interested in what I could see people doing in the present than listening to what they had to say about their past.

An understanding of some of the most important, most commonly practiced, and most discussed rules for living informed my work. People taught me what every Yup'ik child already knew. Yet the detailed *alerquutet* (prescriptions) and *inerquutet* (prohibitions) surrounding daily interaction with animals, life-cycle changes, and encounters with the spirit world were largely beyond my ken. During the last decade, however, I have learned more about, and increasingly come to recognize the importance of, the complex and elaborate regulations that circumscribed daily life along the Bering Sea coast into the early 1900s and that continue to shape daily life in the communities there today.

The material on which this book is based derives in part from two sources—taped interviews gathered as part of the Nelson Island Oral History Project, and a study of Yup'ik law and governance initiated by the Yupiit Nation. A handful of young men and women living in the village of Toksook Bay on Nelson Island, where I had done fieldwork in 1976–77, began the oral history project in 1985. Their goal was to record, transcribe, and translate the history of their area. The material they gathered included both *qulirat* (legends or tales told by distant ancestors) and *qanemcit* (historical narratives related by known persons).[1] They asked me to help get funding for the project as well as to work with village researchers on recording techniques and problems of translation and transcription. I had the opportunity to listen again and again to dozens of hours of taped interviews. I began the project thinking that I knew something about Yup'ik oral tradition and ended it recognizing the limits of my knowledge.

The second experience involved the Yupiit Nation, a tough-minded contingent of Yup'ik Eskimos who joined together in 1983 to declare their status as a sovereign nation of Yup'ik people. By 1988 nineteen of the fifty-six villages in the Yukon-Kuskokwim Delta had joined this sovereignty movement, including all three of the modern communities located on Nelson Island—Toksook Bay, Tununak, and Nightmute. As part of their efforts to confirm their independent status and their right to self-government, the Yupiit Nation sought to document forms of leadership, law, and governance that characterized Yup'ik society into the early 1900s. In 1988 they received a grant from the Administration of Native Americans to support research on traditional Yup'ik law and governance and thereby provide an alternative to the common assertion that they had no law (Honigmann and Honigmann 1965:241; Jenness 1922:93; Nooter 1976:8). Members of the Yupiit Nation were to do the work. The grant also provided for an anthropologist to guide

1. The Iñupiat of north Alaska make the same distinction between legends (*unipkaat*) and personal narratives (*quliaqtuat*) as do the Siberian Yup'ik Eskimos (Serov 1988:242).

the research and write a final report, and the Yupiit Nation hired me to help document governance from the Yup'ik point of view (Fienup-Riordan 1989). The pages that follow draw upon the knowledge I gained through involvement with both of these projects, supplemented by additional interviews carried out independently with men and women from other coastal Yup'ik communities. The result is not an ethnography describing what I have observed, but a history in which I have used the oral texts as an archive, citing the orators as authors. This act of individuating is a two-edged sword. Though regional variation makes it critical to place the statements of particular elders in time and place, the elders who "authored" these texts would likely eschew such a label. Rather than a creative enterprise, they view their words as the conduit for immortal facts about the way the world is. Through speech they have attempted to repeat and pass on what they have witnessed and apprehended, never claiming to be complete (see also Mather 1986).

I, too, am attempting to repeat what I have heard and do not claim that my knowledge is complete. I offer the apology of Yup'ik orators who fear that their narration has omitted something of importance: "Alas, I am throwing away a lot of bones!" My hope is that I have included enough to enable readers to do with the contents of these pages what Yup'ik elders continue to advise their listeners to do with their words: "What you have just been told, tie it to your ankles, so you will not have to stumble on it in the future" (Eddie Alexie, Togiak, March 10, 1988).[2]

I have quoted the words of Yup'ik elders at length in the following pages. The translations are retained in the text both to convey the quality and variety of Yup'ik oratory as well as to give readers, especially Yup'ik readers, access to the words of individual elders whom they know well.

This book exists only because knowledgeable Yup'ik men and women were willing to talk to me. Although I have organized and commented on their statements, I have tried to let them tell their story in their own words as much as possible. Yup'ik orators expect different listeners to interpret what they have to say differently. They would want readers to have the opportunity to see new meaning in their words, meanings that I have missed or not understood. This can happen only if I let them speak for themselves.

Some limitations adhere to this description of the past based on the remembrances of elders of the 1980s. All the elders cited were born between 1898 and 1930. Along the coast they were the last generation to be raised with these rules and the first to see them put aside—sometimes quite violently—in favor of Catholic and Moravian practices.[3] Orators could re-

2. I have cited quotations from the testimony of individual Yupiit by orator, location, and date. For tapes associated with specific recording projects I have added tape collection (NI for Nelson Island Oral History Project, YN for Yupiit Nation Traditional Governance Project, and BIA for the Bureau of Indian Affairs ANCSA office oral history collection), tape number, and transcript page number.
3. Nelson Island elders gave vivid accounts of the efforts of the Catholic priest Father Paul

call only a fraction of the rules and personal rituals that circumscribed activity in their youth and could provide only limited information on the all-important gift distributions and ceremonial exchanges that formed a vital part of community life before the introduction of Christianity. Nonetheless, this book represents a true picture from the point of view of contemporary Yup'ik elders. Although it may lack some of what an outsider might consider necessary for a "full history," it includes many concepts essential to the Yup'ik view of the world. These accounts represent what contemporary Yup'ik elders remember as most important in the past, and with much finer detail than many scholars and ethnohistorians thought could be within their recall. Most social scientists in the 1960s predicted the imminent demise of rural village life in Alaska. They considered "traditional native culture" already dead. In fact, villages in western Alaska remain vital and growing. Although the ceremonial cycle of the nineteenth century is a thing of the past, both the Yup'ik language, and the unique view of the world that it enables contemporary Yup'ik people to express remain intact.

This book draws on oral texts recorded as part of two locally initiated projects. As such, the elders' recitations simultaneously confirmed the value the orators placed on the oral traditions they recalled and the contradictions they saw between these "rules for right living" and "unregulated" modern life. Moreover, the sharing of information between elderly historians and inquisitive young men and women was by no means an apolitical act. On the contrary, the interviews affirmed the centrality of the elders and the importance of their speaking out in community life. The perception of the present as threatened by disorder from without gave special urgency to their recitation of the rules of the past. Orators did not discourse on all aspects of their past in equal detail but emphasized those parts they perceived as most important for correct action in the present.

Finally, this book is an attempt to organize what I have learned in hope that it will inspire others, both natives and nonnatives, to consider these same issues in other times and places. Although some comparative information is included as elaboration, the focus of the discussion is on the rules for living and the ceremonial cycle of the Yup'ik people living on and adjacent to Nelson Island at the turn of the century. As I know best the people of that part of the Bering Sea coast, I ground my discussion with them. What remains to be done is to record comparable histories for other parts of western Alaska. Although a common value system and ceremonial cycle characterized the Yup'ik people, regions differed dramatically in precisely how people played out these values and ceremonies. To ignore this rich variability would be to deny the creative elaboration within Yup'ik cosmology that it embodies.

Deschout to suppress practices he viewed as "heathen superstition." Although priests had visited Nelson Island from the 1880s, Father Deschout was the first priest to learn the language and live among the people, remaining from 1934 to 1962.

ACKNOWLEDGMENTS

THANKS FIRST AND FOREMOST to the Yup'ik men and women who spoke to me over the years and shared their knowledge with me, especially Billy Lincoln, Brentina Chanar, Paul John, Frances Usugan, Theresa Moses, Mary Worm, Thomas Chikigak, and Herman Neck. I was privileged to listen to them. They often reminded me of the Yup'ik admonition that people must not be stingy with their knowledge. They must give away what they know or it will rot their mind. Although I am not Yup'ik, I feel bound by the same rule.

Along with older orators, I am deeply grateful to David Chanar, Louise Leonard, Marie Meade, and Cathy Moses for their work in recording and translation, their advice, and their encouragement. They always made me feel that what we were doing was important, and that it was essential to get it right. David Chanar especially worked through tape after tape beginning in 1987, and I could never have written this book without his expert knowledge. I am also grateful to both the Yupiit Nation and the Toksook Bay Traditional Council for allowing me the opportunity to work with them on their oral history projects.

Colleagues who gave their time to read and comment on the manuscript include Tiger Burch, Julie Cruikshank, Steve Jacobson, Margaret Lantis, Elsie Mather, Suzi McKinnon, Phyllis Morrow, Irene Reed, David Schneider, and Jim VanStone. Their help was invaluable. As in every book I've ever done, Jim Barker has enlivened my text with a number of fine photographs. The National Museum of the American Indian also provided photographs of Yup'ik ceremonial masks collected by the trader A. H. Twitchell in Bethel in the early 1900s. Additional photographs were provided by the Moravian Seminary and the Yugtarvik Regional Museum (both in Bethel, Alaska); the

Anchorage Museum of History and Art; the Alaska and Polar Regions Department, University of Alaska Fairbanks; the Oregon Province Archives of the Society of Jesus, Gonzaga University, Spokane, Washington; the University of Washington Library, Seattle, Washington; the Thomas Burke Memorial Washington State Museum, Seattle, Washington; the Moravian Archives in Bethlehem, Pennsylvania; the University Museum, Philadelphia, Pennsylvania; the Phoebe Hearst Museum of Anthropology, University of California at Berkeley; and the Smithsonian Institution, Washington, D.C. Karl Johansen (the great-grandson of John and Edith Kilbuck) and Patrick Jankanish generously provided the maps.

Thanks also to the National Endowment for the Humanities for their continued support of my work, and to the Alaska Humanities Forum for supporting the Nelson Island Oral History Project and the Yupiit Nation research on traditional governance. Without Forum support of these projects I would never have become involved in the detailed recording that led to this book. More recently the National Historical Publications and Records Commission of the National Archives has granted the Association of Village Council Presidents funding to pay for the complete transcription and translation of the two-hundred hours of taped material on which this work is based. My hope is that the entire tape collection can be made available to both Yup'ik and non-Yup'ik people in libraries and cultural centers accessible to them. As a step in that direction, the money this book earns will go to the new Yup'ik Cultural Center in Bethel to create cultural resource materials and collections that people can use not only in Bethel but in the surrounding communities.

Last but not least, Judith Brogan's fine editorial skills have contributed to the clarity of this book, and Dawn Scott continues to patiently teach me everything I need to know about computers. John Drayton and the editorial staff at University of Oklahoma Press gave thoughtful attention to the innumerable details of publication. And to my mother and father, Dick, Frances, Jimmy, and Nick—I love you all, and I hope you like this book.

TRANSCRIPTION AND TRANSLATION

THE CENTRAL YUP'IK LANGUAGE, of which there are four dialects (Norton Sound, Hooper Bay/Chevak, Nunivak, and General Central Yup'ik), is spoken by Yup'ik Eskimos living on the Bering Sea coast from Norton Sound to the Alaska Peninsula, as well as along the Yukon, Kuskokwim, and Nushagak rivers. The majority of Yup'ik speakers cited in this book speak General Central Yup'ik, while a handful of orators speak the Hooper Bay/Chevak dialect of Central Yup'ik. All four dialects of the Central Yup'ik language are mutually intelligible, with some phonological and vocabulary differences (Jacobson 1984:28–37; Woodbury 1984a:49–63).

The Central Yup'ik language remained unwritten until the end of the nineteenth century. At that time both missionaries and native converts began to develop a variety of orthographies. The orthography used consistently throughout this book is the standard developed by linguists in the 1970s and detailed in *Yup'ik Eskimo Grammar*, by Irene Reed, Osihito Miyaoka, Steven Jacobson, Pascal Afcan, and Michael Krauss, and *Yup'ik Eskimo Orthography*, by Osihito Miyaoka and Elsie Mather. Miyaoka, Mather, and Marie Meade have also recently completed a summary overview of Yup'ik grammar.

The standard orthography represents Central Yup'ik with a total of twenty-six letters or letter combinations, each corresponding to a distinct sound or sounds: vowels *a, e, i, u;* stop consonants *p, t, c, k, q;* fricative consonants *v, l, s, g, r, vv, ll, ss, gg, rr, y, w, ŭg, ŭr;* nasal consonants *m, n, ng*. Doubly written fricatives are voiceless, whereas single fricatives are voiceless at the beginning or end of a word, next to a stop, or after a doubly written fricative, but otherwise voiced. A nasal is voiceless either after a stop or a doubly written fricative or when written with a bar above the nasal (Miyaoka, Mather, and Meade 1991:6–7). The standard orthography has the advantage that the same Yup'ik sound is never represented by different spellings, and the same spelling is never pronounced in two different ways.

The Yup'ik language, like all Eskimo languages, is a "suffixing language" made up of noun and verb bases to which one or more postbases and a final ending are added to denote such features as number, case, person, and position. For example, the word *Yup'ik* is derived from the noun base *yug-* (person) to which the postbase *-pik* (real or genuine) has been added, literally "a real person." Similarly, the word *yua*, "its/his/her person," is the same noun base *yug-* with the third-person possessive ending.

Yup'ik is complicated by the fact that pronunciation and stress patterns of a Yup'ik word depend on the sounds before and after a given base or postbase. In Yup'ik each base and postbase generally has only one basic sound shape. But when bases and postbases are combined into a word, various sound changes take place at the boundaries, including dropping, adding, and fusing of sounds. Some of the changes are very regular, while others are more specific. One type of suffix may cause a different sound change at a boundary from another type. Both *Yup'ik Eskimo Grammar* and *Yup'ik Eskimo Orthography* give detailed discussions of the rules regulating the pronunciation of Yup'ik words (Miyaoka, Mather, and Meade 1991:12).

Because of its reliance on the process of suffixing in the creation of words, Yup'ik and English often appear as mirror images of each other. For example, the English phrase "my little boat" would be written *angyacuarqa*, literally "boat little my" from *angyaq* boat, plus *-cuar(ar)* small, plus *-qa* first person possessive. The English sentence "I want to make him a big box" would translate "*Yaassiigpaliyugaqa*," from *yaassiik* box, plus *-pak* big, *-li* make, *-yug* want, *-aqa* I-to-him,—literally "Box big make want I-to-him." Translation is thus a continuous process of reordering.

As these examples indicate, Yup'ik words generally show a clear division between bases, postbases, and endings, which are "glued" rather than "fused" together, making them easy to identify. Yup'ik is also generally characterized by a one-to-one correspondence between the meaning and the sound shape of a base or postbase, albeit with regular sound changes. As a result, linguists designate Yup'ik an "agglutinative" language, a term derived from the word "glue" (Miyaoka, Mather, and Meade 1991:13–14).

Several features of the Yup'ik language make for potential problems in the translation of oral accounts. First, relatively free word order characterizes the Yup'ik language. For example, the meaning of the English sentence "The man lost the dog" can only be conveyed by placing the words "man" "lost," and "dog" in this order. But a Yup'ik speaker can arrange the three words *angutem* (man), *tamallrua* (s/he lost it), and *qimugta* (dog) in any of six possible word orders with no significant change in meaning. However, as Miyaoka, Mather, and Meade (1991:15–16) note, it does not follow that word order is totally irrelevant to interpreting Yup'ik sentences. On the contrary, word order may be the sole key to appropriate interpretation where the ending alone would give two different interpretations. For example, the sentence *Arnam atra nallua* (literally "woman name ignorant") can mean either "The woman does not know his name" or "He does not know the woman's name." The same three words in a different word order, however, are less ambiguous. *Arnam nallua atra* is commonly taken to mean "The woman does not know his name." As contrasted with relatively free word order, the relative position of morphemes inside a word is very rigid. Consequently, a word may have internally such syntactic problems as a sentence has in other languages (Miyaoka, Mather, and Meade 1991:16).

Translation is also complicated by the fact that the Yup'ik language does not specify gender in third-person endings. When elders describe rules for a girl's first menstruation, I have translated the pronominal ending as "she," as that is the way an English speaker can best understand the Yup'ik orator's intent. Conversely, pronominal postbases are translated as "he" when men discuss rules for hunting. In general discussions, "s/he" is used.

The Yup'ik language also handles verb tense differently from the English language. Although some postbases place an action clearly in the future and others place action definitely in the past, a verb without one of these time-fixing postbases may refer to an action that is happening either in the past or present (Jacobson 1984:22). This is why many of the accounts of events or customs that are no longer practiced in western Alaska have been translated in the present tense. Where tense is specified, it is translated accordingly, for example, "In the past they ate a little bit of ash before eating the season's first king salmon."

Throughout this discussion, I have also nominalized the terms that refer to ceremonial processes for consistency with previously published sources (Morrow 1984) and to make the discussion easier for English readers to follow. Thus, I refer to the Bladder Festival as Nakaciuq. In the Yup'ik language, however, the noun *nakacuk* (bladder) would appear with a verb ending as in *nakaciuryaraq* (the process or way of doing something with bladders) to designate the ceremonial process. Similarly, speakers commonly refer to the seal party as *uqiquryaraq*, not Uqiquq; the Messenger Feast as *kevgiryaraq*, not Kevgiq, and so on.

I carried out some interviews by myself over the years, but during most I had a native speaker present. This worked well, as my status as an ignorant nonnative allowed us license for numerous odd questions that no self-respecting Yup'ik interviewer would have asked and many that elicited useful responses. Cathy Moses, Ruth Jimmie, and Marie Hopstad were the most enthusiastic participants of the Nelson Island Oral History Project, and we did many interviews together during summer 1985. David Chanar and I carried out dozens of interviews with Nelson Island elders visiting in Anchorage, especially Billy Lincoln and David's mother, Brentina Chanar, between 1986 and 1991.

The translations have also been a collaborative endeavor. Louise Leonard, born and raised in Chevak, worked on all translations appearing in line/verse format. Her translation style is more literal than David's, and the line/verse format is her attempt to reflect on paper the delivery pattern of the oral accounts. Each line break indicates a short pause in the speaker's delivery. Each time a more pronounced pause occurs, a line is skipped (see Woodbury 1984b for a detailed description of this transcription style). Louise's translations are sometimes difficult for speakers of English to follow. At the same time, they provide an accurate representation of the spoken Yup'ik on which they are based.

David Chanar, born and raised on Nelson Island, translated most of the material appearing in paragraph form. David is a confident English speaker with knowledgeable word choice, as in his translation of the Yup'ik word *qengaq* (nose) as "proboscis." David was less interested in reflecting the nuances of the spoken word on paper than in producing a flowing English translation complete with "fifty-dollar words." He preferred translating in paragraph form.

My job working with both translators was to check translations for consistency and accuracy, to research etymologies, and to clarify English sentence constructions. Marie Meade, originally from Nunapitchuk and presently teaching Yup'ik language classes at the University of Alaska Anchorage, reviewed the entire manuscript to double-check translations and clear up unanswered questions.

Finally, readers should note that the last quarter of the book dealing with the nineteenth-century ceremonial cycle could not have been written without the ground-breaking work carried out in the early 1980s by Elsie Mather and Phyllis Morrow. Mather's book, *Cauyarnariuq* (A time for drumming), and Morrow's seminal article, "It Is Time for Drumming," give detailed descriptions of the five major ceremonies: Nakaciuq, Elriq, Kelek, Kevgiq, and Petugtaq. Moreover, Elsie Mather accompanied me to Nelson Island in the spring of 1986 to give a workshop on recording and translating oral accounts. Their comparative research inspired many of the questions that elicited the area-specific account of the Nelson Island ceremonial cycle.

Morrow and Mather are presently in the process of producing a definitive text on Yup'ik ceremonies. The following pages supplement their excellent accounts. I stand on their shoulders in an effort to frame the ceremonial cycle as it occurred in one part of western Alaska—Nelson Island—and to follow through the central theme of this book: the capacity of ritual acts, both public and private, to bound off, and create pathways between, the human and nonhuman worlds.

YUP'IK ORATORS

Name	Residence	Birthdate
Billy Lincoln	Toksook Bay, Nelson Island	1906
Anna Kungurkaq	Toksook Bay, Nelson Island	1908
Albert Therchik	Toksook Bay, Nelson Island	1908
Cyril Chanar	Toksook Bay, Nelson Island	1909
Brentina Chanar	Toksook Bay, Nelson Island	1912
Frances Usugan	Toksook Bay, Nelson Island	1913
Gertrude Therchik	Toksook Bay, Nelson Island	1920
Theresa Moses	Toksook Bay, Nelson Island	1926
Paul John	Toksook Bay, Nelson Island	1929
Tim Agartak	Nightmute, Nelson Island	1903
Clara Agartak	Nightmute, Nelson Island	1915
Magdeline Sunny	Nightmute, Nelson Island	1915
Dennis Panruk	Chefornak	1910
Elsie Tommy	Newtok	1922
Thomas Chikigak	Alakanuk, Yukon Delta	1913
Camille Joseph	Alakanuk, Yukon Delta	1917
Agnes Tony	Alakanuk, Yukon Delta	1930
Sophie Lee	Emmonak, Yukon Delta	1922
Mary Mike	St. Marys, Yukon River	1912
William Tyson	St. Marys and Anchorage	1916
Joe Friday	Chevak	1906
Joe Ayagerak, Sr.	Chevak	1915
David Boyscout	Chevak	1922
Kurt Bell	Hooper Bay	1910
Mary Worm	Kongiganak	1898

Adolph Jimmy	Kongiganak	1904
Billy Black	Kongiganak	1915
Kenneth Igkurak	Kongiganak	1915
Sam Carter	Quinhagak	1915
Joe Beaver	Goodnews Bay	1909
Mary Beaver	Goodnews Bay	1913
Eddie Alexie	Togiak	1910
Evon Albrite	Kasigluk	1908
Herman Neck	Kasigluk	1909
Nastasia Kassel	Kasigluk	1910
Wassilie Berlin	Kasigluk	1916
Matthew Frye	Napakiak, Kuskokwim River	1901
James Lott	Tuluksak, Kuskokwim River	1908
Joshua Phillip	Tuluksak, Kuskokwim River	1909
Mary Napoka	Tuluksak, Kuskokwim River	1916

BOUNDARIES
AND PASSAGES

CHAPTER 1

METAPHORS TO LIVE BY
The Boy Who Went to Live with the Seals and the Girl Who Returned from the Dead

The angalkuq *[shaman], observing the ways of our ancestors, compelled a young person to go with the seals out to sea.*
He was a young person just like you.
He lived with the seals for a whole year. Then at the end of the winter, he finally came back.
He was a young child like you, and he was the only child of his parents.

—Paul John, Toksook Bay

A LONG TIME AGO there was a couple who wanted their only son to become a great hunter. They permitted a powerful shaman to send the boy to live for a year with the seals. At the close of the annual Bladder Festival, the shaman took the boy to the ice hole and let him depart with the seal bladders returning to their home under the sea. There the boy stayed in the seals' *qasgiq* (communal men's house), where an adult bearded seal hosted him and taught him to view the human world from the seals' point of view.

While staying with the seals, the boy would sometimes look up through the skylight, seeing the people from his village as the seals saw them. He observed whether they were acting properly—shoveling doorways, clearing ice holes, and generally "making a way" for the seals to enter the human world. For example, when he heard snow hit the undersea skylight, he knew that hardworking youths were clearing entranceways in the village above. When he looked up at the skylight, he saw the faces of the young men who cleared the ice holes, while those who failed to perform this action were obscured from view.

The boy's parents would sometimes miss him very much during the year of his absence. The shaman would tell them to make *akutaq* (literally, "a mixture") and let the shaman eat. When the parents gave *akutaq* to the shaman, the boy received *akutaq* in the seal world.

In the spring the boy swam through the ocean with his host, viewing human hunters from the seals' perspective. After encountering a number of unworthy hunters, he and his host approached a good hunter, whom they allowed to overpower them. When hit by the hunter's spear, the boy lost consciousness and was taken back to his village. There he remained invisible

3

to his parents until the end of the Bladder Festival, when a young woman found him naked and shivering at the edge of the hole in the ice where the bladders had, once again, been returned to the sea. The boy was crying because his companions, the bladders, would not allow him to follow them. The woman brought the boy to his parents, who rejoiced at his return. When he became a man, he was indeed a great hunter. From his accounts of his experiences, people came to understand how the seals saw humans and how humans must act to please them.

Paul John of Toksook Bay told me this story in 1977. The story is well-known throughout western Alaska, and I have since heard many versions. Billy Lincoln, also from Toksook, told me another well-known tale in 1985, which, along with the story of the boy who went to live with the seals, can best introduce the general themes of this book.

The second story concerns a girl who journeyed to, and subsequently returned from, the land of the dead. She also was a beloved only child, but she died. In the land of the dead she regained consciousness and found that she was traveling down a path off of which smaller trails led to different villages. She eventually arrived at a village where she met her grandmother, and they stayed together.

When they received an invitation to a feast, the "grandmother-related ones"—the girl and her grandmother—traveled together back to their village, where they received gifts through their namesakes. On their return trip, the grandmother realized that she had forgotten a bowl she had been given. She sent the girl back along the way they had come to retrieve it. Before they parted, however, the grandmother advised the girl that if she came upon a fallen tree, even though she could go under it or around it, she should go over it.

The girl went back along the path and did indeed come upon a fallen tree that had not blocked the path before. Following her grandmother's advice, she tried to go over it but tripped. In some versions she intentionally fell on the tree and immediately lost consciousness. When she came to her senses, she found herself in the village beside an elevated food cache. Picking up her grandmother's bowl, she tried to find the path, but it had disappeared. Weeping, she was discovered by a young man who came out of the *qasgiq* to urinate. When he tried to bring her into the *qasgiq*, he could not take hold of her. Finally he was able to grasp her after he rubbed his hands with food scraps, covering and protecting himself as he reached between worlds. But he still could not pull her up into the *qasgiq*. Only after an old man rubbed the girl and the floor with soot from a seal-oil lamp were they able to enter and stand on the *qasgiq* floor.

The people recognized the girl as the one who had died four years before. They found that she was wearing the same number of parkas that her father had given to her namesake during Elriq, the great feast for the dead. Her namesake died soon after the girl's return, but the girl lived to be an old woman. Throughout her life, she told the people about the place she had been, which she referred to as Pamalirugmiut (the place back there obscured from view). She also recalled what they must do to make their dead relatives who dwell in that place more comfortable.

Just as the tale of the boy and the seals goes a long way toward clarifying the relationship between seals and humans in their parallel but closely related worlds, the story of the young woman who returned from the dead provides a vivid image of the relationship between the living and the dead. The stories are complementary accounts and have a structural similarity. Both recall the departure of a young, uninitiated person from the human world, their arrival in another world where a knowledgeable elder of their own sex hosts them and schools them, and their subsequent return. In short, both recount physical journeys along paths between worlds, resulting in special knowledge.

Though the similarities between the two stories are striking, differences are equally revealing. First, all versions of both stories agree on the sex of the person who made the journeys. A boy visits the seals, and a girl returns from the dead. The sex of their hosts supports this dichotomy. Whereas the boy is hosted by an adult male bearded seal, the girl goes to live with her grandmother.[1]

While the boy and girl remain outside the human domain, their relatives continue to feed and care for them. In the case of the boy, his parents send him *akutaq* through the shaman who engineered his departure. The girl receives clothing when her father dresses her namesake in new parkas. Like feeding the shaman, dressing the namesake transfers gifts from one world to another.

The boy's return to the human world resembles the young girl's return to the land of the living. In both cases the children's mentors send them back. When they arrive at their destinations, both lose consciousness. Both are subsequently discovered (the girl by a young man during the night and the boy by a woman at dawn) and brought into the human world—the girl to the *qasgiq* and the boy to his parents' home. In both cases the young people emerge into the human world through a carefully prepared passageway—the boy through an ice hole and the girl through the entrance in the *qasgiq* floor after someone has carefully encircled the hole with soot. When the girl returns from the dead, the young man who finds her must apply food scraps to his body to allow him to make contact with the spirit world and pull her back into the world of the living.

The length of stay in the nonhuman domain differs in the two stories. The boy remains away for an entire harvest cycle, from the close of one Bladder Festival to the end of the next. The girl is gone for four years. In some accounts this period of time corresponds to the years prior to Elriq during which the dead were in a regular host/guest relationship with their living

---

1. In Nelson's (1899:488–90) version, the girl's grandfather brings her to stay with her grandmother, and she travels with both of them to her old village to attend the feast.

relatives. Though people always sent gifts of food and water to the dead, individual dead were particularly honored through gifts given to their name-sakes soon after the death. Thus, although the length of their stays varies, both the boy and the girl are absent for a period corresponding to that in which their mentors—seals in one case and the human dead in another—journey away from and subsequently reenter the human world.

Finally, on their return, both the boy and the girl think often and fondly of the places they have left behind. They also teach their fellow villagers what they have learned about their former hosts. When the boy returns from the seals, he teaches people to make a "removal motion" after they drink from a bowl so that their faces will remain visible and attractive to the seals they seek. The girl likewise instructs people in essential ritual practices, teaching them to explain carefully the origin of their gifts to the dead when they present them during Elriq. If they fail to do so, the spirits of the dead will be reluctant to take them.

Both children advise people of the perpetual "thirst" of the human shades and the seals' *yuit* (literally, "their persons"). From the time of their return onward, people have been careful to greet freshly killed seals, and amply supply their dead relatives, with fresh water.

A parallel exists between the rituals surrounding a human death, as de-scribed in "The Girl Who Returned from the Dead," and the celebration of the rebirth of animals, as described in "The Boy Who Went to Live with the Seals." Just as people once concluded the five-day Bladder Festival by moving the bladders out of the smoke hole and placing them down through the hole in the ice to begin their journey to their underwater home, they also moved the corpse out through the smoke hole and down to the grave to begin its four- or five-step journey to the land of the dead. Just as the seals had been drawn into the human world, hosted, and sent out to be drawn in again the following season, so the name-soul was ritually drawn into the body of the child at birth and sent out again at death to return in succeed-ing generations.

In *The Nelson Island Eskimo*, I described Yup'ik views surrounding the relationship between humans and animals and the relationship between the living and the dead. I emphasized the cyclical nature of this journey—the cycle of departure and return. *Boundaries and Passages* focuses on the journey itself and the ways in which Yup'ik people describe this cycle as move-ment along paths, some of them clear and others obstructed. I remember in March 1985 hearing Catherine McClellan describe the nuances of traveling among Athapaskans, and I naively chalked this up to a marked difference be-tween the people she had come to know and the Yup'ik people of western Alaska. I practically had to be hit on the head with Yup'ik descriptions of "making the way clear" (*tumkegcaarturluki*, from *tuma* footprint, trail, path, plus -*kegte*- to be good), "following the path" *(tumyaraq maligluku)*, and "not thinking of removing the obstacles from the path of his future catch" *(pitarkami tumkaa carrillerkaa umyuarqevkenaku)* before the importance of following and clearing pathways in Yup'ik discourse sunk in.

If I had written this book ten years ago, I would have focused on the structural similarities and inversions that these two tales represent. In fact, true to my training, I would likely have taken the formal analysis a bit further. But over the last decade, anthropology has embraced a closer reading of texts from the natives' point of view, and I have learned more about Yup'ik discourse. Today what I find most remarkable in thinking about these two stories is their common use of metaphors simultaneously depicting paths between worlds (human and animal, the living and the dead) and the obstacles or barriers that sometimes block these passages. Many contemporary anthropologists argue that there is no culture, only discourse with permeable boundaries between groups. Ironically, in Yup'ik discourse the creation and maintenance of boundaries and passages between worlds and between different categories of persons are of central importance.

The first story of the boy and the seals describes the relationship between hunter and prey as a cycle of reciprocity in which seals—the focus of ceremonial activity for the Yup'ik people—visit the human world, where they are hosted and sent back to the sea to return the following season. The Yup'ik Eskimos view this response on the part of the seals as intentional. The seals willingly approach the good hunter in the ritual of the hunt. Clearing a path for the animals to come to you is a constant theme in Yup'ik moral discourse. In Paul John's version of the story, the bearded seal advises the boy as follows:

> When you arrive at your place, you might be lazy to shovel the doorways of others in your village when the weather is bad. Listen to someone up above, one of the men from your home who is taking care of doorways in such weather instead of lounging. And as he hurls the snow off his shovel, you can hear it land on the roof of our house. Listen to him cleaning the pathway so carefully, as he clears the way he will use when he comes to catch one of us in the spring.
>
> "The things that would block him on his journey are landing on our roof." . . .
>
> And sometimes the boy would hear something faintly from way in the distance. Someone was actually shoveling. And when he tossed the snow, the impact would be hardly audible.
>
> The mentor would say, "Now observe this very carefully. You may sometimes shovel aimlessly without thinking about the path of the animal. You can hear someone shoveling up there now who is totally unaware of removing the obstacles from the path of the animal. And the snow from his shovel is landing in the path of those that will come to him."

Ideally, a young man focused all his efforts on "making their way clear," both by keeping the thought of the animals foremost in his mind as well as by physically working to clear water holes, entranceways, and windows, allowing the animals both a clear view and a clear path into the human world. Paul John concludes his version of the story as follows:

They say that the person who had stayed with the seals down in the ocean used to speak in the *qasgiq*. When he became an elder, he spoke to others and talked about the doorways, ice holes, and the floors of the houses. He would urge the young boys to take care of these places. He would say that when they kept these places clean, they were clearing the way between them and the animals.

This is where the story usually ends.

The pathway metaphor is also explicit in descriptions of the shade's journey to and from the land of the dead. In the past when a person died, relatives carried the body out through the skylight instead of the doorway used by living persons. After burial the relatives would circle the grave and return to the house, following the same way they had come and cutting across their path with a knife or scattering ashes behind them to prevent the dead from following them. Numerous prohibitions applied so as not to cut or block the path to the land of the dead. It was especially important to avoid cutting, sewing, or making loud noises for the first four or five days following a death, corresponding to the four or five steps separating the land of the living and the land of the dead.

A variation of the story of the girl who returns from the dead describes how a child comes back to comfort her parents. She, too, must travel a fixed route past logs, creeks, hills, and over an obscure trail. Before her departure from the land of the dead, she had been warned never to reveal the path she had taken there. She disobeys these orders and, as a consequence, is not permitted to return to the world of the living (Anderson 1940:106).

At Elriq, the great feast for the dead, people planted wooden stakes at the grave site to invite the dead to journey into the human world, where they feasted and hosted them as honored guests. In the story of the girl who returns from the dead, she follows such a path to her parents' village but finds it blocked when, after the feast, she tries to return.

In E. W. Nelson's (1899:489) version of the story, the girl finds a river blocking her path to the place of the dead. This river was made up of the tears of people who weep on earth for the dead. As the girl watches, a mass of straw and refuse floats down the stream and stops in front of her, enabling her to cross. This is the refuse she had dutifully cleaned from houses and doorways while she was living. Just as young men removed obstacles from the path of the animals by shoveling snow, young women created a walkway for themselves by clearing the refuse from floors and doorways.

At the close of Nelson's account, the girl remains among the living. Her grandfather pushes her while they are leaving the feast, causing her to fall and lose her senses in the underground passageway of the *qasgiq*. She waits in the passageway for her companion shades, but they do not come. Eventually she is discovered by an old man who sees her floating with her feet above the floor.

In Billy Lincoln's version, she is pulled into the human world on her arrival among the living by arms protected with animal scraps and through an entranceway encircled with soot. Without these coverings, she would not have been able to pass between worlds. The food scraps and soot acted simultaneously as boundary-maintaining devices and protective coverings, allowing people to reach between worlds. All eight versions I know of the story describe the girl's path as blocked at some point during her journey. But what blocks the path is never the same.

In my previous work on Eskimo cosmology, I focused on action observed— the countless exchanges of gifts and services that continue to shape life in western Alaska. More recently I have been overwhelmed by the eloquence of the ideal "rules for living"—the *alerquutet* (prescriptions) and *inerquutet* (prohibitions)—that forged the shifting and permeable boundaries between the human, animal, and spirit worlds and the ritual acts that created the pathways between them.

In their rules for living, Yup'ik people paid particular attention to the senses of human and nonhuman persons, both the living and the dead. They believed all persons possessed thought; the senses of sight, smell, hearing, taste, and touch; and hunger and thirst. Passages could be opened between persons by appealing to these shared senses. The hunter, in the guise of a bird, invoked the power of breath when he breathed out air to overcome the seal. The healer provided a passage for disease to "walk out" of the body by rubbing it with dirt or through a laying on of hands. Shamans with super-natural sight followed the path to Pamalirugmiut to bring back spirits of the dead or dying. Boys prepared a path for the seals by shoveling snow and clearing passages while keeping thoughts of the seals foremost in their minds.

Just as human action might open passages and extend the boundaries between worlds, the thoughtless use of one's senses blocked passages and created unwelcome obstacles—breathing a woman's air, sleeping late, exiting the house carelessly, drinking sloppily, eating wastefully, squandering one's vision, making inappropriate noise. Conversely, the proper boundaries be-tween persons were held in place by restricting one's breath, sight, thought, speech, and bodily movement—avoiding contact with women's air, going belted and hooded, covering the body with paint, oil, or food scraps, lower-ing one's eyes, cutting across one's trail with ashes or a knife.

Numerous private ritual acts worked to keep persons separate while other actions pulled them together. The major ceremonial sequences involved a complex combination of these acts to draw animal spirits and the shades of the human dead along the path into the human world while maintaining the differences between the two.

Again and again, Yup'ik orators select one piece of their past—the meta-phor "clearing the path"—to explain their view of the world as well as to communicate what they hope listeners will incorporate into their own lives. This image of Yup'ik activity, both physical and mental, is an indigenous articulation. Rules form "boundaries" and ceremonies create "passages" among many people. In western Alaska, however, "clearing the path," "making a way," "creating a barrier," and "cutting off one's future catch" are not only implicit in the ritual process, they are the explicit metaphors people use to describe their view of the world.

THE PEOPLE OF WESTERN ALASKA

Yup'ik orators speak of "clearing the path" and "making a way for the seals," and these actions always occur in a particular setting. Who are the Yup'ik Eskimos and what part of the Arctic do they call home? To be able to talk about the creation of boundaries and passages between human and nonhuman worlds, we must begin with their manifestation in a particular time and place.

The name Yup'ik (plural Yupiit) is the self-designation of the Eskimos of western Alaska and is derived from their word for person *(yuk)* plus the postbase *-pik,* meaning "real" or "genuine."[2] Like the Inuit to the north, they consider themselves "real people," in contrast to unspecified and presumably less real outsiders. They are indeed members of the larger family of Eskimo cultures, extending from Prince William Sound on the Pacific coast of Alaska to Bering Strait, and from there six thousand miles north and east along Canada's Arctic coast and into Labrador and Greenland. Within that family, however, they are members of the Yup'ik-speaking, not Inuit/Iñupiaq-speaking, branch.

Archaeologists tell us that the Yup'ik Eskimos of western Alaska and the Inuit of northern Alaska and Canada had a common origin in eastern Siberia and Asia. They date the original peopling of the New World from Asia by men and women moving across the two-hundred-mile-wide Bering Land Bridge, exposed during periods of glaciation somewhere between twenty-thousand and eight-thousand years ago (Dumond 1977:154–59). The ancestors of modern Yup'ik Eskimos were originally shore dwellers, settling primarily on the coastal headlands of western Alaska as many as three-thousand years ago (Shaw 1982:59–73). By A.D. 1400 population pressure combined with the search for a more reliable food supply to produce migrations up the drainages of the coastal rivers of western Alaska (Oswalt 1973:125). By the late nineteenth century, Yup'ik territory extended upriver to the vicinity of Paimiut on the Yukon River and Crow Village on the Kuskokwim River, at which point they came into contact with Athapaskan Indians, with whom they had largely amicable relations.

The coastal landscape into which the ancestors of today's Yup'ik Eskimos first moved is nothing like the glacial fjords of their Greenland relatives or the rocky coastline of the Canadian Arctic. Rather, it consists of a broad, marshy plain, the product of thousands of years of silting action by the

2. All Yup'ik definitions and etymologies given in the text derive from the *Yup'ik Eskimo Dictionary,* compiled by Steven Jacobson and published by the Alaska Native Language Center in 1984.

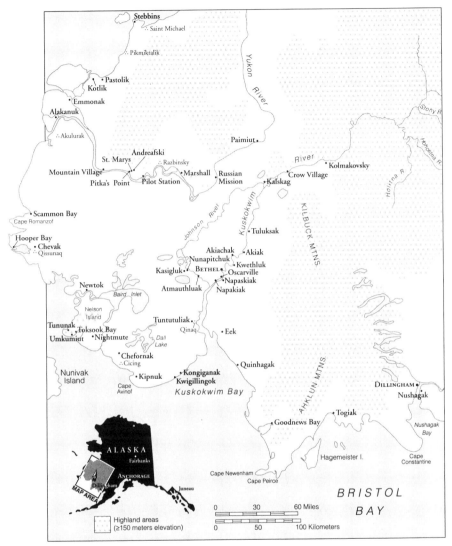

The Yukon-Kuskokwim Delta region.

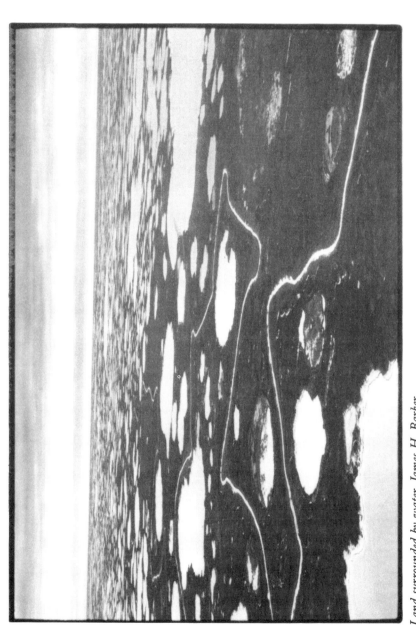

Land surrounded by water. James H. Barker.

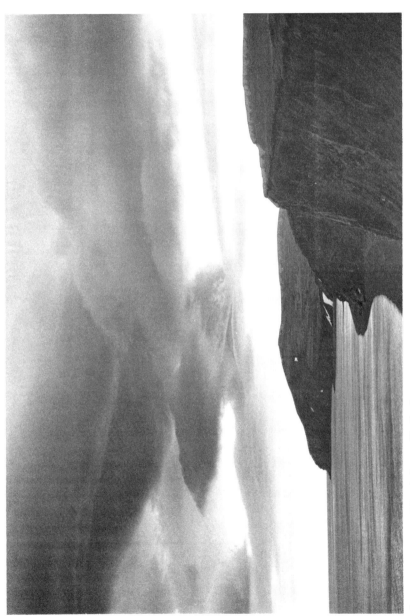

Clouds over Nelson Island. James H. Barker.

Yukon and Kuskokwim rivers. Innumerable sloughs and streams crisscross this seemingly endless alluvial prairie, covering close to half the surface of the land with water and creating the traditional highways of its native population. Low volcanic domes on Nelson and Nunivak islands, and outcroppings of metamorphic rock in the vicinity of Cape Romanzof, provide the only relief. Along the coastline the sea is shallow and the land is flat.

Frequent storms gather force as they race uninhibited across the delta landscape. Although not as frigid as the interior, wind chill can drive temperatures to the equivalent of -80°F in winter. At the other extreme, a sunny, windless day in July can reach temperatures of +80°F. The abundance of surface water gives the impression of a moist environment, but the climate is actually very dry. Precipitation averages no more than twenty inches a year, including fifty inches of snow. Unlike their Iñupiat neighbors to the north, the Yup'ik Eskimos live far enough south to avoid the sunless winter months characteristic of the Arctic coast. Even during the darkest months of the year, the sun rises above the horizon for at least five hours a day.

THE BOUNTY OF LAND AND SEA

Early Euro-American visitors to western Alaska were quick to remark on the austerity and desolation of this broad lowland plain, calling it a wasteland at the world's end. In fact, the natural environment supports abundant plant and animal life. No wonder the relationship between humans and animals became the focus of cultural elaboration in a land where the rapid appearance and disappearance of a variety of living things characterizes nature's cycles.

The subarctic tundra environment nourishes a rich array of vegetation, including numerous edible greens and berries harvested by the local people. Shrubs and trees, including willow and alder, crowd the shores of streambanks. River drainages sustain a mixture of spruce and birch from above Bethel on the Kuskokwim and Pilot Station on the Yukon. Breakup releases an ample drift of logs downriver every spring. Though living beyond the reach of the dense forests of the interior, the Yup'ik Eskimos were well supplied with wood, which they used to build their homes, boats, tools, and elaborate ceremonial accoutrements.

The western Alaska coast supports an equally rich fauna. An impressive variety of animals and fish appears and disappears as part of an annual cycle on which the Yup'ik people focus both thought and deed. The annual entry and exit of animals into the human world inspired elaborate regulation. Far from viewing their environment as the insentient provider of resources available for the taking, Yup'ik Eskimos continue to this day to view it as responsive to their own careful action and attention.

Winter begins to give way by the end of February. In the lengthening light, hunters emerge bent on replenishing the stores of food their families depleted during winter. As leads begin to open in the nearshore ice, men hunt seals in earnest. Adult bearded seals *(Erignathus barbatus)* appear first,

Moving through the ice out of Toksook Bay for seal hunting. James H. Barker.

Simeon and Paul John hauling an adult bearded seal onto the ice. James H. Barker.

followed by the yearlings and two-year-olds. The availability of these seven-hundred-fifty-pound sea mammals is fraught with uncertainty. Seals congregate near floating ice floes, and strong north winds that blow the ice away as it breaks off from the shore pack mean poor hunting. An onshore wind that pushes the ice landward closes the leads and prevents pursuit. Men hunt in the crack between winter and summer, when the ice has given them room to approach but still lines the shores as protection from a treacherous open sea. Coastal hunters continued to use skin-covered kayaks into the 1940s and 1950s, but today wooden and aluminum skiffs and outboard motors have replaced them.

Daylight stretches to a full twelve hours by April. Rock ptarmigan *(Lagopus muticus)* begin to flock in the willow and alder, increasingly visible as the melting snow leaves their white-plumed bodies showing against the brown tundra. On fine days women and children adjourn to the shoreline, where they hook through the ice for tomcod *(Eleginus gracilis)* and sculpin *(Cottus species)*. The reflection of the spring sun off the snow turns their faces and hands a dark brown as they wait for the fish to come with the tides. As the snow melts, children range the nearby tundra in search of last year's berries. Young men and boys go farther afield, hunting for Arctic fox *(Alopex lagopus)*, snowshoe hare *(Lepus americanus)*, and Arctic hare *(Lepus othus)*. They may also harvest an occasional musk ox from the herd introduced onto Nelson Island from Nunivak Island in 1963 and gradually spreading up and down the coast.

The Yup'ik name for April is Tengmiirvik, translating literally as "bird place" (from *tengmiaq* bird, fowl, duck, plus +*vik* place for). Millions of birds annually make the long journey north to nest and breed in the ample coastal wetlands of western Alaska. These include Canada geese *(Branta canadensis)*, emperor geese *(Philacte canagica)*, white-fronted geese *(Anser albifrons)*, and black brant *(Branta nigricans)*. Sandhill cranes *(Grus canadensis)*, whistling swans *(Olor columbianus)*, and numerous varieties of ducks and seabirds, including pintails *(Anas acuta)*, old-squaws *(Clangula hyemalis)*, and king eiders *(Somateria spectabilis)* also abound. Traditionally taken by blunt-headed arrows or spears within earshot of the hunters' homes, the noise of technology has forced men to range far afield to fill their game bags. Over the last decade the decline in geese populations has resulted in stringent state and federal regulation of both hunting and egg gathering. Debate continues today about these restrictions in the coastal communities of western Alaska, where the arrival of the geese means the first fresh food in many months and a source of nourishment difficult to resist.

The inexorable melting continues all through May, and the shore ice begins to dissipate. Men continue to hunt seals in open water. The smaller ringed, or hair, seals *(Phoca hispida)*, spotted, or harbor, seals *(Phoca vitulina)*, and ribbon seals *(Phoca fasciata)* follow the bearded seals on their way north. Hunters also occasionally take sea lions *(Eumetopia jubatus)*, walrus

(Odobenus rosmarus),[3] and belukha whales *(Delphinapterus leucas).* Off the coast of western Alaska, men hunted seals from kayaks rather than harpooning them at their breathing holes, as in the Canadian Arctic. Today they work from wooden boats in pairs and trios. Fathers may take the opportunity of a long season to give their sons an opportunity to make a catch rather than add to their own take. Although hunting techniques have improved, the quantity of each species a family can process and use in a year still limits the harvest.

The ringed seals and spotted seals are small, and women bring them into the house and butcher them on the kitchen floor. The men do an equally precise butchering job of the larger bearded seals out on the ice to facilitate transport back to the village. The real work begins in mid-May, when women adjourn to their storehouses to cut and prepare for drying the thousands of pounds of meat that have accumulated between the beginning of hunting and the time when the days are warm enough to defrost the stock of frozen carcasses. They will also cut the seals' blubber and store it in plastic or skin containers in a cool place, where it gradually renders into the ubiquitous oil that accompanies every meal.

As men continue to harvest from the sea, women venture into the space between villages, territory dominated by male activity during the winter. There they pursue a varied quarry, supplementing the meat-rich diet of spring with the greens of marsh marigold *(Caltha palustris)* and wild celery *(Angelica lucida)* and the roots and shoots of wild parsnips *(Ligusticum huttenis).* In the past, women gathered willow leaves *(Salix glauca)* and pond greens such as sourdock *(Rumex artica)* in great quantities and stored them in seal oil for winter use. They continue to gather them today but in smaller amounts. Through the 1970s both men and women collected eggs from the thousands of nearby nests made by gulls, cranes, geese, and ducks. Although egg gathering is largely a thing of the past, coastal residents continue to harvest fresh clams and mussels from the tidal flats along with last year's berries from the adjacent tundra.

The fishing season begins in earnest by early June, and modern coastal communities bustle with twenty-four-hour activity. The first arrivals are herring *(Clupea pallasii),* which residents harvest in abundance and dry for winter use. A man's mother, unmarried sisters, and wife all work together to process his catch. The same configuration of women uses the same herring pits and drying racks year after year, in some cases at sites used for decades. Like bird hunting, the herring fishery has undergone dramatic changes over the last ten years. In the 1970s villagers, especially on Nelson Island, vehe-

3. In the past, walrus were not relied upon because they were not dependable from year to year and were dangerous to pursue, as these huge animals travel in aggressive herds. Materially they were important, but culturally they were not. Today, when during a good year one day's walrus hunting could supply one-third of the protein produced through the toilsome herring season, the hunt is abandoned to ready fishing nets (Fienup-Riordan 1983:88).

Frank Woods's family and friends travel out to the tundra. James H. Barker.

Women gutting herring, Toksook Bay, 1981. James H. Barker.

Processing herring on Nelson Island. James H. Barker.

Getting ready for commercial fishing, Toksook Bay, 1981. James H. Barker.

mently fought against a commercial herring fishery, but the early 1980s saw the opening of such a fishery. Although not without its problems, especially the unwelcome competition from nonnative fisherman, local commercial activity has neither interfered with nor diminished the subsistence herring harvest. In fact, the thirty-foot boats fishermen built or bought to help them in their commercial harvest have facilitated fishing for local use. Just as villagers began to adjust to the new commercial fishery, however, low returns due to by-catch harvest of herring offshore forced commercial closures in 1989 and 1990, threatening the stocks that islanders rely on for their subsistence harvest.

Herring breed along the coast and do not enter the Yukon and Kuskokwim rivers. Instead, the riverine summer harvest focuses on the regular succession of five major species of salmon, including king, or chinook, salmon *(Oncorhynchus tshawytscha);* red, or sockeye, salmon *(Oncorhynchus nerka);* coho, or silver, salmon *(Oncorhynchus kisutch);* pink, or humpback, salmon *(Onchorhynchus gorbuscha);* and chum, or dog, salmon *(Oncorhynchus keta).* From June through August, millions of these fish struggle up the major waterways to spawn. As they begin their ascent, thousands are taken in gill nets, dried, smoked, and stored away as food for the winter for both people and dogs.

Herring and salmon are only two of the many fish species taken by the Yup'ik Eskimos of the Bering Sea coast, and all through the summer boats come and go with the tides. Fishermen harvest halibut *(Hippoglossus stenolepis)* and flounder *(Platichthys stellatus)* with long lines and four-pronged jigging hooks. As the summer comes to a close, men also use dip nets, spears, and traps to harvest an impressive variety of freshwater fish, including sheefish *(stenodus leuichthys),* northern pike *(Esox lucius),* Dolly Varden, or salmon, trout *(Salvelinus malma),* burbot *(Lota lota),* and blackfish *(Dallia pectoralis).* Various species of whitefish *(Coregonus species)* also abound in the tundra lakes to the east of Nelson Island.

Coastal villagers organized goose drives in late July until fifteen years ago. Men and boys worked together to round up the molting females and goslings on Nelson Island, and the event elicited both tremendous camaraderie and quantities of fresh food.[4]

4. When describing this exclusively male get-together, men talk of "gathering" the geese. Conversely, women talk about "hunting" eggs, berries, and greens. The English glosses *hunting* and *gathering* that differentiate and oppose these activities are misleading. In Yup'ik, the postbase +*ssur* means obtaining anything from nature as food or for some other purpose (for example, *pissurluni,* literally "getting it," including both *nayirrsurluni* "getting seal" and *ikiituggsurluni* "getting wild celery"). When the men talk of gathering the geese, the meaning of gathering is "to cause to converge." They would say *quyurtellrunauraput* "we rounded them up, caused them to converge" using *quyurte-* "to make (plural object) come together." The Yup'ik language thus differentiates "round up" from the general case of "getting from nature," whereas English emphasizes the difference between getting unmoving objects in nature (gathering) and catching and killing moving animate things (hunting) (Fienup-Riordan 1983:121–22; Anthony Woodbury, personal communication).

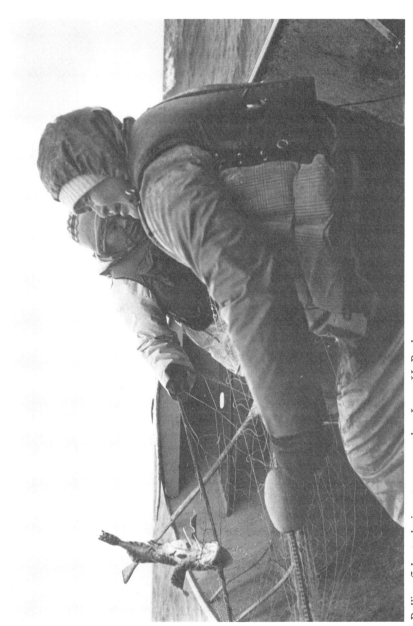

Pulling fishnets during stormy weather. James H. Barker.

Fishing slows by the first of August as the berries begin to ripen, and families disperse over the soggy tundra to harvest salmonberries *(Rubus chamaemorus)*, crowberries *(Empretum nigrum)*, and blueberries *(Vaccinium uliginosum)*. People enjoy the fresh fruit mixed with sugar and condensed milk. Later in the season, women whip the stored berries together with Crisco and sugar to make the festive *akutaq*, or "Eskimo ice cream," which remains to this day a requisite to hospitality during winter entertaining and intervillage visiting.

Their daily diet is more rich and varied at the end of summer than at any other time of the year. It includes fresh greens and berries, shellfish and ducks, smoked salmon strips, and the newly dried herring dipped in freshly rendered seal oil. Villagers continue to gather tundra plants into September, including mushrooms and medicinal herbs, such as *caiggluk* (wormwood, *Artemisia tilesii*).

The wind blows mostly from the east during early autumn, and the coastal waters are often cold and rough. Temperatures regularly drop below 35°F at night. The seals return to the river mouths, and men hunt them in open water. Men formerly used nets for fall sealing, as the seals, with their depleted stores of fat, tend to sink. Today the weapon of choice is the .22 rifle and, at the mouths of the Yukon and Kuskokwim rivers where the water is less salty, the harpoon. Seals are not nearly as numerous as in the spring, and people do not relocate for hunting. Both ringed and spotted seals outnumber the larger bearded seals, and hunters pursue them into December if the winter is mild. Schools of belukha whales again enter the river mouths and are sometimes beached, butchered, and shared throughout the village. Hunters may take as many as ten belukha in a single day and see no more for several years.

Men stay busy before freeze-up checking nets and traps on day trips away from the village or leaving in pairs on overnight hunting ventures. Some Nelson Islanders follow a circuitous inland river route up the coast to the Yukon River to hunt for moose and bear. The freezer has replaced the underground cache, so it is no longer necessary to bury the fall catch for storage and protection against the rainy autumn weather. Women tend to the last of their annual harvesting activities. On clear days they search the tundra for caches of "mouse food"—the stock of small roots and underground stems of sedges and cotton grass gathered for winter use by unsuspecting tundra lemmings. Women boil these sweet, dark tubers and serve them either in soup or mixed into an *akutaq*. They also gather rye grass blade by blade and dry it to use for weaving baskets during the long winter. This gathering used to be a major fall task, as winter boot insoles and household mats required a huge supply. Though much less important now, the gathering of grass remains part of the fall routine.

Men travel out to nearby sloughs and streams during September to set wooden or wire traps for the small but tenacious blackfish as well as the more substantial burbot. These cone-shaped, spirally bound traps are set with

Belukha whale alongside boat, 1930s. Oregon Province Archives, Gonzaga University.

their mouths upstream and rely on underwater barriers to channel the fish. The same fishermen set them in the same channels year after year. If checked regularly once or twice a week, these traps can provide hundreds of pounds of fresh fish through the fall and early winter. Blackfish are remarkable in their ability to hold on to life even when confined in a trap for weeks at a time along with hundreds of their two-inch relatives. Many oral accounts of starvation end with the protagonist's salvation upon miraculously harvesting one of these small but durable creatures.

Fall is also a time for bird hunting, today less so than in years past due to declining bird populations and increasing state and federal restrictions. From mid-August through mid-September, geese, cranes, and swans begin their journey south after their summer nesting season. By mid-October the ducks are gone as well, and the berry-fattened ptarmigan remain the only fresh fowl available for the table. Except for processing the daily catch of fish and fowl, the major gathering and butchering tasks end with the frost in early October, and women retire into their houses for the winter. Men continue daily hunting and fishing trips away from the village.

November brings freeze-up. Tomcods continue to run upstream, and men fish for them through the ice with barbless hooks. Fishermen also net thousands of sticklebacks *(Pungitius pungitius)* through the ice with large *qalutet* (dip nets). In the not-too-distant past, men gathered these tiny "needlefish" in tremendous quantities for dog food, as the rivers flowing into the Bering Sea support them in abundance. This activity gives its name to the people of

Collecting rye grass in the fall. Moravian Seminary, Bethel, Alaska.

Nelson Island, who continue to identify themselves as Qaluyaarmiut, people of the dip net.

As the rivers freeze and the first snows cover the ground, men leave the village on a daily basis to set and check traps for mink *(Mustela vision)*, muskrat *(Ondata zibethica)*, and beaver *(Castor canadensis)*. Later in the winter, they may set trap lines for Arctic fox *(Apopex lagopus)* and red fox *(Vulpes vulpes)* within snow-machine distance from the villages and check them every four to five days. Alternatively, a man may set metal spring traps near his fishtrap and check it irregularly. Not every man traps. For those who do, the pelts provide a modest supplement to their income as well as the raw material for parkas for family members.

December temperatures can fall to -20°F, too severe to allow much ocean hunting. No birds fly, and the ice is too thick for tending fishtraps and nets. Only an occasional gust from the south mitigates the cold north winds of January and February. This is the season of indoor work, when villagers mend nets, repair motors, tan skins, and sew new fancy parkas. On clear, calm days, young men and boys pack water, pump stove oil, and shovel the snow that has blown into porchways and covered up windows.

Fresh food is scarce through February, and in the past famine was an all-too-common antecedent to spring renewal. Though tomcod, needlefish, and blackfish remain available, a rainy summer season during which few fish are put by, combined with prolonged cold weather the following winter, still can produce real hardship. Cash-poor households in coastal communities set a sparer table in March than in May.

Freeze-up in western Alaska corresponds to a marked social thaw. While blizzards gather force across the tundra, men tighten walrus-stomach or plastic coverings over the circular wooden frames of large hand-held drums. Women and children join them in the community hall, bringing their dance fans out of storage. Community leaders may also make plans to invite neighboring villages for an intervillage dance. Such celebrations traditionally required months, even years, to prepare the food and gifts. Even now residents strip food caches and store shelves bare to insure their guests' satisfaction. Women whip berries and fat together into *akutaq* and boil fresh-caught seal meat and store-bought turkeys into rich soups. Families give away what they have gathered during the previous seasons, and by the close of the winter they are ready to begin the process all over again.

CHANGES FROM WITHOUT

From the beginning the Yup'ik Eskimos of western Alaska built on their rich resource base. They developed a complex and internally differentiated cultural tradition prior to the arrival of the first Euro-Americans in the early 1800s. Sometimes referred to as the "cradle of Eskimo civilization," the Bering Sea coast traditionally supported and continues to display a cultural diversity and vitality unsurpassed in the Eskimo world. As many as fifteen-thousand people may have lived on the Yukon-Kuskokwim Delta in the early 1800s, divided into at least twelve socially and territorially distinct regional populations, of which the Qaluyaarmiut were but one. Each of these groups was internally divided into a number of territorially centered village groups, ranging in size from fifty to two-hundred-fifty persons and joined together by ties of blood and marriage.

The abundance of fish and game available in western Alaska allowed for a more settled life than that enjoyed by Eskimo peoples in other parts of the Arctic. Like the northern Inuit, the coastal Yupiit were nomadic; yet their rich environment allowed them to remain within a relatively fixed range. Each regional group demarcated a largely self-sufficient area within which people moved freely throughout the year in their quest for food. Under good conditions, there was no need for travel between the regional groups, as each had access to a complete range of resources. Dramatic fluctuations in animal populations and variable ice and weather conditions, however, often made interregional travel and trade expedient. A number of social strategies facilitated this movement, including the regular exchange of food, spouses, names, and feasts.

Interregional relations were not always amicable, and, prior to the arrival of the Russians in the early 1800s, bow-and-arrow warfare regularly characterized delta life. Ironically, death itself brought this killing to an end in the form of a dramatic population decline resulting from the diseases that accompanied contact with Euro-Americans. Although few Russians settled in western Alaska, the larger Russian trade network, to the northern end of which the Yupiit were attached, subsequently introduced smallpox into the region, devastating the native population. Entire villages disappeared. As much as 60 percent of the Yup'ik population with whom the Russians were familiar in Bristol Bay and along the Kuskokwim were dead by June 1838 (Oswalt 1990:51).

The effects of the smallpox epidemic of 1838–39, combined with subsequent epidemics of influenza in 1852–53 and 1861, produced not only a decline but also a dispersal and shift in the population. It undercut interregional social distinctions and left undefined the boundaries over which the bow-and-arrow wars of the seventeenth and eighteenth centuries had been fought. Although the introduction of communicable diseases damaged traditional social groups and patterns of intergroup relations, it largely left intact the routines and rhythms of daily life throughout the remainder of the nineteenth century. Small bands of bilaterally related extended family groups continued to move over the landscape, seeking the animals they needed to support life, as well as to gather in winter villages for an elaborate annual ceremonial round.

Significant Euro-American settlement did not occur in western Alaska until the end of the nineteenth century. Though rich in the resources necessary to support a scattered and seasonally nomadic native population, the Bering Sea coast is notoriously lacking in significant amounts of any of the commercially valuable resources that first attracted nonnative argonauts and entrepreneurs to other parts of Alaska. The shallow coastline is blessed with neither the sea otters that first drew Russians to the Aleutians nor the bowhead migrations that later brought American whalers into Arctic waters farther north. Prospectors never discovered gold or mineral deposits comparable to those found in either northern Alaska or the upper Yukon drainage. Although furbearers were present, the scattered human, as well as animal, populations undercut the ability of nonnatives to exploit them.

Outsiders virtually ignored the Yukon-Kuskokwim Delta during the first three-quarters of the nineteenth century, as a result of its geographic isolation and lack of commercial resources. Russian traders and Orthodox priests migrated inland along the delta's major rivers from the 1840s, but the people living along the Bering Sea coast between the mouths of the Yukon and Kuskokwim rivers did not experience extended contact until nearly one hundred years later.

The first nonnatives to come to western Alaska were the Russian traders and explorers who sought to extend the purview of the Russian American Company north from the Aleutians. According to oral tradition, the shaman Issiisaayuq, who lived at the mouth of the Kuskokwim River, foretold the coming of these Kass'alugpiit (literally "original white people"). Issiisaayuq saw a vision of a freight ship approaching, and an identical vessel arrived the following year. The shaman told his people not to trade with the newcomers, warning them that when the ship departed, the goods would likewise vanish. The people did not listen and suffered the consequences (Fienup-Riordan 1990:50–51). Just as the appearance and disappearance of game was a central focus in the relationship between humans and animals, the power to predict and control the appearance and disappearance of Western goods was the original focus of accounts concerning the relationship between Yup'ik and Euro-American peoples.

The appearance of Russian traders had relatively little impact on the population of the Bering Sea coast. Neither dramatic innovation nor a substantial increase in the nonnative population accompanied the establishment of trading stations at St. Michael in 1833 and at Kolmakovsky Redoubt on the middle Kuskokwim in 1841. The traders were mostly Yup'ik-speaking creoles (people of mixed Alaska native and Russian ancestry), not white Russians, who settled down with local women. Although the traders made available a variety of utilitarian goods, the Yupiit were more interested in luxury items such as beads and tobacco. The scarcity of imports also meant that Russian traders often dealt entirely in local goods. The Russians ultimately failed to get local people to increase substantially their harvest of furbearers such as fox and beaver and were unsuccessful in fostering a system of paternalistic dependence.

The arrival of missionaries dramatically altered life along the Bering Sea coast. First came the Russian Orthodox priests working out of Ikogmiut

Eskimo angels in a Moravian pageant. F. Drebert; Moravian Archives, Bethlehem, Pennsylvania.

(Russian Mission) on the Yukon River from 1845. Orthodox hegemony was challenged in 1885 by the establishment of a Moravian mission at Bethel on the Kuskokwim River and three years later by the founding of a Catholic mission on Nelson Island, which moved to Akulurak at the mouth of the Yukon a year later. These two missions made a much more sustained bid to convert the "baptized heathen" to whom the Russian Orthodox laid claim. Moreover, both made concerted efforts to alter the Yup'ik way of life, especially along the Yukon and Kuskokwim rivers in the vicinity of their mission stations.

The year 1900 constitutes a major marker of change in the Yukon-Kuskokwim delta region. The influenza epidemic that arrived in western Alaska with the annual supply vessels would, over the next three months, cut the native population in half. Although the coastal communities were not as severely affected, numerous winter villages on the Yukon and Kuskokwim rivers were abandoned.

A sharp increase in the region's white population matched the decline of the native population. The gold rush at Nome had spawned a concerted effort to locate mineral deposits along the upper Yukon and middle Kuskokwim rivers. Stern-wheelers relocated from Nome by the beginning of the twentieth century to transport and supply the growing number of prospectors working along the two rivers. Although mining camps typically sprang

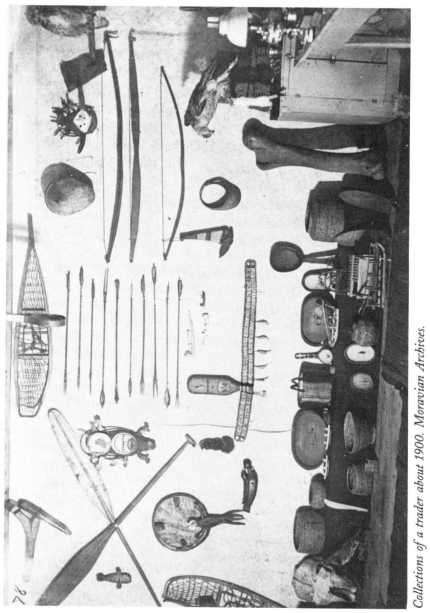

Collections of a trader about 1900. Moravian Archives.

Technology in transition. Oregon Province Archives, Gonzaga University.

up at the headwaters of streams away from major centers of native population, their presence along the rivers increased availability of trade goods and
helped establish a local cash economy.

The Yup'ik people supplied fish and cordwood to miners and steamship
captains and participated in an expanding fur market. This activity brought
substantial changes to their domestic economy. In 1916 the regional superin-
tendent for the U.S. Bureau of Education, John Henry Kilbuck, wrote with
satisfaction that most Kuskokwim natives lived in log cabins heated with
cast-iron stoves, ate homegrown turnips and potatoes from graniteware
dishes, possessed at least some Western clothing, which they mended on
treadle machines, and received education, health care, and Christian teachings from federal employees and missionaries. Although cognizant of the
changes nearby along the rivers, coastal residents continued to live in extended family groups in semisubterranean sod houses, focusing their energy
on following the seasonal migrations of the sea mammals, waterfowl, and
fish on which they relied.

Much had changed in western Alaska by statehood in 1959, but much
remained the same. Even along the Kuskokwim, where contact between
natives and nonnatives had been the most intense, the continuities between
past and present were as significant as the innovations. Missionaries, traders,
and teachers had introduced a variety of technological, social, religious, and

political innovations by the 1920s. Nevertheless, the people continued to speak the Central Yup'ik language, enjoy a rich oral tradition, participate in large and exuberant ritual distributions, and focus their lives on extended family relations that were bound to the harvesting of fish and wildlife. They never converted to gardening or reindeer herding, regardless of sustained missionary and federal encouragement to do so. The coastal population had declined dramatically and was physically weakened by introduced diseases, but its geographical isolation and commercial insignificance had inhibited change. Their seasonal cycle of activities remained much the same as that of their ancestors'.

TURN-OF-THE-CENTURY COASTAL VILLAGE LIFE

The riverine Yup'ik Eskimos became objects of missionary efforts and commercial interests from the 1880s. The Yup'ik people of the Bering Sea coast, however, were left largely to their own devices into the early decades of the twentieth century. When the orators cited in this book were born, their parents still followed the seasonal round of their forebears. People lived scattered across and around Nelson Island in dozens of seasonal camps and winter villages. Travel remained primarily by skin boat, including both the single-man kayak and the larger wood-framed, skin-covered *angyaq*.

The bilateral extended family, numbering up to thirty persons, was the basic social unit. Consisting of from two to four generations, including parents, offspring, and parents' parents, the group might also include married siblings of parents or their children. An overlapping network of consanguineous and affinal ties, both fictive and real, joined the extended families making up a single community. Members of a residential group usually were related to one another in several different ways within four or five degrees of consanguinity. In larger villages most marriage partners came from within the group, though regional recruitment also occurred.

Extended family groups lived together most of the year, but normally they did not live in family compounds. Rather, winter villages were divided residentially between a communal men's house or houses and smaller sod houses. Married couples or groups of hunters often moved to outlying camps for fishing and trapping during spring and fall. Family groups would gather when temperatures dropped below freezing and, in some cases, during the spring seal-hunting and summer fishing seasons. Winter villages ranged in size from a single extended family to as many as three-hundred people. In these larger settlements there might be as many as three men's houses with up to fifty men and boys living in each.

The *qasgiq* (men's house) was the social and ceremonial center of village life in which all men and boys older than five years ate their meals and slept. In winter men rose between three and four in the morning to begin their day's work and be home by sundown. Men spent their spare time together in the *qasgiq* talking and carving tools, weapons, bowls, kayaks, and elaborate ceremonial equipment. Their daughters and wives brought their meals, wait-

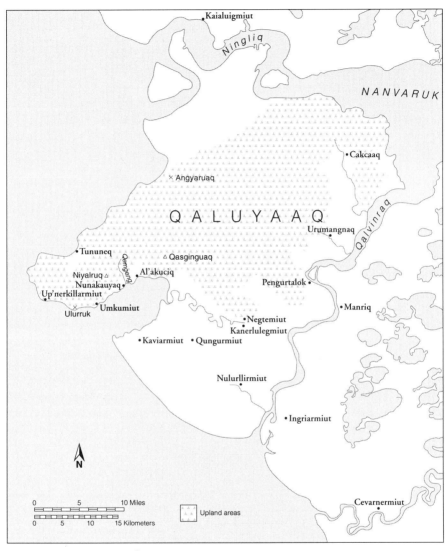

Qaluyaaq *(Nelson Island), early 1900s.*

The qasgiq, *or men's house. Moravian Archives.*

ing demurely by their sides while each man emptied his own personal bowl. The *qasgiq* was also the scene of the ubiquitous sweat bath, when occupants opened the central smoke hole and fed the fire to an intense degree. After enduring this heat, the men rubbed their bodies with urine aged in wooden buckets. The ammonia worked to cut the grease and, combined with a rinse of fresh water, effectively cleansed the bathers.

Every man's place in the *qasgiq* reflected his social position, and the men's house framed a number of internal distinctions, including that between young and old, married and unmarried, and host and guest. The social structure of the *qasgiq* also mirrored that of the natural world. The coastal Yupiit believed that sea mammals lived in huge underwater *qasgit* (plural), where they ranged themselves around a central fire pit in ranked fashion, comparable to that displayed by their human counterparts. From these underwater homes they could view their treatment by people and, based on what they observed, could choose, or refuse, to give themselves to human hunters.

The hunters who gave the most thought and care toward the animals they sought were richly rewarded, both socially and materially. The *nukalpiaq*, or good provider, was a man of considerable importance in village life. Not only did he contribute wood for the communal sweat bath and oil to keep the lamps lit, he also figured prominently in midwinter ceremonial distributions.

The position of the *nukalpiaq* was not, however, comparable to that of the *umialik*, or whaling captain, of northern Alaska, who had the power to collect the surplus and much of the basic production of individual family members and later redistribute it. Instead, the less centralized system in western Alaska had every local extended family vying with the others in their ability to gather and redistribute surplus during both informal and ritual redistribution.

Social status and power accrued to those who could afford to give. Without the existence of a central authority figure, political integration was loose, at best. Although the prowess and generosity of the *nukalpiaq* was a primary focus of both political and economic integration, the counsel and valued knowledge of elders, who not only advised when to harvest but when distribution was appropriate, mitigated his authority. Dispute settlement within the group was also informal, operating chiefly through ostracism and indirect confrontation of the offender through gossip and avoidance.

As youths contemporary elders had listened to their fathers and grandfathers discuss the hunt and discourse on the rules for right living in the *qasgiq*. The tradition of oral recitation continues, but their generation was the last to be raised within the *qasgiq*. Young men received an essential part of their education as they listened to and observed the older men at work. Elders encouraged them to try their hand at carving and fixing tools. They also admonished young men and women alike to perform helpful acts, while keeping their minds filled with thoughts of the animals on whose goodwill their lives depended. People believed that thoughtful actions cleared a path for the animals they would someday hunt.

Women and girls lived and worked in a distinct but parallel social setting. Each men's house was surrounded by a number of smaller *enet* (sod houses), in which resided four to a dozen women and children. The sod houses were frequently cold and damp, as cooking was done in the entryway and sweat bathing was reserved for the men's house. Given the small size of the structures and the many people often present, body heat as well as the heat generated by seal-oil lamps warmed the interior of the dwellings. Some sod houses also had central fireplaces instead of entryway cooking places, which provided an additional source of heat.

Families sometimes lived together in seasonal camps in multiroomed dwellings. Passageways connected a large central compartment to smaller sleeping and storage chambers. Although both men and women lived within a single structure, their work space remained separate. Ivan Petroff (Porter 1893:111–12) described a settlement on Nunivak Island, which consisted of a central room surrounded by domestic apartments connected to it by subterranean passageways: "The Nuniwagmiuts occupy large subterranean communal dwellings, consisting of a number of square or circular cavities opening upon a common hall or corridor but with a single entrance from the surface of the ground. Each family compartment has its separate smoke hole,

Sod house. Moravian Archives.

but these are rarely used, as the object of crowding together is warmth through exclusion of all outside air."

Recent archaeological survey work on Nelson Island and the lower Bering Sea coast indicates that this "honeycomb" pattern may have extended beyond Nunivak in the nineteenth century. Nelson Islanders also described three- and four-room dwellings commonly used at seasonal camps into the 1940s in which each extended family occupied its own apartment. Residents considered each "room" a separate house and the common area a "mutual porch." Only at small camping places would a man and his wife stay in one house.

YUP'IK ESKIMOS ENTER THE MODERN WORLD

Coastal village life has changed considerably since the turn of the century. The influenza epidemic of 1900 and pandemic of 1918–19, not to mention subsequent bouts of smallpox, measles, and tuberculosis, compounded the population decline produced by the epidemics of the early nineteenth century. Yet during the last seventy years the population has grown to surpass its aboriginal number. Today, nearly 20,000 Yup'ik Eskimos reside in western Alaska, scattered among seventy small communities of from 150 to 600 inhabitants. Each of these modern villages has both an elementary and a secondary school, city government or traditional council, clinic, church or churches, airstrip, electricity, and running water and flush toilets in a few places. The residential separation of men and women has been abandoned in favor of single-family dwellings, and children divide their time between public school, video movies, and playing basketball games in the new high-school gymnasiums rather than listening to their elders tell stories in the *qasgiq*.

These changes are relatively recent, dating from the early 1900s along the Yukon and Kuskokwim rivers and the 1930s in the more isolated coastal communities, including Nunivak and Nelson islands. Until sixty years ago the majority of the coastal population lived much as they had a hundred years before, in sod houses located at scattered seasonal camps.

At the time of statehood, Americans viewed Alaska natives generally as extremely disadvantaged, and they regarded the Yup'ik Eskimos of the Yukon-Kuskokwim delta region as one of the most impoverished groups among them. Relative to most other areas of rural Alaska, the availability of Western material goods was minimal, modern housing nonexistent, educational levels extremely low, and a tuberculosis epidemic, as destructive as earlier influenza and smallpox epidemics, ran rampant.

The federal government launched a number of "War on Poverty" programs in the 1960s aimed at rectifying these inequities. Passage of the Alaska Native Claims Settlement Act (ANCSA) followed in 1971. The act completely transformed land tenure in the state and is the major determinant of land status in Alaska today. It extinguished aboriginal land claims, giving in return fee-simple title to 44 million acres of land and nearly one billion dollars. ANCSA also set up twelve regional (and one nonresident) profit corporations, as well as individual village corporations, to administer the land and money received under ANCSA. The Calista Corporation (from *cali-* to work, literally "the worker") was established to manage the corporate resources of the Yukon-Kuskokwim Delta.

The "Molly Hootch decision" in 1976 mandated sweeping educational reform. Local high schools sprang up in all of the smaller communities of the region, which had previously sent their children to boarding school in Bethel, St. Marys Catholic Mission, or outside the region. Both ANCSA and the Hootch decision dictated changes that redefined village organization and economy. These acts and decisions of the 1960s and 1970s jointly are responsible for shaping the modern villages of western Alaska.

The coastal communities of western Alaska experienced steady growth during the 1970s and 1980s, supported in large measure through ANCSA village corporation activity and the state education industry. Residents have not saved and invested income to escape the village. Instead, the villages have burgeoned in both population and modern facilities, and employment income and cash transfers of other kinds provided some support for local subsistence-harvesting activity.

By the 1960s the traditionally mobile and dispersed Yup'ik population had established churches, schools, and stores at centrally located sites throughout the region, and gradually became more settled and centralized. Creation of the modern village of Toksook Bay typifies the process of village formation that occurred throughout the delta. Half-a-dozen Nelson Island families established Toksook in the spring of 1964 when they moved their small plywood houses on sleds pulled by dog teams over from Nightmute, located fifteen miles up the Toksook River. The new location obviated the need to move every year between the traditional fall and winter fishing site of Nightmute and the coastal spring sealing camp of Umkumiut. Toksook Bay has steadily grown, and in 1989 had more than sixty houses (double its size ten years before), a new high school, community hall and clinic, village corporation store, cable television, telephones in most homes, and daily flights to and from the regional center of Bethel.

The regional economy shifted radically as the delta's population coalesced at permanent sites. Along with the continued importance of subsistence-harvesting activities, the most significant feature of village economy in western Alaska today is its dependence on government. Commercial fishing and trapping, craft sales, and local service industries provide a small portion of the aggregate local income. As much as 90 percent flows through the village economies from the public sector. Wages and salaries of teachers, administrators, construction workers, health aides, and social-service workers provide some of this government-source income. Various state and federal transfer payments and grant and loan monies supply the remainder. Most local service and distribution businesses in the private sector consequently depend on purchases made by persons and organizations which themselves rely on public-sector income transfers.

Men and women in contemporary coastal communities participate in the economy as clerks, welfare recipients, commercial fishermen, and bureaucrats but also partially maintain themselves through subsistence hunting and fishing. Integration into the larger economy is marginal, and domestic activities focus on extraction and consumption rather than investment and production. Dependence on public sources of income limits economic diversity. The combination of wage employment and the harvest of local resources for both commercial and subsistence use still dominates.

High rates of alcoholism, child abuse, sexual assault, suicide, violent crime, and mental-health problems continue to plague the region. True, the rate of infant mortality has dramatically declined during the last twenty years, but the regional suicide rate has increased from 5.5 to 55.5 per 100,000 during the same period—five times the national toll. In nearly all cases, alcohol is a contributing factor (Lenz 1986:4,5).

A suicide epidemic in the Yukon Delta village of Alakanuk, in which seven young men and one young woman killed themselves over a sixteen-month period in 1985 and 1986, is an example of the violence besetting many Alaska native communities today. The expression of personal and family problems tends to be inner-directed or directed at close relatives. Overt conflict more often occurs in interethnic confrontation. The more traditional and tightly integrated communities of the Bering Sea coast have so far

Off-loading freight at Toksook Bay, 1981. James H. Barker.

escaped tragedies comparable to Alakanuk's, but they, too, have experienced a dramatic rise in alcoholism, suicide, and domestic violence.

The traditional Yup'ik value hierarchy places the natural and human world in a highly structured, reciprocal relationship. This perception continues to shape actions and ideals in the region today. Residents struggle to find solutions to village problems and ways to continue to live in their traditional homeland. Coastal dwellers, especially, see themselves as living in a mutually beneficial relationship with the resources of their environment, not merely surviving off them.

The Central Yup'ik language continues as the first and primary language for the majority of residents living in the coastal and tundra villages. Coastal villagers also continue to employ Yup'ik kinship terminology and traditional naming patterns. Recently the hours spent in formal schooling plus the introduction of television in the 1970s have undermined the use of the Yup'ik language by many young people. Yet Yup'ik remains the language of choice in the majority of coastal communities.

Public-housing programs of the last twenty-five years have made single nuclear-family houses available in rural Alaska on an unprecedented scale. Nevertheless, elaborate patterns of interhousehold sharing, adoption, hunting partnerships, and work-group configurations continue to provide numerous contexts for maintenance and expression of extended-family relationships. Labor intensive and time consuming, subsistence-harvesting and processing activities provide many such opportunities.

Coastal residents remain strongly committed to traditional harvesting activities, which often involve modern equipment. Most villagers view the cash economy as supportive of and subordinate to hunting and gathering activities. Cash gained from commercial fishing or part-time employment is used to facilitate, not obviate, such subsistence pursuits as seal hunting, herring fishing, bird hunting, and fall moose hunting. Money is a means to an end, not an end in itself. Villagers continue to share the products of the harvest, and families are defined and distinguished by the quantity and quality of the gifts they are able to receive and repay.

The passage of ANCSA and, more recently, the heightened awareness of domestic problems has created a diffuse yet important cultural reformation in much of western Alaska. Consciousness raising has led some to work for substantial changes in the political system, which nurtures restorative powers. Today Yup'ik residents concentrate with an unprecedented sense of urgency on maintaining control of their land, resources, and local affairs; improving residents' health and sense of well-being; and adhering to cultural and linguistic traditions.

This renaissance reflects a certain nostalgia for the "old ways." In political and economic terms, "old ways" refers to the 1920s, after many positive technological improvements had been introduced into western Alaska but before the Yup'ik people had experienced subordination to federal and state

Toksook Bay, spring 1985. James H. Barker.

Paul John dancing at St. Marys Dance Festival, 1987. James H. Barker.

control and related dependency. The Yupiit Nation sovereignty movement is one embodiment of this reformation. The common message in its diverse activities is a deep concern for and commitment to the environment and the animals it supports; its aim, often frustrated, is to regain control of Yup'ik land and Yup'ik lives.

These trends have not yet coalesced into a single, concerted, region-wide movement. Even so, increasing articulation of issues of native cultural identity and political control indicate a growing awareness of the value of being a Yup'ik person in the modern world. This book, in fact, owes its existence to two recording projects dedicated to preserving and communicating the nineteenth-century Yup'ik view of the world. Many of the rules for living recounted in the following pages emerged from the Nelson Island Oral History Project and the Yupiit Nation's Traditional Governance Project. These efforts, in turn, reflect the desire of many Yup'ik people to gain recognition of their unique past, parts of which they hope to carry into the future.

CHAPTER 2

THE RELATIONSHIP BETWEEN HUMANS AND ANIMALS

Only connect.

—*Virginia Woolf,* To the Lighthouse

They taught the young people in those days to keep things separate, never to let them touch each other, always to watch out that we never connect with those animals in the wrong way.

—*Frances Usugan, Toksook Bay, July 1985*

VIRGINIA WOOLF'S austere admonition seems a fair sum of the fundamental task of many of those trained in the Western tradition to explain the meaning and motivation of the actions of others. Following Hobbes, Euro-Americans begin with the assumption that society—their own as well as others—is made of a diversity of individuals ultimately united through self-interest. Contemporary anthropological analysis continues in this tradition insofar as it assumes the innateness of cultural differentiation, and that a fundamental "problem" of social analysis is the explanation of the relation of analytically distinct categories and separate domains. These categories are not seen as man-made but as facts of nature.

Viewed in gross terms, Western ideology and the cosmologies of many of the societies it seeks to understand are very differently constituted. Certainly this is true in the case of the Eskimos of the Far North. If the fundamental existential problem of the Hobbesian individual was to forge a unity out of the natural diversity of humankind, Eskimos traditionally viewed themselves as confronted with an originally undifferentiated universe in which the boundaries between the human and nonhuman, the spiritual and material, were shifting and permeable. Moreover, these boundaries, they believed, were not naturally given but depended on human action to keep them in place. The rules for living and ritual activity—both public and private—focused on the construction of boundaries and passages to circumscribe and control the flow of activity within an otherwise undifferentiated universe.

Written descriptions of Eskimos have often ignored this fundamental preoccupation. From their "discovery" four-hundred years ago, Westerners have alternately viewed Eskimos as noble savages—pure until corrupted by civilization—and uncivilized heathens in need of everything from a bath to baptism. Whether observers emphasized the positive or negative side of the Eskimo image, they increasingly represented them as the ultimate individualists. Contact with the small, dispersed populations of the Canadian Arctic engendered a view of Eskimos as independent, hardworking, and resourceful. Far from recognizing their character as unique, Euro-Americans increasingly viewed Eskimos as the original embodiment of the Protestant ethic (Balikci 1989). Their ability to survive in a harsh and inhospitable homeland continues to exert a tremendous fascination on the Western mind (for example, Malaurie 1982). To this day the Euro-American assumption that Eskimos embody an original image of themselves underwrites much popular discussion of arctic peoples.

Ironically, much of what has been written about Eskimos emphasizes their character as rugged individualists, and the premium that they placed on personal freedom unencumbered by social constraints. As theirs was presumably a simpler reality than ours, analysts assumed they required fewer social encumbrances and viewed their social interaction in the Hobbesian tradition as a form of "contained anarchy" (Oswalt 1963:54).

What might at first blush appear as self-serving, individualistic maneuvering (Graburn 1969) on closer scrutiny reveals itself as complex and highly regulated social hierarchy. Eskimo cosmology recognizes detailed distinctions between different categories of humans and animals, and innumerable rules regulate their interaction. Moreover, these recognized differences are culturally constituted rather than naturally given. Far from perceiving social differentiation as something innate and requiring relation in a deliberate sense (Wagner 1977:624), many Eskimo peoples perceived the identity of humans and animals as a given and prescribed rules both to create and to maintain the proper boundaries and enact the proper ceremonial exchanges between them.

Arctic anthropologists have compiled detailed lists of these rules, articulated primarily in terms of the prohibitions and prescriptions that guided Eskimo peoples in their interaction within and between the human, animal, and spirit worlds (for example, Lantis 1946:182–95, 223–35, 1959:27–36; Nelson 1899:285-322; Ostermann and Holtved 1952:35–37, 118–20, 124–27; Rasmussen 1929:169–202, 1931:258–82). Described variously as taboos (Boas 1888:609; Hoebel 1964:70), magical acts, and ritual injunctions (Oosten 1976:64–78), these rules for living have rarely been the focus of discussion. The power of systematic distinction that they embody—their power to create difference—has either been underestimated or entirely dismissed. More often anthropologists have dealt with them in summary fashion as less-than-critical ethnographic detail in support of more general statements. As in my earlier work, ethnographers often have focused on the description of observable behavior, including Eskimo subsistence techniques, social interaction, and ceremonial activity. Whereas chroniclers of the Arctic have written a tremendous amount about what Eskimos do, they have paid much less attention to why Eskimos find it necessary to perform such actions.

A paradigm fundamentally different from that of most Western peoples organized Eskimo cosmology. It was originally founded on the assumption of an undifferentiated universe, wherein human attention to the rules was an act of participation necessary both to create difference and maintain connections. If Yup'ik social interaction was "contained anarchy," these rules were the container and a more carefully contrived one than we have previously allowed. The rules that guided interaction between persons not only built bridges but helped create boundaries between them. Western ideology, specifically the Judeo-Christian tradition, assumes an inherent differentiation between humans and animals and focuses on the explanation of the relationship between originally independent parts. It holds that humans have souls and the ability to attain salvation, whereas animals do not.[1] The Yup'ik Eskimos stand this basic assumption on its head and assume, for instance, that humans and animals are analogically related as human and nonhuman persons (see Hallowell 1960).[2] The focus of explanation shifts from the unification of independent beings to the creation of difference out of an original unity. Roy Wagner (1977:623) first proposed this reversal in the reorientation of kinship analysis from an original assumption of homological difference to one of analogical solicitude (epitomized by David Schneider's [1984] "diffuse, enduring solidarity") between categories of kinsmen. His suggestion invites extension.

The differentiation of persons into humans and nonhumans was for Eskimo peoples at the foundation of social life. The Yupiit believed all humans and animals—both male and female, the living and the dead—shared personhood; however, within this category they distinguished human and nonhuman persons. The elaborate exchanges that characterized their relationship constituted a "deliberate controlled analogy," a regulated flow of goods and services that replaced the substantial flow of shared personhood by the imposition of the original differentiation (Wagner 1977:631). Once the initial differentiation between human and nonhuman persons had been established,

1. Modern science, essentially ignoring the question of a soul, deals with the human species as it does with all animals, noting degrees of difference as in the development of the forebrain, means of communication, period of gestation, and period of fertility. Different genera and families may have different numbers of toes or teeth, but the more ethology we learn, the more science emphasizes similarities in social organization, emotional behavior, and other behavior patterns. Through science other animals are now more respected, and the human species is not seen in the image of God but as a highly developed, complex animal, also worthy of respect. Because of science we can say, "We are all part of one world, on earth together." There was, however, a period of two thousand years when humans and animals were differentiated in European and some Asiatic communities because of religious beliefs (Margaret Lantis, personal communication).

2. In "Ojibwa Ontology, Behavior, and World View," A. Irving Hallowell draws the distinction between humans and living "persons" of an other-than-human class.

their relationship in perpetuity depended on their carefully regulated interaction.

The distinction between humans and animals seems so "natural" to the
Western eye that its character as a culturally manipulated distinction is
largely invisible. There is, however, nothing in nature that requires the
choice of this relationship over and above other relationships as the focus for
cultural elaboration. Other peoples have chosen to elaborate quite different
"natural" facts. Recent work in Melanesia, including that of Wagner (1977:629)
and Strathern (1987:5), suggests that the "germinal social differentiation"
that motivates social life in that part of the world is the differentiation
between male and female. Work in Africa by British social anthropologists
reveals the hierarchical relationship between ancestors and others as an important focus (Evans-Pritchard 1940; Fortes 1969). Although Eskimo peoples certainly make important distinctions based on gender and age, these are
not the primary relationships for them.

The essential relationship in the Arctic is between humans (male or female) and animals. Just as gender may be seen to provide the "master code"
for Melanesia (Biersack 1984:134), the relationship between human and
nonhuman persons may provide a comparable master code in the Arctic. Out
of the "sameness and difference" of humans and animals, in various states and
genders, comes an "indigenous conceptual vocabulary" (Strathern 1987:8).
Beginning from the recognition of an essential similarity, humans and animals distinguish themselves from each other by their acts. The difference
between them is thus an "activity rather than a state" (Strathern 1987:21).
Boundaries are dynamic and transitional, and passages between worlds are,
for better or worse, always a potentiality.

The ritual process creates the passages between worlds as cultural rules set
the boundaries between them. Food sharing and gift giving constitute the
core of Yup'ik social life. During the annual cycle of ceremonies, dead
humans and animals were gradually drawn into living society, feasted and
hosted, and finally sent away again. This analogic flow and the resulting
continuity in the relationship between human and nonhuman persons through
time and space preoccupied the Yup'ik people. For instance, in the rules
surrounding seal hunting, the gift of fresh water to the recently killed seal
produced the possibility of receiving that same seal in the future. If people
did not host the animals, they jeopardized their future relationship to them.
The Yup'ik Eskimos were concerned with the capacity of acts of differentiation to create the possibility of future relation (Wagner 1977:626). What
goes around comes around again.

Yup'ik cosmology, as described by Yup'ik elders in the 1980s, presents
human and nonhuman persons as engaged in a constant cycle between birth
and rebirth, and this process of reincarnation constituted Yup'ik society
ideologically as an ahistoric entity. A perpetual cycling of names and souls
connected the living and the dead. But this cosmological cycle did not exist

separate from human activity. People maintained it by rigorous attention to ruled boundaries and ceremonial passages.

The rules and rituals that circumscribed Yup'ik life derived from the essential relationship between humans and animals. As in Wagner's (1977:638) discussion of Daribi kinship, the impression of both complexity and "naturally" imposed differentiation of kinds of beings was an illusion fostered by the consequences of the imposition of the original distinction between human and nonhuman persons, most dramatically between seals and men. Following Keesing (1987:46), Yup'ik categories did not deal primarily with "substances and essences" but with "boundaries, invasions, and dissolutions of form." Seal bones or animal blood did not of themselves portend danger, but bone or blood in the wrong place did.

ANIMALS AS NONHUMAN PERSONS

In every animal and every plant and really in everything, oil lamp or river or mountain, dwells a human-like being which one occasionally is allowed to see.

—*Hans Himmelheber,* Eskimo Artists

The Yup'ik people traditionally relied on a wide variety of fish and game, and their relationship with these animals continues to structure their lives into the present day. The centrality of the relationship between humans and animals in everyday life is but one indication of its significance. The Yupiit considered humans and animals similar in a number of important respects and believed society included both human and nonhuman members. They extended personhood beyond the human domain and applied it as an attribute of animals as well. They did not view themselves as dominant over dumb, mute beasts that served them. Neither did they see themselves as dependent on or subordinate to animals. In contrast, they viewed the relationship between humans and animals as collaborative reciprocity by which the animals gave themselves to the hunter in response to the hunter's respectful treatment of them as nonhuman persons.[3]

According to Yup'ik oral tradition, animals originally possessed the ability to transform themselves into humanlike creatures. Humans might be visited by animals and were capable of visiting the animal world, where the animals appear to them as human persons (Fienup-Riordan 1983:177–81). Dozens of stories recall how a person (usually a young boy or girl) loses the way and happens upon a sod house. The person enters the house and is subsequently fed and cared for by a husband and wife who appear in human form. The hosts invariably betray their animal identity by some peculiar trait during the visit. On departing, the human visitor sometimes looks back and sees the host in animal form, or the human visitor is warned not to tell about the visit.

3. Robert Brightman's (1983) discussion of the relationship between humans and animals among the Rock Cree provided the starting point for my work on this topic.

In one story a young girl, who had stayed with a bear in human form, is pestered by her fellow villagers until she finally leads them to the house where she had wintered, which is actually a bear's den. The bear emerges and kills the girl and her companions.

Within the larger class of living things, human and nonhuman persons shared fundamental characteristics. The Yupiit believed that the perishable flesh of both humans and animals belied their immortality. All living things participated in an endless cycle of birth and rebirth, contingent on right thought and action by others as well as self.

The Yup'ik Eskimos identified aspects of both humans and animals that sustained life. Each animal's *yua* (the possessive form of *yuk*, person, literally "its person") had an anatomical locus—the bladder—to which it retracted at death to await rebirth. An animal's *yua* might appear as its spiritual double in human form. People believed inanimate objects also possessed *yuit* (plural, "their persons"). Hunters decorated their implements not only to please or "draw" the animals they hunted, but also to impart life into and please the objects themselves. Even a lowly boil *(aninguaq)* was believed to possess a *yua*.

A *yuk*, or human person, was more complex and possessed no single spiritual entity that Yup'ik people translated as "soul." Rather, the human body was animated by, among other things, breath *(anerneq)*,[4] mind *(umyuaq)*, and life spirit *(unguva)*, qualities without which it could not sustain life (see also chapter 7). The human shade or visible image *(tarneq)*[5] remained near the body after death for a specified time before going to an extraterrestrial realm, where it received food and clothing from living relatives. A person's *ateq*, or name, like the *yua* of an animal, was believed reborn in subsequent generations, usually within his or her namesakes.[6]

Along with this belief in spiritual continuity bridging the past to the future, the Yup'ik people believed that humans and animals alike possessed awareness *(ella)*. Belief in such awareness dictated proper treatment of animals, as people considered them privy to all a hunter thought and did. Animals, like people, could appreciate how they were treated. According to Tim Agartak of Nightmute (June 1987 NI98:10), "It is told that even when seals are killed, they do not forget their consciousness. They know the exact manner in which they are handled after they have been caught. For those who handle them carelessly, they know about those people. They would not go to them anymore."

4. *Anernernirtuq*, literally "s/he has no more breath," means "s/he is dead."

5. Yupiit also translate *tarneq* as spirit. Terms derived from this base include *tarenraq* (image, picture, likeness, reflection) and *tarenriur-* (to look at one's reflection). A person observing someone who is ill sometimes reports seeing two people, as when a person is dying, his or her *tarneq* starts to leave them (see also Lantis 1960:120).

6. As described in chapter 7, a person can have more than one namesake. Just as they had no single word for "soul," the Yupiit did not confine the concept to a single reincarnation.

For this reason a hunter must always cover any trace of blood remaining at the kill site. Failure to do so would doom the hunter's future efforts, as his negligence would cause the animals to avoid him. Likewise, a hunter must never boast or brag of what he intended to do or had already accomplished. Animals could use this knowledge and hide from him. As a result, people spoke little about the hoped-for outcome of harvesting activities. Parents taught their children to give thanks verbally for what they acquired, yet not to brag about what they planned for the future: "Because we are so grateful when we catch something, we have to smile every time. Those that hook fish must always smile; they will call to others because they are so grateful. They must not refrain from smiling" (Brentina Chanar, Toksook Bay, June 30, 1989).

This awareness, which allowed individuals a sense of control over their destiny, resulted from experience. Persons, both animal and human, lacked a sense of self at birth and only gradually became aware of their surroundings. The Yup'ik language designates this process by the verb *ellange-*, which literally translates "becoming aware," "coming to one's senses," or "getting a glimpse of reality." Once acquired, awareness continued throughout a person's life and into death:

> Because like us, when they are killed, they momentarily lose consciousness but regain it later. They know the individuals who are taking care of them. But after we have eaten and defecate, the dogs immediately eat our feces. That is when they no longer are conscious. All *pitarkat* [game animals, prey, literally "things to be caught"], including the seals, know if they are handled properly after they are caught. They try to go to the one who takes care of them properly. But some of them say they will never go to the one who does not take care of them properly. (Camille Joseph, Alakanuk, August 9, 1987)

RULES FOR LIVING: THE POWER OF THE MIND

> *So those were always our alternatives because they were told to us. They were there all the time for us to think about right away in the event that we had to do something.*

> —*Frances Usugan, Toksook Bay, July 1985*

The Yup'ik Eskimos believed that animals and humans alike shared a common code for conduct, emphasizing personal integrity and respect for others in their interaction. These rules for living marked the crucial boundaries both between and within the human and animal worlds. They were known collectively as *qaneryarat* (from *qaner-* to speak, literally "that which is spoken"), and specifically as *alerquutet* (laws or instructions, from *alerqur-* to tell to do something, to advise, to command, to order) and *inerquutet* (admonishments or warnings, from *inerqur-* to admonish, to tell or warn not to do something). The rules enabled a person to "stand up properly."

As both human and nonhuman persons grew to maturity and gained awareness, they learned a multitude of *alerquutet* and *inerquutet* for the proper living of life:

Alerquun [singular] . . . is passed on orally. They tell it so that it is strongly encouraged for people to live by. The *alerquun* gives strict guidelines for a person to live by.

And *inerquun,* a warning, which will cause bodily damage to a person or that will cause that person to be irritating to others, or cause unfavorable attention to [that person], that is strongly discouraged. (Kenneth Igkurak, Kongiganak, June 1988 YN14:6)

The rules for proper living took a lifetime to learn and to fully understand. Three related ideas underlay their detail: the power of a person's thought; the importance of thoughtful action to avoid injuring another's mind; and, conversely, the danger inherent in following one's own mind (Fienup-Riordan 1986a).

Regarding the power of a person's thought, the message was that people's attitudes were as significant as their actions. Thus, hunters admonished young men to "keep the thought of the seals" foremost in their minds as they shoveled snow, carried out trash, and hauled water. In all these acts, by the power of their mind, they "made a way for the seals" they would someday hunt. In the same way a pregnant woman must keep the thought of her unborn child first in her mind to insure its well-being.

Animals also complied to this stricture. For example, oral tradition describes how young seals were admonished by their elders to "stay awake" to the rules, both literally and figuratively, so that their immortal souls might survive the hunter's blow. If they were asleep when they were hit, they would "die dead, forever" (Fienup-Riordan 1983:179).

Both humans and animals assisted individual elders to avoid their displeasure because of the "power of the mind of the elders" to affect their future. Matthew Frye of Napakiak (June 1988 YN18:3) put it this way: "And they have an oral directive that anyone who is an elder, they should try to make him grateful all the time. If one is grateful . . . and even now if I am grateful, I cannot wish anything bad toward someone who makes me grateful. But I wish him toward something that is good."

One contemporary account admonished young people to perform good deeds at night so that no one would see them:

Only at night he clears the path.
If he does it during the day,
letting the people see him,
already then,
through the people he has his reward.

But if he does that with no one watching him
and nobody is aware of him,
only the one watching him,

the ocean or the land, . . .
the *ellam yua* [person or spirit of the universe]
will give him his reward.[7] (Toksook Bay Elders, November 3, 1983 NI57)

Traveling in the wilderness demanded that people keep their minds calm and focused and follow the rules their elders had taught them.

If that person is traveling down in the ocean, the nature of panic is such that one gets scared. One will think, "I am going to perish now!" A person that thinks like that never lives, but the one who uses the *alerquun* and does not panic survives. It is as if that person knows that s/he is not the only one who causes him/her to live anyway. . . .

Because the mind of a person goes before a person. The body of a person is controlled by the person's mind if [the person] is thinking. (Sam Carter, Quinhagak, May 11, 1989)

Corollary to the positive power of the human mind was the negative power of jealous thoughts. Withholding information or nurturing bad feelings ultimately would harm a person.

This is what they used to tell us. When one of our members is not instructed, wishing he does not catch anything, if he did that, it would not happen to that person we have bad wishes for. Instead it will happen to us. If I was wishing that one of my companions didn't catch anything, I will not be able to catch anything. But then if one of my companions or someone who is there to go hunting, if I was supportive of him, that is when they would say there would be many things available for me to catch. . . . One who is supportive of another hunter becomes a success himself, and is referred to as a *nukalpiaq*, one who is successful at hunting. But then the person who is unsupportive, not wanting another person to have a good catch, that person will be unsuccessful. And so, he is referred to as an *arrsak* [poor person]. (Joshua Phillip, Tuluksak, August 1, 1988 BIA48)

If a person wishes bad thoughts to another "by the mind," illness and death can result.

I had four children like this every year, these two boys and these two girls. And so it was that this younger sibling would die when the older sibling would die. So it was Andrew. . . . By his mind he probably did not want me to have children.

So even though my grandfather told me not to, when he was going to eat, I invited [Andrew]. . . .

So when they were both finished eating, I said to [Andrew], "Cross-cousin, what is the matter with you that you always want me to have you in my dream? You always make me scared all the time. No wonder that my children do not live long."

7. This contemporary account of a traditional rule parallels (or perhaps appropriates in Yup'ik terms) the advice given in Matthew (6:1–6) that a person not pray and perform charitable acts standing on street corners to be seen by others but rather in secret to be rewarded by God.

And then he said to me, "Let it be. That Qerruralria will live." . . .
And then when I got through telling him, I gave him those mittens and
those socks. He was so grateful. He would say to me, "Do not be worried and
be pregnant; it will live!"
And so that was the truth. After that my children lived. . . . So somehow,
that Andrew wished me bad by his mind. . . . He had a bad mind. (Mary
Napoka, Tuluksak, May 5, 1989)

Father Segundo Llorente (1990:183–84), a Jesuit priest who served in
western Alaska for many years, recorded a succinct example of the potentially
negative power of the human mind: "An old Eskimo told me that they
believed that one person can kill another by thought. . . . When this man
feels indisposed, he knows that death is trying to get him. So what does he
do? He mentally places another man between him and the coming death."
    Just as a person must refrain from thinking bad thoughts about another, so
people must avoid saying unkind or hurtful words. According to Kurt Bell of
Hooper Bay, "Never make fun of someone who you think is ugly or wears
strange clothes. That person will always remember what you said" (Madsen
1990:101). Just as the power of a person's mind can work for good or ill, so a
person's thoughtless words can injure another's mind, causing hurtful thoughts
in turn.
    The second basic rule was the importance of thoughtful action to avoid
injuring a person's mind. Evon Albrite of Kasigluk (June 1988 YN26:6)
remembered, "According to what their elders tell them to do, and if they live
by that, they live right and proper. But those who go against what they have
been told, they cannot live a long life. If they are breaking the minds of their
fellows or if one does not obey what their fellows told one to do, that is also
the reason why they do not live long."
    As proper thought could affect success in the domain of human and
animal interaction, so careful thought must reign over thoughtless action to
avoid injuring the mind of other persons, whether human or animal. A
person's mind is both powerful and vulnerable. Yup'ik reticence derives from
this belief, as well as the value placed on a person's ability to retain control in
a tense situation. Ideally, calmness and amiability should mask a person's
emotions.
    Within the group, consensus was the ideal:

This nature of having consensus of minds, if people have consensus and don't
go against one another's mind, when they do that people are strong, when they
help each other and work together.
    When they deal with anything and when people have one mind, they have
strength and they are strong.
    But if they are against each other and break each other's mind, when people
do that they cannot be strong. But if they have one mind and cooperate, they
have strength. Then they are able to fight back.
    Even if other people do not think highly of them, if they have one mind

when they do that, they have strength and can fight anything; people are able to fight back. (Adolph Jimmy, Kongiganak, May 13, 1989)

Masking one's emotions in the presence of others was as important in animal/human interaction. The same consideration or respect for the animal's mind or awareness that prohibited the hunter from bragging about his accomplishments also motivated his verbal apology when dispatching his prey.

The third basic rule was the danger of "following one's own mind." Joshua Phillip of Tuluksak (June 1988 YN22:15) recalled, "This is the worst act of breaking the rules. If a person lives using his own mind, he will not walk through life properly. One will encounter many problems. If one uses one's own mind, disregarding proper advice, one is breaking the traditional ancestral *alerquutet*. . . . One will not live long if one is standing using one's own individual mind."

If a person followed his own mind and did not live according to the rules, Ungalek ("the one with facial hair," from *ungak* whiskers) might come and "shake one up" (Mather 1985).[8] The implication was that the experience would alter one's path. According to Billy Lincoln of Toksook Bay (January 15, 1991), "Those old men used to advise a young person about the way he must live so he may not get into an accident. They teach him to live so that he would not meet up with misfortune by telling him [advice]. And then if he acts contrary to what they tell him to do and he meets mishap, but he still lives, then they would say to him, 'So? Did the Ungalek tell you?' . . . It is because that disobedient person realizes his mistake, that is why they told him thus."

A number of traditional tales recalled the consequences of people following their own minds as opposed to following the advice of elders. Results were usually disastrous. Retribution often involved the wrongdoer as well as the person's companions. The original differentiation between animal and human persons described in the *qulirat* is most often framed as the result of people's disregard for the rules and subsequently following their own minds.

If people followed their own mental dictates, they were impossible to instruct and educate; their minds were said to "go bad." Conversely, a person who attended to the rules and the words of others could acquire the knowledge adult life demanded.

At that time, they always talked by letting them gather in the men's house. And that door, they put a stick of wood there. So one of the people would be talking. And then one of them rushed out by breaking the wood. And he slams the door. That person will never listen to *alerquutet*. That is how he is. His mind gets angry when he hears what is being said.

But that person who follows the *alerquun*, his mind does not get bad, but in

8. Ungalek may be another name for Raven, whom Nelson Islanders describe as having whiskers made of willow trees. The bearded Raven once came to live among humans, but people laughed at him and then fell down dead. Seeing that he was causing the death of his descendants, Raven departed and has not been seen since.

his mind, he is grateful even though he does not say anything. (Sam Carter, Quinhagak, May 11, 1989)

The consequences of following one's own mind were often incorporated into Yup'ik oral tradition as stories or *neq'ayarat*, literally "devices that help one remember or call something to mind" (from *neq'ake–* "to remember, to keep in mind with consideration," plus *+yaraq* way of V-ing):

> Those kinds of stories, they call them *neq'ayarat*. . . . When this action is done, they say that it is *neq'ayaraq*—they say that it is something to keep in mind with consideration. . . .
> But whatever action a certain individual has done, they try to use that as an example to remind people of the ensuing consequence if one does something. That is what they mean by *neq'ayaraq*. . . .
> If a person does something so that it merits to be told, it is a *neq'ayaraq*. If one is haughty, [that person] is *neq'ayaraq*. These people that are so bad, one becomes a *neq'ayaraq* by their pitiful state only . . . those things that people have actually done. (Brentina Chanar, July 7, 1989)

True to Yup'ik instructional style, Brentina Chanar followed her general statement with an example (see also Morrow 1990). She related how a man named Kinguqalria refused to give his former lover a poke of seal oil that she had taken from his cache. Against the advice of his wife and following his own mind, he entered his lover's house and retrieved it. Immediately regretting his actions, he tried to return it, but the woman made no reply. Kinguqalria made a *neq'ayaraq* about what he did. The lesson of his particular experience was that a man could not follow his own mind and take back food, regardless how valuable and desirable the disputed object. His relatives told his *neq'ayaraq* to future generations so that they might learn by his experience and not make the same mistake.

Closely related to but distinct from the proscription against following one's own mind, people were also instructed *"Umyuan niicugniuraqsaunaku"*: Do not listen to their own mind. To brood unduly, turning one's bad thoughts inward, was potentially as dangerous as failure to follow the rules, as it prevented a person from being aware of and responsive to one's surroundings. In one well-known story, a deserted wife used a bearskin to give her the power to travel overland to find her deceitful husband, and in the form of a bear, she tore him apart. Her extreme and uncontrollable anger, however, caused the bearskin to attach itself permanently to her body: "Therefore we have the admonition to meekness and moderation, eventemperedness and slowness to anger" (Kawagley 1989).

The essential similarity between human and nonhuman persons created the common ground of their interaction. Because of their mutual possession of awareness, an immortal aspect of their being, and a common code for conduct, humans and animals shared the ability to volitionally act upon, and react to, their surroundings. Just as human hunters were capable of conscious decisions as to what and where to hunt, animals were capable of conscious decisions that affected the success of individual hunters, such as the decision of a seal not to approach a hunter who appeared to him as careless in either thought or action (Fienup-Riordan 1983:180). Although human conduct was an important factor in the interaction, it was not sufficient to guarantee a hunter's success.

MUTUAL RESPECT

The qualities of personhood shared by humans and animals established the basis for a mutual and necessary respect. People understood respect in both positive and negative terms, including love and fear. The Yup'ik language uses different terms to denote this state of being, including *kencike-* (to watch over with respect, from the base *kencig-* to be careful with one's clothing) and *qigcig-* (to look sideways without turning one's head). The most often-used term is *takar-* (to be shy of, respectful toward, or intimidated by). This term, combining both admiration for and fear of the person designated, is used in reference to elders and certain animals. It may also refer to the weather, as in "the cold does not respect people with fancy parkas" (Jacobson 1984:353).

The respect a hunter demonstrates for his prey is only one special example of the general respect relationship between and among humans and animals. Numerous examples of this respectful attitude circumscribe harvesting activities to this day. These include the placement of food at the base of a plant or the return of its roots to the place where they were gathered, both to show appreciation to the plant as well as to insure that it will grow again at the same location. Himmelheber (1987:33) observed, "Before we go berry-picking we always bury some food, for example fish, in the tundra. It is for the little men [*yuit* "their persons," plural possessed of *yua*] who live in the berries so that they will provide a rich harvest." Yup'ik men and women still commonly bury small amounts of tobacco, tea, and dried fish when camping on the open tundra, saying "Eat, whoever passed away before us." As we shall see, such acts of "feeding the land" or "feeding the trail" fed the human dead as well.

Hunters may also leave the paw from a trapped beaver at the kill site as "thanks" to the animal as well as insurance that its *yua* does not "run away." One must pick berries neatly without stems or leaves to please the plants. And when passing a piece of driftwood, one should turn it to give it relief from the tedium and discomfort of lying in one position. If people perform these acts thinking about shedding their sickness, the plants and animals will thank them and provide them with good health and good fortune.

Other aspects of the treatment of animals derived from the fact that they were thought of as persons worthy of respect. For example, respect dictated that a hunter dispatch an animal quickly to minimize pain. The failure to do this had practical as well as moral consequences. The meat of seals that have died slowly is saturated with blood and bad to the taste.

Parents advised children never to tease animals, especially with food, or they could expect similar treatment in return. At an elders' conference at Toksook Bay in 1983, one person recounted a *neq'ayaraq* to illustrate this theme.

And this food, when people are lacking it, or even when they are not lacking it, a dog or any other animal, one is never to tease it with food.
This was a warning of the Yup'ik people.
And the reason behind it, at some time, one of the women had a dog, it was her own dog.
When she ate, she would tease it with the food she was eating.
Then she would not even let the dog eat, she would not even give it some food.
After some time had passed, suddenly they found themselves without food.
Because they had no food, because they had run out of food, one of the evenings the one who was always teasing with food went outside to urinate.
When she went out, she found that one, that dog she was always teasing, nearing the house with a lochefish in its mouth.
She tried everything to get at its food. And because she persisted in going after it, after it had let go of it, she went over to it. It was a willow root!
She suddenly felt disappointed, feeling very sad.
Finally, she understood that no animal is to be teased with food, being aware of the great disappointment it can cause.
It causes great discomfort, especially when one's stomach is empty. She placed herself in the dog's position. (Toksook Bay Elders, November 5, 1983 NI59)

HUMAN AND ANIMAL DIFFERENTIATION

The relationship between humans and animals is made possible by their mutual possession of some essential aspect—either *yua* or *ateq*—that is capable of rebirth, a common code for conduct, and a mind meriting respect. In traditional tales, animals often transform themselves into human form by lifting up their beaks or muzzles. In 1936 Lame Jacob told Hans Himmelheber (1987:33), "A mink comes forward, and suddenly throws off his pelt and is a person." Nelson (1899:394) made the same point: "It is also believed that in early days all animate beings had a dual existence, becoming at will either like man or the animal forms they now wear; if an animal wished to assume its human form, the forearm, wing, or other limb was raised and pushed up the muzzle or beak as if it were a mask, and the creature became manlike in form and features."
Orators sometimes equate gaining awareness *(ellange-)* with peeling back the skin of an animal, as in the story about the puppies born to a Nelson Island woman who had married a dog. The puppies peeled back their fur and revealed themselves to their mother in human form. Nineteenth-century transformation masks vividly portray this perception of reality (Nelson 1899:393–414; Fitzhugh and Kaplan 1982:180–216).
Along with depicting animal-human transformations, oral tradition also

Kuskokwim mask representing the yua *of a seal. J. H Turner, 1885; National Museum of the American Indian.*

recalls the subsequent process of differentiation by which the physical and behavioral contrasts between humans and animals occurred. For example, the origin of the vicious wolverine is attributed to the frustration and subsequent transformation of a man following his desertion by his spirit wife (Charlie Pleasant, Quinhagak, 1981:263). These tales identify contemporary animal species as descended from transformed human beings.

To this day Yup'ik people ascribe different human personality traits to each species of animals. For instance, they depict spotted seals *(issuriit)* as ill-tempered people.[9] Ringed seals *(nayiit),* on the other hand, are seen as gentle, sensitive people whose feelings can be easily hurt. Great care must be

9. Hunters on the Yukon Delta report that during the fall hunting season spotted seals can be quite aggressive and have been known to bite at kayaks and oars when cornered.

taken not to offend them. The bear is an unpredictable person, a trait attributed to the woman who was transformed into a bear in her search for her unfaithful husband (Kawagley 1989:7). Bearded seals are known as "old men" meriting particular respect, and belukhas are personified as peaceful and hardworking. Clara Agartak of Nightmute (June 1987 NI98:8) recalled, "They say that belukhas did not have any weapons and that before they go out to hunt, they only take a grass basket and nothing else, because they are people."

Animals thus differ among themselves based on shared features with certain classes of humans. As we shall see, humans are likewise differentiated from each other on the basis of the character of their relationship to animals. As important as the differences between animals and humans are the individual differences between persons (both human and nonhuman) who are ill-tempered, sensitive, scary, or gentle. To the present day many Yupiit construct their universe through a process of analogical differentiation. For example, young girls on Nelson Island are told that when gathering mouse food they will find some mouse caches full of twigs and droppings and others laden with tasty roots. The lesson is that mice are like people in their range of housekeeping standards—some are slovenly and some are neat.

In the Yup'ik view, as revealed through their oral tradition, society begins in unity and coactivity. The traditional tales explain how this original reciprocity between humans and animals and between people was in specific instances broken. A common theme recounts the fate of persons following their own minds and losing sight of the rules. As a result, either figuratively or literally, they lose their humanity.

Perhaps the most vivid accounts of interaction between animals and humans, and those that best portray both the similarities and the differences between animal and human society, are tales that describe humans visiting animal society and animals living within human society (Brightman 1983). An example of the first is the story of the boy who goes to live with the seals (Fienup-Riordan 1983:177–81). On arriving in the seals' underwater home, the boy perceives his hosts as humans of differing sizes and shapes, depending on their species identity:

> So when they got to the *qasgiq*, just like the people had at his home, when they entered he saw that there was a bed going all around the *qasgiq*. And on the floor in front of the ground bed were people with sores on their bodies. They didn't stay still but kept scratching themselves. And those who were sitting on the ground-level beds were small people with round faces, they had big eyes that were wide open. But those who were sitting on the bed going all around the *qasgiq*, these were men of obvious established skills. . . .
>
> Then he soon discovered that the people on the floor who were covered with sores and constantly moving were spotted seals. And those people who had big eyes were harbor seals. But he saw them as real people. But those who were sitting on the elevated beds which were situated around the walls, these were the bearded seals. (Paul John, Toksook Bay, February 2, 1977)

The same perception of their animal hosts as human is described for two brothers during their sojourn with walrus people (Fienup-Riordan 1983:236). Conversely, animals can enter human society, as in the case of the wolf who takes human form and comes to dwell with the hunter Ayugutaar. The animal nature of the wolf-man is apparent in his propensity to crunch bones when he eats.

These tales simultaneously depict animals as humans and underline the differences between them. For example, the story of the boy who goes to live with the seals describes the seals' experience with humans from the seals' point of view. From the seals' perspective, humans who failed to live by the rules appear distorted, alternately comical and scary.

Following Brightman (1983:227), oral tradition represents the perceptible differences between humans and animals as masking the underlying resemblances between them. In Yup'ik myth and story, animals thirst for fresh water and hunger for *akutaq* (literally "a mixture"). Seals arrange themselves in their underwater *qasgiq* comparable to the Yup'ik social hierarchy. Smaller seals sit on the lower benches while the large bearded seals, the "old men," occupy the place of honor. Carcasses of spawned salmon on riverbanks are not their bodies but their "canoes" that they have abandoned on their journey inland over the mountains to return the following year (Himmelheber 1987:32). Just as some aspect of the human person is reborn in the next generation, so animals, too, experience rebirth. For example, the boy who goes to live with the seals observes the spirits of the seals killed the previous year not merely arriving at the underwater men's house, but subsequently departing in the spring to return to the hunters who had cared for them in the past. This rebirth following their mortal demise is still a firmly held tenet of many Nelson Islanders.

On Nelson Island many people today view animals as direct descendants of mythic ancestors. The view persists that animals were once closer to humans and used human clothing and speech. Gradually, however, they diverged from their human counterparts (Brightman 1983:237) and today are only encountered in human form by the occasional lost traveler. Yet their possession of mind, attention to the rules, and rebirth after being killed and eaten by humans remain essential aspects of their personhood. The treatment given animals by Yup'ik people today—care of their bones, circumspection in discussing the kill, care and distribution of the catch—presupposes these shared aspects of personhood and sets the stage for everyday experience.

EXTRAORDINARY PERSONS

In traditional Yup'ik belief, still another range of persons shared features with humans and animals and interacted with them on a regular basis. These persons possessed a mixture of traits requiring special treatment. Like human and animal persons, they possessed both mind and awareness, and so merited careful treatment and respect. Rules for how these nonhuman persons should be treated often exaggerated or reversed proper rules for interaction between humans and between humans and animals. As with the rules for living in general, people ignored them at their peril.

Although nonhuman persons often had special traits, they were not supernatural. Rather, they were a part of the world that might or might not be experienced. Accounts abound, some quite detailed, concerning encounters with such persons. What follows is a sample of some of the nonhuman persons that orators had heard about or encountered in western Alaska, particularly in the Nelson Island area.

Unlike narratives recorded in northwest Alaska (Burch 1971), none of these accounts identifies sites or localities that should be avoided to escape encounters with these unusual beings. Rather, they describe persons one might encounter at any place and any time. Parents tell the stories so that young people will know how to act if they have such an experience. As in life generally, the encounters are dangerous only if people lack the knowledge and the ability to deal with the situation.

Although sightings of such persons today are not as common as in the past, they still occur frequently enough that young people require instruction. The tracks and footprints of these persons can still be found, along with an occasional tool or piece of clothing. People can also sometimes hear their singing, stamping, and thumping, proof that they are still present in the land. In the past, when the earth was thin *(nuna-gguq mamkitellruuq tamaani,* from *nuna* land, and *mamkite-* flat object that is thin), encounters with unusual persons were quite common. According to Brentina Chanar of Toksook Bay (February 4, 1991):

> Things were available long ago when the land was thin. Kegluneq said that her grandmother used to say that when the land was thin things like that used to appear. And now that land has become thick, they do not appear, and *ircenrrat* and those others are never seen anymore. That was what was said when *nevuq qecigkitellrani* [the dirt/soil *(nevuq)* was thin-skinned].
>
> When it was thin and when it freezes, you know things going on top of it become resonant. You could also easily hear people walking outside. At that particular time, haunts become many, what they call *carayiit* [literally "terrible, fearsome things"]. So when the earth was thin-skinned, those footsteps would wake them up.

Ircenrrat are perhaps the most commonly encountered of these extraordinary persons. Brentina Chanar reported that they appear as just ordinary people. Although she had not seen them herself, she had heard their songs—proof of their reality. Others say they are small people, two to three feet high, and some people describe them as dwarves on this account. Occasionally a person encounters *ircenrrat* as *yuut* (people), and later sees them as wolves or foxes or other small mammals. At other times, humans encounter wolves or foxes who later reveal themselves as *ircenrrat.* When someone encounters an *ircenrraq*, that person at first will not perceive it as an *ircenrraq*, but as another normal human being. Encounters with extraordinary persons generally are not remembered until days later, as the experience affects a human's perception of time.

Although *ircenrrat* can be seen anywhere, they generally prefer to live in hilly areas, and some people say that these hills were once their houses. People believe *ircenrrat* inhabit specific places, such as the low hill known as Qasginguaq (literally, "a place that looks like a *qasgiq*,") on Nelson Island. Sometimes people find small, toylike sleds or tools in these places.

Brentina Chanar (February 4, 1991) described an encounter with an *ircenrraq*, perceived as a person, in which it gave advice on food preparation. As in many descriptions, the *ircenrraq* appeared clean and radiant, surrounded by a bright light:

> There was this man who went by kayak in the spring. When he saw a kayak, he intercepted it and saw his kayak was radiant. It was an *ircenrraq*. And his kayak and double-bladed oar ornaments were moving. So they talked after their kayaks were side by side. That *ircenrraq* wanted to share his food with him. So they ate. When he took out his food, the *ircenrraq* told him that he could not eat them. And he told him that women should first tie their sleeves while preparing food for the men to take. If they did not, they would pour *caarrluk* [dirt] on the food through their open sleeves. He could not eat his food. And then that *ircenrraq* told him that he was going to go home. And then he went directly toward Ulurruk and he was watching him. . . . He penetrated into the cliff. And then he wondered if the *ircenrrat* were like that. And that is how the story ends.

Although people usually encounter *ircenrrat* in the human world, some stories tell of a person traveling in the hills who happens on the window or door to the world of the *ircenrrat*. That person might look through that opening for what seems like only a moment but is actually a long time. Frances Usugan of Toksook Bay (July 22, 1985) related how a person once heard the songs of the *ircenrrat* while they were celebrating in their underground *qasgiq*. The songs of the *ircenrrat* are easy to remember, and people who have heard them have later used them as songs for the Messenger Feast.

What were those *ircenrrat* in the times through which we came?

My brother,
Cyril Chanar,
from Qasginguaq
he heard drums and singing.
And when winter came, during the time they had Kevgiq
[Messenger Feast],
they had songs that were from the *ircenrrat*.

It is said that when one hears *ircenrrat* singing like that,
they always learn them right away.
He, Nuyaralek's dad,

by walking, he went to get red clay from Angyaruaq,
so far, way over there!

When he was a young men, he walked far during the summer.

Then, as he was going home,
he heard singing.

Evidently, it was from Qasginguaq.
Even though they were far away,
these *ircenrrat* that were singing,
he kept hearing them.

As he neared Qasginguaq,
the singing was becoming less audible.

Then reaching it,
they became quiet then.
(see also Brentina Chanar, February 4, 1991)

Not only could a person encounter *ircenrrat* in the human world, or view
them in their own world, but a person might also visit the *ircenrrat* in their
home—just as the boy visited the seals in their underwater *qasgiq*. There the
human visitor would see his hosts as people. The visitor's ability to return to
the human world depended on his reception. Frances Usugan (July 22, 1985)
gave a detailed story to illustrate this general point:

Also the *ircenrrat* used to bring in . . .
some people to their land.
When they brought them in,
they would sleep overnight.
And when they let them go out,
they would go out
and find that they were coming out a year later.

This after they had just slept overnight.

That was how I used to hear about *ircenrrat*.

I heard a *qanemciq* like this.
They brought in this man,
he was not a *nukalpiaq*,
his parka was a patchwork of different materials
that were not the same.

See, like this, in those times,
when they were destitute, the ones who were not *nukalpiaq*,
they used to have patchwork parkas.

Then,
when the *ircenrrat* brought him in,
in those days when the poor things used to wear parkas
and they had no such things as *qaspeq* [cloth parka cover],

their parkas that were made of bird skins,
the men would wear them fur-side out.

After trying to do something with him,
the *ircenrrat* began to question him,
asking him about his parka.

What had he caught this one with?

The one with the parka
would answer that he caught it with his whatever.

When he asked about a certain one,
he would answer that his father caught this one.
This one, someone else caught.

And also when he asked about another,
he would answer that this was his uncle's catch,
that one was his cousin's catch,
that one was his grandfather's catch,
all of them he said were his relatives' catch.

Then,
the *ircenrrat* said,
"Let us then, the one down there,
without doing things to him,
let him go,
he apparently has a lot of helpers."

They were afraid of him.

"He apparently has a lot of helpers,
let him go
without trying to do things to him."

Like this,
I hear about the *ircenrrat,*
when they are going to go out,
their doors are like this,
the three of them.
Whatever those *ircenrrat* are,
they say to him like this,
for him to go out through the middle,
and the others say to him to go out through the bottom,
or to go out through the top.

Then,
one of the old men said,
"Don't mess around with him,
let him go out through the middle."
Like this,
some of those,
they think he has no relatives.

So if he went through the bottom, he would not make it.
He would be too far down,
or he would be too far up.

They feared him
because he attributed his parka to his relatives,
because they never used to think they lied in those days.

Thinking that he really did have helpers,
those *ircenrrat* feared him,
those elders,
when they used to have them for leaders.

For that reason one of the elders said,
"Without messing around with him, let him go."
And the others had urged him to go through the top and bottom.
[The old man] scolded them to let him go without messing around.

When he went out,
he went out to our world.
That was how I heard that *qanemciq* [story].

If a person spends what seems like a night with the *ircenrrat*, it will actually take a whole year. Parents warn children that if a person they do not recognize asks them to spend the night, they should refuse, as that person might be an *ircenrraq*. Mary Napoka of Tuluksak (May 9, 1989) recalled, "And then from then on, if they could not recognize a person, they came to have an *inerquun* that even if that person tells them to spend a night, they should not spend the night. They say that they only let them go out after one year. For them it is just the next morning."

Some people say that a person should try to take something from the *ircenrraq*, such as a tool or piece of clothing, as it will bring good luck to its owner. Possession of the hunting tool of an *ircenrraq*, for example, will make that person a better hunter. People may also acquire good fortune by exchanging something with an *ircenrraq*. Eddie Alexie of Togiak (March 10, 1988) told the story of a man who had killed a caribou. While he was sleeping, two people (who were actually *ircenrrat*) appeared to him and said that they wanted to trade for his catch. When he awoke, his caribou was gone, but the following spring he was able to catch belukha whales, which had avoided him in the past but were an animal form that *ircenrrat* sometimes take.

Many accounts of encounters with *ircenrrat* contain the implicit moral that if animals are treated poorly, their "persons" will call the offender to account. Billy Lincoln of Toksook Bay (July 21, 1985) related this version of the well-known story of a man's encounter with wolves who were actually *ircenrrat*.

In that time before,
when he was traveling in the wilderness like this,

in the summer,
he apparently came upon these two wolf pups.
They were small wolf puppies.

So, after eyeing them,
because their parents were evidently not around,
he departed, leaving them behind.

Then, as he was traveling,
in the summer of the fall that it was going to happen,
those two wolves began to gain on him from behind.

Then when they came up on him,
repeatedly going past close to him,
they would thrash him with their tails
on his legs.

They would hurt him when they whipped him here,
on his legs.

These were the wolves they used to tell about.
They say that wolves were *ircenrrat*
in that time.

He apparently would say to them,
admonishing them,
that he did not do anything to their kids
and not to do anything to him.

He said to them
that if they didn't stop it, with this one [his gun],
with its load, the weapon against *ircenrrat*,
he was going to hurt one of them.

Its bullet which is never seen,
its load which is never seen.

Saying that he would hurt one of them he would show them it,
but they would not be deterred.

So because it kept doing it,
he shot the bigger of the two
at the area around here,
without trying to kill it.

When he shot it,
they suddenly went away from him.
He then went home.

So, during that particular fall,
when he traveled, he began to hear singing.

When he went to bed,
he began to hear them from somewhere under his pillow,

those singers,
singing from below.

Then, when he went to bed one evening,
from under his pillow they began to sing.

Then, those two strangers were around at his place.

When he opened to them,
there were those two teenagers,
with noses of wolves.

(How do they have their noses?)

They told him that they had come for him.

So when they told him they had come for him,
getting his things together, he went out.
Going out, he saw this sled;
when he sat in it, they secured him to the sled inside a caribou skin.

They told him then
not to inquire about them.

From inside
he could hear them speed off with him.

Because he was curious,
because caribou scratch a lot when being infested with lice,
through that place, he saw two wolves.
Oh, how they were bounding!

Then after bounding, they stopped.

When they stopped,
doing something they took their hoods off.
It was those two teenagers.

They said to him,
"So now you have seen us.
You are going to let us be late in arriving.
Now that you have seen us, don't be curious about us anymore."
They then started out there.

Then they suddenly stopped.

When they stopped,
from his wrap they undid the ties,
and going out
he saw that they were inside a river.
It was deep,
and there were big villages on either side of it.

Those two, without uncertainty
landed right in front of the *qasgiq*.

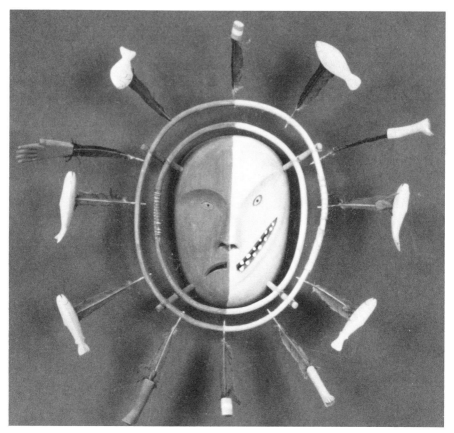

Human/fox mask made for a Messenger Feast, Nunivak, 1946. Many accounts depict ircenrrat *as half human and half animal. Dance masks representing* ircenrrat *often have human features running down one side of the face and animal features on the other. Margaret Lantis; Thomas Burke Memorial Washington State Museum, Seattle.*

They said to him,
"The one who is to come and get you will come for you,
the one who is to bring you up."

As he was there, from the men's houses
a half-man came out, a one-sided human.

Then from the other, its mate came out.

These two came down.
And when they reached him,
placing him between them,
they brought him up to one of the men's houses.

They brought him in
and leaving him in the entrance way
they went in to get the one who will bring him in.

The area under the house had no food in sight.

Then something came for him and brought him in.

The one who was to bring him in
brought him into that *qasgiq*.

Then he sat down
on the corner of the floor.
And the one over there,
the one sitting to the left of the area where one enters,
he was moaning back there.

The one back there
at the end of the floor plank
was a *nukalpiaq* [good provider].

Rolling back and forth,
he would expel puffs of smoke.
Then someone against the wall asked
for what reason had he injured that one?

He then tried to remember who he had hurt,
because he had not hurt any person.

He told them he didn't know,
that he didn't know of doing anything to anybody.

He then said
that while he was out this past summer
he suddenly remembered what he did to those two wolves.

So he related to them about those two
about how he came to these wolves during this trip out this summer
that he had left them alone,
but that their parents had gone after him,
and how they had whipped him with their tails as they passed by,
how he had tried to admonish them to stop,
that he had done nothing to their children.

He told how he had shown them his weapon,
telling them that if they didn't stop
he was going to hurt one of them
with the one whose load cannot be seen.

So then, because they didn't stop bothering him,
without mortally injuring him,
when he could have killed him if he wanted to,
he had injured him.

He told how they finally went away from him
and quit whipping him.

Then that one said,
"And here he is saying that you injured him with no provocation on his part.
Bring him out somewhere and throw him away."

Rushing to him, they dragged him out somewhere.

Then they began to deliberate over something.
The man who was sitting to the left of the entrance,
hanging right above him was a drum.

They began deliberating,
"What is to be done to him?
How are we going to deal with him?"

They decided to hang him.
They instructed someone to go get the one who was to pierce him
because that one had lied.

Then the woman
whose lips were long
told them to hang him with the unbreakable root of the earth.

Then they hung up
the braided root,
the one with no end.

Threading it through there they hung him,
somewhere around the skylight.
As he was hanging there, he fell down,
the thing having broken off.

"Iiii!
See the root that is hard to break,
he has finally made it break."[10]. . .

Only when he spoke like that,
the one near the exit,
the man said . . .
for them to quit messing around with him, to stop it,
that he has come to the conclusion that he has not hurt one of them.

That if they kept messing with him
he was going to throw one of them in the men's place.

So they ended up not killing him.

Then that man,
because he had been told by that one to come,
he sat down near him.

10. Another version of this story told by Wassilie Berlin of Kasigluk refers to hanging the
man from the bridge of his nose on the *taqeq* (vein) or *nunam taqra* (land's vein or artery),
which also breaks, after which the *ircenrrat* free the man (see chapter 8).

That one then,
they thought that he might have been some part of them,
they regarded that man
as though he might have been some part of their ancestors.

As he was there in the *qasgiq*
they said
that a village was approaching for Kevgiq [Messenger Feast].

So they kept going out,
those who went out to watch
the [arriving guests] who had come to "attack."

Then—probably when they were the only ones left—he said to him
that if he was curious, why didn't they go out to watch?

Then that one,
taking his drum down,
they sat down on his drum
and they went outside, flying on that drum.

When they went out
there appeared these two Canadian geese
looking out towards the ocean.

While they were there
the ones out there would come into view.
And after coming into view, they would disappear.

The village was approaching for a Messenger Feast
all grouped together.

And around them
these two,
the ones who are circling around them,
they went back and forth in front of them.

Then, when they were not too far away,
one of them said,
"Has not that stranger become sleepy yet?"

Then the other one said,
"Has a woman done anything to him?"

He responded that a woman has not hid him.

Then that one said to him
that if he has not been that way
the ones circling down there will go for him,
that it is not good for him to be here,
that maybe he should be sent home.

Then fleeing, they went somewhere,
and his companion said to him
that he is to somersault four times.

So following his order he somersaulted four times,
and sitting up he saw
he was somewhere in the wilderness.

Looking around he saw
that he had sat up right in front of his house.

Those things that were hanging outside his house,
the one on his sled, too,
had become white.
They had become old.

To him he had only stayed for a while,
through the night to the next day.

So after having gone through that, he went home.

And when he arrived,
they were surprised about him,
for he had been gone so long, doing something,
and he had arrived home.

So now it has ended.
And that's how long a *qanemciq* it is
that one.

Ircenrrat could also take the form of killer whales, and rules forbade hunting
or injuring these whales for that reason. Anyone who did doomed an immediate family member to die. According to Frances Usugan (July 22, 1985):

And those down there,
the ones they refer to as Kalukaat,
at the bend,
when we go around them, the ones high up there,
they say that they are *ircenrrat.*

And these *arrluut* [killer whales],
they say they are *ircenrrat.*

And down there at the bend,
when a person hears them,
after they make kayak sounds,
the killer whales resubmerge from near the shore, going out.

These are the *Kalukarmiut* [the people of the bend]
who make kayak sounds
as ones who are preparing,
even though they have not seen anything,
the killer whales resubmerge going out,
from near the shore here.

Not only do people believe that wolves and whales—similar in that both
hunt in packs—are sometimes *ircenrrat* in animal form, but they believe

belukha whales occasionally transform themselves into wolves[11]. Brentina
Chanar (February 4, 1991) related this story:

That man went seal hunting. He has another name but I refer to him as
Tumaralria. And so he was sitting upright, using *tupigat* [grass mats, literally
"woven things"] as a windbreaker. He was by the shore of the ocean. As he was
there, from down in the ocean, belukhas came "smoking."

And then he thought, "A long time ago when belukhas are about to come on
land they do that according to what the old men say." So he hid his kayak
among the *unret* [?], and he hid somewhere where he could see the ocean shore.

So they approached toward the shore upwind from him. And then they
emerged from the water from down there.

And when they had landed on shore, they shook and they spew with *mangtak*
[belukha skin with fat attached]. After *ungullerqulnguameng* [?] and they no
longer had *mangtak*, they scurried to all of the spots where things had odor.
And not far from him was a small dark thing. They would all go to it, and
having smelled it, they would shake their head and avoid it. And after they
tired of doing that, they howled like wolves, those belukhas that had come on
land. After they howled, they went up toward the mountains. And soon, maybe
because they had reached the mountains, they howled again.

When they couldn't harm him anymore, going to that small dot that they
kept going to without touching, he saw that it was a shrew. That was the only
thing that they did not eat though they had eaten snow and any kind of feces. It
is that those who first come on land eat everything. It was fortunate that he was
downwind from them. So because he would not stay there indefinitely, he went
home.

That is the length of that story[12].

To this day some people attribute the fluctuating wolf population in
western Alaska to the emergence of *ircenrrat* from their underground homes.
When *ircenrrat* take the form of wolves, they deplete other food resources
such as reindeer and caribou. When elders saw belukha whales ascending the
Kuskokwim River in the summer of 1990, they predicted that the wolf
population would increase during the coming winter.

Finally, *ircenrrat* reveal the future of the people, as in this account by
Brentina Chanar (February 4, 1991):

But those *ircenrrat* revealed the future of the village, for they would have things
or do things that they will experience later on in the future.

Because that may be true that they did that, when we used to always stay at

11. On the killer whale/wolf transformation see Edward Nelson (1899:444) and William
Fitzhugh (1988:47). Also see Sergie Serov (1988:244) on the Koryak belief that killer whales
could transform into wolves in winter when the sea is frozen to hunt reindeer on the land, as
they hunted belukha whales in the sea.

12. "Other spirits that were white whales in the water could come out on land and turn into
wolves. People were afraid to go around the coast alone for this reason. However, beluga
would not transform itself and attack unless the unwary person should stumble and fall"
(Lantis 1946:199).

Nunakauyaq and it was fall, when we didn't move to Nightmute for a long while, only when it is time and it used to get dark, your father would go out and come in and say, "There beyond Qemqeng [river], two lights were traveling very fast and then they disappeared. And then one of you got up. There is a flashlight coming down on this side of Niyalruq!"

But when we went out to check, we did not see it. And sometimes, from the end of Qemqeng, we would hear something roaring. And across from us, there would be lights but nothing would happen to us.

And now Ski-dos go by light across there and coming down from Niyalruq. I used to suspect that [ircenrrat] revealed what is to be and roaring Ski-dos used to approach from over there! . . .

It was probably them, revealing what people will do, the coming generation.

Not only did *ircenrrat* often possess technological innovations prior to their introduction in the human world, but *ircenrrat* might also foretell death or disaster. When people heard thumping noises, they believed that the *ircenrrat* were stomping their feet or banging their doors, making noise at their pleasure in receiving someone. These sounds warned that someone was about to die. The association between *ircenrrat* and awareness, or understanding, of death is extended in Nelson's story (1899:480–81) of the dwarf couple who came to reside at Pikmiktalik. After the death of their tiny son, they introduced the people to the making of grave boxes and the custom of mourning the dead for four days.

A second category of extraordinary persons are the *egacuayiit*. People described them as tiny, harmless "errand people," who, when humans wanted something at night, would throw the desired object in from the entryway. By most accounts, they filled their flowing sleeves with fish stolen from fish-traps. They might also have dark faces and eyes in a vertical position. Some people considered the *egacuayiit* a kind of *ircenrrat*. Others viewed them as simply another category of person:

They apparently were people, too.
They had the name of *egacuayiit*.

They didn't have a house for a home.
They had legs like a small animal.
And these
were like the legs of those animals over there,
that hop around to walk,
and keep their young here.

They were not lazy.

And they spoke Yup'ik with a different dialect,
but they were understandable.

So in the *qasgiq*, then,
they used to have *qerrutet* [urine buckets]
that were round and made out of wood.

After he had dumped his bucket outside,
his wooden bucket,
he would come in,
forgetting his *qerrun* outside.

Outside in complete darkness.

And their floor had boards of wood.

One of them would say like this,
"Oh dear!
I have just left my *qerrun*!"

The language of the *egacuayiit* is a little different,
but it is understandable.

And just after he finished saying that,
down there,
the area where there had been nobody,
his *qerrun* would be going fast towards the inside,
and someone out there would say,
"Here is your *qerrun*!"

It was that person, understandable.
(Tim Agartak, Nightmute, July 18, 1986)

James Lott of Tuluksak (May 9, 1989) told a parallel account, adding this additional detail:

And when they want to heat their house, having no stoves, they light fire at the middle of the floor, they open the window above.

When a man or woman said, "I did not get a fire," those *egacuayiit*—they were not lazy—would throw that stick with a cinder at the end into the house and say, "*Kincici tamaai!*" [*Kencicin tamaa-ii*, "Here comes your fire!" from *keneq* fire] They did not know how to speak proper Yup'ik. They look like regular people, but they used to disappear when they went into the shade. They would look, but he would not be there.

Thomas Chikigak of Alakanuk (August 11, 1987) reported another commonly asserted characteristic of *egacuayiit*: "The *egacuayiit* take fish out to the fishtraps. It's known that they do that. And the fishtraps, even though they are made of wood, I don't know how, they turn them inside out."

Brentina Chanar (February 4, 1991) described *egacuayiit* as "extraordinary but hilarious."

They were not amazing, but they had big sleeves, probably because they used to see them. And they used to always take the fish out of fishtraps and put them in their sleeves, because they probably eat fish.

Once there was a man who went to check his *taluyaq* [fish trap]. He saw that *egacuayak* [singular] taking fish out of it. And when he scolded him, the *egacuayak* left having a hard time lifting his sleeves.

So while it was leaving, that man answered him saying the *egacuayak* had taken fish from his *taluyaq*.

And those *egacuayiit* always mimicked what people said to them. So the man said to it, "You will get bad when you eat!"

And then it said the same thing back to the man. They would always say exactly what is said to them by anyone.

And then the man said to it, "You will start scratching and . . . your rectum will start issuing!"

And the *egacuayak* said the same back to the man.

So the time passed. And the year after that, the man became like that, just like the *egacuayak* had said to him. He started to scratch all the time; just the way he said, he started issuing from his rectum.

So it is that they should not be talked to in that way.

And also one of the men answered it like this: "It is good that you will become strong!" And then it answered him the same.

"May you never be ailing anymore!" And it said the same thing to him.

It was because that man was always ailing and sick. And it was true that he became just like the way the *egacuayak* had said. He was no longer sick, he became well. And he regained strength.

A third variety of extraordinary person sometimes encountered on the tundra is the *cingssiik,* from *cingik* (point, tip), referring to the being's pointed head and conical hat resembling a fishtrap. Brentina Chanar (February 4, 1991) recalled, "I've heard that they use a thimble as a hat and a needle as a cane. As one is coming into the *qasgiq,* he could hear the pitter patter of small feet inside. When he peeked in, he saw small people wearing thimbles as hats, and they say that they have pointed heads, and their canes are shiny needles. And when they detect a person present, they scurry around and go behind the cracks in the wall. That is how I've heard about the *cingssiiget* [plural]."

Magdeline Sunny of Nightmute (July 17, 1985) described observing *cingssiiget* through the window of their *qasgiq* much as others described looking into the world of the *ircenrrat:*

I wonder how big I was,
up in that direction at Cakcaaq?
I probably was a young girl.

As I was, I observed,
I was going up a house.
And then,
when I came to it, I saw it had no window,
this old house.

Then, lying low, I stayed that way.

Then as I was there,
this little tiny person went down.
Then another went down.
Soon there were many of them down on the floor.
They had heads that were pointy.

And what they held in their hands
were what they used to call *mingqun* [needle].

They were going about on the floor,
doing things.
Then gathering together my saliva,
I let it fall.
It splashed.

When it splashed those people,
in a flurry,
they began to go up.
And down there, shining
were what had been their walking sticks.
Then after watching them,
I went down.

According to Eddie Alexie (March 10, 1988), *cingssiiget* made noise in the *qasgiq* when no one was there. But they were never seen, only their footprints. James Lott of Tuluksak (May 9, 1989) said much the same thing: "In those days when the land was thin, everything was available. And those little people that were this big, only at night they could be seen in the dark, in the old houses. Even though they talk, they cannot be understood. They talk like little birds, as if they were chirping, they could not be understood. And a person could not get hold of them, they scatter in smoke. Even if one tries to take them, they cannot be taken. Those are what they call *cingssiiget*—the little people. Those people used to be visible when the land was thin. When one makes calculations, it must have been 400 to 500 years ago."

Thomas Chikigak (August 11, 1987) gave a detailed account of a man whose curiosity about *cingssiiget* made him lie in wait for them in the *qasgiq*. In the dark he could hear them but could not see them. When they arrived, the man grabbed out and captured one. All of the other *cingssiiget* disappeared into the ground. Although small, his invisible captive was strong and began to pull him toward the wall of the *qasgiq*. The man then called to a boy companion to light the lamp. When the boy did so, the *cingssiik* lost all his strength and became visible as a small person. The man then began to tease and torture the *cingssiik*, holding it close to the flame of the lamp. The boy, however, through his thoughts, silently communicated to the *cingssiik* that he disapproved of the man's ill treatment. After this encounter, the man gradually lost his ability to hunt, while the boy became a good hunter. When the man sighted game, something always seemed to startle the animals, and they fled from him. In contrast, when the boy sighted animals, they were driven in his direction and he was able to make a catch. It was said that the *cingssiik* was repaying them, one for his good thoughts and the other for his bad treatment.

Another kind of extraordinary people are the *tenguirayulit* (from *tenguk*

liver), literally "the ones which like to take the livers" of people. Joshua
Phillip of Tuluksak (July 1, 1988 BIA48:2–4) gave this description:

> The *tenguirayulit* people . . . are true beings, and that still holds today. And
> they are really fast. Once before, they saw a person behind the area of the
> village of Akiachak. And when he took off through the air, he only left a trace
> of the trees being wind blown with snow. That is them there, the ones which
> travel through the air. They are real and are alive today. And those beings, with
> my own eyes, I have seen their trails. Here he had crossed the Elaayiq, and once
> he had crossed, before he got to the trees, his path disappeared. Those are what
> they call *tenguirayulit*. They look just like us, and they wear the same types of
> clothing and eat the same types of food as us. But they are very fleet-footed and
> travel through midair. And we were told by some white people that down in the
> middle of the ocean, in some instances, they come aboard ships. And when they
> come aboard, they eat and change their clothing as much as they please. And if
> they wanted to take money from the ship they also took as much as they
> pleased. The white people say not to bother them whatsoever. . . . The white
> people refer to them by a different name. . . .
>
> If a person should shoot one, they will die just like we would. But it is a rule
> not to bother them. This is what the white people say, should the *tenguirayulit*
> miss one of their members, and they find him dead, within a half hour, no
> matter how large an area, they can destroy every living soul within that half
> hour, should they counterattack. That is the reason why one should not disturb
> them in any way.
>
> Whenever I think about it, I always think maybe the white people may have
> killed one of those people. Because why would they know that if they were
> counterattacked they would destroy so many people within just half an
> hour. . . .
>
> I have heard a number of times of sightings of the tracks of those beings.
> They even say that their footprints would end abruptly at open ice holes. . . .
>
> When they were across the old village of Qinaq, at Pailleq, they were missing
> a boy. Two of those beings dragged him away, and then when they got further
> back, one of the people found a liver of a person. Then from there, that person
> who was dragged away kept in step with those beings, leaving a trail behind
> them of their footprints getting farther and farther apart with each step until
> they disappeared. When the time came, that person came back to pay a visit to
> his parents, just once. And he told his parents that they should not pity him, he
> said that he was supplied with any food that he wanted to eat, anything that he
> had in mind. He said he was not pitiful. . . . That is how he became one of
> them, the ones they call *tenguirayulit*.

Another being that sometimes appears in human form is the *amikuk*.
These huge creatures also have unique pathways, as they can travel through
land or air; it is said they pass through land as if it were water. When they
alight, they make a thumping sound. These strange creatures can also have a human incarnation. According to Joe Friday of Chevak (July 6, 1984 BIA40–49):

> It has been said that these *amikut* can turn into another form when they get
> tired of being *amikut* for a long time. When they reveal themselves, they turn

"Mask representing 'Amekak' [amikuk], which lives in the ground and leaves no hole when it emerges. It dislikes men and will jump through them, leaving no mark. The man then lies down and dies." A. H. Twitchell, 1910; National Museum of the American Indian.

themselves into a human form, and they would be pulling a sled. When they turn into that form, they would be referred to as *qamungelriit* [from *qamur-* to drag or pull something].

Our ancestors have been passing down advice on what to do if you run into this person that is pulling a sled. You are to sit with your back to that person dragging a sled, and you should always go in front of his path and sit.

Our ancestors' advice said to do just that. And they never used to tell about those beings coming around to our area, but they just wanted to make sure that a person knew what to do in case s/he comes across one. They would say that those beings have always been seen in the northern part of our area.

Our ancestors say that the *amikuk* can't go around the person sitting in front of him/her. The *amikuk* will be surprised and will ask the person why s/he is sitting on his pathway. Our elders long ago said never to converse with the *amikuk* when it first starts talking. These rules were strictly emphasized by the elders long ago.

At that point the *amikuk* will start offering gifts but saying that the person sitting on his path should let him pass. But still the person sitting on his pathway should not answer. The *amikuk* will continue to offer another gift as long as the person sitting will not answer. From what I heard about these beings, a person that sits on the *amikuk*'s pathway can become very rich. The person sitting on the pathway of the *amikuk* is advised to answer the *qamulek* [the one pulling a sled] only when the *qamulek* has named everything that the person needs, or that anything is mentioned that is on his mind.[13]

According to Joe Friday (Pingayak 1986), the *qamulek* looks like a normal person when it is in human form. If a man meets a *qamulek*, the "prized catch," he should block its path. The *qamulek* can walk only in a straight line, so the hunter should sit in its path and avoid looking at it. This is the opposite of the appropriate behavior for a hunter, that is, clearing a path for animals and looking directly at them with one's strong vision. The *qamulek* will then name gifts, and to acquire them, the person should identify what he wants, then leave, still without looking at the *qamulek*. The first question the *qamulek* will ask is why the person is blocking his path, but the person should not answer. It is said that the *qamulek* will remain standing forever unless the human gets off his path. It is also said that the *qamulek* will tell the human not to watch him as he leaves. When he leaves, he will look back at the human under first his right, then his left, arm.

Joe Friday (Pingayak 1986:16) told a story of a man named Quran who encountered a *qamulek* and started shooting at it. The *qamulek* asked Quran why he was making him suffer, and Quran asked the *qamulek* why the *qamulek* was in his way. The *qamulek* answered that Quran's mind was causing him to be in Quran's path. As he collapsed, he told Quran not to look in his sled. After this encounter Quran lost his ability to catch animals even when they were readily available, and people assumed that this was because Quran had, in fact, looked in the sled of the *qamulek*.

Another story tells of a man living north of the Yukon River who encountered a *qamulek* and did not answer it until it promised to fill his bag with gold. The *qamulek* did so, and when white people heard about the money, they rushed to Nome. Many froze to death along their way. This story constitutes one Yup'ik explanation of the gold rush to northern Alaska at the turn of the century.

Just as people believed that it was the power of the mind that drew the animals to be hunted, putting them in a person's path, so the power of a person's mind put the *qamulek* in one's path. When asked, "What are you doing in my path?" the *qamulek* would answer, "You put me here." If people handled the situation correctly, they were rewarded with good hunting in the future; if not, disaster followed.

Another extraordinary person sometimes encountered out on the ice is the *qununiq*, a male seal-person (see also Lantis 1946:199). At first approach, this

13. John Pingayak (1986:13), also of Chevak, reported that often there is a small nest close by, and the *amikuk* will act like a bird and try to protect it: "If you find the nest, you wouldn't find any eggs, only small pieces of fur. When these nests are taken home, they produce many riches of furs, skins, and other items. A person can place small portions of furs, skins or other items inside the nest and they will become whole the next day. . . . It also applies to other things not just to furs and skins."

being looks like a person wearing five rain parkas. Brentina Chanar (February 4, 1991) gave this account:

> When Kanglek and Taulen went to it, it was a person who was waving like this. When they approached it, it was on top of the ice, lying down wearing sealgut rain parkas and *arilluuk* [waterproof fish-skin mittens (dual)] and *ivrucik* [waterproof skin boots]. And so when they got to it, they waited. So they waited, and soon he took his spear, and [*qununiq*] was wearing five rain parkas. [Kanglek] pierced the last strand of the gut on his hem, and then it fell into the water! Then that *usaaq* [line attached to a spear] went out.
>
> So his line went out. When it surfaced it was a *maklassuk* [two-year-old bearded seal]; that is what those *qununit* are, but they were not scary. So having caught it, they went home. So when they brought food to the old men, one of them was given a shoulder blade. When he was eating the bone clean, he recognized it as *qununiq*. Its shoulder blade had a hole just like a human [shoulder blade]. So by that he found out that he had caught a *qununiq*.
>
> And after that Kanglek said, "I will never get *qununiq*." . . . After that, although he heard one make noise like that while his son was with him, he turned around and didn't hunt it. He would never hunt it though it beckoned him—it had almost expended him. So he left it behind.

John Pingayak (1986:15) of Chevak added that the transformation of the *qununiq* into a seal predicts how long a person's life will be: "If the *qununiq* turns into a bearded seal in the morning, your life will be short; noon transformation means half a life; late afternoon or evening means a full life into ripe old age." He also noted that when approaching a *qununiq*, a hunter will encounter seals and other sea animals that are the *neqcaq* (bait) of the *qununiq*. These are to be avoided if a person wants an opportunity to get the *qununiq*.

Another category of person sometimes encountered is the *agiirrnguat*, "the ones looking as if they are approaching from a distance" (from *agiirte-* to approach from a distance). If people look around anxiously watching for someone's arrival, they might invoke the presence of the *agiirrnguat*. Frances Usugan (July 22, 1985) told this *neq'ayaraq* (story) recounting a past experience with *agiirrnguat*.

> The ones looking as if they're approaching
> up there at Cakcaaq,
> we see tracks of the *agiirrnguat*.
>
> They used to tell us like this,
> that we were not to be anxiously looking around.
>
> With my own eyes,
> I have seen the tracks of the *agiirrnguat*.
>
> To Cakcaaq
> they travel nowadays.
> At the "throat" of the Qalvinraq is Cakcaaq.

Those people apparently *curukarluteng* [attend a challenge feast, from *curug-* to
    go over to attack, physically or verbally]
to the other side of the mountain,
these Cakcaarmiut.

Then,
these two, a grandmother and a grandchild,
they were the ones that stayed behind.

So the *curukat* [invited villagers, literally "attackers"]
did not arrive when they should.

They did not come back.

Then,
her grandchild,
on account of his being impatient for their arrival,
he looks for them from on top of the house.

As he was looking,
from near the small mountain,
towards the evening,
he sees them coming down.

Then,
his poor grandmother,
when he went in,
taking her up, he tells her that they are approaching.

So, then,
through the whole evening, from the mountain,
they have been coming down.

Through the whole night,
through the whole day.

They were going down very, very slowly.

So,
many, many times
he would go out and check them,
they would just have come only this far.

With the coming of the evening they became faster.

These were the *agiirrnguat.*

So for that reason,
they used to tell us not to look around too much.

That [if we did] we would turn into *agiirrnguat.*

That one we used to be afraid of.

Then, in the evening, when they became fast,
when their sound became audible,
they were creaking.

When I asked about that,
they said that came from a whole bunch of *citaat*
[old-style coffins in which a person was buried with knees
   folded and drawn up to the chin].

So,
when he told his poor grandmother
that they were coming faster,
and that their sound could be heard,
his poor grandmother,
with whatever she had,
some way, maybe with just her mind,
she wished that they could be missed.

She was doing whatever she could do
so that the village would not be in their direct path.

They used to do just some poor little things,
and an elder's, an old woman's or an old man's, mind used to
   be strong.

And like this,
it used to be like praying when they lived.

That place,
just barely missing them,
those *agiirrnguat* came.
Up there then, right near Cakcaaq is a trail,
the trail of the *agiirrnguat*.

So like that, it ends.

Other extraordinary people believed to inhabit the Bering Sea coast are the *tengmiarpiit*, people who appear as giant birds and who nest at known sites on low volcanic domes and hills scattered throughout the region. The relationship of these bird-people to humans is sometimes friendly and protective and sometimes hostile and destructive. Nelson (1899:486–87) describes the destruction of the last of these "giant eagles" or "thunderbirds" by a hunter in retribution for the death of his wife. Having killed the young birds in the nest, he waited for their parents, which he shot. But they flew away, never to be seen again. Although contemporary elders agree that many *tengmiarpiit* were killed in the past, they still believe some remain in the low mountains to the north of the Yukon River (Pratt 1993).

Along with extraordinary persons, various categories of creatures also inhabit the Yup'ik world. Among these is the *itqiirpak*, the huge hand that lives in the ocean and has mouths on each finger and a mouth in the palm. If children make too much noise at night, it might rise from the ocean and devour them. The *meriiq* (from *meq* water) is a creature that sucks the blood from one's big toe if there is no water in the house or tent. The *muruayuli* (from *muru-* to sink, literally "the one that is good at sinking") is a creature that sinks into the ground when it walks. The *arularaq* (from *arula-* to be in motion, to move back and forth) is described as a monster with three toes on each foot and six toes on each hand. *Quugaarpiit* live underground and swim on land ("land is like water to them when they travel"), and they are identified with mastodons, whose bones are sometimes found in western Alaska: "They say that those are muskrats that have transformed into those kinds of creatures. You know that muskrats have big incisors and *quugaarpiit* have ivory teeth. . . . But though they have been muskrats, they are huge. Their teeth and bones are extremely hard, and [people] carve them. They only find their bones under the ground and never in the water. . . . When the waves erode the ground, they become visible. . . . But now they are never seen anymore" (Brentina Chanar, February 4, 1991).

Amllit (from *amllir-* to step over) are abrasive creatures that live in shallow, milky-colored lakes. If they are encountered in the water, one must step over them, not try to go around them. Even though the water is not deep in those lakes, if a person tries to go around them, that person will not live. *Ingluilnguq* (from *inglu* other one of a pair, literally "one lacking the other one of a pair"), or *ingluperayugaat*, have one leg, one arm, one eye, half a head, and half a body. The *miluquyuli* (from *miluqu-* to heave or throw with malicious intent) is. a legendary rock-throwing creature, the size of a small human. And the *ulurrugnaq* is a sea monster said to devour whales. These creatures do not exhaust the list.

EXTRAORDINARY PERSONS, STRANGE TRAILS

What seem to us simple differences between humans and animals belie the complex interrelationship between numerous categories of human and non-human persons in the Yup'ik world. Appearances are often deceiving. The man encountered on the tundra might be an *ircenrraq* in human form. Conversely, the wolf cubs seen playing in the grass might be *ircenrrat* in animal incarnation. Just as animals might be encountered in human form, so extraordinary persons might be encountered as animals.

Extraordinary persons are often characterized by their unusual paths. *Tenguirayulit* leave visible tracks that end abruptly at open ice holes or that get farther and farther apart with each step until they disappear. The *amikuk* also has unique pathways and can travel through land as if it were water. In some cases people are told that, if they encounter an extraordinary person, they should place themselves in the creature's path. People who come across an *amikuk*, for instance, must block its path and refuse to look at it—as compared to the good hunter, who should clear the animal's path and fix it with his gaze. Conversely, the *agiirrnguat* appear when a person watches the trail too closely. They approach slowly from a distance, and people can avoid disaster only by moving out of their path. People also may encounter creatures blocking or otherwise obstructing their paths. People must step over the *amllit*, or they will die. A person who meets an *alangruq* (ghost or apparition, literally "thing which appears unexpectedly") blocking the path should push it down with the palm of one's hand. People are also instructed to let the weight of their hands push down *amiingitulit* (those who obstruct passageways, from *amik* entranceway). If they turn and flee, they will en- counter that same person in the opposite doorway. If they keep running back and forth, the space between the doorways will become smaller and smaller. Only by touching the person's skin and pressing it into the ground can they successfully enter.

The variety of persons and creatures that one might encounter in one's path is immense. Moreover, human action or thought—and thoughtless- ness—often produces their presence. The man who injured the wolf was called to account by *ircenrrat*. The boy who kept looking for people's arrival evoked the *agiirrnguat*. Just as the power of a person's mind clears a path for the animals, the mind's power caused the *gamulek*, the "prized catch," to appear in the hunter's path. The Yup'ik universe is a moral one, and each human action is believed to produce an appropriate reaction. Knowledge of the many forms in which things might appear is a person's best preparation for both ordinary and extraordinary encounters with human and nonhuman persons. Listening to accounts of the experiences of people who have lived before them provides such knowledge. In this way a person learns both what to do to keep the path clear and how to remove obstacles that one might encounter.

CHAPTER 3

CLEARING THE WAY
The Entry of Animals into the Human World

When people from your home are taking care of the doorways during bad weather, they make the way clear for the seals which will come to them during the springtime.

—Paul John, *"The Boy Who Went to Live with the Seals"*

ANIMAL GUEST AND HUMAN HOST

Because of their shared qualities of personhood, humans and animals treated each other with mutual respect. People did not consider animals a nonsentient resource to be harvested according to the dictates of human need, but rather classes of persons with whom they had established relationships, complete with mutual obligations. When animals entered human space, men and women treated them as honored guests to be hosted and sent away satisfied.

Beginning from the recognition of this essential similarity, animals and humans were systematically differentiated in thought and deed. A plethora of rules and regulations for the interaction and exchange between animals and humans established and maintained their difference. Boundaries were in place that the Yup'ik people did not believe existed when the earth was new. Now humans and animals inhabited their own worlds. For interaction to take place, properly prepared human hunters must move out of the village into animal space, and animals must accompany them back into the human world.

Many obstacles blocked the path between human and nonhuman domains, and only careful attention to the rules by both humans and animals made crossing through possible. The boundaries between the human and animal worlds could not be crossed randomly, thoughtlessly, without consequence. The passages had to be carefully prepared and an invitation sent to "draw" the animal guests into village space. If the animals approved the hunter's actions and state of mind, if they felt the power of his mind, they would follow the path he had cleared. On their arrival in the village, animals were given valued gifts (water or oil) and their bodies rigorously cared for to insure their return. During the winter ceremonial season, villagers likewise feasted and hosted the animals' *yuit* (their persons).

Hunters at the mouth of the Kuskokwim. Moravian Seminary, Bethel, Alaska.

To fail to host animals properly invited disaster. If people treated an animal's body thoughtlessly, or carelessly wasted or trampled on food, *ellam yua* (the person of the universe) would come and "wake them up." Elaborate rules circumscribed human behavior toward animal guests to guard against such an eventuality and insure that the animals return in the future. Although many of these rules are no longer followed, elders in the 1980s vividly recalled these practices as well as their significance.

RULES SURROUNDING TREATMENT OF SEALS:
PASSAGE FROM SEA TO LAND

Among the different animal-persons hosted by humans on the Bering Sea coast, the most important were the sea animals *(imarpigmiut* "people of the ocean" or *imarpiim unguvalriit* "living things in the ocean," from *imarpik* ocean, plus *unguva* life). The focus of activity and concern was on neither whales nor walrus but three varieties of *taqukat*[1]—bearded, ringed, and spotted seals—abounding in the shallow coastal waters.

With the return of light and the receding ice pack, March and April found hunters and their families preparing in earnest for spring seal hunting *(qamigarluni)*. The seals who had remained in their underwater homes

---

1. Although *taqukaq* (singular) is the generic name for seals along the coast, it means "brown bear" inland and upriver.

through the winter would begin their journey to the human world. In antici-
pation men and women alike worked to prepare the passageway to permit
their entry. According to Theresa Moses of Toksook Bay (August 1987
NI94), "During the beginning of spring, when hunters start catching seals,
they had *inerquutet* [warnings] not to use tools at the door. Not to chip or
carve wood at the door. . . . No one, including the children, could use tools
at the door through which seals were to be brought in."

Likewise young men were admonished to keep the doorways and water holes
clear of snow. Joe Ayagerak, Sr., of Chevak (December 16, 1987) recalled:

> Those *inerquutet* that I know . . . tell me that if there is drifting snow to clean
> the doorways. . . . And they told me to think that while I am cleaning the
> paths of the people or somebody's doorway this is the way I should be thinking:
> the bearded seal that I am hunting will be on top of this spot. It will be sleeping
> here, lying here. That is how I will be thinking while I am cleaning. . . .
>
> Those *nukalpiat* [men in their prime, good hunters and providers] especially
> used to work on clearing off the doorways. And it is said that the one below
> whom he will catch will hear it more and more until the time he is actually
> caught. . . .
>
> It is as if those who take care of doorways are throwing snow on the window
> of the seal world. And it is easy to tell when that happens.

Mary Beaver of Goodnews Bay (June 1988 YN30:6–7) concurred:

> And at night when they used to have *qasgiq*, and the men slept in the *qasgiq*, he
> shoveled the doorways. Sometimes while he shoveled he would dig up the
> whiskers of a bearded seal, and they would be throbbing. . . .
>
> Then people did not indulge in sleep, and they kept waking up more than
> once in the night. And they did not let the snow collect in the doorways . . .
> and the ice hole.

Conversely, clearing the passageways without proper thought and concentration created a barrier the seals would not cross. An analogy existed between the clear mind of the hunter and the clear path he hoped to make for
the animals' approach. Humans know to perform these acts because of the
experiences of the boy who spent the winter as a guest in the seals' underwater men's house. During the boy's stay in the seal world, his seal mentor
warned him, "Be a witness to it. . . . You will dare not to think of the
animals you will catch and randomly throw away the contents of your shovel.
And you will not be thinking of anything. You hear that person over there,
because he is not thinking about making the way clear for what he will catch,
wherever the contents of his shovel lands is creating an obstacle for the game
he should catch" (Paul John, Toksook Bay, February 2, 1977).

Just as hunters must keep the doorways clear to allow the seals' entry, so
they must keep the water holes, the "windows of the world below," clear to
allow the seals to view the preparations for their arrival that their human
hosts were making.

And while they were staying [in the seal world], during that winter, when the weather was bad, a person up above would clean [the window] off. . . .

When the person looked down that water hole, the window of their *qasgiq*, that boy who was from his village, and that boy [living with the seals] would recognize him.

So his mentor would say to him, "See and observe him. See that person up there who is one of the people from your village.

So just like the way he did it, if you go back to your village and you are making a living, do not clear off the water hole carelessly. And if you are thirsty, stoop down and drink like that.

We will see you exactly the way we just saw him." (Paul John, February 2, 1977)

Throughout the winter men and women worked carefully and diligently to encourage the seals to come to them in the spring. Men prepared new and attractive hunting equipment, as they believed that the seals appreciated being killed by beautiful weapons. They set new kayak covers to bleach in the sun and painted their bentwood hunting hats with white clay, as the seals preferred clean, white things. Women likewise carefully stitched new gut parkas and hunting boots, both to protect and empower the hunters, and to attract and please the seals.

The Yup'ik people believed the seals came of their own volition, motivated by their thirst for fresh water. Seals were believed to come to a hunter and his wife to quench this thirst and were thankful when the hunter helped them out of their holes and the woman let them drink. The hauling and handling of water was an important part of the preparation for the seals' arrival and was carefully regulated. According to Theresa Moses of Toksook Bay (August 1987 NI94), "During the wintertime, the men who were preparing to go seal hunting were encouraged to keep fetching water and take care of the refuse. The reason was that the seals long to go to them because if they are going to cook them they would not be without water. They fetch water and wood to use."

As boys fetched fresh water from the ice holes, they were admonished never to urinate by the hole or contaminate it with unclean water. If they did so, the hole's *yua* (its person) would experience their urine as rain beating down on its head and would be seriously offended.

Just as fresh water was attractive to seals, the smell of the land also pleased them. It was said that the smell of dirt and "trash" (unspecified) overrode unpleasant human odors. People considered both disposing of refuse and cleaning of floors honorable and advantageous occupations. The dust of the land imparted power to human workers and made them attractive to the seals. Men fumigated their bodies in preparation for hunting with the smoke of wild celery, Labrador tea, and blackberry bushes for this reason: "They try to smell like the land so the ones they could catch cannot go away from them. So through the smoke or some other way, by wiping some product of the earth on themselves, they tried to be the same smell as the land. Then [the dirt] on his body is like a barrier to these misfortunes. With the trash of the people spread on one's person, they used to say misfortune cannot touch one" (Toksook Bay Elders, November 3, 1983 NI57).

Each hunter acted as *ek'eralria*, literally "the one crossing over," every year in preparation for the first seal hunt of the season. He purified not only his body with smoke but his equipment as well, including his sitting mat, pack basket, food supplies, and kayak.

> When those who had kayaks were going to the sea for the first time in the spring season, they did that. If they were going to go, they collected all kinds of plants and dried them. And when they were going to leave, they burned those [plants] by their kayaks with those they were going to take. Having shaken those things over the fire, they would put them in the kayak. They shook all of them. And when they have done that to all their things, the kayak would be here and the fire here, and they let the smoke through here [inside their clothing], and dragging the kayak, they let it go over the fire. And then they leave. (Brentina Chanar, Toksook Bay, June 30, 1989; see also Billy Lincoln, Toksook Bay, January 15, 1991)[2]

It was particularly important to perform this act of purification following a human death.

> Like in the spring, some people do die. So before they go seal hunting, they *tarvarluki* [fumigate with smoke] their equipment, their kayaks.
> And when we are going to seal hunt for the first time, even though we have hunted seal before, but when we are going to hunt seals during spring camp, after we build a fire we shake our equipment over the fire. And our kayak, we spread smoke over it, and then we put it upright. We put it on top of the sled. . . .
> They did that so that the catch of the ocean would be attracted to the individual. (Joe Ayagerak, Sr., December 16, 1987)

The hunter and his wife also offered food to the seals. According to Paul John (February 2, 1977), "When they actually got to the ocean they made food offerings to the seals they would catch, giving them something to eat. They took a little bit of their food and threw it into the water. Even though it was a small amount, they threw it. It is said they gave food offerings for the seals that they were going to catch to eat."[3]

The hunter's state of mind was as important as the acts he performed. A hunter ideally must keep the thought of the seals first and foremost in his mind during, as well as prior to, the seal hunt. If his thoughts were scattered and unfocused, the seals would see him as paddling his kayak suspended in

2. Lantis (1947:39) notes that on Nunivak a hunter would carry a lamp around his kayak and thrust it under the kayak. Then he would walk around his boat east to west, launch it, paddle around clockwise three times, and head out to sea. Compare Paul Ivanoff's description of the spring hunt on Nunivak (Sonne 1988:172).

3. See also Curtis (1930:13–15), Lantis (1946:193–94), and Rasmussen (1927:351) on boat-launching ceremonies.

air. At the time of seal hunting, seals would not allow themselves to be taken by men they viewed in this way.

> And then sometimes [the seals] would see a kayak in midair. He would be rowing not touching the water.
> But occasionally the tip of his oar would barely dip into the water.
> His mentor would say to him, "You see him there in the distance, because he has no awareness of actually rowing in the world of us who live in the ocean, you see him there rowing elevated from his particular location. . . . Because he never ever thinks about the ocean seriously, he is rowing like that." (Paul John, February 2, 1977)

Rules not only required hunters to act in certain ways to "draw" the seals, numerous *inerquutet* prohibited certain actions if a man wanted to be successful in the hunt. People who failed to live by the rules would appear distorted to the seals in one way or another. For example, men were forbidden to walk under lines hung with clothing or other objects. If they did so, the seals would see them bedecked in hanging paraphernalia, encumbered by "a necklace of many things such as old mukluks" (Theresa Moses, August 1987 NI95A). For the same reason, a man must not pick lice from someone's head using his teeth but must carefully pull them out with his fingers. If he used his teeth, he would appear to the seals with a mouthful of hair. This would so scare the seals that they would be too terrified to approach him.

Another rule required a person to make a stylized "removal motion" after drinking water from a bowl or dipper. This was done by passing one's right hand back and forth across the face to clear one's vision. If a man failed to perform this motion, he would not be able to see animals, even though they were well within his view. Furthermore, the animals would see him as having the bowl or water dipper or bucket stuck to the front of his face. The story of the boy who went to live with the seals portrays the consequences of this action.

> Sometimes that old man would say to him, "Now look at where you came from at a man who picks up the water bucket and drinks from it."
> The child would look and see a man with a bucket hanging on his neck like a necklace. When the man turned his head, the bucket would make noises.
> Those are the men who *aug'aruayuilnguut* [never make a necessary motion to remove the object in front of their faces]. These men would never see the seals even when they were in full view.
> And there were times when the old man directed the attention of the child to look at one man. The man's face would be covered with a wooden bowl. These were times when people made bowls of wood. Even when such a man looked toward them, he could not see them. He would say to the child, "See how a man looks who does not make a removal motion." (Camille Joseph, Alakanuk, August 9, 1987)[4]

4. Joe Ayagerak, Sr., of Chevak (December 16, 1987) compared the bowl covering the face to a mask: "In those times they had drinking containers. . . . And after we drink and put it

A hunter who slept facing his wife would impair his vision, and the seals would see him with a woman's braid covering his eyes.

> One of them would be rowing a kayak biting on a tuft of hair. But even though he was biting on those hairs, he was turning his head around, looking. The boy's mentor would tell him about that person.
> "See! That person up there, even though his wife is turned away from him, he is the one who lies facing his wife!"
> And so that person would pass them; and even though they look at him, that person would never see them! He would pass them not too far away from them. (Joe Ayagerak, Sr., December 16, 1987)

If a man used his pants for a pillow, it had the same effect. According to Camille Joseph of Alakanuk (August 9, 1987), "Even when they look around at [the seals], they would never see them, even when they were in full view. Such a man would pass by unaware of their presence. His face was covered. And sometimes some men fold their pants and use them as pillows when they go to bed. Their faces would be covered with their pants."

The seals also regulated their own behavior:

> They did not want them to be caught by their hunters while they were sleeping because they would lack speed in rushing into their *qamenqut* [?].
> So that was their law that they must try to stay awake when they were being hunted.
> And then when the one who will catch him harpoons him, using all his agility, he then should rush into the very end of his captor's kayak.
> It was that . . . they told them so that their living spirits *(yuucian unguvii)* would rush into their bladders.
> So the ones who indulge in sleep too much, if they did not rush into their bladders, they probably died for good. (Paul John, February 2, 1977)

At the same time that a hunter and seal must carefully control their thoughts and actions before and during the hunt, a woman must also regulate her actions. Her passivity and inactivity worked to keep open the passageway between the human and animal worlds. Theresa Moses (August 1987 NI95:1) recollected:

> Females did not work at all but stayed still doing nothing at all.
> For those who were made great hunters by the powers of the shaman they had warnings.
> They just stayed put. And they never worked by the door using any knives. They absolutely could not do that.
> They were told not to sew but to stay put just as if it was Sunday.
> They always used a belt. The woman was never to be without it.
> But after a man had caught a seal, even if he was out seal hunting the woman could work. But even if they were able to work, they were never to do that by the door.

---

down, we made some motion to take it away. Because that person there did not make that motion, he has a mask. Those that do that motion take away their masks."

At the time they are going seal hunting the woman didn't do anything. The women were always on guard so they could not do anything. . . .

The women never washed their hair. And the lap of her *qaspeq* [hooded garment or parka covering] was extremely dirty in the springtime.

Brentina Chanar (May 7, 1989) added detail to Theresa Moses's account:

Before [the hunters] went on the seal hunt, we prepared everything which they had to take along. And during the time of spring seal hunting, those who were taking care of the seals could not gather grass, could not handle grass. And they could not wash their hair, they could not fix their hair. Only the air took care of her hair. That was observed during seal hunting season. . . .

Only after [her husband] has caught a seal, the woman *eyagluni* [abstains]. And they were unable to work with grass inside the house. Women could not take grass inside the house.

And if they did take grass inside the house, because they had a window up there, they pretend and make a motion to take them out. They say they take them out.

So when I take in grass, my mother and my mother's sister used to make a motion to take them out of the window after they had taken them from me. And I used to do the same thing with grass that I took into the house. I pretend to take them out through the window. . . . They could not work inside the house. They could only work outside and in the food cache.

People reported the same restrictions on the Yukon Delta, where women were likewise prohibited from either sewing or working on fur animal skins while their sons and husbands were seal hunting.

Throughout the hunt women quietly waited in the house, refraining from any act that might "cut" the seal's path or otherwise discourage its progress from sea to land. A woman could not sleep while her husband was hunting, lest he lose his concentration in the hunt. Nor could a woman eat while her husband was seal hunting, as some people equated this act with her consuming her husband's flesh. Nor could she tend to her own person: "Only one woman is the one who works on bearded seals. She only works on bearded seals, she does nothing else. As long as there are bearded seals to work on, she does not even tend to herself. She does not wash her poor *qaspeq*. Even her face is dirty. They respected the bearded seal very much" (Gertrude Therchik, Toksook Bay, November 3, 1985 NI87:3).

In western Alaska the wife acted the part of the land for which the seals yearned and which motivated their movement into the human world. Holding water, smelling of smoke, waiting quietly, literally "in the land" in her semisubterranean sod house, the woman was the personification of that toward which the seal moved. Through her inactivity, however, the woman also hoped to evoke a comparable passivity on the part of the seal, who would then allow her husband to take it in the hunt. Also like the seal, she must not sleep during her husband's absence. Thus, at the same time she acted in partnership with her husband to draw seals into the human world, the hunter's wife and the seals he sought were analogically related.

A multitude of rules show the degree to which a woman's actions within the house directly affected her husband's ability to hunt. Unless she followed the rules carefully, her husband would appear unattractive to the seals. Here again it was the woman's action in the house that determined her husband's ability to succeed in the world at large:

> In the house we were told never to hang the boots facing upside down by their shoelaces. We were forbidden from hanging our boots in the springtime during the time of seal hunting. We were told that if we did, our seal hunters would be seen by the seal like one with lots of old boots draped over his neck and looking very terrifying. The seals would be terrified to go near him.
>
> That was how women were told to act. And we were also told that when a woman is making clothing for men to use when they go seal hunting, such as raingear, they were forbidden to hum or sing a song.
>
> And when making raingear care was taken to make each stitch perfect. It had to be perfectly sewn.
>
> If a woman had been singing while making a man's hunting clothes, the seals would see him as one hunting and singing at the top of his voice and making a lot of noise. And the stitches of his raingear if not made perfectly would be abhorrently conspicuous. And he would be so terrifying to the seal that it would never be caught by such a hunter. Even though a hunter is far away he would be that terrifying. . . .
>
> When we were at our seal hunting camp and the men were hunting, the women were told not to make baskets. When the men started seal hunting, we women ceased all basket-making activities. (Clara Agartak, Nightmute, June 1987 NI98A:2–3)

At the same time that a direct parallel existed between a woman's inactivity and the seal's willingness to be taken, men's direct contact with women was carefully circumscribed. Just as people believed the odor of the land drew or attracted the seals, female odor reputedly repelled them. For this reason men must never walk downwind of a woman or take in her air. Whereas circumscribed action on the part of a man's wife contributed to his success, inappropriate actions by, or contact with, women had the opposite effect.

GREETING THE SEAL. As a woman restricted her actions both before and during the time her husband was hunting, appropriate action on her part was also essential when her husband returned with his catch. Clara Agartak (June 1987 NI98A:1, 10) described how women once greeted seals on Nelson Island: "When the men came home from seal hunting in the spring, and when the seals were brought into the house, they had *ipuutet* [wooden ladles]. The women took the ladle and got fresh and pure snow. Then they gave the dead seal a drink saying, 'Because you are thirsty, we are giving you good pure water. If you are thirsty, come here so you can have excellent water.'

They sprinkle snow below their mouth [on their chin] and also on their flippers, all the time talking to them. That is the way our mother did it."

The hunter's wife, mother, or sister performed this greeting before anyone else had touched the seal. First, they brought the seal inside the house, from which it was never removed in one piece. Then the woman would ask someone to bring her snow or water from outside the house in an *angassaq* (ladle), which she would use to anoint the mouth and joints of the seal's "hands" and "feet" (flippers). Leftover water was flung out the door. Billy Lincoln (July 10, 1985 NI77) recalled that on his return from seal hunting, first his mother and later his wife would always pour fresh water or place clean snow into the mouth of freshly killed seals. She also placed water or snow on its joints and over its feet. While performing these actions, the woman would talk to the seal, saying, "See our water here is tasty, very inviting."

This five-point anointing of the seal with water (including mouth, two front flippers, and two back flippers) mirrors the five drinks given to the boy who went to live with the seals in their underwater home, and which, on his return, he taught his fellow villagers to offer to their guests. As we shall see (chapter 4), rules similarly limited boys' intake of water in the human world:

> When [the boy who lived with the seals] became thirsty, that little one began to cry. His grandfather [the bearded seal] as he thought of him would take his drum right above him and beat on it while singing. From underground when his grandfather did that, just between the floor boards, water would start spurting out!
>
> And then he instructed him to swallow five mouthfuls of water and not to go over that amount.
>
> Then one time he drank more than the limit seeing how thirsty he was. That extra drink besides the five was salt, and it could not be swallowed!
>
> That is why that custom of giving water, that is the reason for it. They learned it by that experience. So now when living things arrive, those that are receiving it pour water into their mouth, just the way it is told by that [story]. (David Boyscout, Chevak, December 15, 1987)

The five ritual drinks are repeated at significant points throughout the seals' sojourn in the human world. The ritual welcome by the women is mirrored at the close of the Bladder Festival when men pour fresh water in each corner and in the center of the square ice hole after returning the seals' bladders to the sea.

Chevak women not only offered their guests water, but made a small incision on the seal's forehead to release its "person" and allow it to tell its fellows about the good treatment it had received. Alternately, some women slit the seal's eyes so that it could not see offensive things. As in the case of the ritual drink, only mature, fertile women were attractive to the seals and could perform these acts. A woman who was menstruating or who had recently lost a child was not allowed near the carcass, for it was believed that the air of menstruating women repelled the seals. Just as young hunters must take every precaution to avoid contact with a menstruating woman, dead seals were not allowed in her presence, as they found her bloody appearance frightening:

> When those two people got to them, one of them was all bloody all the way down [on the lower part of her body]. She was just abhorrent! . . .
>
> Fearing that the one bloody person might step over him, [the boy who lived with the seals] really *qungvagyugluni* [felt creepy]!
>
> No wonder, at that time, these *aglenrrat* [girls who had their first menses] were told to step away when they were going to step over the seals. . . .
>
> So that girl was an *aglenrraq*.
>
> So they brought them into the house, and he was so afraid that she might step over him. The [people] used to tell girls in that condition not to step over the seals. It was because of that. (Joe Ayagerak, Sr., December 16, 1987)

The drink of water completed the seals' journey from sea to land, from outside the human community to its center. Through the power of their minds and their careful attention to the rules, young hunters had cleared the entryway of snow to open the seals' path into the village. At its center awaited the women—passive and sexually receptive, within the land and smelling of the land, girdled by a belt composed of the teeth of the caribou, the quintessential land animal—to greet their guests with a drink of fresh water, to anoint their "hands" and "feet," and to open their bodies to release their *yuit*.

SHARING THE SEAL'S BODY: DISTRIBUTING THE CATCH. After greeting the seal, Nelson Islanders handled its body according to set rules to insure its return in the future. They gave special attention to each man's first-caught seal of the season. Here, too, the hunter required the help of his close female relatives. Before the seal even entered the village, the man gave away its ribs to hunters encountered on the ice. Albert Therchik of Toksook Bay (November 3, 1985 NI87:2) stated, "They take one side of the ribs off the bearded seal in the springtime. These are given to the ones they meet along the way. In the ocean, whoever receives [such a share] eats it right away, even though it is raw. But when they begin to catch more [seals], they do not do that to the ribs."

Once the hunter reached the village, special rules regulated the distribution of the meat and blubber of the first-caught bearded seal of the season. Albert Therchik (November 3, 1985 NI87:2) continued:

> When they arrive at the village by themselves, after they have removed the blubber, they pass it out to their containers adding pieces of liver to them. This is what was termed *cuanraq qasqilluk,* the men taking them to the *qasgiq.*
>
> And the women, by themselves, they *uqiqurluki* [distribute seal oil, meat, and gifts when someone has caught a seal; from *uquq* oil, especially seal oil]. [The pieces of blubber] are the size and length to make seal oil, but they are long.

Cutting blubber from a seal, Tununak, 1933. O. W. Geist Photograph Collection (acc. # 64–98-245 N), Alaska and Polar Regions Department, University of Alaska Fairbanks.

And they place their pieces in boxes. They cook them, and they cook their livers, too. Then they take them to the *qasgiq*. Immediately, with much relish, the *qasgiq* people would eat.

People viewed the women's *uqiquq* distribution of meat and oil of the first bearded seal of the season as essential to the hunter's future success, not just in seal hunting but in the pursuit of animals in general. Conversely, the consequences of failing to give over his catch to the women for distribution could be disastrous:

The *uqiqulria* [one who distributes seal meat and oil] knows the meaning behind having it. But I do know this. The man who does not follow the custom of distributing seal meat and oil, even if he goes after animals the way he usually does, he will not catch his animals.

Then in the spring when the seals were scarce and no one had caught anything, a *nukalpiaq* [good provider] went seal hunting.

When he was coming back, whistling, the women in that village quickly started going to his wife, taking their only containers. They congregated at his house because they knew that the seal they were going to distribute meat and oil with was coming.

When he was within hearing distance of them, that *nukalpiaq* scolded the women, asking them why they were at their house! He said he wasn't going through frustration to get something for them.

Oh dear! Those women became suddenly disappointed over the one who said that to them. Backwards, by their minds, they apparently pushed him just by their minds. That poor person was possessive of his catch because it was his.

Seal-party distribution, Toksook Bay. Women still celebrate hundreds of lively seal parties each spring in the villages on and around Nelson Island. James H. Barker.

Seal-party distribution, Chefornak, spring 1977.

> Since those women pushed him backwards through their minds, that *nukalpiaq* didn't catch a single thing through the whole spring.
> That one points to the power of a person's mind. That is its meaning. (Toksook Bay Elders, November 5, 1983 NI59:22)

If a hunter brought home a walrus before he had taken his first bearded seal of the season, his wife would distribute it. The choice parts of the walrus included its intestines, which could be used to make waterproof rain gear; its bladder, which was used as a water container; and its stomach, which made a good container for seal oil.

As seal hunting became more routine in spring, hunters succeeded more often. Still they were obliged to give significant shares to others. Villagers eagerly awaited the return of the good hunters, who sustained not only their own relatives with the rich meat and oil, but the entire community as well.

> This is the way people know when one gets a bearded seal in those days. [The successful hunter] approached the village from the ocean running and without a sled. He would be holding *negcicuar* [a small hook].
> And before he arrives in the village, people would start talking. "This person approaching has caught a bearded seal!" He *uurcaq* [alerts the people that he has caught a bearded seal].
> And sometimes one of them would come to the village holding *negcigpak* [a big hook]. Even though he does not tell a tale, these people would start saying,

Loading seals, Umkumiut. James H. Barker.

"This person approaching has caught a walrus!" (Dennis Panruk, Chefornak, December 17, 1987)

Billy Lincoln (July 13, 1985) detailed the division of young bearded seals into shares *(nengit)* once the hunter had retrieved the carcass:

> The *amirkaq* [young bearded seal] has a head and a face and then there are its *unatek* [two hands/flippers] and its *it'gak* [two feet]. And inside of it is its *keggatek* [chest and shoulder] and below its chest is its *uatek* [haunch, body from the waist down]. That is how they call those parts.
>
> Its chest, its haunches, and its feet. And here are its *qat'gai* [rib, from *qatek* chest]. And inside its body is its *qilu* [intestine], its *anrutaq* [stomach], *tenguk* [liver], *pugtautaq* [lung], and its *ircaquq* [heart]. That is how the insides of the seal are named.
>
> If one man catches a bearded seal, he will give his companion one haunch and also its foot, the meat of its leg. And he will also give him some part of the blubber. He gives him those parts, and also one side of its shoulder. . . .
>
> Following its one side beginning from the head to its feet, he takes off the blubber and gives it to his companion.
>
> If there were three men, if the one who catches the seal has two companions, he splits its haunch. The other man gets the part down there and the vertebrae. He cuts its blubber in half. And his companions share its arms and its shoulders and its legs.
>
> That is how the one who catches *nengirturluku* [gives portions to] his companions.

A different set of rules for distribution applied to an adult bearded seal taken in fall. Seals were not so plentiful then, and the encroaching sea ice restricted hunting activity to bays and river mouths. The seals' bodies, at their leanest during this time of the year, sank easily, and hunters used harpoons to retrieve their catch. Men worked together to insure that their quarry not be lost, and so shared their harvest even more widely. Albert Therchik (November 3, 1985 NI87:1–2) described the process:

> If they caught *maklak* [adult bearded seal] during the fall, those parts are given to different people. The seal belongs to the one who first harpoons it. And the second harpooner has the stomach, even its intestines. If another harpoons it, he gets the *uatek* [haunch]. And the legs and the chest and shoulder, each has its owner. That was how they did it for whoever had a part in handling the seal.
>
> But if it was caught in the spring, he only shares those things with whoever is with him.

At different times of the year and at different times of his life, a hunter shared his catch differently: raw ribs given to the first hunters met on the ice; strips of skin and oil given to the old men; pieces of blubber to the children; large cuts of meat and oil to his hunting companions (often close male relatives). Smaller (but still substantial) shares went to unrelated village women in the spring seal-party distribution.

To this day women play prominent roles in the distribution of their sons' and husbands' catch. Not only are women responsible for the formal sharing of raw meat in distributions such as *uqiquq,* but once the catch is brought home, it is both her responsibility and her right to share it informally, both raw and cooked, with family and friends as she sees fit.

> And they also had the following *alerquutet.* This man who brings home subsistence food, he no longer owns it when he brings it home. But his wife receives it, and she comes to own it so that she will take good care of it. The wife takes good care of it because it is hers now.
>   While the man is in the process of taking it home, he owns it. And when he comes home with it to his wife, he lets it go, the wife comes to own it, but she takes good care of it. (Joshua Phillip, Tuluksak, June 1988 YN22:9; see also Paul John, November 6, 1991)

Here "taking good care of it" entails treating it properly as well as giving it away. Sharing creates and maintains relationships within the human community and between human and nonhuman persons. Animals, especially seals, give themselves to a hunter and his wife in exchange for proper thought and care. They also allow themselves to be hunted on condition that their bodies be shared. If stingy with the harvest, any harvest, animals will not return nor allow themselves to be taken. A direct parallel exists between the animals' willingness to give themselves to the people and the people's willingness to share their catch. According to Paul John (February 2, 1977), "The seals observe me and observe my actions. If they know that I am a careful person, that I take care of them, then they come to me. They allow me to hunt them. Then I share my catch. Then the thankfulness of the people is strong, and I will be able to hunt animals." Finally, after the meat is distributed, women cook and serve it. People eat in silence out of respect for the animals they consume, talking and visiting only after they have finished the main meal, and the hostess serves tea. According to Paul John (November 5, 1991), "At mealtime when they eat, they would be very mindful of their food. They would not leave scraps of food. As they carefully eat their food it would be like a continuous ceremony. . . . If the food was eaten carelessly, it would not be readily available to them." Even a solitary person closes the meal by saying *"Quyana"* (Thanks), not to human hosts but to the animals.

    In the past, the rules for the distribution of seal were more elaborate than for any other animal. Yet seals were far from the only animals shared. Hunters generally distributed both belukha whales and walrus within the community, giving meat and skin to anyone who wanted a share. As with seals, to be stingy discouraged the animals' return.

    Men and women worked together to draw animals into human space and to care for their guests after they arrived. A hunter could not hope to attract animals without the knowledge and forbearance of his female relatives—his mother, his sisters, and, eventually, his wife. Men and women also worked together in distributing the catch. Just as elders must share what they know with young people and must never be stingy with their knowledge, so the hunter and his wife must not be stingy with their catch. Their ability to receive animals depended on their willingness to give.

CARE OF THE SEAL'S HEAD. Nelson Islanders carefully attended the seal's body to insure its return in the future, sharing its meat and blubber widely within the community. The seal's head also received attention, especially that of the first seal of the season. According to Brentina Chanar (August 1987 NI94A:5), "When the sealskin was brought into the house, the woman cut the head off [the first seal of the season] making a circling motion with it around the sealskin . . . following the universe [east to west]. This was after it was given water also." Women carefully placed the heads of all seals inside the house, facing the door where the other seals would come in. The heads remained there until spring, when they were cooked together and their contents eaten with great relish.

Yukon Delta people placed the seal heads facing toward the inside of the house. Although their position was the reverse of the tradition of their coastal neighbors, the meaning was comparable. The heads' placement encouraged the seals' comrades to follow them into the human world. Thomas Chikigak of Alakanuk (August 11, 1987) described their treatment:

> When they bring seals into the house they make them face inward so they can come in again.
>
> And if they are not going to keep the heads of the seals, before they throw them in the water when they sink them, they say to them, "If and when I start thinking of you come again!" Saying that, they throw them away.
>
> Saying to them in that fashion, they let the seals' heads sink. And some of them give them to the kids to eat, having cooked them. But some sunk them. Sinking them they tell them, "Come again if I come to think of you."

The seal's skull was not the only animal skull to receive special treatment along the Bering Sea coast. The people of Nunivak held a dance at the end of summer during which a walrus skull was brought into the men's house and subsequently speared by little boys. Young men then brought salt water in a small cup and poured it over the skull. A participant then took the skull out and placed it below the village, facing the village, all the little boys accompanying him. A distribution of gifts followed the ceremony (Lantis 1946:195). The men's treatment of the walrus skull in the *qasgiq* forms a striking parallel to the women's ritual treatment of the seal's head in their dwellings. Aside from this attention to the walrus's skull, walrus bones were neither buried nor replaced in water but used in various practical ways on both Nunivak and Nelson islands.

Siberian Yupiit also reportedly celebrated a "head festival" in early summer, during which men took the heads of walrus and bearded seals from the caches, set them in a circle, and gave them food. The *umiak* team tied a line to the largest walrus head and dragged it across the ground, as they did after a successful walrus hunt. Then followed a feast of head meat, after which people burned the remains (Serov 1988:255).

Although Nelson Islanders denied that they had given belukha skulls special treatment, Porter (1893:100) observed rows of belukha skulls lined up from the shore inland along the coast just north of Goodnews Bay. The skulls were "laid one by one beside each other, with the pointed jaws to the south.[5] . . . These rows, of which there are between thirty and forty within a few miles, were begun at the beach, where the skulls are half decayed and moss grown, and continued inland where the newest specimens are found. I have counted nearly 200 in a single row." Nunivak hunters also routinely placed the heads of slain caribou with their noses toward the hunter's home (Lantis 1946:195). Orators on the middle Kuskokwim described the careful treatment the bear's head receives to this day, either being buried or placed on the ground facing the sunrise. Dr. Joseph Romig reported in the early 1900s that along the middle Kuskokwim, the head of the first kill of the season would never be taken home with the rest of the carcass. Instead, the hunter severed it from the trunk and placed it upright so it could see the rising sun (Anderson 1940:87). Food offerings to promote successful hunting were reportedly made to stone heads located on the tundra on both Nunivak Island and the mainland, and also in Greenland and the Canadian Arctic (Boas 1901–7:149; Pratt and Shaw 1992; Søby 1969–70:54–55). On Nunivak an animal with a special relationship to a particular family sometimes approached a family member, allowing itself to be killed. The hunter preserved the head, and he or his son wore it on his forehead during the Bladder Festival (Lantis 1946:183–84).

Human skulls also received special treatment in some areas. Lantis (1947:18) reported that a few years after a human burial on Nunivak, people removed the skull when the next burial at that spot occurred. They set the skull on a mat on a high place facing east, and passersby placed grass over it. In the Bering Strait region, people arranged the skulls and scapulae of large game animals, including bear and caribou, atop the graves of accomplished hunters (Garber 1934:216). At Point Hope, Rainey (1941:369) unearthed human skulls with carved and inlaid ivory eyes, ivory cup-shaped mouth covers, and, in one case, ivory nose plugs.

The story of the boy who traveled with the seals contains information critical to understanding the significance in western Alaska of the severed head, both animal and human. In fact, the parents of the boy allowed their son to sojourn with the seals as a last resort to give him superior hunting power. Before his departure the shaman had tried to give the boy the same power through ritual decapitation, requiring the father to cut off his son's head as the boy came up through the entrance hole into the men's house. In

---

5. South is the direction of the modern village of Platinum. It is unclear whether this was also the direction from which the belukha hunters had come.

effect, the father was asked to butcher his son as he would a seal after it had been hunted and pulled through a hole in the ice. This he could not bring himself to do, thus losing his son's first chance to gain superior hunting power.

Although the bladder, not the head, was the seat of the seal's *yua* (person) or *unguvii* (its life), the belief was widespread in many parts of the Arctic that spiritual entities animated the joints of both human and nonhuman bodies. People may have believed that these spirits animated body parts—the head in particular—once the joints had been severed. In fact, frequent references exist in Bering Sea mythology to the power of the part to call forth the whole (Fienup-Riordan 1983:187). Although dismemberment and severing the head destroy life on one level, the potential for the regeneration of life continues to animate the body part. Recall here the shamanic initiation ritual in which the initiant underwent ritual dismemberment before attaining the ability to see into and travel between worlds.

The head, although severed from the body, still possessed the ability to observe human action and to recount its experiences to its fellows. By feeding and honoring the seal's head, and placing it to face in the proper direction, human hunters simultaneously celebrated the seal's successful passage into the human world and its special power to communicate with and return to its underwater home.

THE TREATMENT OF SEAL BONES. Another example of respectful behavior considered important to this day is the care given animal bones in general and seal bones in particular.[6] Ideally, people never chopped or broke seal bones, but cut them on the joints and cooked them whole. They took great care to remove every scrap of meat. If the bones were not cleaned, the seals would perceive them as loudly singing, warning them not to give themselves to such careless people. Alternately, animals would reward a hunter if he took proper care of the bones of his catch. Tim Agartak of Nightmute (July 17, 1985 NI71) tells the story of a starving hunter who takes a walrus head and carefully cleans it, placing it in his food cache. When he goes to check it five days later, the skull is covered with meat.

In the past Nelson Islanders buried seal bones or placed them in nearby freshwater lakes. As it was the smell of the land that originally drew the seals from the sea, people placed the bones in the land. They never scattered bones around for fear someone would step on them or allow dogs to chew on them. People were supposed to keep these stored bones moist to prevent the hunter's own bones from drying out when he died, indicating a partial

6. What follows is the ideal and is not entirely borne out by evidence from historic Yup'ik archaeological sites where bones have been found scattered all over. At the Paugvik site at the mouth of the Naknek River, for example, a variety of bones were evident, including seal bones. Foxes, however, may have been responsible for this disarray (Jim VanStone, Tiger Burch, personal communications).

analogy between hunter and hunted. Some people said they placed the bones in water to await the bladders that were placed through a hole in the ice during the Bladder Festival. They believed the bladders joined the bones and became living seals again.

Anyone who received a gift of meat was obliged to return the bones to the donor. Frances Usugan of Toksook Bay (November 5, 1983 NI59) observed the careful treatment of bones in her youth:

> That way whatever a man catches, a woman is to receive and handle it with much care, and not be messy with it.
>
> We never saw anyone be sloppy with anything! Even a piece of bone of a bearded seal, we did not see it on the ground.
>
> When spring came upon them whatever they caught, a hair seal, a bearded seal, we buried their bones.
>
> And the bones of the ones they had brought over to someone, to old women and to old men, the bones of the meat they had been given, they placed in a bowl and had them returned to the one whose seal it was.
>
> Then, in the time they refer to as *cikuqami* ["ice forming time," from *ciku* ice] when they would not be catching seals, during the fishing season, when they began to catch fish down at Umkumiut, the ones that I saw down there, those bones, they would put them in an *issran* [grass carrying bag] and packing them, they would bring them up, so far away! Those two lakes at the area of the bluffs, only to there, they took the bones.
>
> Wow! What a way of not throwing things in any old place! What marvel that the ground was not an eyesore.

Not only did they take seal bones to fresh water but to a point high above the sea.

Clara Agartak of Nightmute (June 1987 NI98:2) also described this careful attention to bones: "The bones were collected and kept and never discarded. All through the spring, the bones of the seals were never thrown away. They were collected in one place. Only when spring seal-hunting season was over, they were taken up to the lake and thrown away there. They were thrown all together at the same time then."

The treatment given to a young hunter's very first seal was a significant exception to the careful treatment prescribed for seal bones. According to Brentina Chanar (January 25, 1991), "If a person gets his very first seal, the bones are never kept. They throw the head to the dogs, and they fight over it. And whoever was given a part of that seal, they do not keep the bones but throw them away. I wonder why they used to do that."

Thomas Chikigak of Alakanuk (August 11, 1987) recalled the same requirement that people return seal bones to fresh water in the Yukon area. There people placed only the bones of belukha whales on land.

> During spring seal hunting, seal bones were gathered. When seal hunting was finished, bones were gathered and thrown in the water. . . .

Umkumiut fish camp. James H. Barker.

Storing dried herring in an issran (grass bag). James H. Barker.

Other seals are able to go on land and ice, but belukhas could not even if they wanted to be like the others. That is the reason why their bones are thrown on land, not in water.

[Belukha bones] were just thrown on top of the ground. That was what was done around here. Seal bones were not to be chewed on by dogs but were thrown in the water both in lakes and rivers. They mostly threw them in the river. If there was no river, they could be thrown in the lakes.

Seal bones were thrown in water because they were able to go on land. But belukha bones were thrown on land.

It was all right for dogs to chew on belukha bones. I have seen people feed them to the dogs. Belukha rib bones were used for net sinkers. They were cut in pieces. And belukha hand bones [flippers] were used to make a *nanerpak* [seal spear head]. The rest of the bones were thrown away or fed to the dogs if they chose. . . .

But seal bones were thrown in the water and not given to the dogs to chew, because they are able to go and frolic on land. But belukhas are not able to go on land except when accidently landed because of a receding tide. Although they envy others who are able to go on land, they are unable to. Because of this, their bones are thrown on land and chewed by the dogs.

Unlike seals, belukhas could be hunted and butchered only with stone or bone-tipped weapons, as iron was considered unclean. Moreover, John Kilbuck (1887:727–28) reported that at the mouth of the Kuskokwim the death of a belukha whale required the same period of rest as that following the death of a man: "Those who take part in the killing observe absolute rest for four days after the killing. . . . The natives declare that they would die if they worked within these four days." Nelson (1899:438) added that no one in the village could use a sharp instrument during these four days "for fear of wounding the whale's shade, which is supposed to be in the vicinity but invisible; nor must any loud noise be made for fear of frightening and offending it."

People believed that belukha whales could transform themselves into wolves and attack unwary persons. Although the belukha, when taken, provided food in abundance, the boundary between humans and belukhas was apparently less clear cut. The whales' desire and ability (as "wolves") to hunt on land, and the ritual abstinence they required after death, indicate shared features with human persons. Although these shared features did not prevent their harvest, they required special ritual acts on the part of the hunter not so much to overcome the difference, but to mitigate the similarity, between them.

Finally, the treatment of seal bones on Nunivak provides a variation on the coastal theme. After people on the island found the first bird eggs of the season, they took out the seal skulls and all other bones and buried them in a special place among the rocks, together with wooden bird images and a wooden dish in bird form containing seawater (Curtis 1930:30; Lantis 1947:43). As we shall see, the bird image may have signified not only the hunter's totem, as Lantis suggests, but also the hunter himself as the seals perceived him.

EATING RESTRICTIONS. Just as men and women cared for seal bones following precise and detailed rules, they also carefully regulated their consumption of the seal's body. Although they considered most of the flesh and innards edible, they proscribed specific parts.

On Nelson Island, rules prohibited young men and women from eating the ligaments found in the seal's spine. Clara Agartak of Nightmute said that boys who ate the soft part of the seal's spine section would lose their way and travel in circles. Brentina Chanar (August 1987 NI94A:1) extended the rule to girls as well:

> It was said that if us girls eat them when we are getting grass and the fog came, we would be lost and would not know where we came from.
>
> And for the boys who eat those and went hunting and the fog came, they would also be lost.
>
> Because of that they forbid the young from eating the ligaments of the spine bones. And they are one of the best tasting parts of the seal!

Joe Ayagerak, Sr. (December 16, 1987) reported this same proscription in the Chevak area, along with an additional restriction:

> And also the tail parts of the spine would cause one to tip over in the kayak. They did not want their children to eat them. They say that if they are rowing they would keep capsizing. The spine causes one to capsize. . . .
>
> But because the shoulder parts have lots of meat and make one tired of eating meat, saying that they make one a good hunter, they let the boys eat them. . . .
>
> And even when we are fully grown, when we see someone with head spasms we think about them eating the tail part of the spine. We think that s/he probably ate those when s/he was young. His/her head makes motions.

Eating the seal's diaphragm *(capuraun)* was also prohibited, whereas the consumption of other internal organs was prescribed:

> The seal also has a meaty part which encloses the lungs known as the *capuraun.* Do not feed the boys such meat. If they are fed that part and they go seal hunting, the ice floe will close in on them and surround them and impede their mobility in the water.
>
> I guess that is true. And the part of the seal that looks like a liver but flat and very distasteful,[7] they say that it is called the seal's *elavngigcaun* [spleen, from *elave-* to crouch, literally "makes them able to lie so they are undetectable"]. Even though it is acrid to the taste, we were encouraged to feed the boys this part. If they get down in a prone position while hunting, the game will not be able to see them *(elavnertunarqut-gguq).* (Clara Agartak, June 1987 NI98:4)

---

7. Brentina Chanar (August 1987 NI94A:2) maintained that this part was not distasteful but very soft.

This precaution also aided young hunters in the event that they encountered something frightening in the wilderness. Brentina Chanar (August 1987 NI94A:2) recalled, "It was told that if a boy is in the wild and he encounters some fearful animal, if he gets in a prone position he would not be seen by the animal. Those were the two reasons." Unmarried boys and girls were also prohibited from eating seal kidneys. When a girl who did so had children, she could expect that the top of her hands would always get blisters.

Billy Lincoln (August 1987 NI96A:1) added detail to these restrictions, noting that the prohibited parts for the younger people were the preferred parts for the older men and women: "Those people before us warned us not to eat the delicious parts of the seals, those crunchy parts by the seal's heart. They told us not to eat those parts. Because if we go to the wild, if we lose our bearings we would be lost. But they encouraged us to eat the parts that were very distasteful."

According to Thomas Chikigak (August 11, 1987), the consumption of the seal's diaphragm also was prohibited on the Yukon Delta, but the restriction had a different meaning than on Nelson Island.

> Girls were forbidden from eating the seal's diaphragm. As I know, they were given to the dogs, cooked or raw.
>
> If a pregnant girl is about to give birth, the baby will have a tendency to go up if a girl eats seal diaphragm. All girls were forbidden from eating them. Boys could eat them and do. Also the dogs. . . .
>
> You know where the liver is? There is an organ long and flat. . . . Around here in the Yukon area they call them *mamcayit* [literally "something flat"; *mamcaq* spleen].
>
> We were forbidden from eating them, I do not know why. Even when we were in the wild, we were not supposed to eat them but to throw them in the water. We throw the bladder and biles away.

Different areas of western Alaska had different restrictions. In Alakanuk, for example, "the young boys who would someday become hunters were told not to eat the hearts. If they see a seal, their hearts would throb because of fear" (Camille Joseph, August 9, 1987). Other areas prohibited the consumption of the heart but for different reasons. The one constant was the category of person for whom the restrictions applied. The majority of rules circumscribed the behavior of children and young adults. After the young people had borne children themselves, they were no longer subject to the restrictions.

THE TREATMENT OF LAND ANIMALS

Strict rules surrounded sea-mammal hunting in the coastal villages of western Alaska. The rules governing the harvest of other species were fewer and less detailed, but they were still important. Land animals included rabbit, fox, mink, caribou, musk-ox, moose, wolf, and bear, and they were designated in Yup'ik as either *nunamiutaq* (from *nuna* "land" plus + *miutaq* "one whose proper place is") or *ungungssiq* (quadruped). Large land animals were rarities in the coastal environment. Native caribou and musk-ox, present in the past, had subsequently died out. Brown and black bear and moose were available only upriver.

Some Kuskokwim hunters, when caribou hunting, carried a small wooden doll if their wife was pregnant. Others wore or carried a woman's belt. A man might be given the cloth parka cover of a particularly long-lived woman as a talisman for luck in hunting. All three practices are comparable to the cooperation between coastal men and women during seal hunting.

In addition to the careful placement on the open tundra of caribou and bear heads, the hunter would also try to capture the breath *(anerneq)* of the first land animal he took each year. Before severing the head and placing it where it could view the rising sun, he held *ayuq* (Labrador tea) under its nose until the animal died, then kept the plant's leaves as a charm to guarantee future luck in hunting.[8]

Animals that had eaten human flesh could be recognized by the fact that their stomachs and sides were bare, without hair. If a hunter killed such an animal, he was to bury his catch immediately, for people should never eat the meat. A brown or black bear that cringes and covers its eyes when it sees a hunter could also be identified as having eaten human flesh.

People living along the Yukon and Kuskokwim rivers considered bears potentially powerful allies. After a bear kill, elders might mark young children with its blood on their head, hands, and feet—an act reminiscent of applying fresh water or snow to the seal's mouth and flippers. Such an act both protected the children from bears and gave them the spirit of the bear to protect them in the future.

Bears, like seals, could hear what people said about them. One story tells how a young boy wintered with a family of bears in human form. During his stay, his host would sometimes listen for a moment and say in exasperation, "Aaa, the awful human beings when they are taunting us!" He then advised the boy:

> Now, when you return to your village, you have always called us the wicked animals. Don't ever scorn us. Even though your people talk, don't ever participate and ridicule us. It is just like this. When the people in your home continue to insult us, we can hear them even though we are sitting here in our house. (Paul John, February 8, 1977)

Like seals, the boy's hosts were also sensitive to human odors. Sometimes they would become impatient with their guest and exclaim, "You smell like a human!" After this encounter, people were warned never to speak about bears and to cover their scent when dealing with them. Although there are words in Yup'ik for different varieties of bear, they are rarely referred to by

8. Compare Romig's description of a comparable ritual on the lower Kuskokwim (Anderson 1940:87).

name but rather as *ungungssiq* (quadruped), *unguvalria* (one that is alive), or *carayak* (terrible fearsome thing).

Still today moose hunters on the middle Kuskokwim are told to shoot a moose only once if someone has died in their family that year. If the hunter fires more then one shot at the moose, it will regain strength instead of dying and may attack him. It is as though the death of the hunter's relative gives his first shot power to produce a comparable death in the animal world. However, if he abuses such power, subsequent shots will have the opposite effect.

The wolf was the only large land animal along the coast for which the elders recalled specific rules:

And also when they get wolves by that *petmik* [pit trap], they treat them just like a person who had died. . . . And they put *uullaq* [cooked belukha skin] in its mouth, and dried whitefish. . . .

So they prepare the dead carcass of the wolf as they do a dead human. It used to have a song, but I have forgotten it. . . .

After they did that, they are finished with the ceremony, and then they skin it. . . .

They do that to all wolves that are caught because they say that [wolves] are human, because they were once human.

It is that one time, when they are skinning one—and they did not know anything about *kass'aq* [Caucasian] stuff—here at its buttock they found smoking tobacco in a steel container, right there between its skin and its flesh.

It is that which revealed what those people will be doing in the future. And so when smoking tobacco came, they kept them in their back pants pockets like that. But they found that first in the wolf that they were skinning. That was probably their pockets, too, the one that was in his buttock. (Brentina Chanar, July 7, 1989)

Not only were some wolves transformed belukhas, but wolves shared with belukhas certain humanlike qualities that required people to treat them like humans after death. As a skilled predator, the wolf was admired and emulated, and elaborate wolf masks appear prominently in ceremonial regalia. As we have seen, *ircenrrat*, nonhuman people with special powers, also often appeared to humans as either wolves or belukha whales and, less often, as foxes. Treating the wolf after death "just like a person" may reflect the human desire to minimize, rather than accentuate, the difference between wolves and people. Some wolflike characteristics were considered desirable in a human. Thus, the ritual treatment of wolves, like whales, focused on points of similarity rather than on points of difference.

More detailed rules about the harvest of large land animals likely applied in the past, but most *inerquutet* (proscriptions) articulated by elders in the 1980s applied to small mammals such as fox, otter, and mink. Coastal Yupiit sometimes referred to mink and otter as "fishtrap-caught animals," as they were often taken along with freshwater fish in wooden *taluyat* (fishtraps).

Perception and consequent treatment of land animals differed from that of sea mammals. Whereas people believed that sea mammals resided in underwater villages from which they annually emerged to return to particular hunters, they believed that land animals originated in the skyland. Just as the shaman might journey down through a hole in the ice to visit the seal people and request their return to the human world, so he would journey up through the star holes to request the same favor from the spirits of the land animals who made the skyland their home (see chapter 8).

The greeting of land animals was also the reverse of that of sea mammals. Women greeted sea mammals with pure snow or fresh "sweet" water, a product of the land that the mammals were thought to crave, whereas people greeted land animals with seal oil, a product of the sea for which they supposedly yearned. According to Brentina Chanar (August 1987 NI94A:1), "For land animals, when mink is caught in the fishtrap, they are always put in the plate. And when they brought them in the house, when they used to have oil lamps, from right under the wick they dab oil on the nose of the mink caught in the fishtrap. This was done to greet it."

The people of the Yukon Delta as well as on Nelson Island greeted land animals with oil.

> And when they catch mink, when they first catch some in the fall or if they catch a fox or any fur animals, when they first catch them they apply a small amount of seal oil to their mouth, to the tips of their ears, and here [on their feet], and at the tips of their tails.
>
> That was the way they greeted it. They hosted it so that they would come again. They give them water at the mouth even when they are dead. Oil is used on mink and foxes. At that time there were no otters or beavers.
>
> But in recent years beavers and otters have come. Around here there was only mink, muskrat, white fox, and red fox. So if they catch those for the first time, they greet them with oil as such. They dab oil on their mouth, ear tips, feet, and tail tips. (Thomas Chikigak, August 11, 1987)

Ritually anointing the extremities of land animals with oil both recalls and inverts the anointing of the seal's "hands" and "feet" with fresh water along the coast and the anointing of the child's head and hands with bear blood on the middle Kuskokwim. All three acts prefigure the five drinks of water given the *yuit* of the seals at the ice hole at the close of the Bladder Festival, as well as the placement of the bladders in each of the four corners and the middle of the hole before submerging them. It may be these ritual acts, among others, that are iconographically represented by the paws, flippers, heads, and tails appended to Yup'ik dance masks (Phyllis Morrow, personal communication). Often attached to the hooped masks by means of flexible feather quills, the appendages would come to life with the dancers' movements in the same way the animals' *yuit* would come to life again if the human hunter and his wife "fed" their appendages and otherwise gave them proper treatment and respect.

Anointing land animals with oil makes good cultural sense in terms of traditional Yup'ik cosmology. It is possible, however, that this ritual act originated in the mid-1800s following the observation of the Russian Orthodox and Catholic customs of anointing human body parts with oil during sacramental services. Even if the Yupiit adopted the practice as a "new" tradition, the manner in which they applied it to animals is peculiarly their own.

People gave special attention to the animal's head, although they anointed all the appendages of land mammals with oil. They placed the heads of sea mammals inside the house to greet their fellows, after which they ritually buried them. They put the heads of large land animals (caribou and bear) out on the tundra facing the sunrise. They covered the heads of foxes, otters, minks, and other small land animals while they skinned their bodies. In an act reminiscent of the woman's incision on the seal's forehead, as soon as the hunter had skinned the animal, he cut its body at the neck and feet so that the animal's "person" would be free to run and tell its companions of the good treatment it had received.

Yukon Delta people put seal bones into the river to insure that they would reunite with the bladders and return the following year; however, they buried the bones of land animals or put them in a lake. James Lott of Tuluksak (June 1988 YN21:5) described a variant of the Yukon practice: "And the bones of these land animals, at that time, they never threw them in the river but into the lakes, because the fish travel in these rivers. And small animals also walk and travel on them. And if the carcass of an animal had rotted at one particular place, they would not go near it. Or if a fishtrap has had some fish rot in it, during those times when they used fishtraps. . . . And fish slime should not be discarded carelessly." Mary Napoka, also of Tuluksak (May 9, 1989), contrasted the treatment of the bones of land animals to that of the bones of water animals (including fish and seals) on the middle Kuskokwim: "These land animals, they always throw them in the water. Long ago, they filled that small lake across there with bones. It is now filled with bones. But these water creatures, they bury them in the ground. They do them the opposite way. . . . Water creatures into the ground, and land creatures into the water."

Women prepared and served land animals and sea mammals in separate containers. If they had only one cooking pot or serving dish, before reusing it they carefully cleaned it and rubbed the insides with ashes. In some areas people could not eat the meat of important land animals and sea mammals on the same day. Joe Ayagerak, Sr. (December 16, 1987) reported that in Chevak, "If one has eaten belukha meat on that day, they were told never to eat caribou that same day. They say that mixing the meat of those two makes one die. That is what we heard."

Finally, land animals were similar to sea mammals in their presumed ability to see, hear, feel, and smell human actions. Hunters bragged about their capacity to capture animals at their peril. They were advised to dispatch their prey quickly, lest its cries disturb other animals. Most important, a hunter must never allow his catch to rot in his traps, or animals would no longer come to that area. If he found a dead animal, he must bury it at once before its odor contaminated the site.

Contrary to the general assumption in the literature that the distinction between land and sea animals (so important in the eastern Arctic) lost its importance along the Bering Sea coast, people carefully maintained the boundary between sea mammals and land animals in western Alaska. Nonetheless the Yupiit perceived animals of the land and sea as similar in that their destinations in death were the opposite of the space they inhabited during life. Seals yearned for fresh water. Belukha whales sought to rest on dry land. Conversely, wolves were feted with cooked belukha skin and small land mammals with seal oil—both products of the sea. Just as coastal and riverine dwellers traded with each other to get seal oil and furs, animal persons relied on the knowledge and ability of the successful hunter and his wife to supply their needs. In return for these services, human persons received the right to harvest the animal's body at the same time they incurred the obligation to care for the animal's *yua* until it was reborn the following year.

CARE OF FISH

Fish were a primary resource on the Bering Sea coast. The word *neqa* simultaneously signified fish and food in the Central Yup'ik language. Although fishing and fish processing were less circumscribed than seal hunting, fish were critical to the people's well-being and were carefully attended.

In the articulation of the opposition between land and sea, fish were divided in their allegiance. Whereas the larger, seagoing fish such as salmon were in some respects treated like seals, freshwater fish taken in fishtraps were classed along with small land mammals and treated as creatures "of the land." The difference between sea and land was not articulated as an overarching opposition between creatures of the water and creatures of the earth. Rather, the opposition was between saltwater/sea and freshwater/land, reflecting the distinction between sea mammals (especially seals) and "fishtrap-caught animals," including freshwater fish and small land mammals. Large land mammals, birds, and fish taken in nets figured much less prominently in the system of regulations recalled by Nelson Islanders in the 1980s.

Nelson Islanders prescribed special rules for the care of fish as well as small mammals taken in fishtraps. According to Brentina Chanar (August 1987 NI94A:1–2):

> All game and fish caught by fishtrap were always put on the plate. And the sack to get fish with always had a plate under it or was carried into the house with a ladle under it.
>
> These were the traditions then. . . .

They do that so that they do not stop catching more food in the future. And if there was a lot that was caught, they put them in the large plates and brought them into the house.

They took special care of the fish, and if a mess had been made on the floor with the fish when they had mud floors, they took special care to wipe the area.

And if fish was to be put in the caches, they never threw them in but put them in the plates and poured them into the fish pan. . . .

They did not do that to fish caught by nets. They only took special care of the ones caught by the fishtrap. The fish caught by net even though they also took proper care of them, they did not handle them like fishtrap food.

Although small in size and apparently insignificant, the products of the fishtrap were a critical food resource, especially in times of general food shortage or famine. The diminutive but plentiful blackfish were particularly important in this respect, and the coastal Yupiit surrounded their harvest with special restrictions. Rules strictly prohibited cutting blackfish with a knife or other sharp object:

As to the blackfish, they told us not to use an *uluaq* on them. That was one of the ultimate taboos.

It was a warning never to cut a blackfish because that would cause the river to be depleted of fish. *Kelgurluteng-gguq* [telling the others what had been done to them] the fish would disappear if we cut the blackfish. I have never seen anyone cut a blackfish to this day.

You have heard of *aninit* [name for blackfish in some areas and under certain conditions]. That is when the blackfish surface. Their bodies are dry. If they were caught using a *qalu* [dip net], a small one, instead of using a blackfish trap, there would be no more blackfish. That is when blackfish tell the others. And there would be no more blackfish.

Kaialuigmiut told us that when the blackfish surface like that one should never use a dip net to catch them. They made us use a special dipper for removing ice from the fishing hole. They call it *qenuirun*. If a dip net is used, blackfish will become extinct and be depleted. (Clara Agartak, June 1987 NI98:5; see also Mary Napoka, May 9, 1989)

Eddie Alexie from Togiak (March 10, 1988) recalled the same prohibition: "They never used to let them use an ax on them. They used to tell them not to do that, with the fishtraps anyway. *Kelqutuniluki, kelgait takniluki* [If you cut them, you cannot invite them.]" No one should ever cut fish or animals caught in a fishtrap with a sharp object. To do so would be like cutting off the fishtrap's future catch. Here again, analogic thinking compelled the people to treat the body of the fish and the trap's future catch as comparable.

Also, if a blackfish accidentally fell to the floor, someone must immediately wipe and apply ashes to the place where it fell. This action prevented the blackfish from becoming extinct. The Yupiit used ashes in numerous ritual contexts to close a passage, create a boundary, or prevent a spirit from moving from one world into another at an undesirable time.

Not only did people refrain from cutting blackfish with a knife or other sharp object, but they took special precautions not to "cut off" the path of any fish. Neither a menstruating woman nor a corpse could cross over a river, as fish would experience their movement as a barrier and be prevented from coming up the river the following year. The path of anadromous fish would also be blocked if they encountered fish bones or human refuse in the water. According to Joshua Phillip of Tuluksak (May 8, 1989), "And they say also, these fish that will go upstream, they are very particular and very clean. If the water that they will go through is mixed with bad stuff, they will not go into it." James Lott, also from Tuluksak (May 9, 1989), concurred: "So now, those places that have fish, we are told to keep them clean and not to throw anything in them. If we did that, they would be good like in the old days. . . . These fish, because water is where they live, smell. . . . If something is wrong, we smell it. Fish are like that too."

Dead salmon and their unused parts must never be left lying around or be thrown into the river. Once human hands had touched them, they were marked. If other fish saw them in their path, they would not continue upstream but return to the sea. Like the fishtrap, the river was a passageway between the world of fish and people. Humans must take care to keep it open and clean (see also Wolfe 1989:14).

People treated the bones of trapped and netted fish differently from one another. Whereas they carefully kept away from dogs the bones of fish taken in traps, they cooked the bones of fish taken in nets and gave them to the dogs as food. Ideally, they never left bones around to be trampled.

People must also avoid argument during the fishing season, as the fish would exaggerate any appearance of discord and refuse to approach the offender. Maggie Lind of Bethel told a story in which two old women cooked a fish but fought over who should have the bigger share. That evening they heard a voice threatening to cut them in half and eat them. They were so scared that they packed up all their belongings, including their house. They even folded up the paths where they went for berries and wild spinach and put them in their canoe. In the end they found the culprit was a needlefish that they then cut in equal halves and ate (Koranda 1966:23).

At the same time that humans refrained from certain actions so as not to block the upriver migrations of fish, they believed other actions encouraged their progress. The noise of thunder, for instance, scared the fish in the ocean and encouraged them to run upriver (see also Llorente 1990:183). Although people should never replace river-running fish such as salmon in the water after handling them, they could release other coastal and tundra species, including codfish, herring, and blackfish, to encourage a large catch in the future. Brentina Chanar (June 30, 1989) noted that people sometimes let fish go intentionally.

Some fish, when someone lets the fish go, they tell it to *angagcaasqelluku* [to get more catch, from *angu-* to catch]. . . . So they did that wishing that they will get a lot of fish. . . .

They let it go, merely saying, "*Angagcaa*!!" . . .

While it is alive, they let it go, let it swim away. . . .

Not necessarily the first one they catch, but if it escapes they say, "*Angagcaa*!"

Conversely, after they finished eating dried herring, Nelson Islanders routinely broke the backbone so that the fish would not follow the people. Here, instead of a ritual act clearing the animal's path, people broke bones to effectively end the animal's approach.

Just as people gave the heads of sea mammals special treatment, they also gave fish heads special consideration. As in the case of seals, the people of the Yukon Delta bestowed this treatment to encourage the fish to return to the human world the following year:

When they hang the fish heads to dry, they face them away from the river. And if a fish rack is facing toward the river current, they make the fish heads face toward the current. They think about the time they will spawn again someday, so they may come again next year. And those who are facing away from the river, they hope that they will come on land again. That is what people said. They took precautions with everything.

All the Yup'ik people hang the king salmon heads facing away from the river after cutting them. And they dry them facing the current hoping that they will come through the Yukon again. Thinking of that happening again they do that. (Thomas Chikigak, August 11, 1987)

Although the consumption of fish was relatively unrestricted, Clara Agartak (June 1987 NI98:4) described one prohibition applying to *manignaq* (burbot or loche fish):

Also in regards to burbot, right at the end of the liver is an organ called the *tengugngalguq* [from *tenguk* liver, literally "one that resembles a liver"].

We were told not to eat such organs.

Both male and female but especially the males. They are conducive to preventing anyone from catching game of any kind. It seems so meaningless. I have never eaten them, even now that I am an old woman, because it is advice from time immemorial. . . .

That is called the fish's *urruit* [gall bladder? possibly *iiraq* gland?].

This particular organ resembles a blood clot. It has been there for eternity. It could never be eaten by youngsters. That is a traditional taboo of the land. Anyone eating that organ will stop catching game.

According to one well-known story, a lazy wife once fed her husband this tabooed part on purpose to diminish his prodigious hunting ability. Her plan had the desired effect and more. Soon she lacked both work and food and eventually died of starvation.

According to Brentina Chanar (August 1987 NI94:3), rules prohibited people who were ill from eating some species of fish taken with line nets or dip nets:

> I have never heard of taboos for fish. But anyone who is sick, there are fish that they should not eat. King salmon, Bering cisco, burbot, smelt, those are the only ones. They were not good to eat for someone who was sick.
>
> And during the spring the blackfish get bloated with water. Those were not to be eaten by one who is sick.
>
> Those were the fish which were to be avoided and not eaten among the other fish.

People living at the mouth of the Yukon and Kuskokwim rivers took salmon in abundance and relied on them as a central part of their food supply. They marked the beginning of the harvest by small but significant ceremonies. People must not eat the year's first king salmon, the first of five salmon species to make their annual appearance in the rivers of the Bering Sea coast, until the day following its arrival. On that day they consumed every part of it. In the Chevak area people cut and hung salmon as well as other fish caught for the first time during the season at either end of the drying racks to insure that more fish would eventually fill the poles.

In some areas limits were placed on the number of king salmon they could harvest. Camille Joseph of Alakanuk (August 9, 1987) reported, "I have known times when one family was allowed to catch only forty king salmon. It was standard advice not to exceed that number. This was long ago when I first came to be aware of it. It was said that if they exceeded this amount, there would be sickness. There would be *cangerlak* [bad season, famine, epidemic]. But they could catch any amount of other fish *(neqpiat),* small fish other than king salmon."

Camille Joseph (August 9, 1987) also recalled rules surrounding the consumption of the season's first king salmon.

> They did not tell us of any parts of the fish which were forbidden to eat. But during the spring when the king salmon first came, before we eat our first salmon, our late mothers and fathers used to let us eat small amounts of ashes.
>
> After that, they let us have our first salmon. This practice applied both to men and women. This was done to protect us from the possibility of becoming nauseated during the summer while we are eating salmon.
>
> That practice of eating ashes only applied to king salmon and not to any other fish. And even now, personally, because I have learned this, I always let my children exercise that tradition. During the spring before they have their first salmon, I let them eat a pinch of ashes. Just the way I have been told from the beginning.

Here again, ashes marked a boundary, in this case between the parts of the year focused on seal hunting and fishing. As the coastal Yupiit considered both freshwater fish and "fishtrap-caught animals" to be "of the land," the boundary designated might also be viewed as one between land and sea. As in the treatment of bones, this distinction was differently drawn by the people of the middle Kuskokwim, who classed their primary resource of salmon with seals in opposition to fishtrap-caught animals.

Joshua Phillip of Tuluksak (June 1988 YN22:8) articulated a regionally specific version of the principle that "opposites attract," underlying not only the disposal of the unused parts of the fish, but also of land and sea animals in general.

> Food, first and foremost, had this *alerquun:* Never ignore any bits of food which are lying around. One should pick it up right away and bury it in a place where people will not walk on it. They took care of food especially. . . . They were told to bury the fish parts on land. Keep them picked up. But something not from water, if it is a land animal, the bones are thrown into water, either a river or a lake. Their bones are put in the opposite elements from where they have existed. It should never be wasted in the element it had been taken from. They kept their bones or their furs well picked up.

Although the care of fish was not as ritualized or rigorously controlled as the harvest of sea mammals, it still required thoughtful action and attention to detail. People must never waste fish, must handle their bodies properly, and must dispose of their bones appropriately.

King salmon and blackfish were particularly valued among fish species—king salmon because it was the first salmon up the rivers after breakup, and blackfish because of their reliability during times of scarcity of other food resources. Just as coastal people learned how to treat seals from the boy who lived in the seal world for a winter, and a young man spent a winter living with and learning from a family of bears, so residents of the lower Kuskokwim tell how people learned to care for king salmon and blackfish by spending time traveling with them.

In both the story of the blackfish people and the salmon people, a young person spends the winter with an older couple who appear to him as people. In spring the child travels with these fish-people as they swim through creeks and rivers searching for their human hosts. As in the story of the boy who travels with the seals, the salmon-people pass by nets and see some above the water, some just below the surface, and some at the bottom of the river. Only those nets that appear in the water belong to people who take proper care of the fish. The wooden *taluyat* (fishtraps) also appear differently—either floating in the air, just below the surface of the water, or at the bottom of the creek—depending on their owner's attention to the rules. When the fish-people have found their hosts, they leave their human apprentice. Telling their guest to watch them, they go to the net or trap, swim under water, and start splashing. Thus they reveal their true identity.

Note the similarity between the three positions of the net or trap and the three paths leading out of the world of the *ircenrrat*. In each case the middle path is the one leading to safety and an abundant harvest in the future.

Fishtrap and river alike provide a path between the worlds of fish and humans. If people work to keep this passageway open, fish will come to them. Some, like the smelt that run along the coast and up the rivers in the spring, are to this day viewed as literally bringing food to the people *(pa-yugte-* "to take food over to a friend or relative"). Here, as in their sense of smell, ability to hear arguments, and general sensitivity to human thought and care, the fish reveal their human character as they engage in exchange relations not just as objects given, but as gift givers.

THE TREATMENT OF BIRDS

Birds, designated collectively as either *tengmiat* (from *tenge-* "to fly") or *yaqulget* (from *yaquq* wing, literally "thing with wings"), held a special place in the Yup'ik world. Their importance in ritual and myth is undisputed. Like humans, some birds travel on both land and sea, and they may have been especially valued for their ability to cross boundaries between worlds. Raven created the first people, and he later brought sunlight to the earth's inhabitants (Nelson 1899:452–62, 483–85). By one account Nelson Island itself was created when Raven threw dirt on an ice floe to provide firm footing for his wife so that she would not be swept out to sea (Fienup-Riordan 1983:372–73). Raven's footprint can be found on the underside of wooden bowls carved in the late 1800s, and his feathers were regularly used in ceremonial regalia.

Tengmiarpak, literally "big bird," was another important creature in Yup'ik oral tradition (Nelson 1899:486–87). Capable of human speech, they were in fact believed to be humans who became *tengmiarpiit,* taking the form of giant eagles, only after putting on their bird skins (Pratt 1993). Their nests can be found to this day on the mountaintops and highlands of southwest Alaska.

Just as they did with animals and fish, the Yupiit differentiated between birds of the sea and birds of the land. Some say that this division originated in a quarrel between Raven and Loon during the days when the earth was new. Thomas Chikigak (August 11, 1987) tells the story this way:

> In the beginning those two, a raven and a loon, were partners. They were sidekicks. They helped each other. When the sky came to be, they were helping each other. They painted all kinds of birds. They were partners in that endeavor.
> So they painted them differently, some black, some white.
> And the cranes, they painted their brows with red dye. That is how they painted the brows of the crane.
> They said, "People to come will see you like this." So that is how those two were.
> So they painted them to be like they are so that people to come would see them as such. That is the reason they painted them.
> Then one day they came to the small birds. When they got to them they went on painting, having a lot of fun in the process. They were on very good terms with each other then. They liked each other. So there came a time when they were still painting when they were about to finish with all of them. Then

there came a day when they came to what we call *cuqcurliq* [rusty blackbird]. They are black birds. They call them black birds. It was said that they had been white before. They had been shiny white before.

So one day when they got to those birds they said, "These birds have to be painted. They should not be without design." So they palavered with each other. One would suggest that they paint them like this. The other said that even if it was white it would be just fine.

That is what the loon said. Then they started to argue as they went along. But that raven wanted to paint it jet black like him.

Then while they were arguing they got angry at each other. This was after they had painted it. So they exploded with anger at each other!

The loon fled into the water because the raven could not dive or even swim.

So walking on land that raven fetched a handful of ash. The raven followed the loon. Loon's wake was visible, and he was about to surface. Running, the raven rushed the loon when he surfaced. At the back of his head the raven threw ash at the loon. Then the loon got his design with some white. That is why he was named *tunucellek* [from *tunu*- back of, area in back].

From then on they came to be what they are now. They were not partners anymore.

The loon was always in the water then because he could not walk on land. But the raven was on land only, and he could walk around but he could not swim. . . .

So the raven and the loon had been partners in those days. They were sidekicks. But from that time when they got angry with each other, they split apart. One was always by the water, and the other was always on land. But loon was not too confined. He could go by water and air but could not go by land. Having told the story this much I am finished.

This original distinction is important, and significant rules surrounded the treatment of birds and waterfowl. Of those, several concern the effect of a woman's activity on the bird's ability to reproduce. For example, Nelson Island women must refrain from touching an empty nest, lest it remain barren in future. Also, if they found a nest with eggs, they could touch only the eggs, never the nest itself. Theresa Moses (May 9, 1988 YN19:2) reported, "When the birds came [in springtime], they warned us not to touch their nests with our hands before the eggs are laid or if there are eggs in them. This is how the birds see: a hand in the nest where they are going to lay their eggs. It was because when we stick our hands inside those nests, and if we do thus, when the bird goes back to them, here are these hands. So the nest would be filled with hands only."

Some Nelson Island women said they would routinely spit in an empty nest and turn it over after gathering its contents so the bird would return to lay more eggs the following spring. Although people harvested the eggs of most species, the eggs of swallows, which built their nests near human houses, were proscribed. To disturb their nests would give one a "bad mind."

Joe Ayagerak, Sr., of Chevak (December 16, 1987) noted that when people find the eggs of the *kukukuaq* (common snipe), they must walk straight by and pretend not to see them. A person can then return and gather the nest's contents. Failure to follow this rule will bring injury to the person's eyes, sometimes causing blindness.

Children's activity was also directly tied to the activity of birds. For example, boys were to wait until the first snowbird left before using new bows and arrows made during the winter. Throughout the delta, parents admonished their daughters never to bring their dolls out of doors before they sighted the first cranes in the spring, nor could a girl use her *yaaruin* (story knife) to draw in the mud. If they forgot these rules and took their dolls or knives outside during winter, the weather's eye *(ellam iinga)* would see them and turn bad for a long time. According to Joe Friday of Chevak, "There was a village one time when people were playing with dolls during the wintertime. The season came about to be spring and in this certain village it was still winter and all those birds—ducks—were walking around town on the snow. They didn't realize that the place around them was summertime but the village inside was winter" (Eskimo Doll Project 1981:3). In both cases the activity of children is directly connected to the presence of the birds and their ability and willingness to reproduce.

The coastal Yup'ik Eskimos ate all birds except ravens, songbirds, and sea gulls. They had at one time eaten gulls; however, once a gull ate the eyes of a drowned man, and since then people have avoided them as food. Some Yup'ik orators claimed that they do not eat the raven because he was their ultimate ancestor. Others stated that scavenger birds, including ravens, were never eaten except in an emergency

The Yupiit considered most birds edible and surrounded their consumption with detailed rules. Brentina Chanar (August 1987 NI94A:3) said that after a person had eaten young birds, including swans, he or she was not supposed to eat berries. Ptarmigan, like rabbits, were proscribed for young men lest they likewise become fearful and easily startled. Rules also circumscribed the consumption of geese. Billy Lincoln (August 1987 NI96A:1) remembered, "They did have prohibitions. They told us not to eat their wings while we were boys because we would not be able to row as well using double oars. That seems to be the only warning as far as the birds were concerned."

According to David Boyscout of Chevak (December 15, 1987), it was not the flesh of the geese but the delicious wing-bone marrow that was at issue: "There is an *inerquun* [prohibition] regarding the marrow of the geese wings. They told us not to eat those. They said that it would cause us to row slowly. They had prohibitions attached to those foods which are the most delicious. They told us not to eat them."

Boys were also prohibited from eating cormorants because they were "like females." Billy Lincoln (August 1987 NI96A:1) continued, "Now what else were prohibited for the boys? I think it was the cormorants when they ate them. They used to eat them a long time ago. They ate them with no qualms at all because they were birds. But for us, when we were boys, they told us not to eat them. They said that they were like females. The females ate them and also the old men. The old men didn't have any taboos." According to Brentina Chanar, rules prohibited pregnant women and mothers of young children from eating cormorants for the same reason.

Breaking the rules surrounding the consumption of birds endangered the productivity of the offender and, in some cases, the entire community. Like the prohibited parts of the seal, the rules primarily applied to active young hunters and fertile women, not the older members of the community no longer occupied with either production or reproduction. As in so many prohibitions, analogic thinking was employed. Insofar as the wings of the bird were like the arms of the hunter, the latter could not partake of the former. They were to remain separate, and the boundary between them carefully preserved. Their perceived "likeness" was the basis of the prohibition, which functioned simultaneously as a boundary between like things and a mechanism of differentiation.

The story of the boy who went to live with the seals elaborates a crucial identity between birds and hunters, specifically small seabirds and seal hunters. After traveling with his mentor, and viewing a variety of careless hunters, the boy finally comes to the good hunter:

> And there as he was seeing it, was a *tengmilqurraq* [small bird] approaching right toward them. His grandfather [the bearded seal] said to him, "See him, this one approaching is the one who will catch us!"
> When it was very near to them, he said to the boy, "When something happens to you immediately, as fast as you can, rush into your bladder!"
> It was because he saw that one that was hunting them as a bird. As soon as something happened, just the way he had been told, [the boy] rushed to his bladder. He knew he did that! That is when he lost his consciousness! (David Boyscout, December 15, 1987)

In another version of the same story, Joe Ayagerak, Sr. (December 16, 1987), specified the small bird whose form the hunter took as an *aarraangiiq* (old-squaw duck).

> And then his guardian told the boy that they were about to be caught by the person who would catch them.
> Eventually, two *aarraangiyaak* began to approach them. Then his guardian looked at the boy and said, "See how they look so unworthy, the ones who are going to catch us, those two that are approaching us."
> And his guardian told the boy, "See how they are when their minds have made a determination to catch us. They approach us like this, and by the way they keep shoveling, they keep approaching us until the time they actually catch us." So his guardian kept telling that boy the way it was.
> And then when those two got to them, they speared them. When he was

killed, he went down to his bladder; his awareness did not change at all. And what his guardian did not explain to him, he realized right then and there; that is where his awareness was supposed to have gone to.

In his narration of the same story told to him by a man from Hooper Bay, Billy Lincoln (January 17, 1991) describes the hunter appearing to the boy and his mentor as another oceangoing bird, a *metraq,* or common eider *(Somateria mollissima):*

> Soon there came a noise like someone handling the kayak from the village. [The bearded seal] told [the boy] that their host was preparing to go to the ocean to hunt. So they were lying side by side. And pretty soon that person came down into the ocean.
>
> While they were lying on the ice, that eider duck began to approach them, swimming. And his companion said to him, "That is him. Even if you are sleepy, try not to sleep!"
>
> Soon, as it was swimming toward them, a fine mist came out of its mouth and drifted toward them. And when it got to them, irresistible sleep hit him and his companion.

The transformation into an eider duck in this version is significant. Like a kayak, the eider duck (a relatively large ocean bird) can move quickly and can cover long distances in low flight across the ocean's surface. In commentary following his narration, Lincoln did not clearly distinguish between the human hunter and his craft as the object of transformation: "The way that boy saw it was an eider—it may have been a kayak in reality. . . . That is how that person was seen as an eider." The Central Yup'ik association of the eider and the hunter in a kayak is particularly striking in the context of Asiatic Eskimo hunting ceremonies in which images of birds are said to have been analogous to the *angyaq.* In the Saiak fall hunting festival, for example, the wooden bird and boat images could reciprocally be substituted (Mikhailova 1990; Krupnik 1990).

The analogy between the eider duck and the kayaker is also present in Jack Williams's unusual rendition of the well-known story "Dog Husband" recorded by Robert Drozda on Nunivak in 1987. According to Williams, the woman who was married to the dog was starving and near death when some men from the mainland, possibly Nelson Islanders, discovered her. These men were designated "eider people." The woman traveled with them underneath the skin of their kayak, where she could not see out. She "understands sometimes she is travelling on the rumbling waters, sometimes smooth." This is an analogy to an eider duck, which, when flapping its large wings, resembles a kayak on rough water; when gliding, the travel (water) is smooth. Extraordinary hunters as well as human kayakers might appear as eider ducks. Speaking from personal experience, Jack Williams also described a trip he took with his grandfather. They were out in kayaks together when they saw a pair of *ircik* ("little people," comparable to coastal *ircenrrat*) paddling kayaks. When they pursued them around a large chunk of ice, two eiders flew away (Robert Drozda, personal communication).

In Paul John's (February 2, 1977) version of the story of the boy who went to live with the seals, the kayaker appears to the boy and his mentor as yet another variety of seabird— a *ciguraq*, or Kittlitz's murrelet *(Brachyramphus brevirostre)*. Moreover, his account details the transformation of the human hunter wearing a bentwood hunting hat into a seabird, in the eyes of the seals he is hunting.

> Those hunters had a hat made out of bent wood, sharp pointed and tall, that they used solely for hunting and sneaking up on the seals sleeping on the ice. . . .
> So putting on that kind of hat, [the good hunter] came to hunt them. And when he disappeared on the other side of the ice, while [the boy] waited for him to appear again, that small waterfowl began to appear from the other side of the ice. Those small birds are called *ciguraat* [murrelets], those ocean birds that are white [with black coloring on their wings]. They are always diving around in the ocean. . . .

Hunting hats continued into the 1950s to be an important part of seal-hunting equipment of coastal Yup'ik hunters. These cone-shaped hats were traditionally made out of wood and painted with white clay to blend with the sea ice. Kurt Bell of Hooper Bay models a hat that he made out of linoleum, painted with flour paste, and decorated with ivory and eider feathers in 1972.

After [the hunter] had disappeared on the other side of the ice, when it came around, that kayak did not appear but only that bird. But when that bird came around the bend, it began to swim right directly toward them! And as it was swimming it burped a little bit. And its burp was a fine fog which began to spread toward them! And when that fine fog got to them, right along with it, though he tried to resist, a very pleasant drowsiness came upon him!

Oh my! When it came to him though he resisted, as he was getting sleepy his companion nudged him, "Poor you! I have told you to try and stay awake!"

So when he tried hard to snap wide awake, drowsiness left him instantly!

When he was no longer sleepy, [his guardian] said to him, "Now he will do that again after this, but this time, you see, a very strong sleepiness will hit you. But even I will not resist sleeping. And I also got sleepy just a little while ago. Just in case you fall asleep, as soon as your awareness is violently disturbed, dash instantly into your bladder!". . .

So just when [the bird] got near to them, and he seemed to burp out a small fine fog, just like before that fine fog came to them, a fine small fog. When it got to them, though he resisted, he blacked out and fell asleep!

And while he was sleeping, his awareness was violently disturbed, it was jolted! And just the way he had been instructed to run into his bladder if his awareness was violently disturbed, he rushed into his bladder!

So [the hunter] had killed their bodies! But because they had rushed into their bladders, their *unguviik* [life (dual), from *unguva* life] were in their bladders.

All four narratives recount the transformation of the human hunter, riding in a kayak and wearing a bentwood hunting hat, into a small seabird in the eyes of the seals he seeks.[9] The identity between human hunters and birds is an important theme in Yup'ik iconography, and the stories add greatly to our understanding of these representations. For example, it may be a murrelet or other small seabird, rather than Raven, that is depicted on the bentwood hunting hat collected by Edward Nelson in the 1870s at Kaialuigmiut, just north of Nelson Island (Fitzhugh and Crowell 1988:14). The old-squaw feathers inserted in a loop of grass on another hunting visor collected by Nelson may also relate to the identity between bird and hunter (Fitzhugh and Crowell 1988:48). A hunter painted designs on his kayak representing his "inogo" (patrilineally inherited animal helper, probably *iinruq*), which Lantis (1946:239) noted was usually a bird. Wearing hunting hats decorated with either the feathers or the images of oceangoing birds, and paddling a kayak decorated with a bird motif, the hunter became such a bird in the eyes of the seals he sought.

Significantly, neither the image of Raven nor powerful birds of prey were represented, but ocean birds of less renown. Just as the apparently powerless shaman actually possessed the greatest skill in the story of the boy who lived with the seals, so it was the humble human hunter in the form of an insignificant seabird to whom the seals were irresistibly drawn. In fact, seabirds had their own special abilities. They were diving birds that, unlike Raven and the giant eagles, could swim as well as fly and thus had ties to both the upper and

9. The story "The Terns" (Lantis 1946:291–92) reverses this process. Instead of hunters going behind an ice floe and reappearing as birds, two terns approach a woman, disappear in back of her, and reappear as men. These men subsequently catch many seals: "When one of them made a catch in front of her, he took it up and gave it to her. Then, when they disappeared in back of her, they became men."

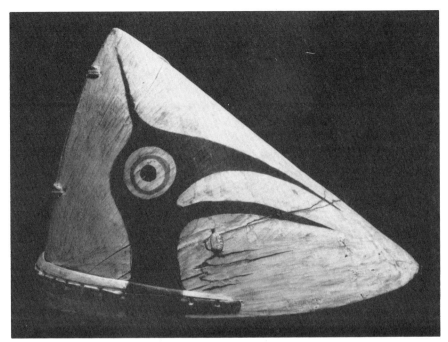

Bentwood hunting hat collected by E. W. Nelson from Kaialuigmiut. According to Billy Lincoln, who was born near Kaialuigmiut in the early 1900s, "They called those big caps elqitellriit [from eliqiaq wooden visor]. *They put those on when they are stalking the seal resting on top of the ice so that they won't be seen as they are. Big caps with pointed tops. They use those in the ocean and though a wave breaks over him, he could see in front of him." National Museum of Natural History, Smithsonian Institution.*

watery worlds. Seabirds that feed offshore during the day and return to nest on the land at night also acted as guides to land for disoriented hunters. Several Nelson Islanders described following seabirds toward the mainland when caught offshore in thick fog at the end of a day's hunting.

That Paul John's story named the Kittlitz's murrelet is of special interest. Associated with seals near ice, these small seabirds hunt singly or in pairs and alert seals and birds to the fish they stir up. Although small in size, they can fly up to fifty miles per hour, dive underwater, and swim with their wings. Unlike many other varieties of seabirds, Kittlitz's murrelets do not nest in colonies on cliffs but in individual nests located slightly inland on high ground. They visit these nests at dawn and dusk to feed their chicks. Moreover, these chicks fledge the nest before they can fly, riding down to the sea on small creeks that empty into the ocean. Perhaps it was their inland homes and kayaklike ride to the sea that supported the Yup'ik comparison between these small birds and human hunters.

A question posed by Margaret Lantis (personal communication) is whether

*Bering Sea Eskimo visor ornamented with ivory gull beaks and walrus heads, crested by
a clutch of old-squaw feathers. National Museum of Natural History, Smithsonian
Institution.*

or not water-repellent bird-skin parkas were once worn by seal hunters under
their gut parkas during the hunt. Birket-Smith (1936:115) notes that the skin
of the eider duck, like that of the hare and the fox, combines great warmth
with extreme lightness but is too delicate for general use. We know that
Yup'ik hunters wore bird-skin clothing (Nelson 1899:31), as did the old man
photographed by Father John Fox at Qissunaq, near modern Chevak, in 1928
(see also Woodbury 1984b:52). What is unclear is to what extent men used
this attire during seal hunting.

Small birds of various kinds play a prominent part in Yup'ik ritual and oral

Qissunaq man wearing a bird-skin parka. Father John Fox, 1928; Oregon Province Archives, Gonzaga University.

tradition. Numerous tales recount a poor boy or girl receiving advice or supernatural aid from a tiny bird. For example, in "The Mask Story" told by Cyril Chanar of Toksook Bay, a young boy's helper-bird created a fog to overcome the human enemies of the people he had come to assist (Fienup-Riordan 1983:243–45). According to Lantis (1947:93), Nunivakers believed that every person had his own little bird spirit hovering over him.

Parents on Nelson Island gave special care to the bodies of small birds killed by young boys, carefully drying them, hanging them with the bladders at the following Bladder Festival, and burning them at its close. In the early 1800s F. L. Kolmakov reported that mothers strung together the skins of the birds and small animals that their sons had killed during the year, adding a bird carved of wood in the middle (Liapunova and Fedorova 1979:78). They were hung in the men's house above a lighted lamp during the Bladder Festival. Lantis (1946:186; 1947:6) reports the same practice on Nunivak in the 1940s, where the birds were hung at the back of the *qasgiq* and burned at the close of the feast to release the birds' souls for future reincarnation. According to Curtis (1930:73–74), when a boy caught his first bird, his father covered the bird with the skin of a young hair seal under three years of age. His son then offered the sealskin to an old man who skinned the bird in return. Bird bones and feathers also constituted powerful hunting charms.

Bird images were central to many Yup'ik ceremonies, especially those associated with seal hunting. Nelson (1899:352) records numerous instances of images of birds in the plastic arts, including a drum handle in the shape of a murre. Dance fans and masks, both carved in the form of birds and decorated with bird feathers (primarily owl and swan) allowed the dancers, with arms extended, to appear as birds in flight. Not only were a young boy's birds hung with a wooden bird image in the presence of the seal bladders, but on Nunivak seal bones were buried together with wooden bird images and a wooden dish in bird form. The bird and the bladder, the hunter and the hunted, were closely associated.

Lantis (1946:194) reports that Henry B. Collins, Jr., excavated some of these seal burials and found wooden figures five or six inches long with the bones. Most of the figures resembled loons, which Lantis supposed to be the hunter's "inogos" (animal helpers). In describing the Nunivak system of patrilineally inherited helping spirits, Lantis (1946:239–40) provides this example: "One inogo of a certain man was Crane. He owned a frayed specimen of a crane head which he wore in a certain part of the Bladder Feast. Also, at various points during the Feast, he imitated his inogo; for example as he burst the seal bladders and put them down under the ice (to return as seals next year), he made the cry of a crane. . . . Although the men had the crane all over their seal-hunting gear, there were no carvings or etchings of a crane on any of the women's implements. The point is easy to see: *the* inogo animal, among several belonging to the family, gave seal-

Mask representing a swan that drives white whales to the hunters. A. H. Twitchell, 1910; National Museum of the American Indian.

Vernon John using dance fans with owl-feather "fingers." James H. Barker.

hunting power, the greatest of all." And "the inogo animal" was most often, although not always, a bird.

Ethnographers have recorded little concerning these inherited helping spirits for other parts of western Alaska. In a description of the Bladder Festival on Nelson Island, however, Billy Lincoln (January 17, 1991) described dances imitating birds as well as other animals, passed on from parent to child:

> During the Bladder Festival they do that—*nayangarluteng* [dance nodding their heads]. They also say "*Yar Yar*" and they put on [wooden] caps. They keep making this motion like this—*yaryarraarluteng*. And whoever wants to would sit down on the floor and dance pretending to be a white fox, a loon, just pretending to be anything. If he pretends to be a bird, he flaps his arms. During *apalluk* [lyrics of a dance song], he makes that bird's sound. They are so entertaining to watch.
>
> So they dance every night for five days, only the men. . . . I danced what he taught me, pretending to be a hawk.
>
> In those days, whoever does a certain dance taught it to their children.

Bird images also played a central part in Asiatic Eskimo ritual activity. Asiatic Eskimos often included images of birds, specifically sea ducks, in hunting ceremonies (Mikhailova 1990). These wooden birds, along with images of whales, boats, and paddles, were tied to nets hung to a central pole. Bogoras (1904–9:393–95) points out that in the Kere'tkun Ceremony of the Maritime Chukchi, a net is suspended from the vent hole of the house, and wooden birds and toy paddles are hung all around the net: "The birds represent probably sea-gulls: at least, the heads of sea-gulls figure in the boat charms of the Maritime Chukchee. A similar net figures in the fall ceremonial of the Eskimo of St. Lawrence Island. It is spread on a wooden frame made of small paddles, with the bodies of four sea-gulls carefully preserved for the purpose. A few heads of walrus or seal are put on the ground as in the 'genuine thanksgiving ceremonial.'"

Bogoras (1904–9:401–2) also describes the Eider Duck Ceremony of the Asiatic Eskimo, in which, besides the usual net with wooden sea gulls, wooden images of eider ducks (not markedly different from the sea gulls described for the Kere'tkun Ceremony) move on separate leather lines: "Each line is held by one person, who, by a simple jerk of the hand, may make the bird soar aloft or descend the line. Very simple whistles . . . are used to produce from time to time a shrill sound, which is called the 'eider-duck's voice.'"

Thus, not only did images of birds play an important part in Yup'ik iconography, but humans often took the part of birds in ceremonial activity. As another example, Nelson Islanders celebrated the bladders' entry into the men's house with a feast and a special variety of dancing performed by women, known as *ingulaq* (also sometimes performed as a separate ceremony). According to Nelson Islanders, the slow, stylized motions of the dance imitated the mating dance of loons. Young Nelson Island women dancing like loons displayed their status as wives and potential mothers to the entire community (see chapter 5). The newly married woman dancing during the ceremony focused on the rebirth of animals. Just as the Bladder Festival simultaneously invoked images of human and animal regeneration, the *ingulaq* "loon" dance provided a vivid image of the close relationship between the reproduction of human and animal life.

Not only were images of human and animal reproduction complementary, but the regeneration of birds and seals also were associated. For example, when Nunivak children found the first bird eggs, the spring seal hunt was brought to its formal, ritual conclusion, marked by the burial of the seal bones accompanied by wooden bird images and the taking of a sweat bath (Lantis 1946:178, 195). The burial of the bones, like the laying of eggs, was an initial step in the process of the animal's reconstituting itself as a living being.

We have seen that although many rules surrounded the treatment of seals, comparatively few circumscribed the treatment of birds and waterfowl. Those that did, however, concerned how a woman's activity affected the bird's ability to reproduce, as in the prohibition against a woman's touching an empty nest lest it remain so in the future.

Juxtaposed to the women's performance of the loons' mating dance at the outset of the Nelson Island Bladder Festival, men were associated with oceangoing birds at its conclusion. As the men deflated the bladders, they imitated the sounds of birds, perhaps presenting themselves to the bladders as the seabirds that had also "burped" out air when they sighted the living seals in the hunt.

The association between humans and birds adds to our understanding of the Nelson Island Bladder Festival. It also sheds light on obscure but tantalizing details in ethnohistoric descriptions, specifically Nelson's description of the Bladder Festival he observed at Kushunak (Qissunaq), the birthplace of two of the four orators of the story of the boy who lived with the seals. When he entered the *qasgiq* at Kushunak, Nelson (1899:382) observed a bird-shaped image, reportedly a sea gull, hanging from the roof: "It had the primary quill feather of a gull stuck in each side of the body to represent the wings. The body was covered with the skin and feathers of the small Canada goose. It was fastened to a long slender, rawhide cord. . . . By pulling and releasing this cord, the image could be made to glide up and down." In the other *qasgiq* in the same village, the wooden image of a man wrapped in the skin of an eider duck took the place of the bird (Nelson 1899:391).

At the back of the room, men had tied a bundle of wild-parsnip stalks to the top of a ten-foot pole. On the left side of the room, they had attached several hundred seal and walrus bladders to a large sheaf of spears. Beneath the spears and bladders was a pile of thirty or forty wooden hunting helmets, on many of which were painted "female phallic symbols." Behind the entrance hole stood a large walrus skull. In this setting Nelson observed:

> Early in the evening . . . the hunting helmets were ranged around the kashim, forming a circle on the floor inclosing the walrus skull and stake. . . . Two small wooden buckets of water were brought in and placed in front of the hole to symbolize the sea, the hole thus representing a seal hole leading into the sea through the ice. . . .
>
> The men and boys now put on their helmets, and the one who had first taken the grass from beside each hunter again took it up and . . . scattered it in the ring just inside the place where the circle of helmets had been; this was said to represent the drift weeds lying on the seashore [the habitat of small sea birds?].
>
> A young man now seated himself under the spears and bladders and another under the bundle of wild-parsnip stalks. . . . The drums began to beat loudly, and the young men around the room imitated the notes of the *eider duck*. In a short time the men and boys ranged themselves around the room just outside the circle made by the grass, the women and girls behind them. . . . [All the people began to sing.] . . . During this song one of the young men imitated in pantomime *the motions of a loon and another those of a murre*. These men remained seated upon the floor, swaying their heads and bodies about in the most singular postures, *like those of a bird diving and swimming under water, or on the surface, pecking with their beaks, etc., after which they made a flapping motion with their hands as if rising and flying away, imitating at the same time the cries of the birds they were representing.*
>
> A short interval followed. . . . Then various others of the dancers began similar bird movements. (Nelson 1899:382–84, emphasis added)

Here, in the presence of the bladders by the symbolic hole in the ice, the hunters donned their hunting helmets and acted out the part of the birds in whose form the seals perceived them. We also see here the loon and the murre dancing side by side, recalling the women's loon dance at the opening of the Bladder Festival and the hunter's appearance as a murrelet during the hunt. The "female phallic symbols" on the hunter's hat also point to the efficacy of the hunt deriving from a combination of male and female elements.

At one point in the Nunivak Bladder Festival, men hung the seal-oil lamp in the middle of the *qasgiq* and sat around the lamp: "Some wore pointed wooden hunting hats, some wore various birds' heads and wolves' and wolverines' heads on their own heads or tied to their wrists" (Lantis 1946:184). Lantis notes that these were actual heads, not wooden masks.

At the close of the Nunivak Bladder Festival, after the men had returned from making the holes in the ice but before they submerged the bladders, one man wearing his wooden hunting hat and two little boys imitated a mother eider and her young, stretching out their arms like wings and whistling like eiders, as in the Asiatic Eskimo Eider Duck Ceremony. "Mother eider" sang, followed by two old men. Immediately after this, a young man representing a seal spirit showed his head through the entrance hole, and another young man "hunted" the spirit with a toy spear. Lantis (1946:185–86) described this sequence as the high point of the Bladder Festival.

In discussing a native drawing representing the Kere'tkun Ceremony in the house of a Maritime Chukchi, Bogoras (1904–9:394) described an event in some respects parallel to that described by Nelson and Lantis: "A pole protruding through the vent-hole supports a wooden image of a gull. The net with paddles and gulls is suspended in the middle. Two walrus-heads are lying on the ground. A lamp is fastened to the pole, and another lamp stands on the ground." Men stand and sit around the pole, performing incantations both inside the house as well as on the roof and in the entryway. As in the Kushunak and Nunivak Bladder Festivals, the Chukchi Kere'tkun ceremony joins images of seabirds and sea-mammal hunting in a ceremony both enacting and predetermining the successful hunt.

The use of bird images in Yup'ik iconography has in the past been interpreted as the hunter's desire to present himself to his prey as less human and more birdlike (Fitzhugh 1988:48). The symbolic identity between humans and predator birds has also been stressed, wherein the hunter takes on the special qualities of birds (speed; clear sight; ability to live on land, sea, and air) (Black 1991:102; Ivanov 1930:502; Morrow and Volkman 1975; Sonne 1988:62). This enhancement of ability was part of the representation in some ceremonies and shamanic rituals. Additionally, however, in the ritual of the hunt, the hunter not only took on birdlike qualities but became a seabird—a murrelet or an eider duck—in the eyes of the seals he sought, a bird that is apparently worthless but actually hard to detect.

CONCLUSION

A close look at the Yup'ik view of the relationship between humans and animals has proved full of surprises. Contrary to scholarly opinion (Fitzhugh 1988b:90), the Yupiit carefully maintained the distinction between sea animals and land animals, not so much to avoid contamination as to promote their successful passage between worlds. Whereas sea animals yearned for the products of the land, land animals hungered for the products of the sea, products only their human hosts could provide them. The success of human hosts rested in part on their ability to supply the special needs of their animal guests, needs that animal-persons could not supply in their own world. In return, humans received the right to use the animal's body while at the same time incurring the obligation to care for the animal's *yua* during its tenure in the human world.

Just as shared personhood created the common ground for the relationship between human and nonhuman persons, the rules surrounding their interaction elaborated the differences between them. Every action performed by the hunter and his wife affected their ability to attract animals. A plethora of rules were in place to guide human action. These rules, if followed, would clear the path for the animals to approach the hunter and his family. Con-

versely, unfocused thoughts and careless actions blocked the animals' path—
with snow, with hanging clothes, with menstrual blood, with human hands.

Land and sea animals shared with human persons the ability to see, hear,
feel, and smell human action in relation to them. Of all animal species, seals
were depicted as the most sensitive, and the greatest number of prescriptions
focused on keeping their path into the human world clear. Conversely, the
identity between birds and humans—both men and women—appears to
have been the strongest. As humans were originally created by Raven, it was
in the image of a seabird that human hunters appeared to the seals, and of a
loon that women danced in their honor. The small wooden birds hung with
the bladders during the Bladder Festival and buried with the seals' bones
provide a vivid image of this relationship—hunter and hunted side by side.

The circle is complete. Whereas people might encounter animals as human, seals perceive hunters in animal form. In fact, in all hunting and
gathering activities people must appear industrious and humble (like a little
bird?), never counting on getting a catch. Humans and seals alike share
personhood; the ideal hunter shares aspects of a bird's animal nature. Stories
of seal persons and birdlike hunters emphasize different sets of contrasts in
the active construction of the boundaries and passages between human and
animal worlds.

The seal hunt, like the pursuit of all animals for food, involves a contradiction. On the one hand, the Yup'ik people described the outcome of the hunt
as the seals' willing entry into the human world. According to oral tradition,
seals come to the good hunter of their own volition, and on their arrival in
the human world the hunter and his wife feast and host them as honored
guests. Yet to bring home the "guest," the hunter must first kill it. Rather
than directly celebrating, let alone confronting this lethal act, the Yupiit
represent the hunter's killing of the seal as a seabird breathing out a fine
soporific mist, which the seals find irresistible. The reference to the power of
the bird's breath also functions to clothe the seal's death in an image of life, as
breath *(anerneq)* is associated with life and regeneration. The situation remains ambiguous. The confrontation is indirect (Morrow 1990). Presenting
the kayaker as a bird not so much gives the hunter superior qualities, but
allows him to shift the negative implications of his act. Hunters do not
appear to seals as they are. Their new identity both protects and empowers
them.

The question of why the hunter appears as a seabird rather than a raven or
a fox is more difficult to answer. Is it because of shared features between the
seal hunter and the seabird, such as the similarity between a kayak and an
eider duck as they travel over the surface of the water? In fact, the seabird is
like both the human kayaker and the seal in that all three are ocean hunters.
Cultural systems often play on natural connections, and the Yup'ik representation of the seal hunter as a seabird is no exception.

The human hunter also may have taken the form of a seabird because of the structural place of birds in general in Central Yup'ik cosmology, as mediators between land and sea, the human and nonhuman. In many accounts, the shaman took the form of a bird when he traveled between worlds in supernatural flight. Siberian shamans considered their coats to be bird skins that empowered them to fly during trance (Fitzhugh and Crowell 1988:241). Again, the world was created by a bird—Raven. Thus, it makes good cultural sense that a bird be chosen to mediate between the hunter and the hunted—specifically a seabird in the case of ocean hunting, a bird that could dive and swim as well as fly. Although neither "culture" nor "practical reason" can provide an unequivocal answer to the question "Why is the hunter perceived by the seals as a seabird?" the representation of the ocean-going hunter as an oceangoing bird simultaneously makes good cultural and natural sense.

CHAPTER 4

PREPARING THE PATH
Becoming a Real Person

It is said that if a person lives in such a way that everything is not handed down to him or given him, this person uses his head, he becomes wise.

—*Frances Usugan, Toksook Bay, December 9, 1985*

THE CARE OF YOUNG CHILDREN

"Living in such a way" took a lifetime to learn. Children were instructed about what to eat, what to watch, and how to behave from an early age onward. Parents assumed that very young children lacked "awareness" or a lasting memory of their experiences. To *ellange-* (obtain awareness, from *ella* awareness, plus *-nge* to begin) was an essential aspect of personhood that children did not usually experience until the age of four or five, and then only sporadically.

Young children, referred to as *mikelnguut* (from *mikete-* to be little, literally "little one") or *yun'erraat* (from *yuk* person, literally "to begin to be a person"), were treated with indulgence partly because of this lack of awareness, but also because of their identity with recently departed and much respected ancestors. Like the bits of food regularly offered to the shades of the dead, it was important never to deprive a child and always to give it some little morsel:

> They considered a child's hands tiny, and they were to be given a little. They were to be filled with some little thing, whatever is available, a piece of food, something given towards the satisfaction of their hunger.
>
> And nowadays too, since the *kass'aq* things are available, a little piece of something, a piece of bread that might satisfy [the child's] hunger, because they have these things to give.
>
> Even this sugar, a piece of sugar satisfied its little body. These things were important for the time when one first became aware.
>
> That was what they did to them, and it is an instruction to this day that a child's hands are small. (Toksook Bay Elders, November 5, 1983 NI58)

Because very young children had not as yet gained awareness, people considered their minds vulnerable and susceptible to injury. Like the animals,

143

they must never be roughly treated or talked to in a loud or unkind manner. Joe Beaver of Goodnews Bay (June 1988 YN31:3) reported: "Toward their children they must not act impulsively. This habit of yelling is a strict prohibition against the children. And a woman must not be rough with a child. That is the duty of a woman inside the house. She takes care of a child gently, not scolding too much."

This proscription against rough treatment applied particularly to boys. People said that when boys grew to manhood, they would live their lives out in the weather. The universe (ella) was harsh and would give them enough rough treatment without their parents doing the same. Frances Usugan (December 9, 1985 NI69) recalled: "Then again, when a couple had their baby, if it was a boy, they were told never to slap him or mistreat him in any way. When he came of age and began to go out hunting, the rugged land would have its way with him. When they have begun to go out hunting, they will work hard at it as if they are mistreated by ella [the weather or the universe]. And it does. Some told stories of young boys getting so frustrated that they cried."

If a child cried for something, it should be given what it wanted without scolding so that its mind might be satisfied. If adults listened and catered to their children when they were young, the children would presumably grow into good listeners and willing helpers in their turn.

Adults tolerated a certain amount of misbehavior by very young children because of their immature minds and lack of awareness. Verbal correction was considered appropriate even for the very young, but not in a harsh tone. Mary Worm of Kongiganak (May 14, 1988 YN17:6) reported: "Even if our minds are bothering us, as far as small children are concerned, especially by our mouth, we are not to ever handle our children with oral abuse. . . . But we talk gently to them. . . . We warn them in a gentle and quiet voice and do not shout or yell at them. . . . Even when they are grown, talk to them in a gentle way. Do not scold them. . . . When the day goes on, we have plenty of time to reprimand them orally. So there was a warning when they first open their eyes. It was strictly prohibited to talk to them in a hard voice when they are just waking up . . . and also at night when they are about to sleep."

Because young children lacked mind or awareness, parents could not use reasoning to control them. They could, however, startle or surprise children into obedience. To hush a crying child, an adult might loudly exclaim "Carayak!" (monster, literally "terrible, fearsome thing") and pretend to listen for its approach. This scare tactic usually won the child's attention and is regularly employed on very young children even today. Each child had its own ingun, a particular endearing set of made-up words adults used to coo to the child. Adults also employed teasing, both friendly and otherwise, to influence the behavior of young children (especially those named after their deceased "teasing" cousins) and teach them to control their emotions. Both friendly teasing (ilangciarluki) and deliberate provocation *(qinucetaarluki)* were regular modes of interaction between adults and children.[1]

CHILDHOOD TRAINING

> *There are many stories to tell and much advice to be given, things we used to be told. It was a part of our everyday life to be told things.*
>
> —*Frances Usugan, Toksook Bay, September 12, 1985*

As boys and girls reached the age of five and six, their lives began to change. By that time they had attained awareness of their surroundings, and their minds were considered receptive to oral instruction. To become "aware" implied that they had reached a stage of maturity in which their memory of their surroundings and the events of life were continuous rather than fragmented, as is characteristic of a small child. As they reached this stage, parents replaced the indulgent treatment of infancy by careful and continuous training according to a strict set of rules designed to help them develop in the correct way.

Mothers, grandmothers, and older sisters instructed young girls *(nasaurluut* from *nas'ak* unmarried girl, virgin, plus *-r(ur)luq* poor dear one) in the sod houses. According to Joshua Phillip of Tuluksak (June 1988 YN21:2): "Inside the house, the one with authority was the mother. The mothers talked to their children on how to work, how to clean up the house, and how to sew too. They teach them how to sew starting from the time they are young girls."

At the age of five, young boys *(tan'gurraat* or *tan'gaurluut* from *taneg-* plus *-r(ur)luq* poor dear one) "moved out of their mothers" and went to live in the men's house with their father and other male relatives. According to Paul John:

> Only the *qasgiq* was the home for the men and the young men and boys. . . . Those were the people that stayed in the *qasgiq*. And even though they go to their own home, they did not stay long. . . . Those young men would not stay in their own house for no reason at all. If he comes into his house and sits down, his grandmother, if he has a grandmother, will say to him, "Instead of just sitting there, go over to the *qasgiq* and keep listening to what they say, all the things that you will use to live."
>
> They say that if a young man stays too much in his real house he will not hear anything that has to do with his life. . . . At the *qasgiq*, too, they would say, "Why do you stay in your own home with nothing to do?" Even though these *yuunrat* [children] are really small, they start to retain knowledge because they have started to try to be in the *qasgiq*. (Paul John, Toksook Bay, February 4, 1977)

1. See Jean Briggs's "Mazes of Meaning" for a detailed discussion of Inuit socialization. A central idea of Inuit education, she argues, is to "cause thought." As in western Alaska, the techniques for causing thought also stimulate feelings: "Whereas we . . . like to imagine that emotions and 'rational' thought are in opposition, Inuit utilize the relationship in powerful ways, creating intense emotions as a means of stimulating thought" (Briggs 1991:5).

The boy's parents often marked their son's introduction into the men's house with a small feast. Not only might they present food and gifts to the occupants of the *qasgiq*, but sometimes they also gave a gift of a new gut window, lamp oil, or food to the *yua* of the men's house.

In the *qasgiq* the young boys listened to the oral instructions. Billy Lincoln recalled: "When I became aware, men never stayed anywhere but in the *qasgiq*. There used to be many men in the *qasgiq*. From the front all the way back, getting younger. The younger boys would be in the back. The *qasgiq* would be very quiet. The young people would be down on the floor" (Alexie and Morris 1985:37). Speaking at great length, the elders encouraged the boys to try to "steal" their words and keep them safe in their minds for future use. According to Paul John (November 5, 1991), "Some of them would say to the young boy, 'Go over to the *qasgiq* and try to steal a few words from the others who are speaking.' It would be like when he hears something said by another, he would always remember." An orphan from St. Marys introduced his recollections by saying, "These things I tell you I stole. I had no father or mother so when my friend's father spoke, I listened."

In the *qasgiq* the young boys listened while the men gave instructions on what they should do and on how to live: "So they learned that way of life before they were fully able to hunt. That is how they did it. . . . And then these young boys were talked to by one man on the way of life. And while he was talking one could not even hear anyone whispering. But that one particular speaker who was giving the instructions of life talked alone" (Dennis Panruk, Chefornak, December 17, 1987 NI107:4).

The words of the elders guided the young hunters as they matured. According to Eddie Alexie of Togiak (March 10, 1988): "It happens that some people say, 'A person who is never jealous loves to tell things to his fellows. . . . So the one that is not jealous likes to instruct others.' . . . When he finishes, he would say, 'What you have just been told, tie it to your ankles! So you will not have to stumble on it!'" John Nicholas concurred: "The things that my father spoke to me about, I tied to my ankles so that they were always with me. Today, I remember them when I come across them. Back in the old days, everything that was said was received as a scolding" (Alexie and Morris 1985:59).

Some contemporary Yupiit remember the traditional teaching practices as *alingnarqellruut* (frightening). The speaker was *takarnarquq* (intimidating, making one feel shy and respectful). Conversely, elders say that contemporary youth *takaunateng*, they lack respect *(takar-)*. Young people are not properly shy or bashful and do not attend to what they say.

Many stories vividly portray the consequences of inattention to those early lessons. One well-known account is the story of *Itqiirpak*, the gigantic hand that rises from the sea and devours a group of noisy children. Billy Lincoln (April 1986 NI83:1–2) told the story as follows.

In those days, when we were being mischievous in the *qasgiq* at night without the supervision of elders, they used to tell us not to make noise because if we do, *Itqiirpak* [a giant hand with a mouth in the palm and at each fingertip] would get us.

The story that I heard was when the *Itqiirpak* entered into the *qasgiq* when children were being mischievous in there.

It came in as a big hand, felt around and did away with the boys who were playing, except for this poor boy who hid in the pit dug in the inner portion of the *qasgiq*. This hole was dug to channel off the incoming water into it. When it gets full, they would haul the water out with containers.

So that boy went into that pit.

So that hand did feel the pit, but because it was covered, it did not harm the boy.

So the next day, he told about that incident to the people in the village.

So that next day, they hung a big steel blade over the door. They tested it to see if it would work by placing a log underneath it. When they let it fall, that log broke in two.

So they set it up like that.

So, on purpose, they made noise in the *qasgiq* that night but they kept checking to see if that *Itqiirpak* was coming.

Pretty soon it surfaced from the ocean. You have seen the rising sun. It is crimson and big. They say that it looked like that when it surfaced. When it was near, they went into the *qasgiq*, and while they were still making noise, it entered.

When it came out of the floor-entrance, they let the blade drop and cut that hand off. And it became suddenly dark, and that thing disappeared. They probably couldn't see exactly what was happening because it was dark.

The next day, they found nothing but ice instead of a hand.

That was how I've heard the story.

Especially at night children were instructed not to make noise or they would attract *nepengyat* (from *nepa* noise), ghosts believed to present themselves at night accompanied by noise and a cold mist. They never let people walk around outside when auroras were present, as noise might disturb the auroras and cause them to take people away. Noise was not always proscribed. Men intentionally made noise during the ritual cleaning of the *qasgiq* to drive away evil. Nunivak hunters are said to have beaten on their kayaks to drive away bad weather (Lantis 1946:196). Nonetheless, the punishment for random noise in the *qasgiq* was severe. Moravian missionary Arthur Butzin observed in the 1920s: "Should the boys become loud, one of the young men would be instructed to punish him. The young man would take the boy and strip him of his parka, flop him on his back and seizing him by the legs would drag him over the rough planks over the fire pit until the boy's back would be well bruised and then the boy would be shoved out into the exit. Even a father was not allowed to interfere. The respect for the order and quiet of the kashige must be preserved" (Fienup-Riordan 1992:40).

An important contrast existed between the ideal behavior of young men and women and that of the elders who instructed them. Young people were encouraged to be active workers in the village to enable their parents to "sit

Men seated on the back bench of the qasgiq. *Moravian Archives.*

down."[2] According to Billy Lincoln (January 15, 1991): "When his children are able to hunt, having taught them about the ocean and land hunting, that father sits down. That is the truth." Children listened closely to the advice of their elders on proper action. Whereas, ideally, young people were active but quiet, their elders sat down and spoke.

> Because they loved [their children] and didn't want them to go the wrong way, they talk to them so that they could be more aware. But some of these men that are really old would just exist without talking or anything like that. And they did not tell [the young people] what to do in the men's house, even though they might have grandchildren in the men's house.
>
> These men that just exist without saying anything at all are referred to as the ones who do not goad. But if he lives with that goading spirit, he is cheering for the ones who come after him to succeed. He sees them and he thinks, "How can I help them to live a better life?" . . . The one that feels like this will be telling *kinguvri* [his descendants, from *kingu+* time after, literally "the ones who come after him"] the things he learned. (Paul John, February 4, 1977)

To selfishly instruct only one's own children was considered even more reprehensible than neglecting to instruct altogether.

> They used to say like this. Some man at the men's house doesn't try to make his children aware of things. But he would only tell his own kids how to do things at

2. One term for adopted child is *aqumkengaq,* from the root *aqum-* (to sit down) and $\simeq$ *kengaq* (one that is being V-ed). It may relate to the adopted child letting its parents sit down by working for them (see also Morrow and Pete 1993).

his own house. And they would refer to this person as the one who is jealous. These things that he is telling to his own kids he doesn't want another child to hear. But another person who has no jealousy would tell any young person. When he tells them about life like that he would only tell them at the men's house because he wants everybody else to live good with each other. He tells them all with no exceptions. These people then looked at life only a set way, and there should be no deviation from what they taught. (Paul John, February 4, 1977)

Even though they are warned, some children never modify their behavior. It is said that later in their lives, when they encounter the obstacles that the elders anticipated, such children will "live with recognition." Paul John (February 4, 1977) continued, "And this older person will say to this young man . . . 'You don't ever let go of the life that you are living right now. And in your life ahead, while you are living your life the way you are living, you will hear what I am saying and you will say that you live with recognition.' Whatever this old man says, he is saying exactly how it is going to be."

PREPARING THE PATH

Parents and other adults taught an attitude toward life and work as important to their children's future as specialized skills. Regardless of their technical knowledge, if young people failed to perform certain acts "to prepare the path for the animals," they put their future life in jeopardy.

The training of the boys in the *qasgiq* and girls in the smaller sod houses was far from indulgent. Anna Kungurkaq of Toksook Bay (December 1976) recalled:

> Poor! The ones in the *qasgiq*. The young boys would be sleeping with their legs folded in as far as they can. They used their hair seal mittens as pillows. If it was too cold, they could put their feet in the inside of their boots.
> Saying that it was not time to be lying down, one of the men would call out loud to them from the side. He would tell them that it was not time to lie anymore but to get up. And if one of the boys did not wake up, his *iluraq* [male cross-cousin of a male], taking the urine from one of the men, would splash him on the head. And without sleeping anymore, he would get up, put on his boots, and go out. And he does not act as if he is getting angry because these people always tried to follow the sayings. They followed whatever their speakers said.[3]

Getting up and out early in the morning were important cleansing actions that elders taught children to perform from their earliest years. Theresa Moses (August 1987 NI95:2) recalled: "In the mornings we were told not to lie around. It is said that if a person walks in the morning, his refuse emits profusely from him like smoke from the fire. If that happens that refuse is

3. Butzin reported the punishment meted out to sleepyheads along the middle Kuskokwim. There "early rising was the rule," and men considered it shameful to have the women and children awake first: "If the night chambers of the children were emptied before a boy was up, that boy would become a poor hunter. Boys were strapped with belts having horn and ivory fastenings in order to rouse them for the day's program" (Fienup-Riordan 1992:40).

strewn all over, and it comes to rest on a person who is lying down in the morning."

People traditionally considered illness to be an animate force, and how they chose to live determined whether or not illness could enter their bodies. Paul John (February 1977 NI39A:2–4) explained the requirement to be a *tupagyararatuli* (early riser, from *tupag-* to wake up) as a way to avoid illness:

They tell us what we are to do in the evening so that in the morning, as soon as we wake up, we will get up.

While s/he is lying down, a person will not acquire things s/he needs. But if s/he breaks sleep by getting up early and doing things, then s/he finishes things. . . .

Before they began to depend on a hospital, they would tell us, "So then, when you wake up in the morning try to get up as soon as you wake up." They liken the one who starts doing things early to those who contradict their *caarrluk* [bad stuff, dirt], that which they are going to have as illness. It is as if the one who is lying down is being showered with the *caarrluk* of the one who is up and about.

Young girls were likewise instructed to be early risers. Anna Kungurkaq (December 1976) reported: "My mother would wake me up in the morning and tell me that the men were going hunting for food. She would tell me to get up. And when she told me to get up, I would not just lie there but get up right away because we used to try to follow what was said to us."

On rising, parents instructed boys and girls alike to go outside and check the world and the weather before doing anything else. According to Mary Worm of Kongiganak (May 13, 1989):

I would wake up, and my mother up there is putting on my mukluks while I sleep. We used to have boots that were long. . . . She would lace up my boots. And when she put me down and stood me up, I would open my eyes right away. And when I wake up, she would say to me, "Go outside right away, and when you do, urinate in the refuse place: if you do that, you will not be sleepy at all!"

And I would rush out, rushing to the refuse, taking down my old pants when I urinate, I would be wide awake suddenly! Who would be sleepy at all?

A child learned early to pay attention to the direction of the wind: "Asking one where the wind is blowing from teaches one how to be observant according to our ancestors' traditional ways. That is the beginning lesson of how to be observant" (Joshua Phillip, Tuluksak, June 1988 YN21:2).

Paul John (February 1977 NI39:5–8) described the importance of this rule to check carefully the new day and the consequences of not attending to it:

In the morning,
after waking us up,
our mothers would say to us,
"Well then,
put your boots on and go outside!"
Even to the girls,
to the young girls like you.

"Do go outside,
by putting on your crummy shoes
and not asking when!"

When they told us to go out,
they said to us,
"Well then,
as soon as you go out,
be certain as to which direction the wind is coming from.
Be aware of it.
And also scan the sky.
Then after looking at how it is,
come in!". . .

Only by looking with their own eyes
they try to understand the condition of *ella* [the weather or world].

And also,
even if the one they have instructed was a girl,
she will look at the weather.
"Oh, it is like this."

So then, when she becomes a mother . . .
when she has children,
and if she learns the weather
for the purpose of instructing her children,
even though she was a girl they instructed her. . . .

I recognized this particular saying
from the one who was the mother of Nick. . . .
His mother was an old woman
but she would try to get around.

In the springtime
before we used outboard motors
when we were preparing to leave,
she had warned us,
"So you are leaving." . . .

So my companion said to her
that we were going to overnight across there.

Then when he said that to her she said,
"Alas, the weather is not conducive to going out
since it seems unpredictable.
This morning Nunivak Island has become visible.
It is going to be windy from the south,
the wind will be strong."

An old woman tells us two
who are going out to the wilderness.

So we left,
depending on the ice like the one out there,
the one that is floating away.

We went down from the shore
towards the water.

I then paid attention to Nunivak Island
the one I never paid attention to,
and it was like that,
it was visible.

Then I looked at it, thinking,
"I wonder how the old woman's saying will be,
with Nunivak Island being like this?"

So, that time, we went out,
and the night came,
the wind started to pick up.

The next day,
the dawn came with really bad weather.
It was exactly like the old woman had said.

There then,
because she watched the weather like she was told,
knowing it exactly as she learned it
she told it to us.
But because we did not understand how the weather is
mistakenly, we went out.

After rising and checking the weather, boys and girls alike were kept busy
with numerous manual tasks:

And those who are young boys keep shoveling entranceways when it is snowing
even though they are not theirs.
    Or if one is a young girl, instead of just lying around in the house, whatever
needs tending to, whatever needs working, these are the ones that the early
morning workers do.
    These are the ones the illness finds uncomfortable and so cannot be with
them. (Paul John, February 1977 NI39B:4)

Young people were trained to embrace willingly even the most distasteful
chores. The performance of such tasks provided important protection in their
future life. Herman Neck of Kasigluk (June 1988 YN28:3) stated that "even
though something might be dirty and abhorrent they tell us to handle it, put it
away someplace, and not leave that dirty refuse where it is. Clean up that dirty
thing. Just handle it with your hands, because they say that starting from our
hands we would not begin to wear out even though we work on those dirty
things. And that dirty thing will not stick permanently to our hands."

Just as the women anointed the seals' "hands" with snow and the land
animals' paws with oil, so children covered their hands with dirt. Dirt was
considered a pathway for illness out of a person's body as well as a barrier
preventing entry of disease in the first place. According to Joshua Phillip of
Tuluksak (June 1988 YN22:18), "If a person is such that s/he always sweeps

and s/he always works on any refuse, any epidemic of sickness is not able to conquer that person! Any sickness will not be able to bring down his/her body. Even if the people are going through some great sickness, that person will not die. It is because the refuse that one works on makes that person strong, and they do not let any sickness touch his/her body."

Joshua Phillip (June 1988 YN22:16–18) recounted a dramatic consequence of a person's care of refuse. The things that people helped to clean up, such as grass and ashes, opened a way for them in times of great need.

> During spring, she went across the river to do something, and when she was on her way back, the ice had gone out, and there was a current just like it was summer. She was panic-stricken because she was going to be stranded right across from the village, and it was nighttime. So while she was in the state of panic, because she had a staff, when she checked to see how deep it was, it was very shallow. So continuing to do that with her staff, she started and crossed that river, and the water came up this much. . . . And probably it was wide. . . . So like that, she continued to cross it, the water . . . had not gotten any deeper than that. And the bottom of it that she was stepping on was hard and firm. And eventually, she had crossed that big river all the way to the other side. She was so grateful and happy when she got to the other side. While she was thus grateful, when something caught her eye and she looked at the way she had crossed, there drifting down the river were discarded grass and also ashes. It was the ashes that come from the *qasgiq* and from the houses of the people. So those things that she had swept had formed a walktrail through the river when she was in the state of panic. The refuse had helped her. . . .
>
> That is not the only experience that those people had. Even down there in the ocean, a person was also rescued by those things. He would step on those ice chunks in the water. After he had stepped on them, he would look back to them, and they would be ashes and grass. Those people who were grateful for his past deeds helped him in his time of great need for assistance. They rescued him from his inevitable death by using those ashes and grass.

Here the power of the minds of the people he had helped, as well as the power inherent in the refuse, provided a barrier to misfortune and a pathway in time of need.

Not only must young people care for the refuse, thereby creating a "walktrail" for assistance in their future life, they must also regularly travel and care for the pathways within the village. It was the job of young girls to carry food from the sod houses to the *qasgiq* to serve their male relatives. Anna Kungurkaq (December 1976) recalled this task and how the people of the *qasgiq* regarded her as their *tegussuun* ("handler," from *tegu-* to take in hand):

> This was how I brought food to my father
> after my mother prepared the food,
> and also to my aunt's husband
> and my mother's brothers.
> These are the ones I brought food to,

including the bowls of the visitor, if there was one.
We would go to the *qasgiq* with our parkas belted. . . .

My work was to be ready to serve them.
It was the reason why I went to the *qasgiq*.

Then when I would go out one of the people would say,
"Go then and tell them over there to go ahead and bring us food."
Or the one with no helper would tell me
to get something to bring to him,
the one who has no girl for a helper.

One of the ones who stayed in the *qasgiq* that I am bringing food to would say,
"Alright then, do not go out, but come in and eat with me."
This was how I ate at the *qasgiq*.
I ate with the one I brought food to.

At this time the girls might also receive verbal instruction. According to Billy Black of Kongiganak (May 13, 1989), "Those females, according to their ways, when they came to the *qasgiq* to bring food, they would let them sit down on the floor just in front of the men, and then someone from around there would tell her about how to live and how to take care of her husband. [She was told] how she should live while she was alive."

Frances Usugan (December 9, 1985 NI69) recalled the care young girls took when entering or exiting the *qasgiq*: "When the women brought food, they were told to enter past the entryway instead of appearing through it. . . . There used to be two walrus tusks on each side of the entryway to grab onto, to aid entrance and exiting. When a woman or girl was getting ready to leave, she was instructed to stoop down and make sure her hem was spread around her, making sure her legs were not showing. Then she would grab on to the tusks and exit by dropping down onto the ditch to be on her way. If her legs had appeared, the men poked her bottom because she ignored their instructions."

Anna Kungurkaq (December 1976) described her entry into the houses as a young girl when the women sent her to fetch fire to light her mother's lamp:

In the evening my aunt would say to me . . .
that if one of the people had a light in their window
to go and ask them to provide a fire for us. . . .
Going out I would look around the village for a lighted window.
Then seeing a lighted window,
I would run over and when I went in,
when they say to me, "*Waqaa?*" [Hello, what can I do for you?]
I would say, "I have come for fire."
"Then fire up your lighter from down there and go."
Then lighting up the lighter I would run home.

Even today children do not enter houses in a thoughtless manner. Instead, they stand quietly by the door out of respect to the occupants and wait to be invited to come in. In the past children could not leave a house any more freely than they could enter. While the elders were speaking, a person left the *qasgiq* at his peril. A stick was placed over the exit to block the boys' departure. The consequences of inattention were as dangerous as the unruly behavior of young children. According to Matthew Frye of Napakiak (June 1988 YN18:13), "One of the individuals used to break that strip and rush outside. He would flee from being talked to, probably because he will never listen at all. So when he does that, the speakers would say, 'Let him be like that so that he will have very fine-looking teeth at the beginning of the snowdrift.' It was so that, when he freezes to death, his teeth will be showing at the spot where the snowdrift has its reason to form. They curse them in such a fashion."

Young boys worked throughout the village, clearing all manner of passageways—shoveling house entries, clearing the *qasgiq* skylight of snow, tending water holes to keep them free of ice. According to Billy Lincoln (July 13, 1985 NI78B):

> When the weather is bad,
> the boys, the teenagers,
> the ones able to shovel
> would be told by their parents
> to clear their porches.
> One of the boys would go out,
> he would go after getting ready.
> The one who uses his mind
> would take a shovel and go out
> and go from house to house.
> He would go through the whole village,
> clearing their porches,
> shoveling them.
>
> He would think like this,
> that when he begins to do things,
> he hopes that his catch will come to him.

Removing snow from passageways—an endless task, as the wind and weather filled openings with snow and ice as quickly as they were cleared—was especially important for young men preparing to be hunters. By performing these actions, while keeping their minds focused on the animals, boys cleared a way for the animals, whom they would someday hunt, to come to them. Joshua Phillip (June 1988 YN22:16) told this story: "There was this person who, during the winter, kept the walkway cleared by shoveling. Starting from the night, he would shovel, clearing the walkways of snow. Sometimes when he is shoveling, his shovel hits something and gets stuck before the morning daylight comes. When they check on what it struck, it would be an antler of a caribou. Now where did that come from? And after that happened to him, he started to catch caribou all the time. Because of his consistent activity clearing away the walkways, that made him become a great hunter" (compare Himmelheber 1987:26).

By clearing these passages, whether of refuse or of snow, young people both mentally and physically prepared a future way for the animals to come to them. Paul John (February 2, 1977) came back to this point often: "When he talks, he would tell them . . . that those boys should go ahead and work on those doorways and water holes, sweeping floors, so their future catches will have good trails." By these acts they removed the obstacles from their lives, making their way smooth. According to Eddie Alexie of Togiak (March 10, 1988): "When one does things to make the way smooth, living is not too tough where one does not have any way to go. The person who sets things aside that are in the way is helped, even when there is ice. That is what happens to one who sets things aside from one's path. That is one of the oral teachings that is told to us."

Discipline was not confined to the circumscription of movement, and to the repetition of manual tasks that clear the path to one's future life. Parents also carefully restricted a child's intake of food and water:

Sometimes when we felt hungry
they would say to us
that we would be eating soon.
And because they had windows made of seal gut,
we would be told to look at the window,
anything,
looking for things that looked like people
or like dogs,
and they would tell us to look for things that looked like sleds.

Sometimes when we kept looking at it,
I would also lose my feeling of hunger,
after being hungry.
(Magdeline Sunny, Nightmute, July 17, 1985 NI70:36)

Parents served food to their children carefully and in limited amounts. According to Anna Kungurkaq (December 1976):

When he started to eat
his in-laws would fill his bowl with food
and give it to him saying
that he was to quit eating when his toes became tired.
That was her son's custom at the place they lived,
to squat down on his toes and eat.
Then when his big toes became tired,
he was to stop even when he did not finish his food.
That was how they let their grandson eat.

Ideally, children never played with food or took it without being offered. Anna Kungurkaq continued:

And there were those needlefish out in our hole that we could eat.
Even the needlefish they did not want us to fool around with!
We were not even to eat the needlefish on purpose.
They let us eat things at one time, not at any old time.
We ate early in the morning and had lunch at noon.

At noon they would say, "It is time to eat."
They would then serve us some food
and we did not go after things ourselves.
We would chew the food very well.
They said that if we did not chew them well,
we would get hungry fast.
But if we chewed them well,
we would not get hungry fast.

Oh dear! Those poor people were not the kind in whose presence
you could do anything you wish.
It was not possible for us to follow our wishes or desires
regarding food.
You poor things now just grab something when you want
     and eat it.

Just as eating was carefully controlled, so was drinking. Anna Kungurkaq
repeated what her grandmother had told her:

She said that they did not drink water the way we ordinarily do.
When she was living with her in-laws,
she had a son Amaqigciq.
When her in-laws got up in the morning,
they would dip a sea-gull feather in water
and squeeze it into his mouth.
He would swallow it,
and that is how he drank water.

Then after he ate in the afternoon,
she would do the same thing.
She would dip the sea-gull feather and squeeze it into his mouth.
She said he would become thirsty.

Only after the evening meal,
when he was going to bed,
she would permit him to really drink water.
That is how the little one nursed her baby.
She did not fool around.

The boy who lived with the seals could take only five drinks of water at a
time before it turned to salt. Paul John (February 1977 NI34:2) remembered
the restrictions his mother imposed on his drinking so that his flesh would
grow "firm" and be able to withstand food shortage: "Then, too, sometime
around the time of eating, when I said I would like a drink of water, our
mother would say to me that I have just eaten and that my mouth has not lost

its taste of food. She did not let us drink right away" (compare Himmelheber 1987:75). In numerous accounts children were not allowed to drink water until their spittle came out in a tiny dry ball. Contemporary elders contend that today's young people are weak because they drink too much: "Water, tea, and coffee . . . those things are making people slow" (James Lott, Tuluksak, May 9, 1989).

Traditionally the Yup'ik people would regulate the manner in which they drank as carefully as the amount.

> That mother . . . had told those females like this, "Do not drink water by putting your lips down to the water! People do not drink like that." . . .
> But she told her to drink like this [with her hands]. And that girl down there stooped down and drank.
> And then that person went to her and told her not to do that.
> While she was going up, her face suddenly swelled up. Her face became very big and her eyes closed. And that was because she had drunk by stooping down.
> It is said that those water holes down there are [the seals'] windows. (Mary Napoka, Tuluksak, May 9, 1989)

Parents taught children to take food and water separately. A person should never drink water immediately after eating fish or seal oil. As in the care of refuse, this rigorous separation affected a child's health. Just as people separated land and sea animals in their preparation and consumption, children learned early to make a similar distinction between food and drink in their own diet.

Elders also taught children to distinguish their food from others'. From the time they began to eat solid foods they were given their own wooden bowls, which only they were permitted to use. After they finished a meal, they carefully wiped the dish and turned it upside down to prevent contamination. Not only did people maintain clear boundaries between categories of foods, but they carefully distinguished the foods that belonged to them. Once the bowl was filled, however, people had the right and privilege to share its contents with human and nonhuman comrades, both living and dead.

Ideally, then, all children's activities were carefully regulated, including sleeping, eating, drinking, talking, and moving through village space in the performance of daily tasks. A child awoke early, immediately checked the weather, worked hard without fear of dirt, and ate and drank carefully and in moderation. Through all of these acts, one worked simultaneously to create a boundary between oneself and illness, or ill will, and to clear a passage to good hunting and a good life in the future. Just as the dust of refuse both protected a person from illness and produced a walktrail for one's future well-being, so children were taught that their actions, if performed according to the rules, created a barrier to misfortune and opened a passageway to success in the future. Regardless of their technical skill, if they failed to live by the rules, illness and death rather than animals and offspring would come to them.

CHAPTER 5

THE REPRODUCTION OF LIFE
The Relationship between Men, Women, and Animals

THE RELATIONSHIP BETWEEN HUNTING AND PROCREATION

The foregoing chapter describes the process of social reproduction through time—the process of replication and substitution by which living children came to embody past generations. One way this was accomplished was through the child's inheriting a name-soul (literally "the person" of the ancestor) at birth as well as acquiring a gradual education in ancestral teachings. The knowledge of past generations was passed on primarily by same-sex instruction, with young boys and girls living with and learning from adult men and women, respectively.

The cross-sex relationship between men and women also was critical for the reproduction of life, not only human but animal life as well. As we have seen in the relationship between human and nonhuman persons, it was not the hunter alone but the married couple who hosted the animals. A hunter could not hope to succeed in the hunt without the active assistance and ritual forbearance of his wife.

In the relationship between humans and animals, each was conceived as incomplete without the other. The seal's thirst for water motivated its gift of meat and oil to human hunters, while human hunger required careful attention to the seal's needs. In the same way, men and women, to join in marriage needed first to be regarded as incomplete without the other (Strathern 1986:7). Rather than viewing the single sex state as a "natural" reference point, and the relationship between the sexes as one of opposition, with domains of social life (public/private, political/domestic, sacred/profane) understood as opposed, the Yupiit joined hunting and procreation in a reproductive cosmology focused on insuring continuity in both human and animal life.

The social differentiation between men and women began shortly after birth, when parents dressed their children according to the sex of the person for whom they had been named. Although often corresponding to the biological sex of the baby, this was not always or necessarily the case. Such cross-gender treatment usually ceased by the age of five or six, when young boys were sent to the men's house to learn men's work and their sisters remained in the smaller sod houses, where their mothers and grandmothers saw to their education. Following this residential separation, boys and girls could play together only outside. From the beginning, activity not only differentiated them but established their shared character as persons-in-training (see also Saladin d'Anglure 1986).

As we have seen, parents instructed boys and girls in a common set of rules for living with common consequences for misbehavior. Likewise, children were subject to similar eating restrictions, although the consequences were sexually specific. Both boys and girls worked at numerous small tasks such as clearing refuse, emptying urine buckets, and hauling water, and both ran errands between the men's and women's houses. As a child matured, relationships with both human and nonhuman persons began to change. Adults might excuse the careless acts of very young children because they were not old enough to have gained awareness of the rules for proper conduct. The mistakes of older children provoked both teasing and rebuke.

The Yup'ik Eskimos viewed gaining awareness as a gradual, lifelong process. During the period in which a young person was growing, both simple and elaborate personal rituals periodically marked their physical and social maturation. These ceremonies established their character as "man" or "woman."

FIRST MENSTRUATION: SITTING DOWN AND STANDING UP

A girl's first menstruation marked the most important event in her maturation. She was considered a child until then, but from that point on the community viewed her as a potential wife and mother. On Nelson Island a girl marked her first menses by spending five days outside in a small house called an *aniguyaq* (snow shelter dug into the snow and provided with a door; from *aniu*, snow on the ground), or secluded in a section of the sod house partitioned off by grass mats. During her seclusion, the girl could not work raw skins, eat raw foods, or drink fresh water. Her condition was comparable to that of the fetus in her social invisibility, restriction of movement, and the prohibition against childhood and adult activities. Gertrude Therchik of Toksook Bay (July 14, 1985 NI86) described this period of seclusion:

> Then in the spring time when they become aware that she had become a woman they let her sit down. They put a *tupigaq* [grass mat, literally "woven thing"] in front of her and then behind her they made a door. They did not let her go out through the regular doorway, only through the back door. They only let her go out through that door that they made for her in the corner.
> And they let those girls who had become women wear old clothes, and their mittens had no thumbs. And when they had to urinate they put their hood on

without looking around and bowed their head really low. They went to the area where trash was taken. They would urinate in the dumping place on the ground. This was the only time they left their abode. These are some of the things for the *aqumgalriit* [from *aqume-* to sit], those who had sat down.

A number of elements evokes the power of the menstruating woman to affect the harvest. The image of the thumbless hand, for example, simultaneously signified the idea of impaired grasp and its relation to game productivity (Nelson 1899:395). The use of a hood and restricted sight were considered prerequisite for male hunting power. According to Brentina Chanar (June 30, 1989),

> If she bleeds for the first time, they do what they call *aqumluteng* [(they) sitting down]. When they sit, they put something in front of her bed. They cannot look at a person. They stay like that for five days. . . . And when they are going to relieve themselves, they put on a belt and they make them gloves with no thumb. She puts on a hood.
> She could not look around; she could not really stand.
> But she relieves herself just like an old woman. And she must never relieve herself in the house.
> They call her *aglenrraq* [from *agler-* to menstruate]. . . .
> They used to [let them stay a little ways from the village] before I came to be aware. They called *nalikcaarirluku* [putting a cover or shelter over her]. They made a shelter out of sod and made a flap for a doorway.

Butzin recorded a significant variation on these coastal practices along the middle Kuskokwim, where the period of sitting was preceded rather than followed by the act of standing up:

> A girl coming to maturity first went thru a period of ten days, when she must keep on her feet and when not standing or walking about must lie down, but not sit down. After this first period of ten days either of walking or entirely recumbent, followed the period of sitting still. She sat in the dark corner of the house dressed in an old parka. She was allowed to drink in the morning and evening. This sitting period also lasted for ten days. Upon its completion the old parka was discarded and a new one (or a good one) was put on with a hood up and a belt on. So dressed and with boots on her feet and with fishskin mittens on her hands (but thumbless mittens and thumbs free) she came outdoors again. But she must not look far. She must not go to the creek upon her first exit, nor drink from a stooping position, nor must she eat of migratory birds, nor handle the soil. (Fienup-Riordan 1992:38)

Describing the long-term benefits of these actions, Himmelheber (1987:61) wrote, "Since they only see things at close range in their hut they can still see at a distance in old age: they have thus conserved their eye-sight."

Mary Napoka of Tuluksak reiterated the association between the visibility of the *aglenrraq* (the one who has recently menstruated for the first time) and the occurrence of dangerous weather conditions: "It is said that the northern lights use those females as anchors, and they cannot go away because of them. That is why in those days, when there is lightning, they used to let her stay by covering her. They said the lights might not be able to go away if she is not covered." A girl's behavior during her first menses also affected her own physical well-being.

> They never let them do anything. They never let them walk around or hunt for eggs or pick berries. . . . Nowadays there is no one who abstains. And the one who first becomes a woman runs around all the time. . . . That is why, nowadays, they hurt in their joints [they have joint pain from berry picking during menses]. . . .
> And when they come out they tell them not to look far because they get short-sighted early. . . . Those who go without scarves when they become women have headaches. (Mary Napoka, May 9, 1989)

Following this period of enforced sitting, the girl "stood up" both figuratively and literally as a mature, marriageable woman: "They call it *nanger-rluteng* [(they) standing up] when five days have passed. They say that *aglenr-raq* has stood up" (Brentina Chanar, July 7, 1989). On this occasion the girl gave away her childhood playthings, including small wooden dolls and their clothing, to prepubescent females. According to Theresa Moses of Toksook Bay (August 1987 NI95A), "After those five days have been used, we females were told to go to her to get some of her things. They told us that. . . . And if that girl had dolls, one by one she gives them out to the girls. When we girls did that it was called ⌢*ugayaryaraq* [way of stripping bare of possessions] to get things from her after those five days while she had been sitting down with a covering in front of her bed. And when she goes outdoors she puts on her hood, holds up the hem of her *qaspeq*, and she puts on gloves with fingers exposed. She completely covers herself with clothes."

Gertrude Therchik (July 14, 1985 NI86:5) described the excitement this distribution engendered in the girls who were to receive the dolls:

> Then they would say to us that the woman who was sitting down would stand up tomorrow and for us to get ready to come to her. It was really something that we would think about that whole night. They would tell them to go out early. So they went out early in the morning, trying to be ahead of everybody else.
> Small *inugua* [wooden dolls, from Iñupiaq *inuk* person, literally "imitation person"] of these first-time women before they became women, some of them were in their cloth *kakivik* [sewing kit, from *kaki-* to take a stitch]. These sewing kits had the wooden dolls in them. This was how it was. Before they gave them to us every little possession that they had they gave out.
> They gave the dolls that they used before they became women to the young girls. They also gave away the dolls' clothing. They would try to get up as early as they could. When they woke us up early in the morning, we would get up to ⌢*ugayaryaraq* [strip bare of possessions]. They would get up thinking about those things, the clothes that they had that were going to be given away.

Restrictions surrounding the use of these wooden dolls are particularly meaningful in light of the structure of village life. Young girls were forbidden from playing with their dolls during winter or inside the house. The dolls' dormancy inside the house during winter and their emergence in summer replicated both the transformation of their owners, through puberty restrictions, into women capable of giving birth, and the birth process itself. The timing also coincided with the arrival of the geese and other migratory waterfowl that marked the beginning of the annual spring harvest. People believed that if young girls played with their dolls outside the house before the arrival of spring, the weather would see and punish them: Winter would move into winter with no intervening season. Here again, inappropriate female activity was directly tied to cosmological upset and subsequent disaster, in this case food shortage. At the same time, appropriate female action and control of her procreative functions were prerequisite to the successful harvest.

A young girl's five-day menstrual seclusion paralleled both the five days of rest following a human birth and the five steps that led to the underground land of the dead. As her solitary sitting within the house was comparable to a kind of death or end of childhood activity, her standing signified her rebirth as a mature woman. Her sitting also paralleled the final five days of the Bladder Festival, celebrated annually at the winter solstice when the sun (itself a transformed human girl) "sat down" on the horizon. Whereas the Bladder Festival marked a seasonal renewal and the return of game, a girl's menstrual seclusion marked the renewed potential for human life.

Another parallel between seasonal and physical death and rebirth and the symbolic death and rebirth of the menstruating woman can be seen in the use of ashes to close the young girl's ritual passage. As she emerged from her seclusion, her mother or grandmother took ashes and threw them behind her, "cutting off her past" and thereby insuring the successful commencement of her new productive status. In some cases young women wore a pouch of ashes suspended from their menstrual belts. Alternately, mothers might require their daughters to eat ash to mark the end of their restricted activity and before they were able to pick berries again. People used ashes in a number of ritual contexts, including funerals and birth ceremonies, both to mark a passage and to protect a person from dangerous spiritual invasion.

THE POWER OF WOMEN

After a girl had her first menses and had undergone her menstrual seclusion, she continued to be subject to numerous restrictions. Along with her newly acquired ability to produce human life, she was also believed to have acquired special powers both to draw and to repel the animals that men pursued. Moreover, the Yupiit believed a woman was particularly susceptible to contamination during her menstrual periods and rigorously circumscribed her person and limited her activity to safeguard both her and the community. They carefully limited interaction with her both to prevent the depletion of men's ability to hunt as well as to protect her from harm.

Immediately following a girl's first menses, the very presence of food resources was tied to careful action on her part. On Nelson Island she could not handle fresh food of any kind for five months, or the species she touched would fail to return. She was prohibited from picking berries during the succeeding summer and from helping her father and brothers tend their fishnets. Nor could she touch sea animals, as they perceived her as bloody from the waist down and would be scared away by her appearance. In early summer she was required to tie one end of a hair of her head around a blade of grass and the other around a berry blossom lest the wind blow away the blossoms and with them the year's berry harvest.[1] She could not touch eggs as she gathered them, but instead had to pick them out of the nest with a wooden spoon or ladle.[2] According to Brentina Chanar (June 30, 1989):

And she never eats anything fresh, but something a little old [that is, food caught before she began menstruating]. She cannot go to the river. She cannot pick grass.

Although she keeps on working, she cannot go to the wilderness. When berries come, she cannot pick. Only after a year has passed from the time she bleeds, then she stops doing that.

They used to do that when they already had a spouse. So she and her spouse would do the same things. Her mate would do those things also. Only after the whole year had passed, he could start hunting.

Mary Worm of Kongiganak (May 13, 1989) added detail concerning the eating restrictions imposed on young women following their first menstruation: "Those *aglenrrat* [plural] had *inerquutet* [prohibitions]. They were told not to go to the wilderness and not to eat fresh food. And they did not eat . . . those breads that are cooked with yeast. They did not eat those. So there were certain foods they did not eat. And they did not eat those living things. And they absolutely did not eat belukha whales. They say that belukhas are things to be feared! . . . Walrus, those that are huge! Those huge animals that have tongues. Those, without avoiding them, they eat them. Those that seem to be so scary!"

During this same period the *aglenrraq* must continue to cover her body carefully, belt her clothes, and wear boots both inside and out, even in summer. After she removed them, she had to tie a string around her ankles. When outside, she must wear mittens and always keep her parka ruff close around her face: "Even when she stands she still wears gloves, wears her hood, wears a belt. She will be like that for a whole year from the time she starts bleeding. After one year, she stops doing that" (Brentina Chanar, June 30, 1989). By some accounts, women were to go belted "to hold in their *unguviit* [life]." She was never to look up or around lest she see or be seen by

1. Some people along the middle Kuskokwim modified this rule to require that the girl tie a berry plant to a stick with a piece of string.
2. This was a requirement into the 1980s in some areas, with a metal serving spoon taking the place of the wooden *ipuun* (ladle).

other human or nonhuman persons, or by *ella* (the universe) itself. Failure to follow these instructions was potentially disastrous.

> At that time even when she was able to stand up she could not pick berries.
> And if she had broken the river ice with her foot it is told that the eyes of the fish became red. And sometimes there would be no more fish. The one who was menstruating was told not to get her foot through the ice.
> *Aglerumalrianek* [those who were menstruating]—that is what they did to the females in that stage.
> When a female is like that the male is in want of a girl. After a girl had her menstruation it was told not to be so, and sometimes a girl causes one not to catch animals anymore. One of the women causes the game not to be caught.
> But some females give good luck in hunting. (Theresa Moses, August 1987 NI94A)

The visibility of the *aglenrrat* also jeopardized the harvest along the middle Kuskokwim. According to Mary Napoka (May 9, 1989), "They do not pick berries. Berries fall early if she picks. . . . And they never let them walk in the river. If she keeps going down to the shore, the shore will *merigyugtuq* [(it) keeps folding]. . . . They never let them go on a boat because they might let the fish go away. And if they were going to go in the boat for the first time they make sitting mats. . . . Nowadays they do not abstain; the women are just like men nowadays."

During subsequent menstrual periods a young woman also restricted her activity, if not so severely, avoiding contact with men and animals. She was not supposed either to see or to be seen and therefore went about belted and covered, never looking around. She could not cook or eat fresh food, prepare raw skins, or engage in sexual intercourse. Moreover, she must not conceal her condition but had to make it known to hunters so that they could avoid her. Contact with her menstrual blood could cause a hunter to go blind.

Individual Yup'ik women experienced these restrictions very differently. Some remembered their menstrual seclusion as a positive experience and a time when they were made particularly aware of the importance of their actions for the well-being of the entire community. Others found the experience demeaning and negative, as people blamed them for poor hunting or fishing and bad weather and made them feel these circumstances were their fault.

Although a menstruating woman's activity was always circumscribed, her menstrual blood had positive as well as negative connotations. By some accounts the red clay used as a pigment for decoration of both ceremonial masks and objects of everyday use was the transformed menstrual blood of An'gaqtar, the daughter of Raven. An'gaqtar left pockets of her menstrual blood in various places on Nelson Island, and worthy men could find these places and gather the red clay they needed for painting designs on the many things they carved from wood. Butzin reported that along the Kuskokwim

menstrual blood was also believed to be of medicinal value for certain conditions, including tubercular throats (Fienup-Riordan 1992:47).

Whereas a man's success depended on the support of a woman, young
hunters must avoid clandestine relations with young, unmarried women,
whether or not they were menstruating. Nastasia Kassel of Kasigluk (May 25,
1988 YN27:9) reported, "They used to say at that time that I came to be
aware: a female is death! Those who play around with women before acquiring wives, even though he is still alive, he dies."

Inappropriate sexual activity resulted in specific physical ills. For example,
if a man saw a woman's genitals, it was said that his eyes would rot. Worse
than the direct effects of such an indiscretion were the consequences of
keeping it a secret:

> They used to instruct us in those days of long ago. The boys were what is called
> *qumigituq* [sex crazed, *qumigite-* to be preoccupied with sex to the point of
> mental breakdown] after having been involved with the girl and not telling
> about it. It causes his ruin.
>
> If a male is *qumigituq* his face becomes very pale and his hair stands up. And
> if he gets to the worst stage, if he sees any skin of a female he would be
> unbearable to watch.
>
> The laps of the parkas of those at the worst stage become rotten from this
> secretion. That causes death. A female has death at the end. That was what was
> told. In the present times they do not hear it anymore. (Theresa Moses, August
> 1987 NI94A)

As well as his personal safety and health, a hunter's inappropriate contact
with women jeopardized his relationship with animals. According to Joshua
Phillip (June 1988 YN22:23), "Likewise a man is like a female. Even though
he had been able to catch game before, if he had fooled around with a female,
he can no longer catch land animals. . . . And it is like this also: A female is
death or a male is death. Some male has a pretend wife. Some female has a
pretend husband. That is what was considered to be a terrifying thing to do."
Paul John (November 5, 1991) recounted the teaching that cautioned a young
man not to touch a woman before he got married: "And undoubtedly, when a
boy had been touching a woman before getting married, he would become
weak. And when he hunted or fished, game and fish would become less on
his trail. And if a boy had tried to conform to the *qaneryarat* [sayings], there
would be plenty of game on his trail."

The air of sexually mature women was considered especially polluting to
young hunters, who were advised to pass a woman on the windward side to
avoid her bad air, and to breathe out when passing her so as not to dull their
senses. Conversely, women were told not to walk upwind of the male but
to pass him on his lee side if it was windy: "They used to say that a female is
death at that time. And when a female is grown, he was told not to be near
her. . . . A young boy will not be skilled if he gets a woman's vapor. They
used to say that girls have an *aurneq* [vapor rising from a warm, damp object

in the cold], and the boy is told not to touch girls" (James Lott, Tuluksak May 9, 1989).

According to Paul John, a man's breath soul *(anerneq)* was particularly vulnerable to contamination from such contacts, with potentially disastrous effects. If a man breathed a woman's vapor, his breath soul would be weakened and his mind would become fuzzy and lose its power to focus on the hunt. Here the power of the breath "burped" out by the hunter/bird to overpower seals is opposed to the power of woman's air breathed in by the hunter to repel the seals. A man's air can be strong only if kept apart from a woman's. That such proscriptions affected a man's ability to hunt is attested to in Joe Friday's (August 7, 1984 BIA48) description of a shaman's visit to the underwater home of the seals during the celebration of the Bladder Festival at the coastal village of Qissunaq. While peeking in the skylight, the shaman overheard the conversation of the "bladder people": "Some of them will say they had a good host and will go back to the same host. Some of them will say they had a bad host because the host always made him smell female odor and would say he is not going back to his former host."

Contemporary elders do not fail to remark the replacement of this dangerous odor by sweeter things. Joshua Phillip (June 1988 YN22:11–12) commented, "At the present time, when one passes a girl, she smells really nice, they smell of perfume. In those days before us, that was not the case when one passed a girl. They smelled of something else. At the present time, girls are not like those days anymore. But one's leeside smells of perfume."

A woman's odor was particularly dangerous during her menstrual cycle. Especially during that time she must carefully avoid contact with a man's clothing and hunting equipment, just as he must avoid contact with her. According to Theresa Moses (August 1987 NI95A):

> A female has a stronger scent than a male. If a female is bleeding and if not attended to, she comes to have an odor. If her clothes are not changed the odor becomes unbearable.
>
> The faults of the female were many in those days because she bled. And those who had sons made sure that the young men did not sit on top of the female clothing.
>
> There was special care taken in dealing with females. And if they get husbands they were told to watch their clothing. They did not put clothing on their husbands. They were told to take special care in dealing with their husbands because he was the hunter of the family. They were told to take good care of his clothing.

Nelson (1899:440) noted the belief that certain kinds of uncleanliness produced bad luck in hunting. When people contaminated themselves by coming into contact with something unclean, an invisible vapor attached to them making them abnormally visible to game. Women emitted such a vapor during menstruation. Even when she was not menstruating, a woman was never supposed to step over people who were lying down, as that might cause them to bleed.

At the same time that a hunter must protect himself from the depleting effects of a woman's unclean air, he must also restrict his vision. As restricted social contact was considered necessary to empower a man to hunt, so socially restricted sight produced powerful supernatural vision. Likewise, in most contexts young women were admonished from direct eye contact with hunters. Recall the term for "respect" *(gigciq-)*, translating "to look sideways without turning one's head" (Jacobson 1984:331).

A particularly eloquent example of the relationship between socially restricted sight and powerful supernatural vision as applied to interaction between men and women is contained in the story of the boy who lived and traveled with the seals, thereby acquiring extraordinary hunting knowledge and power:

> And his host [the bearded seal] said to him,
> "Watch him [the good hunter], watch his eyes,
> see what good vision he has.
> When his eyes see us, see how strong his vision is.
> When he sights us, our whole being will quake,
> and this is from his powerful gaze.
>
> When you go back to your village, the women,
> some will see them, not looking sideways,
> but looking directly at their eyes.
> The ones who live like that, looking like that,
> looking at the eye of women,
> their vision will become less strong.
> When you look at women your vision will lose its power.
> Your sight gets weakened.
> But the ones that do not look at people,
> at the center of the face,
> the ones who use their sight sparingly,
> as when you have little food, and use it little by little.
> So, too, your vision, you must be stingy with your vision,
> using it little by little, conserving it always.
> These, then, when they start to go hunting,
> and use their eyes only for looking at their quarry,
> their eyes truly then are strong.
> (Paul John, February 2, 1977)

Today's hunters still recall being instructed in their youth never to look into the eyes of women. This is much more than a matter of etiquette circumscribing their vision within the human world. Rather, restricted human sight is profoundly significant, framing a man's future relationship with the seals and other animals on whose good opinion he depends as a hunter. Here a hunter's vision, like his thought and breath, must not be squandered lest he be left wanting in his relations both within and beyond the natural world. In the past, a man's ability to harvest animals as an infinitely renewable resource was contingent on his careful use of his own finite personal resources. His ability to succeed in the hunt was tied not only to his care of the animals, but also to his relationship with women. As direct eye contact between the sexes was proscribed for successful hunting, successful hunting was the prerequisite for acquiring a wife and sexual access to women.

MARRIAGE

From the time a woman reached sexual maturity, her activity and inactivity, her odor and her sight, contributed to a man's personal health as well as his ability to succeed in the hunt. Rules carefully circumscribed contact with women so that a man could retain his power to pursue game. Living in separate houses, working at separate tasks, eating from separate containers, men's and women's lives were carefully bound off from each other.

Notwithstanding the potential danger of cross-sex relations, a hunter had to take a wife to help him in his work. From the beginning they were partners. A man shared many of his wife's restrictions during her menses. In fact, if his parents arranged his marriage before his wife's first period, he shared aspects of her puberty seclusion as well and, along with his wife, was bound off from both the human and animal worlds (see Nelson 1899:291–92). A woman's menstrual seclusion not only cut her off from the human world, it also excluded the couple from the community.

The partnership of marriage formed the basis of the present and future support and social composition of the community. When a young man or woman was ready to marry, his or her parents did not leave the choice to chance but participated directly in the arrangements:

Only their parents used to prepare them.

In those days,
using their own will,
I do not think all of them used their own choices.
A young girl does not make the first move
towards those young men who were of marriageable age.

A young man,
his mind extended towards a woman he wants as a mate,
prepares himself.

Then when he thinks
he might make a mistake
he will first tell his parents,
asking them about the one that he is desiring.

His parents will tell him,
his father and his mother,
if that girl fits well in their minds
through the things that she does.

"Just-married" couple from Nelson Island, Bethel, 1953. Oregon Province Archives, Gonzaga University.

They will say yes to him.

Sometimes,
even when he tells them,
they will respond negatively,
saying that while he lives
it will not go well for him in their minds.

So that boy,
that teenager,
even though his mind is reluctant,
he does not follow it.
But if he tries to follow what his parents say,
it is also beneficial.

While he lives with that one as his mate,
he will see that he will be in a satisfactory position.

"Let me then go along with them."
This is what he says in his mind first.

His parents are the ones who act as conscience
regarding the one he desires.

If it does not look good that he should have her,
they will tell him that it is not possible,
and when they think it is possible,
they will tell him to go ahead.

And sometimes
his parents first get him ready.

They look at the young girl's activities,
not at the color of her skin,
but at the way she does things.
Watching the way she does things
if she proves to be desirable,
they will let her parents know of their preference for
    her for their son.

After they look over these two . . .
they will mention him to that person
without his knowledge.

Without his knowledge
they get him ready for her,
they will have acquired one for him.

Then they tell him
that if he had her
it seemed she would be good for him as he lived.

Even though it does not go along with what he wants
he tries to follow his parents' wishes

because they can see what the girl is like.
(Toksook Bay Elders, November 1983 NI64:1–2)

In the course of these arrangements, the boy's parents carefully examined the intended:

Nowadays they do not use the custom of examining an intended.
They do not examine each other anymore.
A person visited the house of the intended
to see how the intended acts towards the parents.
They do not use that now.

If the intended was disrespectful towards the parents,
that one could very well be disrespectful towards the mate.

And if one acted in a haughty manner to the parents,
that one will act in that manner to the companion. . . .

If the one is the type that argues,
that one will be like that towards the mate.

And if the one does not respond quickly to the parents,
that one will be like that, too.
(Toksook Bay Elders, November 1983 NI64:4)

Commensurate with the importance of vision in Yup'ik cosmology, parents paid particular attention to the eyes of the prospective spouse. According to Joshua Phillip (June 1988 YN23:18), "They look at his/her eyes only and not at his/her body. Only at his/her eyes. By a person's eye one will know about a person. Those people could easily see because they used all their senses to make determinations."

The most important consideration in choosing a marriage partner was not the person's appearance, wealth, or social standing, but that person's careful, respectful, and honest handling of food. Herman Neck of Kasigluk (June 1988 YN28:24–25) described the parents' search for a good spouse.

And then also some women . . . those are the ones to be scared of! So she says that there is absolutely no more food. . . . But she had stashed food away where her husband could not see or does not know. But after she had waited until her husband had gone and then she would be the only one to eat from that stash. It is said that woman was someone to be afraid of!

And because of that danger, they used to test these young girls who have not acquired husbands yet. . . . A girl, before she has acquired a husband, it is easy to see if she will not take care of food or handle it properly.

They let that particular girl inside their house and feed her and look her over. . . . So she eats, having been given dry fish. . . . So she would be eating, and when she had eaten that dry fish, she would pick up those fish crumbs from her lap. She would eat them also. So she eats all those crumbs which have fallen down. Those dry foods usually have lots of crumbs.

And there is also the girl when the parents are testing her by letting her eat.

When she finishes she would get up and shake off the crumbs from her lap, and then she would go out.

Now that first girl, the one who picked up her crumbs and eats without getting up right away, it is said that one is a real woman, the one who will take care of food properly.

Especially by the way one takes good care of food, that is how they search for a girl.

And that next one who finished eating without bothering to pick up her crumbs but shook them off and went out, that is not a woman.

Paul John (November 6, 1991) gave a concise description of the role that appearance should play in the choice of a husband: "They say a young woman should not reject a homely man. They would say that if a homely man can make a hole in the ice, that man is all right to have as a husband."

Once the parents found a suitable spouse and arranged the marriage, the public announcement of the union was relatively simple and straightforward:

And how did they get married?

They never married,
they just became companions.

When they became companions,
we would know about it.
If they had become companions this day,
the one that became his companion, the woman,
would bring him food.
So by her bringing him food we find out,
after not knowing it,
his acquiring her as his mate.

That one,
the bowl,
the food that she is bringing to him,
it is like saying,
"We are marrying, this one and I."
(Toksook Bay Elders, November 1983 NI64:2–3)

The presentation of food to her husband as well as to other male in-laws was a simple but eloquent expression of the establishment of the couple's productive union. When a woman served a man his catch, she anticipated their future reproductive collaboration. Although not accompanied by elaborate public ceremony, marriage sometimes was marked by hosting a dance and distribution at the subsequent Bladder Festival. The primary focus of the Bladder Festival was on the feasting of the *yuit* of the animals to insure their return the following year. The marriage distribution consisted of the presentation of food and other products of the hunt in the *qasgiq* during the period when the bladders were on display. The bride made this presentation bedecked in new clothing provided by her husband's family. The distribution also included the performance by the bride in the *qasgiq* of a slow, stylized dance, designated *ingulaq*, said to imitate the mating dance of loons. A Toksook Bay elder (November 1983 NI64) remembered:

In those days when there were *qulirat* [traditional tales],
when a little *nukalpiaq* [good provider] took as his companion a *tutgarrluk* [grandchild],
he made the person have *ingulaq*.

With things, he made her put clothes on.
He made her put on clothes that were all new.

Then
when it was time for him,
during the time when they held the Bladder Festival,
those were the things they had for *ingulaq*.

She took them to the *qasgiq* in a bowl with food.

So the woman brought those things in
to the one she had acquired as a husband. . . .

This was how they made her *ingulaq*,
making her his wife they got married.

This celebration and announcement of the renewed potential for human procreation at the Bladder Festival was particularly appropriate given the focus of the festival on the reproduction of the harvest in the coming year. The "marriage dance" performed on this occasion provided a strong image of the complementarity between the production of game and the reproduction of life. While literally dancing the loon's mating dance, the bride held the hem of her skirt and rhythmically "fluffed it up to ward off old age" and to enhance her own future productivity. This expansive gesture, not to mention social visibility, of a sexually mature woman sharply contrasted to the rule requiring young unmarried girls to hold their skirts tightly down around their legs when entering or exiting the *qasgiq* to prevent the old men from grabbing at their vaginas "to teach them respect."

Although *ingulaq* has been performed in the living memory of only the oldest coastal residents, the presentation of new clothes to the bride by the groom's family continues into the present day. The new clothing most often consists of a fancy fur parka, requiring years of planning and preparation in the acquisition of materials, and months of sewing work. The parka itself bares the designs of the groom's mother and grandmother. These designs recall particularly noteworthy events in the family's past. Just as the bride's *ingulaq* dance insured her husband's continued success, the parka is tangible evidence of his hunting prowess as well as the experience, knowledge, and skill of his family:

I did not see *ingulaq*
but wearing new clothes,

this one who he has just acquired as wife brought food in.
With new clothes on she would bring food
to the one she had acquired as a husband.

Holding only his bowl she goes to him and gives it to him.

Apparently their parents got them ready,
making clothes for this man's future wife.

The one that was going to be his wife,
his parents invite her over to their house.

Then the clothes they have prepared,
if she becomes his wife,
the ones his mother has prepared,
she tells his new wife to put them on.

They have her put the new clothes on.
Then providing food,
they have her bring food to her husband.

That was how they got married.

And also,
the ones who have some
bring him food.
And when they bring food to him
his parents follow along and have a *kalukaq* [feast],
providing food to eat for the people in the *qasgiq*.
(Toksook Bay Elders, November 1983 NI64:3–4)

THE RELATIONSHIP BETWEEN HUSBAND AND WIFE:
"LIVING SO AS NOT TO INJURE EACH OTHER'S MIND"

According to oral tradition the basis of a strong marriage was the same as
that for every other relationship between humans and between humans and
animals—care for the mind of the other person. Applied to marriage, the
rules required that both husband and wife continually work hard, always
keeping the welfare of one's partner in mind:

If the young lady does not take good care of his things,
if she just lets them alone . . .
even though he is a good hunter
if she does not mind his things
her husband will experience failure.
Also the men will not arrive at anything
if they live a lazy life
or sleep too much.

If I live trying to live up to the sayings,
if I live without being lazy
and even though my catch may be small,
it has become something to do for my wife.

It is correct
if I do not live as big as my wife,
if I do things without thinking that it will lessen my manhood,
if I help her around with all the work,
and even with cutting fish.

And if we work on things,
work together performing our tasks
it will be as if we are of the same height.
Only if we live that way
can we avoid breaking each other's mind.
(Paul John, February 2, 1977)

In the ideal marriage husband and wife worked together with like minds:

And then I am your husband.
You, my wife, work in the house,
getting food ready,
sewing whatever needs sewing,
doing whatever.
I, your husband, do not sit still
but work around the house.
When it is time for me to go hunting,
I go hunting.
When it is time for me to go fishing,
I go fishing.

When I arrive,
I find you my wife working in the house.
And there is a sense of happiness within the home.
And I, sensing the happiness,
do not come home in a bad mood.
I go whistling whenever I go anywhere.
And you, tugging at your ponytail,
I look upon you with smiles.
We are happy.

This is because we are working with like minds.
(Paul John, February 1977 NI34:5)

Conversely, not living with like minds puts their very lives in jeopardy. According to Evon Albrite of Kasigluk (June 1988 YN26:17), "It is said that if one contradicts one's spouse or if they do not cooperate with one another it will be like that. They will cause the other spouse's untimely death, and it will be like one killing the other. But those who cooperate with each other, those who are of one mind and are peaceful, no one hears anything bad about them from other people."

After a man married and began conjugal relations, he was no less suscepti-ble to the power and danger associated with female procreative functions than he had been before marriage. A man could not get along without a wife—the one who attracted the animals—any more than he could hope to succeed if he engaged in illicit sexual relations. Many people still believe that a man's wife directly influences her husband's ability to attract animals. Theresa Moses (August 1987 NI95A:3) reported, "If one is hunting, animals are available to catch. The animals are attracted to him. Some men, even when they were unable to catch animals before, when they take a wife they are able to make a catch. Some women are conducive to good hunting. Some cause one not to catch game anymore. Some men are good hunters, and when they take on a certain woman as a wife, game is no longer available for them to catch." Marriage is a critical relationship, as a man must have a wife for the animals to give themselves to. A man could not live outside of marriage any more than a woman could.

The strength of the marriage bond in the past is difficult to judge.[3] The missionaries who arrived in western Alaska at the end of the nineteenth century were appalled by the ease with which they believed it could be dissolved. John Kilbuck attributed this to "loose morals" or the woman's inability to bear children. A man on the middle Kuskokwim would not take a woman into his household unless she was pregnant or already had children: "Just as the single man and woman are led to unite for economic reasons, the married couple dissolve partnership if no children come into the home" (Fienup-Riordan 1988:15).

People viewed raising children as a central function of the marriage relationship, and children constituted their parents' "greatest wealth": "Pushing them to marry when they are ready, they would tell them that a child was the greatest wealth. . . . When a child grows up and is able to participate, as it lives it is an infinite product. . . . Our ancestors encouraged everyone to marry, so their children can aid them when they age, saying that their children were their wealth" (Paul John, November 6, 1991). According to William Tyson (August 1, 1991), "We were warned we should have children. . . . So once they have children, they can fall on those children."

Although having children is central to the marriage relationship, childlessness is rarely mentioned today as a reason for separation. If a couple cannot produce a child, they can adopt one with relative ease. What is mentioned over and over again as a reason that couples might separate is the inability of one spouse to take proper care of the animals. Conversely, infidelity is not reprehensible because of its character as an interpersonal offense, but because people believe such behavior offends the animals. According to Theresa Moses (August 1987 NI95A:3):

> Some of them go for other women. If a woman was not going to take good care of them, they left her and got another wife. They looked around for another. That was the way they did it.

3. See Burch (1975:94–95) for a discussion of the strength of the marriage bond in northwest Alaska.

And whatever animals he caught, if the woman was not going to take good care of them, if she caused them to rot and if she continued to let them rot or if she was going to let his catch spoil, he left her and he got another wife.

But a good woman who exercised special care in doing things and who would take good care of him and who did not keep breaking his mind, he stayed with her and never left her. . . .

We women are also told if we get a husband, whatever our husband catches not to think that it is only one but to take good care of it, to greet it well even when it is one goose or duck. It is said that even though it is one at first, soon there will be enough to make a parka. That is the truth.

Never complain because it is only one. Do not throw it away. As they are collected together they will become many, and we will have enough to make something.

Paul John describes four different types of women based on the way they care for animals. First are those who go their own way. Those women will lead their husband away from the animals. Second are those who are too talkative, who will hurt the animals' ears and undercut their willingness to come to him. Third are the women who live as though they have a hole in their bag and are careless with the animals their husbands bring them. Although they are given food, they never seem to have any. As a result of their inattention, their husbands will lose their ability to catch game. Finally, there is the real woman who is quiet and peaceful and does her work willingly, carefully, and without constant talking. A man cannot succeed as a hunter unless he has a real woman as a wife.

PREGNANCY AND CHILDBIRTH

As we have seen, a hunter's ability to overcome his prey was directly influenced by the activity of women, including the imaginative play of young girls, the seclusion of menstruating women, and the more-or-less careful actions of his wife. Not surprisingly, one of the first women to directly influence a hunter's relationship with animals was his mother. Even while carrying the fetus, a woman's actions were believed to influence not only the immediate well-being of her child but also its future abilities as a hunter.

One story describes the efforts of a woman to insure that she had a son who was fleet and strong. She placed one feather in a bowl of plain water and another in a bowl of seal oil. Observing that the feather placed in water floated while the one placed in seal oil became saturated and sank, she proceeded to boil the fat off her food and to abstain from eating seal oil. To this day if a woman wants her future child to be a fast runner, she must abstain from seal oil and drink as little water as possible while she is pregnant.

While a woman was carrying a child, she was thought of as two persons and was referred to using the dual postbase. Moreover, the coastal Yupiit did not believe that the sex of the child was determined at conception. Rather the actions of the woman during her pregnancy determined its character as male or female. If a pregnant woman wanted a boy, she sat with her legs together when she worked. Sitting on a woodpile also increased a woman's chances of getting a boy. To produce a daughter, she dressed especially neatly, sat on her sewing kit, and kept her legs wide apart when she cut meat with her *uluaq* (woman's knife).

Elaborate rules circumscribed a woman's behavior while she was pregnant. Like the restriction against eating seal oil, many of these rules were intended to affect the future ability of her child to attract animals:

> And it was an *inerquun* that never
> through the window
> was she to try to see what was going on.
> She was only to check by going through the door.
>
> When she is curious about something,
> she is to go outside and find out about it.
>
> And if she does that,
> when her son grows up
> and goes hunting,
> when the animals hear him and become curious,
> they would show themselves to him and be caught.
>
> All those things that she is doing
> to that baby of hers, if it is a boy
> toward the times when he will be trying to do things,
> the things she does or does not do while pregnant affect them.
>
> His mother then,
> like the one who makes his catch available,
> like the one who makes his catch visible
> she will give to the one she is carrying.
> (Toksook Bay Elders, November 3, 1983 NI57:1)

Just as rules required a woman to refrain from certain foods to insure the future harvesting abilities of her child, other foods were limited to insure the birth of a healthy baby. For example, on Nelson Island a pregnant woman was prohibited from eating leftover food. If she ate leftovers, the baby might be born missing limbs or other body parts. Similar rules applied along the Kuskokwim River. According to Mary Napoka of Tuluksak (May 9, 1989), "When those that have nets set out, the sea gulls eat holes on some of the fish caught in them. And those that eat those [fish] will have a baby who does not have all its body parts. They have babies that are not whole; they will be different—those that cannot be talked to and do not listen. . . . Some females that eat body parts of geese, their babies come out backwards. But those who eat them starting from their head, their babies are born with their head first. And then those who singe the fish skin and eat them, they get babies that are enclosed in the placenta. . . . It comes out along with that baby."

At the same time that a pregnant woman's actions affected the future persona of her child, they also had a direct influence on the process of childbirth itself. Throughout her pregnancy, a woman was advised to act in certain ways to insure a good birth experience. It was particularly important that she carefully follow these rules during her first pregnancy, as the ones after it would "follow the lead of the first."

A number of the rules surrounding pregnancy focused on the character of a woman's activity within, and exit from, the house, which was equated with that of the fetus within her own body. For instance, a pregnant woman was never supposed to sit directly on the floor but always on a grass mat. She must always sleep with her head toward the doorway to insure that her baby not be born breech. She should not do yarn work during pregnancy, or the baby's cord would get knotted. She also carefully regulated her manner and means of exiting the house. Upon waking each morning, a pregnant woman must quickly rise and exit from the house before she did anything else, so that her child's exit from the womb would be equally expeditious. Theresa Moses (August 1987 NI95A:2) reported, "If they are pregnant they were told to go out right away in the mornings. They were told to be the first to go out through the door. They were told to think that if they want their baby to go out this fast, they were told to go out that fast. They had a hard life to live, and they did not take any liberties with their minds whatsoever."

Any time a pregnant woman left the house, she was told to do so rapidly and without stopping: "And they also told them not to peek out of the doorway. It was said that if women poke their heads out and do not go out completely, when the baby's head was coming out it would not come out of its doorway" (Gertrude Therchik, July 14, 1985 NI86:7). Moreover, any time during the day that she thought about doing something, she was to act upon her thoughts immediately and without hesitation. If she faltered in her work or stopped undecided in the doorway of the house, her child would do the same when it came time to exit from her body. Just as a woman's passive waiting in the house had drawn the seal into the human world at its death, so her active exit from the house allowed her child to exit properly from her womb at birth.[4]

In a variety of contexts the woman's house was depicted as a womb in which biological, social, and spiritual production were accomplished. One story describes a child becoming aware of himself in a house with red walls and no doors, empty save for the presence of an old woman. The child tries repeatedly to exit without success. Finally, a door appears in one side of the house, and the child cautiously approaches. Suddenly he feels the old woman pushing him out of the house. When he again becomes aware of his surroundings he finds himself to be a newborn baby. This story is also given as

---

4. Compare the pregnancy prescriptions recorded by Butzin for the middle Kuskokwim (Fienup-Riordan 1992:38).

an explanation for the origin of the blue spot that appears at the base of a baby's spine, marking the place where the old woman pushed the baby out of its first home.

Under certain circumstances both the woman's house and her womb were equated with the moon, home of the *tuunrat*, the spirit keepers of the land animals. Spring itself was marked by the cutting of a door in the side of the woman's sod house to permit ready egress. People believed the moon was opened in the same way to release the land animals for the new harvest season. Also, as part of their effort to insure success in the coming year, shamans would journey to the moon—a euphemism for sexual intercourse— where they were said to use their power to induce land animals to visit the earth (Nelson 1899:515; Fienup-Riordan 1988:81).

By one account childbirth itself was originally performed by cutting an opening in a woman's side to let her baby out. According to Nelson Island oral tradition, a man named Qukuyarpak floated away on the ice and eventually landed on St. Lawrence Island. While he was staying there, he noticed that all the women walked bent to one side. Some time later he found his host, whose wife was pregnant, sadly sharpening his knife. When Qukuyarpak asked his host why he was so despondent, the man answered that he was preparing to cut his wife's side to let the baby out. Qukuyarpak tended to the woman and taught her how to deliver the baby through her vagina without being cut. Although the husband was grateful for the new knowledge, the people of St. Lawrence Island suspected supernatural intervention and plotted Qukuyarpak's demise. His host warned him of their intent, and Qukuyarpak escaped south to his own people.

When a woman gave birth, she simultaneously created and perpetuated passages between worlds while maintaining boundaries between the generations. She gave birth either alone or with the help of her husband, mother, or another older woman. In the case of a difficult delivery, she tied a band above her belly and applied pressure to push the baby down.[5] Some women said that they had gone outside immediately following a birth, reenacting the child's successful exit from the womb. On the third or fifth day following a birth on Nelson Island, the new mother emerged from her confinement, marking her return to social visibility by circling the house in the direction of the sun's course.

Soon after birth the mother gave her child a taste of seal oil: "When they are *anenerraq* [newborn, from *ane-* to go out, plus *-nerraq* one that has recently V-ed], they smear a little in their mouth. And then, even though they are newborn, they know and they move their mouth. . . . They say something while they do that, 'So that you will live a long time eating these foods!'" (Brentina Chanar, June 30, 1989).

5. In 1887 Edith Kilbuck experienced this painful procedure to help in the delivery of her eldest son (Fienup-Riordan 1988:107).

The woman remained lying down in the house for five days immediately following the birth. Margaret Lantis (1959:32) recorded some women as saying that this period was four days for a boy and five for a girl. As in the five-day menstrual seclusion, the number of days paralleled the number of steps to and from the land of the dead. In both cases the woman was secluded during a transitional period when movement might be expected between the world of the living and the world of the dead. During the five days following childbirth, the Yupiit believed some aspect of the dead was making its way into the world of the living to animate the body of the newborn child. Remaining inactive within the house, the woman continued to act the part of the child waiting to be spiritually quickened. In the same way, the young girl's menstrual seclusion transformed her from unproductive child to fertile woman as she acted out aspects of the birth process.

During her postpartum seclusion, the woman was subject to restrictions similar to those at first menses—she could not eat or handle raw or fresh food and had to use her own dishes; she had to wear her hood up over her head and could not look around; and she was supposed to wear mittens and refrain from touching hunting gear. As in her menstrual seclusion, all of these prohibitions served to bound her off from the everyday world. This seclusion not only protected her during a time when she was seen as particularly susceptible to spiritual invasion, but shielded the rest of the community, especially hunters, from contact with her while she was in a transitional state.

Just as a young man might share the menstrual seclusion of his bride-to-be and a young husband the restrictions of his wife during her monthly periods, the new father shared his wife's postpartum restrictions. Following the birth of his first child, a man remained in the qasgiq for three days and did no work, after which he was free to resume normal activity. Until his child's navel healed, the father had to refrain from using an ax or a knife lest he cut the trail of the name-soul coming to inhabit the body of the newborn child.

At the end of her postpartum seclusion, a woman washed her face and hair in urine and, according to some women, put on new clothes. After the birth of her child, especially a first son, a new mother continued to limit her activities:

> The mother prepares her child while it is inside her
> by having no junk about it.
> When her son is born
> she continues her practice
> of having no junk about him.
> How the things he will catch perceive him
> will also be the responsibility of his mother.
> (Gertrude Therchik, August 14, 1985 NI86)

The actions of the mother and child were analogically related throughout its infancy. For instance, a woman was admonished never to breast-feed a male child while lying down but rather to sit up and unabashedly bare her breast for him to make him tough and strong. Were she to be lazy or reticent to nurse her child, her careless attitude and action would directly undermine her child's future hunting ability. According to Paul John (November 5, 1991), "Our mothers breast-fed us when we were babies with good thoughts of us becoming productive people when we grow up."

One contemporary *qanemciq* describes the supernatural power a child derived from nursing. The story recalls two hunters who come across a house in the tundra in which all the inhabitants had died from starvation. On hearing a baby's cry, they enter the house and find that the child has been kept alive by nursing from its dead mother's breast. Although the woman has been dead for a long time, the strength of her thoughts for the child has kept her milk warm. One of the hunters adopts the child, who subsequently grows up to be the powerful shaman Tengesqaukar.

During the early 1800s, when men still waged bow-and-arrow warfare in western Alaska, nursing mothers sometimes moved into the men's house to better prepare their newborn sons for their future life. Brentina Chanar (June 11, 1989) gave this description: "A long time ago in the time of warfare, the one who first gets a baby boy, they say that she reared him in the *qasgiq*. This was because that boy will be a warrior. And the mother of that baby also moves into the *qasgiq*. And when they are breast-feeding them, they must not feed them with their clothes on. They expose their upper body completely while inside the *qasgiq*."

William Tyson (August 1, 1991), from the lower Yukon, described this ritual feeding as a discrete ceremony: "When a young woman has a boy, after the sweat bath, everybody brings food into the *qasgiq*. And at that time, after everybody brings all the food, the young man is to be there, it's prepared. All the people got their plates, but they didn't eat. The young man is up there. And the woman with the baby on her back brings in the food and gives it to her husband. And then she gets a mat, a grass mat, another one from the *qasgiq*, take the baby down, put it on the mat, take her parka off, put it over her [back], and nurse that child, the boy, from her breast. And everybody eats."

Other, less dramatic acts on the part of the mother fostered the well-being of her newborn son. For instance, she had to regularly empty both her own and her son's urine buckets in the days immediately following birth to promote cleanliness and impress the child's future catch. After birth the mother carefully prepared the child's clothing to fit him exactly to make him a fast runner. Loose clothes would cause him to be clumsy in the future.[6] Or she might move his tiny feet across a cutting board to make him nimble and fleet. The mother must also refrain from eating foods normally proscribed for boys: "If she has a baby boy, there were some things that she did not eat.

6. Women refrained from making clothes before a child's birth for a similar reason: If they made clothes of a certain size, the child would grow that big but no bigger.

She did not eat wild celery and cormorants. That was because she had a baby boy and those cormorants have female flesh. And wild celery also is considered to have female flesh. They believe they have the same flesh as a female. . . . When that little boy grows up, he could not eat those things" (Brentina Chanar, June 16, 1989).

To encourage her child's growth, a Nelson Island mother might gently pull on the baby's right leg and left arm at the same time, followed by the left leg and the right arm. While she pulled, she made a quiet clicking sound. Then she would put her pinky fingers on the child's nose and move them slowly up and over the child's forehead.

As he grew, a mother began to teach her son the rules by which he would live. Ironically, her advice focused on the distance he must keep from women:

A child,
if it is a boy,
he is never to go near a female.
He is not to look at a female squarely in the face.
And he is to pass on the lee side of a female,
and he is never to be stepped over by a woman.
(Gertrude Therchik, July 14, 1985 NI86)

Then, finally, at the age of five or six he was ready to leave her: "Leaving his mother, moving out of his mother, to those men, he joins them" (Gertrude Therchik, July 14, 1985 NI86). Even as he joined the men, his relationship with women would continue to shape his relationship to animals.

BECOMING A HUNTER

Just as first menstruation was the single most important event in a young girl's life, marking her transformation from child to marriageable woman, a young boy's first catch of each species of seal marked his transformation from a boy into a marriageable man. Just as a girl's activity was circumscribed vis-à-vis the harvest and the men who engaged in it, so a young man's activity was also restricted as was that of his closest female relative, his mother.

In coastal villages a boy's first *nayiq* (ringed seal) was the occasion for a special distribution. After his mother brought the seal into the house and ritually greeted it with fresh snow or water, she carefully skinned it. She then cut some of the blubber into four-inch squares, which she placed in a large wooden bowl. People referred to these squares as *aruqsautekat* ("things for distribution," from *aruqe-* to distribute shares), and they were intended as gifts for the children. She cut the rest of the blubber into strips for the lamps of the men's house, placing them on top of the other squares of blubber in the bowl. Children understood what this preparation meant and were said to look happy and pleased for the occasion.

The young hunter's mother then carried the bowl to the men's house and placed it on the floor. All of the children were called over, each entering the men's house carrying their own individual bowls. They would quietly seat themselves at the feet of their fathers and grandfathers, making a circle around the floor.

When it was time to distribute the blubber, the older men who took care of the men's house received the first strips. They would set them aside, and then one of the men would move around the circle putting the squares of blubber into the children's bowls. Young boys received their shares in *aruqsautet*— wooden containers to which a piece of bendable wood was attached, which impaled the blubber. The boys kept these containers inside the men's house when not in use. After they received their portions, each boy took it to his mother's house to be used as oil for her lamp. The pierced piece of blubber was said to represent the boy's future catch, which he would likewise pierce during the hunt and take to his mother.

Once the blubber had been distributed, the men would open the *qasgiq* skylight and cook the meat in a large cooking pot hung over the central fire pit. While the meat was cooking, "helpers" would fetch the men's individual bowls from their houses and then serve them the cooked meat. After they ate, the men would return the bones to the young hunter's family, who collected them and returned them to the water in the spring.

Brentina Chanar (August 1987 NI94) provided a clear description of *aruqsaryaraq* (the process of distributing shares):

> They *aruqsaq* for the one who catches his first seal; they fetch the old men's plates. Then all of the *nayiq* [ringed seal] is cooked, and the blubber is cut in small pieces and put in the plate.
>
> Then food is taken to the old men, and having given food to all of them that plate is taken in. Then the children have *aruqsaq*. All the children have plates that they brought.
>
> The small pieces are distributed in the elders' plates. And all the bones are put in the plate of the person who was giving *aruqsaq*. And then the plate is taken home to the owner. . . .
>
> At the end of spring, they pack all the bones . . . to the lakes. . . . Some of them used to put them on top of the ice. . . .
>
> And for those who got a seal for the first time, the head bones are never kept but are given to the dogs.

Through distribution, the first seal a young man caught became a resource for the entire community. According to Dennis Panruk of Chefornak (December 17, 1987):

> When one finally catches a bearded seal, they take it up to the village. I have experienced that when I got a bearded seal for the very first time.
>
> They did not take it into the house. When that bearded seal was taken up to the village, the one who was taking care of me immediately took all of it to the *qasgiq*.
>
> [They took it to] those men who always got bearded seals, the older and experienced men. So when one brings his first bearded seal into the *qasgiq*, they

put it on top of the floor with a mat under it, and they cut it all up including the skin. . . . They cut it lengthwise and not crosswise. . . .

And while still in the ocean, when a boy gets his first bearded seal, the father of the boy calls on the closest hunter. And when that man comes, he takes out a piece lengthwise, and that is called *aqsataq* [taking a stomach part, from *aqsak* abdomen]. This is before the bearded seal is taken up from the ocean. . . .

Kayaks are within sight of each other while they are watching from the tops of ice floes, and they put their oars in the air whenever they want one to come. And then he watches the one he is calling for, and when he acknowledges him, he puts the oar down. He will not put it down before the other acknowledges his call. . . .

At that time when I got my first bearded seal, they didn't even bring in any part of its meat into our house. It was all given out to the people. . . . The old men used to be so grateful for what they were given. Those who no longer go seal hunting especially are very grateful.

Not only did they cut up and distribute the meat and oil of a young man's first bearded seal, but also its skin. They cut the skin lengthwise into strips used to make spear lines and passed them to the old men.

They cut the bearded seal into individual strips so that all individual elders and men would have a piece of the seal skin to make twine. They also give out the same amount of meat.

And those who are given [a strip of skin] take proper care of the pieces they are given, and they keep the skin until the fur comes off and then they make *usaaq* [sealskin twine]. They cut it in strips with a circling motion. Some of them are long. They do the same thing for young bearded seals.

They make what they call *tutnerkiurluki* [twine to use for snowshoes] and *qamuutaq* [twine for pulling]. They give them to all the older men. That was the traditional way.

When a young man gets his first bearded seal it is cut lengthwise including its skin. (Brentina Chanar, August 1987 NI94:1)

The complete distribution of the young man's first bearded seal was not the only marking of this milestone. On both Nelson and Nunivak islands, the boy's mother sometimes undressed her son and painted his wrists, ankles, and other joints with soot (Lantis 1960:44). Or the boy might be required to wear women's clothing. The boy and his mother then stayed awake and fasted for the next day and night. Both were also subject to a number of restrictions until the close of the next Bladder Festival. Like a girl following her first menses, neither the boy nor his mother could eat any fresh food. Also, neither could eat bearded seal meat. Both the boy and his mother had to use separate dishes, and both kept their hoods raised and wore mittens outdoors, even in summer. Neither could wear ornaments, and both must refrain from sexual activity.

On Nunivak these restrictions ended when the young man ran nude out of the *qasgiq* and down to the beach at the close of the Bladder Festival. When he returned, he took a sweat bath and resumed normal activity (Lantis

1947:6). As in so many ritual acts, physical exit and entry of the human dwelling symbolized the completion of a social and spiritual transformation— in this case the transformation of the young man's relationship with both the human and animal worlds. Just as the menstruating girl bound herself off from the community and hid herself from the weather prior to her transformation into a marriageable woman, so the boy and his mother bound themselves off prior to his transformation into a sexually and economically productive young man, capable of providing the community with both children and meat.

CONCLUSION: THE REPRODUCTION OF LIFE

The coastal Yup'ik Eskimos viewed the daily activity and personal rituals of women as having a profound impact on the relationship between men and animals. Images of female procreation both prefigured and empowered male productive activity. An analogy existed between the production of game and a woman's power to reproduce life.

Both the menstrual and postpartum seclusions temporarily contained a woman's reproductive power. During these ritually charged times, social relations, food intake, and daily activity were all severely restricted. A woman was not allowed to cook for other people, handle fresh meat, or work fresh skins. All a hunter's senses were at risk, and all a woman's senses were bound off to protect his power to attract animals. A woman restricted her vision, sight, smell, taste, and movement to empower her male counterparts. Rather than a boundary between the sexes or between women and animals, these restrictions served to separate the person from the universe during a period when the spiritual counterparts of human and nonhuman bodies were in transition. Just as the woman waited quietly in her house to greet the seal's *yua* after its physical death, so she waited in the home to greet the child's name-soul after its birth, her actions simultaneously prefiguring and enacting the birth into the human community of animals and children.

Moreover, these seclusions were not restricted to women. A woman shared both her postpartum and menstrual seclusions with her husband. In the same way, a mother shared with her son the restrictions following his first seal kill, just as she had shared restrictions surrounding seal hunting with her husband. Rather than an opposition between sacred male and polluted female, men and women alike were bound off at these times to promote a transformation. It was neither man nor woman alone, but the married couple "acting with like minds" and sharing the animals that came to them that were responsible for the production and reproduction of life. As we shall see, the bounding off and reentry of women and men following childbirth, menstruation, and a boy's first seal kill, and the bounding off and reentry of both human and nonhuman spirits into the human community during the annual ceremonial cycle, were mirror images of each other. Yup'ik categories did not deal with unclean substances and essences but with boundaries and passages.

Menstrual blood and female urine were not inherently dangerous. Rather their power for good or ill depended on the context of the encounter.

Under certain circumstances there was an expressed antagonism between sexuality and successful hunting—for instance, the proscription from contact with women required of young hunters. This negative aspect of the relationship between production and procreation is the one most often mentioned in the literature, as for instance by Saladin d'Anglure (1984:496) on the opposition between nonproductive menstrual blood and the blood of slain animals. However, an equally powerful aspect of the relationship between the genders as it relates to the relationship between humans and animals is the idea that properly controlled sexuality works to draw the animals in both everyday and ritual contexts. The relationship between men and women and the relationship between humans and animals are represented as analogous in some contexts.

In their withdrawal from and reentry into everyday life, men and women reenacted the birth process—the movement from inactivity to activity, nonproductivity to productivity, restricted human vision to powerful supernatural sight. These personal rituals circumscribing individual action were essential to the reproduction of life, both human and animal. For animals to be "drawn" and children to be born, both men and women had to abide by rules that simultaneously held them apart and allowed for their productive interaction.

CHAPTER 6

BOUNDARIES AND PASSAGES OF THE HUMAN BODY

CONCEPTS OF SICKNESS AND WELLNESS

Yup'ik ideas concerning sickness and wellness reflected a view of the cosmos as sentient and responsive to human action. The world was enlivened with spiritual essences that could either help or harm. Just as the hunter's ability to catch animals depended on the animals' willingness to come to him, people's physical well-being directly reflected the response of the spirits to their action in the world.

Illness was, first and foremost, a moral state. It was the body's physical response to the way a person chose to live life. The Yupiit generally viewed disease as within their control. If they lived good lives, illness would not easily affect them. The rules for daily living, just like the ritual acts performed to celebrate a boy's first catch or a girl's first menses, served to guarantee continued good health as well as productivity. Conversely, if a person did not follow the rules, illness would "lie on one and make one unhappy." The condition of being ill was directly comparable to the predicament of the unsuccessful hunter. Just as successful hunting and physical well-being were tied to following the rules, so failure in the hunt and failure of the body resulted from thoughtless living. Both the unsuccessful hunter and the sick person bore the double burden of hardship and guilt. According to Paul John (November 7, 1991):

> Those people in the past said that a person who is oblivious is only aware of something [right in front of us] that might pop his/her eyes or that might make him/her fall down. They would say that the instructions and advice were not in his/her mind. It was because s/he was not paying attention. . . .
>
> Apparently they were the kind of people who were very fragile and infirm. They would be easily affected by illness, or they would be easily persuaded to

take part in things that are not appropriate to the society. They would say it was because their perception was very dense. They were quite accurate.

However, those who were alert were not easily affected by anything, and sickness did not affect them as much. . . . They would say they were the kind of people who were astute and aware.

The Yup'ik people interpreted good health as both essential to being a complete person and a reflection of the proper state of mind. They considered an ill person less than whole and guilty for either knowingly or unknowingly disregarding the rules for living. Although illness did not always imply punishment, people believed that their offenses eventually came back to them. Every action had a reaction, as the all-seeing *ellam yua* (the person of the universe) observed transgressions and meted out punishment: "This is what they used to say. The big outside world, up there in the heavens, has a person. . . . That person up there is watching the people of that village. And [that person] is watching that whole village. And then when the people get too crazy and careless about living, [that person] makes them sick or have a great hardship, straightening their lives" (Nastasia Kassel, Kasigluk, May 25, 1988 YN27:21–22).[1]

The Yupiit considered illness to be an animate force, and the way people chose to live determined whether or not illness would be able to enter their bodies and "prey on them." To be cured, people had to care for their bodies, "think good thoughts," and act according to the rules. Many contemporary Yupiit hold a more accommodating attitude toward illness, recognizing that a well-lived life and good health do not always go hand in hand. This is in part because of the tremendous losses they have endured from epidemic disease over the last 150 years. Commenting on the high rates of serious illness among their contemporaries, people will say, "Things today are opposite. Good people get sick." Although many feel there is more disease than in the past, they do not always blame themselves but rather the "upside-down" situation. People do not consider failure to live by the rules the only cause of disease. A person may sicken and die for a variety of reasons, including extreme emotional grief following the death of a spouse or close relative. Still, the manner in which a person chooses to live life is considered a major determinant of general health and well-being.

In the past, to succeed as a husband and hunter or wife and mother, young men and women were expected to perform all manner of tasks while keeping their minds concentrated on the animals they sought or the children they bore. Animals would not give themselves to a thoughtless or careless person. The lazy ran the double risk of ill health as well as loss of the animals' good will.

And also they used to let an illness have a saying.
If an illness went straight to the one who starts going
   about early,

1. See chapter 8 for a fuller discussion of the concept of *ella* in Yup'ik cosmology.

if one starts to do things early while the others are sleeping
one's illness is not comfortable staying with that person,
because one does not stay put,
because one does not stay in bed.
One does not have a comfortable place in [the body],
[illness] finds it disturbing to live there.

So then,
the illness will think,
"Alas, this one is not a comfortable place
because this person does not stay put.
This one is going to cause me to have an uncomfortable place."

Then, when the illness looks around,
over there is one who is lying in bed
although it is time for [that person] to be up and around.
[Illness] will say,
"That one over there seems like a good place."
It will go over to that person
and find a comfortable place.
[Illness's] host is not the kind [illness] finds disturbing
because that person is lying in bed doing nothing
even though that person wakes up and it is time to get up.

Then while that person
is lying in bed,
s/he starts to feel sick.
That person will wake up with a headache
or having body aches
or with some part of the body feeling sick.
(Paul John, February 1977 NI39A:2–4)

Because of contact with unclean influences, all humans were susceptible to
illness. Nelson (1899:431) recorded the belief that epidemic disease came
from the moon and that an eclipse of the moon foretold an epidemic, as
during that time unclean influences descended to the earth. People sought to
mitigate their effect by literally "shaking them off" through their activity.
Moreover, if people did get sick, they could facilitate their cure by remaining
as active as possible. If people lay down and gave themselves up to their
illness, then it would continue to find them "a comfortable place to lie on,"
and they would not get well. According to Mary Mike of St. Marys (October 1, 1992), "When you get sick, always get up and do, and illness will get
uncomfortable and go away from you. Don't give in to it, or it will think you
welcome it. Laugh at it, and it will leave you."

The proscription against too much sleep, as well as the body's suscep-
tibility to unclean influences following an eclipse, indicated a common cause
of illness—the entry into the body of dangerous substances. The Yupiit
believed illness entered the unguarded body as a vapor. If a person lay too

long abed, that person was susceptible to the entry into the body of *caarrluk* (that which you are going to have as an illness; literally "dirt"). Similarly, a man risked encountering "bad air" when he walked downwind from a female. The shades of the dead might also enter a body and cause that person to become ill.

People viewed contagion as introduced from without. Disease sprang from invisible impure air laden with "bad stuff." The Yupiit employed a number of protective measures to frustrate or deflect the entry of disease-carrying vapors into the body. Both men and women fought sleep, lest disease settle on them. The injunction to work ceaselessly at all manner of chores especially stressed the benefit of accomplishing the most repugnant tasks:

> Some worked hard like that, thinking about their future catch. Some did not wish to endure all forms of sickness.
>
> They swept the floors. They cleaned off the dogs' feces. Feces are a lot of mess. After they had swept and the refuse was taken out, they were told . . . not to be repelled by them but to carry them out in their laps.
>
> And after the refuse was dumped, even though our hands were filthy, they told us to lift up the hems of our parkas *(qakegluta)* and wipe our hands on our stomachs.
>
> When I did that it was just cold against my skin. When one does that it is said that sickness is prevented. (Dennis Panruk, Chefornak, December 17, 1987 NI107:9)

Theresa Moses (August 1987 NI94:2) expressed the same idea somewhat differently. As when clearing the path for animals to come to them, young people ideally focused their thoughts on becoming good workers as they handled the refuse:

> During the winters of those times, males did not indulge in sleep anymore. And during the nights when the floor was no more than ground, they scraped it with their hand to clean it.
>
> Dirt was not abhorrent to those who wished to be great hunters. They scooped dirt on the laps of their parkas and having dumped it they pulled up their parkas and wiped their dirty hands on their bare stomachs.
>
> They did that all the time when working with their hands they weren't able to accomplish much. The females did likewise.

According to Agnes Tony of Alakanuk (March 1988), if people rubbed themselves with dirt from the entryway floor, the dirt would provide a path for sickness to leave their body: "Because everybody walks in and out like that, if you take that walking dirt, the sickness goes away, it walks out." As we have seen, it was both the power of the minds of the people who had been helped as well as the power inherent in the dirt to "let the sickness walk out" that provided a pathway for illness to leave the body: "And at that time of sickness, the gratefulness of the people will make one live. And that person will be regarded by one's fellow people as a person who cleans up the air.

That is the nature of helping others, which is one of the *alerquutet*" (Joshua Phillip, Tuluksak, June 1988 YN22:18).

People could also expel sickness from their dwellings by exiting the house, circling it in the direction of the sun's course, and reentering.[2] Here exit and reentry created a passageway for illness to leave the body just as the pregnant woman's rapid exit from the house facilitated the exit of the child from her womb. Rubbing the dirt floor of the house with a rock in a circular motion could prevent sickness. This action might also prevent the realization of something fearful that had been talked about.

Elders enjoined young men and women to care diligently for the village space and to employ the refuse they handled as a protective covering for their bodies. "Encasing" acts were likewise prescribed to keep contamination at bay (compare Morrow 1984). Young women wore belts following puberty, both to protect themselves and to prevent their unclean air from contaminating others. Similarly, young women were told to fold in the hem of their dresses when passing a man and never to step over a sleeping child lest their bad air contaminate them. According to Theresa Moses (August 1987 NI94:3), "Females were warned never to step over a child. Watch the older women nowadays. They fold the hem of their dresses and pass the men. It is said in those days if females step over them they begin to have frequent bloody noses, and they begin to have eye ailments. It is called *aurneraariluki* [from *aurneq* vapor rising from a warm object in the cold]. That is the way they lived."

Covering the body with refuse, clothing, paint, or ashes as well as encircling it with a belt or string had protective power in both everyday and transitional contexts, including birth, death, and first menstruation. Moreover, food and water intended for human consumption had to be carefully covered lest they be contaminated. For instance, Nelson Islanders routinely wiped their individual eating bowls clean with grass or greens after each meal and turned them upside down to prevent contamination from outside influences. Likewise, Nelson (1899:431) recorded that during an eclipse of the moon the people turned all of their utensils upside down to avoid contact with the unclean elements descending to earth during this period. Similarly, villagers emptied and refilled all water buckets following a human death, and close relatives of the deceased were required to hold water dippers under their parka when they took a drink.

Covering the body and food and water containers protected against entry of disease. Keeping one's body covered also protected a person from the departure of one's life force or spiritual essence. Just as disease could be caused by contamination from without, it might also come from within. Nelson (1899:422) noted the belief that a person's "inua," or shade, could be stolen, and accounts of soul loss survive in Yup'ik oral tradition. The extreme depression some contemporary Yup'ik elders display following

---

2. Compare Hughes (1958:80) for the Siberian Yup'ik Eskimos.

surgery may in part reflect their belief that some essential part of them has been removed.

People sometimes held encounters with apparitions responsible for illness. If a person heard a voice calling in the wilderness, one was not supposed to respond, for it might be the spirit of a dead person calling the listener to join it. If a person encountered an apparition in the wilderness, one should ignore it. To acknowledge its presence invited illness, as in this account by Mary Napoka of Tuluksak (May 9, 1989).

Up there at the end of the range, he came upon a person with a squirrel parka. But he had his ruff pulled over his face.

So he tried to move the arms of the apparition, but he could not budge them.

So having done that in vain, and ascertaining that he would not move at all, he would turn around, and that apparition would be just in front of him. When he would turn around the other way, that apparition would be in front of him. The apparition kept right in front of him.

And then because he was right by the bank of the river on the ice, he was wondering why he did not fall through the ice even though these open waters were visible. But he was following the small part that had frozen, and he was skating while checking on his traps.

And after he had tried in vain to get away from the apparition, [the man] suddenly pushed [the apparition]. But when he pushed him, he would go backward real fast because he was wearing his skates. But that apparition was staying in one place.

And then after he had pushed him away, and as he went swiftly backwards, he suddenly turned around and skated away as fast as he could. And he was thinking, "Let me fall through the ice, it will be the same."

So he skated on. And then not too far from that village, because the way he felt was getting so bad, as soon as he lay down, he lost all consciousness.

And then eventually, behind him something was still making noise. "Let him do as he pleases with me as there is nothing that I can do," he thought.

And eventually someone stopped right beside him. When it stopped, that person said to him, "What is wrong with you?"

He did not answer the person but stayed with all resignation. When that person persisted in asking him, he said, "Because I can no longer continue at all, I have lain down right here."

"Why did you do that?"

He answered that he was sick.

And then the person asked him, "But why is your vomit green? I think you may have seen an apparition!"

And then without answering him, he stayed.

Then because he was dragging a small sled, he told him to get in a prone position, telling him that he would take him home. And so he took him home. . . .

And so when he finally got him home and he stopped, he told him that he was going to take him into Cakayak's house. And then when he stood up, his legs were really weak. So practically carrying him, he took him in. . . . When he lay down there, he never moved again. And then pretty soon, he began to vomit all green stuff. And then he went to sleep right away; he was no longer aware of what was going on.

And then soon, someone shook him and asked him, "Are you really feeling bad yet?"

Then when he opened his eyes, he looked around and found that his seeing had improved. So he thought that he was getting better now. And then he said to him, "So if you are ready, go by the river."

Then he said to him, "Give me the cup after you have filled it."

Then when he was drinking tea, he kept vomiting before he could finish the contents of it. But his vomit became less and less.

And when he stopped vomiting green stuff, having drunk coffee, he got up. He wasn't as dizzy as before. So when all that green stuff was gone from his inside, he improved. . . .

So a person who sees a real apparition, that person will vomit green stuff, thus taking out the thing that is making him sick.

In this account, acknowledging the presence of the apparition allowed it to enter the man's body and to make him ill. Had he kept the encounter to himself, the illness might have killed him. Once the cause of his illness was discovered, however, he could expel the illness by vomiting until he completely recovered.

In the same way that encounters with the supernatural had to be acknowledged lest they cause illness, a person was advised to talk about bad thoughts, as to hold them inside would make the person sick: "And then my husband died. He didn't get sick. He shot himself. All those things went together, but I always try not to show it. Every time when it comes to my head I have to speak about it so I won't get sick" (Helen Smith, Hooper Bay, Eskimo Doll Project 1981).

As in so many aspects of Yup'ik cosmology, human action in the world focused on controlling the passage of spiritual essences from one realm to another. Disease prevention was essentially a boundary-making activity in which people concentrated attention on limiting the entry into the human body of outside contagions and, alternately, the departure of an inner spiritual essence. The rules for proper living were also the rules for healthy living insofar as they reinforced the separation between the sexes and an "active" attitude toward life that made it difficult for disease to settle on the body and find a passage inside. The human body was particularly "permeable" when a person was alone in the wilderness; it was also at risk during individual life crises, and during annual ceremonies, at which time the passages between the worlds of the living and the dead were opened and spirits traveled between them.

HEALING

Once contagion had entered the human body, a number of remedies could expel it. Yup'ik Eskimos treated illness with a combination of curing techniques, including plant and animal remedies, bloodletting, purification rituals, amulets, renaming, physical manipulation (a "laying on of hands"), and exorcism by a shaman.

Both Oswalt (1957:16–36) and Lantis (1959:1–75) detail the symptomatic treatment of illness through the application of different types of traditional medication, including medicinal plants and animal products. Lantis (1959:9) denies the existence of a logical premise underlying the use of organic and inorganic substances to cure disease. Limited information obtained on Nelson Islanders' use of medicinal plants indicates that people based the use of plants to alleviate the symptoms of specific ailments on their practical effects.

Although the use of medicinal plants seems to have been grounded in the time-tested efficacy of their use, the employment of both animal products and inorganic materials (including dirt and paint) seems to relate, over and above their practical effects, to a system of beliefs about the spiritual properties of these materials to cure. People primarily regarded healing as a spiritual enterprise aimed at either exorcism of unclean essences or restoring wholeness by recalling something lost. Available information allows comparison only of the uses of different materials when applied to different symptoms. Cures may have varied with the perceived cause of the condition, for example, whether it related to the entry into the body of an outside influence or the exit from the body of a spiritual essence. Contemporary elders recall only the general contours of nineteenth-century concepts of disease causality.

Just as the dust of human and animal refuse provided protection against the possible entry of disease into the body, so the application of dirt or feces worked to cure present afflictions. According to Theresa Moses (August 1987 NI94:2), "In times when one has a physical ailment, they apply dirt which has been trampled on in the immediate area of the ailment. And those applications always had favorable results. Some ailments are rubbed with dogs' feces. Then it is discarded. They spread [dog] feces directly on their bodies, and they always had favorable medicinal results."

Here the application of excrement had the power to elicit renewed well-being. Along with animal feces, menstrual blood and beaver castor also promoted healing. The latter might be chewed to a pulp, spit into the hands, and rubbed over the affected area. Where blood and feces were involved, the illness was "fed" with the opposite of what was considered proper human intake.[3] For example, a person might ingest a woman's menstrual blood instead of water or animal feces instead of animal meat.

> If they have an ailment of dryness of the mouth, the medicine they utilize is the feces of the mice, or they eat something abhorrent. And if their ailment is not alleviated, they drink a small amount of human blood. Those cured their

3. The analogy between illness and living persons in need of nourishment is extended. For example, when a cure did not work and the patient died, some said the disease had already "eaten" the patient.

ailment when they used them as medicine. The males used female blood and the residue that is left after washing the female pants.

Those things cured the ailment. They also use some parts of the beavers which are bitter to the taste for medicine. That is probably in the groin section of the beaver.

When they use those as medicine, they get cured. (Theresa Moses, August 1987 NI94:2–3)

Though consumption of human blood could dispel illness in some instances, swollen joints or muscular discomfort might be bled to restore physical well-being. Nelson Islanders occasionally still employ this operation, referred to as "poking." It is most often performed with a small stone lancet inserted just above the affected area by a person in the community known for his or her skill as a healer (see also Dixon and Kirchner 1982:109). In the past people considered a young woman who had recently had her first menses to have strong healing power, and they might ask her to perform the operation.[4]

The different conditions that required either letting blood out of the body to alleviate pain or taking blood into the body are not known in detail. Both practices, however, were employed to correct an imbalance in the body's condition, and perhaps relate to beliefs concerning the replacement or removal of bodily fluids to restore order and well-being.

Male urine was the single most important human fluid endowed with curative properties. Nelson Islanders regularly used male urine, especially that of young boys, both to cure and to purify. The Yupiit regarded urine as a clean substance that made their flesh "firm," as opposed to the intake of water that softened and weakened one's body (see also Morrow and Mather 1992). After a girl's first menstruation, she carefully washed herself with urine following her seclusion, as did a woman following childbirth and a young man and his mother at the close of restrictions following his first bearded seal kill. Likewise men washed themselves with urine following their participation in the Bladder Festival. The ammonia in urine renders it a potent cleanser, so the use of urine as a spiritual purifier is grounded in practical effect.

Seal oil was the most important nonhuman animal fluid used to maintain and restore human health. In an act somewhat comparable to the anointing of land animals on their entry into human space, parents would dab oil from a lamp on the forehead and nostrils of an ailing child. Rancid seal oil also figured as a valuable ingredient in traditional healing practices. Lantis (1959:8) noted that rancid oil was one of many remedies routinely used in western Alaska to treat wounds. Additionally, Nelson Islanders describe the application of "old" seal oil in case of earache. They also believed fresh seal oil pro-

4. For example, a person suffering from swollen joints might alleviate the pain by asking a young girl who has just had her first menstruation to tie a piece of her hair around the affected area.

moted good health. For example, women rubbed the bodies of newborn babies with seal oil to insure long and healthy lives. To this day people drink fresh seal oil to promote the healing of specific ills as well as general good health. It remains a prized element of the diet of coastal residents, and people identify continuity in its use as positive proof of strong social networks and a good relationship between members of the human and animal worlds.

Recent research in the Canadian Arctic indicates the importance of seal blood in Inuit conceptions of bodily composition and well-being. According to Kristen Borre (1991), the Inuit of North Baffin Island believe that seals and men share common blood and that if their consumption of seal blood declines, they will sicken and die. Seal blood may hold a place in the belief system of certain Inuit peoples comparable to that of seal oil for the coastal people of western Alaska. But seal blood and seal oil may have been viewed very differently in the past. Both the consumption of raw seal liver and ribs by hunters at a kill site, and the rules requiring the sharing of the raw and cooked meat of the season's first seal within the community, point to the ideological as well as nutritional importance of the consumption of the body and blood of the seal for the maintenance of human well-being. On Nelson Island today, eating too much seal meat and oil is believed to be as harmful as not eating enough. Just as people must share knowledge so that their minds will not rot, so they must share seal meat and oil to maintain their physical, not to mention social, well-being.

Along with the consumption and application of seal oil, other food restrictions also were routinely prescribed for illness. Although Nelson Islanders gave little detail on this important aspect of disease treatment, what they did provide indicates an analogic association between the condition and the cure. For example, when a person had an open sore or wound, he or she was not supposed to consume raw foods lest the wound likewise remain open and raw (Snow 1984:43). Such foods were *nernerrluk* (unfit food). Also, the sick person could not eat foods considered "heavy," such as smelts, as these foods would add weight to illnesses that were also considered "heavy," making the patient worse. Certain foods, such as aged fish and salmonberries, were never to be eaten together. The verb base *qaligar-* means to get sick or die from eating incompatible foods (Jacobson 1984:307).

Apart from the consumption and application of seal oil and the proscriptions against raw, heavy, and incompatible foods, the most frequently cited traditional cure on Nelson Island was *tarvaryaraq* (from *tarvaq* wild celery, plus *+yaraq* way of doing), the process of purification with smoke.[5] People used the aromatic smoke of a number of tundra plants, including wild celery *(Heracleum lanatum)* and Labrador tea *(Ledum species,* in Yup'ik *ayuq* literally

5. Lantis (1959:12) noted that whereas purification with smoke was apparently widely used in western Alaska in protohistoric times, it was mentioned only once during interviews she conducted in the mid-1950s.

"carrying away"), both to alleviate sickness and to purify the village after a human death or before the ceremonial entry of spirits into the human world.

When they use it as medicine because of one's illness,
through that smoke
they remove their illness.

They had as *tarvaryaraq*
Labrador tea tied to a stick
and also blackberry branches.

And they also included wild celery.

Using these earth plants,
after lighting them,
the inside of a house, all the way to the front
they would do this with it,
blessing it.

Whatever was bad,
they swept away.

That was how they explained *tarvaryaraq*.
And whatever they were afraid of,
it was afraid of them, too.

They also had words that were said.

If a person experienced something ghostly,
after lighting that,
he would say to it, *"Ayumayurutaat!"* [?]

Those were their customs.

They had things that had stick handles in the home.

They had different things in it,
Labrador tea leaves, whatever,
but it was never without wild celery
that was dead.

Then they did that to their clothes
and they also did themselves.
And they even let the smoke into their parka
and looking up, permitted the smoke to come out through the
    neck opening.

But when they did that in the house,
using that kind as a tip,
those people would bless that house.

You have heard its saying *"Ayumayurutaat."* . . .

It was like they were clearing away their illness,
they were thinking to clear their illness away.
(Toksook Bay Elders, November 1983 NI62)

Theresa Moses (August 1987 NI94:3) also described the curative properties of smoke: "Those who are slightly sick tie sprigs of Labrador tea together and burn the ends. They purify themselves with smoke, and they massage by hitting the body. The use of these for medicinal purposes cures them."

Nelson Islanders consistently described the use of smoke as a boundary-maintaining device employed to prevent illness as well as to expel contagions. For example, a hunter burned plants such as wild celery and Labrador tea to purify himself and his equipment before beginning the spring hunt and to cure illness.

> And in those days when the men are about to hunt in the ocean, when they are going to go down, they gather together land plants and Labrador tea and burn the pile.
> When they start off dragging the kayak on top of the sled, they step over the fire letting the smoke penetrate and billow through the inside of the parka, letting it come out through the neck opening.
> That is to purify himself. *Qumigturluni* [He holds it inside his clothing]. . . . When they are not feeling well they did that.
> And they also drag the kayak sled over the fire. (Theresa Moses, August 1987 NI94:3)

Joe Ayagerak, Sr., of Chevak (December 16, 1987) also described the use of smoke to attract animals as well as to purify hunting equipment following a human death: "In the spring some people do die. So before they go seal hunting they *tarvarluki* their equipment, their kayaks."

People *tarvaryaraq* as a private ritual act as well as in public shamanic healing sessions and ceremonials. Each household kept a supply of dried plants to purify the occupants in case of illness or as protection against spiritual possession. People also regularly fumigated their clothing to take away their unclean, impure human smells and replace them with the pure smell of the land, said to simultaneously attract animals and repel dangerous, outside, disease-bearing influences.

One might also refrain from cutting one's hair to effect a cure. People believed that if they cut their hair with a sharp instrument, they might also "cut" the path of the disease, thereby trapping it in the person's body: "One time I found myself sitting between two boys who were dancing while they were standing. I don't know what motions they made. They had seated me between them. I don't know how they used to do it. I was a *yuungcaraulua* [a doctored one] by a shaman. I came to learn that my hair could not be cut at all. . . . When I came to be aware I never used to cut my hair. I should not cut them. But if I have to cut them, we put them on top of the board and cut them with only a rock, beating on them" (Theresa Moses, October 26, 1987 NI99:1, 95A:7).

Conversely, inappropriate cutting could cause disease. For example, if a man held a grudge against someone, he might cut a notch in a piece of wood while thinking bad thoughts toward the person he disliked. The cure for such a curse was to find the wood and smooth over the cut with a rock. A person could use the cut fragments of another's clothing either to do harm or good, depending on the thoughts of the person who possessed such fragments.

To expedite the flow of disease from the body might require animal assistance. A person would place a frog on top of his head, sit in the sun on the open tundra, and wait for the frog to puff up—presumably filling itself with the vapor of the illness—and then leap away. Nelson Islanders believed that the frog could draw sickness out of the body and carry it away when it left. Lantis (1960:116) also describes the placement of a frog inside a person's clothing. If the animal crawled all the way around the person's waist, that person would live long.

Another main healing technique was the act of encircling or enclosing the illness so as to contain and control it. Evidence from related ceremonial activity indicates that, like placing a tundra frog on one's head or circling the outside of the house to take away illness, these encircling actions also created passageways for contagion out of the human body or habitation (Fienup-Riordan 1987:41–55). The efficacy of the act of encircling was twofold. For example, Nelson Islanders believed that a strip of sealskin tied around the head had the power to cure a headache. A red string tied close to the injured or infected part of the body was believed to provide a barrier to the spread of infection. Women wore valuable belts consisting of overlapping rows of caribou incisors sewn side by side. A woman was never without her belt, lest her life force leave her body or disease enter it. Moreover, when these belts were handed down within the family, they were believed to acquire curing properties. If such a belt touched an ailing body part, people believed that the caribou teeth cut the path of the disease, thereby freeing the body from aches and pains (see also Nelson 1899:435).

Shamans also frequently wore belts during curing ceremonies, as did hunters during the ritual of the hunt. Along with protecting the wearer from intrusion, these belts may also have made them invisible to *ellam yua* (the person of the universe). Lantis (1959:52) records that, on the lower Kuskokwim, a woman whose infant had died would tie a string around her waist so that she could not be seen, and the great "world eye" *(ellam iinga)* would bring no more illness to her and her family.

Nelson Islanders also made use of amulets (*iinrut* plural, *iinruq* singular) to protect them from entry of disease into the body and to cure. Each man, woman, and child had a personal *iinruq,* and people gave the *iinrut* names, sometimes that of the shamans that gave them the *iinrut.* In some cases the owner of the *iinruq* received its name as well. Some people kept their *iinrut* in their homes, while others brought them everywhere they went.

Any object [could be an *iinruq*]. They give them an *iinruq* that they will keep forever . . . miniature weasels, miniature geese, small rocks, just anything. Terns, birds too. . . .

They tell them that person has medicine from that thing.

And I had an *iinruq* of a real tern; but only its beak showed, and the rest of it was wound up with a cloth. It was a real tern but dead and dried up.

We just let it stay. And then, when someone died from this village, my mother would rub that pretend tern all over my body. It is said that it was my medicine.

All the children had *iinrut*. . . .

That thing was kept hanging. Those *iinrut* are always hanging right above them. (Brentina Chanar, Toksook Bay, June 30, 1989)

Lantis (1946:205) considered these objects containing spirit powers a central feature of Nunivak religion: "Nothing that the people considered important could be accomplished without the help of an inogo [*iinruq*]. . . . [The shaman's] real strength . . . was based after all on those same compulsive influences over the supernatural which every man and woman possessed to some degree because he or she knew the right songs and had the right amulets."

A person's *iinruq* could be applied directly to the body for healing. The shaman might also give a person an *iinruq* to cure a particular disease, and specific techniques existed relating to the discovery of a person's *iinruq*, such as feeling for the *iinruq* under the person's sitting mat or clothing. Once the *iinruq* was discovered, people believed its movements could, in some cases, foretell the future. According to Chevak elders, "It is known that a man had a INUQ [*iinruq*] made of ivory, which hung in the middle of his house. It would turn as it is hung with a string or a leather. When someone was going to die, the INUQ would whistle or make noise. Another man had an INUQ made of an old mask which he would carry everywhere he went inside a wooden box. ISSISSI was the name of his INUQ, it was named after Natalia Nayamin's grandfather" (Pingayak 1986:28).

Within the last fifty years, these *iinrut* have largely been replaced by modern medicines to which the term *iinrut* now applies. Brentina Chanar (June 30, 1989) recalled her mother's careful burial of her *iinruq* after the missionaries discouraged its continued use: "When we started believing in Catholicism, we dropped it. We stopped them by telling the *iinruq* to keep going back to its land/place. That is what my mother told my *iinruq*. She buried it in the ground. My *iinruq* is at Talarun."

A person's health and well-being might also be analogically associated with the health and well-being of a particular plant or animal, which that person could not consume. That plant or animal that kept one alive was known as the *napan* (from *napa-* to stand upright, literally "something that keeps one up").

I was finally born. My older siblings kept dying off before I was born. I had been taken special care of to be alive through the help of a shaman.

At that time with wild celery that shaman *napanirlua* [gave me support to live].

At that time when I was able to do things, I would gain weight when plants start to grow, and if the wild celery gets hard I would become skinny again.

That is why even now wild celery tastes terrible to me. I don't like to eat them. (Theresa Moses, August 1987 NI95:7)

Along with plant and animal remedies, purification, ritual acts of encircling, and the creation of an analogical relationship between a person and a plant or animal with healing properties, a major means of curing the sick was to rename them. This procedure was known as *kangilirluni* (from *kangiq* beginning or source), literally "to provide with a new beginning." Renaming was the prescribed cure when a person became ill after someone died. The Yupiit believed that a person might become ill through one's desire to acquire the name of the deceased. Such a person was said to *kangingyugluni* (literally "want to get a new beginning") (Jacobson 1984:187). According to Brentina Chanar (June 30, 1989):

When that baby was getting sick, they would give it another name. So they ask [the baby], "Do you want to understand it?" Maybe this person *kangingyulartuq* [wants to acquire a new name, literally "want to get a new beginning"] about this? And then she bends down to [the baby's] ear and says someone has come, because the baby wants that name while it is like that.

Some people, wanting to acquire a new name, are always sick. And when they give him/her that name, then that one gets well.

That person does not drop [the first *kangiliun* (name)]; one also keeps it as a name just the same. Then when one is given that name, one stops being sick but one keeps all the previous names that one has been given.

Renaming in an effort to cure was once a widespread practice among Yup'ik people. Mary Napoka (May 9, 1989) described the procedure on the middle Kuskokwim:

When a child gets sick suddenly, and when they *kangiliqluni* [rename with the intention of curing], they become wide awake when they understand. . . .

They name it a name of a deceased person. When it wants that name, a child gets sick. The child gets well after it has been renamed. . . .

They use water when they *kangiliqluni*. After they take some of that water when they make a child drink, the child gets well.

And they let it eat.

And the one who was sick no longer has sickness because s/he has that name.

As previously noted, the passage of the name-soul between the dead and the living was tremendously important in Yup'ik cosmology. That there is an association between the bestowal or withholding of a spiritually charged name and the physical condition of the human body is therefore not surprising.

TAKING SICKNESS OUT OF THE BODY: THE SHAMAN AS HEALER

The focus of traditional Yup'ik concepts relating to sickness was prevention rather than cure. "Keeping well" was an underlying motive behind the majority of *alerquutet* and *inerquutet,* with myriad rules prescribing how a person should live so as not to get sick. Homeopathic cures might be prescribed for relatively simple ailments such as headache, earache, cuts, and abrasions. But as Lantis (1959:54) aptly points out, the strength of the Yup'ik system for disease control lay in keeping healthy rather than in getting well.

When the precautions failed and serious illness "descended on the body," the *angalkuq,* or shaman, might be called in to take the sickness out. *Angalkut* (plural) played an important role in community life, functioning as intermediaries between the human and spirit worlds. The shaman was initiated through a potentially deadly experience during which he or she—a shaman could be either male or female—traveled beyond the human world. Returning, the shaman gained recognition as a person with special abilities who would continue to journey for particular purposes with newly acquired agility and speed.

During ceremonies and dramatic trances, shamans communicated with the animal spirits through drumming and chanting. During cataleptic trances, they were believed to die and subsequently be reborn, or they might be killed and come back to life. While dead, their souls left their bodies to travel to the spirit world. These experiences marked them as people apart. In times of food shortage they acted as food locators through the exercise of their clairvoyant powers. They might be asked to divine the cause of bad weather.

Shamans were trained to have visions in which they might see the future in the surface of a pot of water, in a bowl of oil, or in the reflection in an animal's eye. People referred to this act of seeing as *tangrruarluni* or "pretend seeing," and the visions were often fulfilled. Dreams told of the future and might foretell an individual's impending death. The shaman could tell by the "picture" or aura of a sick individual whether that person would recover, remain ill for a long time, or die (Kawagley 1989:10).

Along with their role as seer, *angalkut* also acted as healers in cases of serious or prolonged illness. Their primary aim in this capacity was to extract the intrusive disease from the patient's body. All the normal personal boundaries were inverted to accomplish this. During healing rituals the shaman's touch, sight, and breath were extended, as opposed to the rigorous control of these senses that normally characterized interpersonal relations.

Shamans usually performed their acts of healing in the *qasgiq,* where they employed a number of different techniques. During these sessions grass mats covered the entrance and skylight, and the *angalkuq* wore a gut parka with the hood raised over the head. Devoid of the light required for normal vision, the *angalkuq* employed supernatural sight to determine the location and character of the patient's complaint. The shaman sometimes used a mask for this purpose.

> It was put on, using it as a mask. Then [the shaman] would pretend to be examining this person. . . . And [the shaman] would be able to see that person's ailment. Or if that person did something, or had been mischievous, or had intercourse with a lady, [the shaman] would be able to see it with that device. . . .

When they became old, worn-out, they used to make replacements of their likeness . . . that were identical, out of wood again. . . .

They said back then, no one tried any of the shaman's weapon's, they were afraid of them because belief makes all things come true. If a person believes that a shaman has helped him, [that person] will be helped through his belief. That is how it is. (Joshua Phillip, July 1, 1988 BIA49)

The shaman used supernatural vision to detect invasion from without as well as illness within the human body.

This is what one of those past shamans had done. There was a person who was sick, and sitting near the door was a shaman, sitting on the bench of the *qasgiq*, then after looking over that person, with one of those, he told the ill person, "That person who is sitting by the door is causing you to be ill."

Then the one by the door began denying it, saying that he hasn't done anything towards her. And so, since the person sitting near the door was lying, denying it, he removed one of the floor boards to the *qasgiq* and said to him, "Well you are lying, you have a spell on her. I can see that your weapon is connected to her."

So he took the weapon through the floor board and began tugging at it, whatever it was. Then when he was tugging, the person who was denying it, who was sitting atop the bench of the *qasgiq*, began swaying back and forth with each tug. Then he said, "What about that, what about that." And then he replied, denying it. So he said, "OK. Could you fetch me a knife?" because the person is denying that it is his. And then the person sitting near the door began trembling, "Oh! Don't cut it! Oh do not cut it, I will untie it."

He became frightened and [the shaman] said if he had cut it, the person who was sitting near the door would have died. Because he was afraid for his life, he was saying, "Oh, no, don't cut it, I will untie it. I will take it off." When he had taken it off, then that person was rechecking to see if it was taken off completely. And since he had not taken it all off, he had him take it all off. And once he had taken it all off, that person who was sick became better. . . .

Over at Iquarmiut . . . on the Yukon River, below Russian Mission, that is where the event took place. . . .

And that person who did that was Iluraksuar. . . . But then that person who was doing the pulling, his name was Qellumqitaq, and they would refer to him as Yaayuli. (Joshua Phillip, July 1, 1988 BIA49)

If the *angalkuq* determined that the locus of disease was within the patient's body, he or she might remove the problem through a "laying on of hands." To accomplish this, the shaman either firmly held or gently massaged the affected area. With hands providing a pathway, the healer then drew the illness out of the patient's body into the healer's own body (see also Snow 1984; Turner 1990:14). A person might acquire the power to heal in such a manner through an encounter with magical worms. According to Brentina Chanar (June 30, 1989):

"Eskimo medicine man. Alaska. Exorcising evil spirits from a sick boy,"
Nushagak, 1890s. Thwaits Collection, Special Collections Division,
University of Washington Libraries.

So if one digs up *melquripsaq* [healing worms, literally "one without *melquq* (fur)"],[6] one does this to the hem of their *qaspeq* [covers the worms with the cloth]. Yes [even though one is a male]. Do it like this on top of them. The person's hands will be extremely *qungvagvuk* [ticklish]; and then when they stop squirming, one would take [the hands] off, and that storehouse of the mouse would be completely empty! And it is empty with nothing else inside! . . .

[That person that found healing worms] put his/her hands on the part that has the pain. And the hands really stick to it, they are like those that are stuck. So one keeps moving them, and when they are loosened, one takes off his/her hands. And the pain of that person is gone.

If would-be healers allowed the worms to penetrate their hands, the hands lost their quality as "stiff" or "rigid" and became "open" to the disease. The healer could then break down the boundary between individual bodies and acquired the power to draw out the illness (see also Lantis 1960:114). Just as the hunter and his wife drew seals out of the sea into village space, and the birth of a child drew the name-soul out of the place of the dead, so the *unatelek* (literally "one with hands") had the power to draw illness out of the human body and send it away where it could do no harm. Some accounts depicted disease as an evil spirit which, once ousted from the human body, either was chased away by the helping spirit of the *angalkuq* or killed by the *angalkuq*.

The healers' hands were not the only part of them that could be strengthened in such an encounter. If a person found any type of food in a mouse cache, that person was supposed to eat it. If this was done, the person would become a healer, able to use his or her saliva to heal the cuts, sores, and ailments of the human body. As the incorporation of the magical worms gave the healer's hands the power to draw out illness, the ingestion of food gave the healer's saliva comparable power. Supernatural touch drew the disease out of the body in both cases.

And if one finds two mousefood caches, when one opens the other, one will find it full of *tumagliit* [lowbush cranberries] only. And then that person must take one and eat it; swallow it. And then the person must leave all those other cranberries.

It is said that person has become capable of removing something by sucking. And also by applying their saliva. It is said that those are meant to be saliva.

[The one who found the cranberries] applies his/her saliva directly to the pain or sucks on the part that pains the person. And [that person] takes out that pain in the form of saliva! It would be a mixture of saliva, water, and blood. It would be thick saliva.

6. Elsie Tommy of Newtok (June 9, 1992) notes that there are two different kinds of healing worms, *melquripsaq* and *uguguaq* (furry caterpillar), and each imparts unique abilities to the healer's hand. The healer also uses a variety of plant helpers, depending on the variety of worm encountered. "Furry caterpillar hands" call for Labrador tea as a plant helper, whereas a person who encounters *melquripsaq* uses salmonberry leaves as a plant helper. "They say since those kinds of insects stay on those kinds of plants they used to help them in their work."

And [that person] spits it out on top of the cutting board. They make a proper container using a cutting board.

I witnessed that with my own eyes, when Apacuaralleq sucked my leg, when it got hurt by bending backwards. So I really saw that. The edge of his mouth seemed to really stick to this part! I know that it was really stuck!

It seemed like he was sipping when he did that. And when he finished, they put a cutting board in front of him, when he let it pour out, it was a thick saliva—watery saliva mixed with a small amount of blood. (Brentina Chanar, June 30, 1989)

Along with sucking or lifting illness from the human body, the *angalkuq* also blew on the affected area to expel illness. People referred to a person who possessed such power as someone with "strong breath." *Angalkut* might combine these healing techniques, drawing the sickness from a patient's body with their hands and then blowing on them to dispel the illness from their own bodies.

A long time ago, the shaman made medicine for them. *Tuunrilluki* [from *tuunraq* shaman's helping spirit, literally "using familiar spirits"], they try to make them well. After *tuunrilluki*, they relate what is making them sick. Some of them did get well; they really get well.

They make them know what is making them sick which is called *elucira'arluki* [from *eluciq* "shape, form, what something is like"]. They point out what [the person] must do. It is said that they take it away.

That is called *elucira'armek*. So while [the shaman] *tuunrirtuq*, s/he tells [the sick one] to blow. They really blow out when they say that they *cupniaqameng* [from *cupe-* to blow on]. . . . When [the shaman] is behind that one s/he is making medicine for, s/he has raingear as a covering.

I used to see them. They would blow out. But we could not understand what they said. Occasionally I used to understand what they say. And they say "Whew." They seemed to say, "*Amitataar!*" [from *amik* entranceway]. And then soon, with a big "Whew," [the shaman] blows out!

When they did that, they *elucira'arluki* something; they pretend to do that.

And after that shaman is finished, they feed [the shaman] with real good food. (Brentina Chanar, June 30, 1989)

Although invisible, in some cases the disease-causing agents that entered the body and made people ill were considered to have weight—yet another indication of their personhood. Nelson (1899:433) recorded that when a person from south of the Yukon Delta became ill, *angalkut* would determine the character of the malady by tying a cord attached to the end of a stick to the patient's head or limb and lifting it. The part was very heavy if seriously affected, but it became lighter and easier to raise as the disease passed away.[7]

Along with supernatural sight, touch, and breath, loud noises—especially drumming and singing—were often employed to chase illness out of a

7. Hurtful words give the tongue "weight" and, like disease, cause pain: "They say this tongue, even though it is such a small thing, is like a very heavy object, and when we use it to say bad things to another it can cause heartache" (Paul John, November 5, 1991).

patient's body. According to Brentina Chanar (June 30, 1989), "If they cannot cure him/her by that, *tuunrilluku* [they use spirit powers] in the *qasgiq*. They bring [the sick person] in, let [the sick person] sit on the floor boards. They sing for [the sick person] like they do when they dance. [The *angalkuq*] stomps around [the sick person]. It is said that they know when they find what is ailing the person at the time of *cikingallmeng* [looking down?]. They would really start to jump around; that is when they find what the person's sickness is, when they are able to take it away."

The *angalkuq* also drew disease from a sick person by conducting a seance in which patients were encouraged to confess any transgressions that may have opened a path for illness to enter their body. The rules for living— *alerquutet* and *inerquutet*—created boundaries between human and nonhuman persons as well as between the living and the dead. When someone broke a rule, it opened the way for sickness to enter the body. The task of the *angalkuq* was to ferret out the breach, sometimes by traveling to the home of the animals or the land of the dead. Once the shaman discovered the cause of the illness, the cure could begin.

> And then some of the *angalkut* asked them after they performed medicine on them, "Now, in your past life, you have not fooled around with another woman? Why is your sickness this way? Tell a little bit about yourself even though it may be embarrassing. Reveal a little if you have been with another woman who is not your wife. Even though it is embarrassing, tell a little bit about it."
>
> And some person will admit that he had been with this woman who was not his wife. And then that shaman would say, "Enough said! Because you have volunteered to say by yourself, you have saved yourself. Let me sing a song!" (Joshua Phillip, June 1988 YN22:22)

By confessing their transgressions, patients were freed from the negative consequences of their actions.[8] Public confession of misdeeds provided a framework for the social reintegration of the patient into the human community while it cleared away the ritual obstacles that might block recovery. Only the patient was held to blame for the illness, and only personal confession could provide a cure. At the same time, the other participants continually expressed their sympathy toward the patient and urged that the consequences of the transgression be mild. Here the power of their minds was believed to affect positively the patient's condition. At the same time, the patient was to think only good thoughts and confess bad ones. Wrong thoughts were as damaging as wrong deeds.

8. A recent letter published in the *Tundra Drums* indicates that this belief continues today. Susan Angaiak (1991) of Tununak writes, "When a strong man has sex with a child, he will start becoming weak. . . . The elders would understand that the cause of his illness was what he did in secret. The only way he could heal was if he found someone he trusted and he confessed to that person. When he confessed he would start to heal. . . . If this will help some young people, I will be glad." See also Spencer (1959:309–10) on the importance of confession in healing among the Iñupiat of northern Alaska.

Transgressions were not the only things that might be confessed to provide a cure. People also believed personal encounters with spirits could cause illness if not communicated. One Nelson Island woman recalled an unusual experience she had while berry picking as a young girl. After she went home, she started to bleed and became very ill. During a curing session in the *qasgiq*, the *angalkuq* determined that her illness had been caused by a ghost that she had encountered on the tundra at the time she had picked berries. Once he had established the nature of her encounter, she was cured. The *angalkuq* told her that if he had not discovered the cause of her illness, she would have died.

Along with removing illness from the patient's body, the *angalkuq* was also called on to return a lost spiritual essence, and sometimes had to travel along the path to the land of the dead to do so. Illness was believed to be brought on not only by the entrance of negative forces into the body, but by the departure of a person's *tarnera* (possessed form of *tarneq*) or visible image. Accounts of "soul loss" frequently occur in the oral tradition. For example, Paul John (February 15, 1977 NI26) described the illness of his grandfather following his vomiting up his *tarnera*. His grandfather would have died had a shaman not successfully retrieved and replaced it within his body.

CONCLUSION

The treatment of the body in times of illness was as much a spiritual as a physical enterprise. The Yup'ik people experienced a direct connection between physical problems and spiritual solutions. Conversely, physical ills directly reflected moral inadequacies. People brought on disease by transgressing the rules for living, and only through correcting or confessing their offenses could they hope to free their body from the illness. Animal products used as medicines were primarily an attempt to restore and maintain the boundaries, broken by the original transgression, between the person and the world at large.

In the case of serious illness, the patient employed the *angalkuq* to cure both body and soul. Significantly, all curing techniques involved the reversal of the interpersonal boundaries of everyday life. A person's senses were carefully restricted under normal circumstances—eyes averted out of respect, a woman's bad air avoided, and direct address carefully controlled so as not to injure another's mind. But to draw an illness from a patient's body, the *angalkuq* employed supernatural vision, powerful touch, "strong air," and confession, or "speaking out." By obviating the normal boundaries between persons and between the human and nonhuman worlds, the *angalkuq* opened a pathway either for illness to leave the patient's body or for a lost spiritual essence to return.

CHAPTER 7

DEATH AND THE RENEWAL OF LIFE

THE YUP'IK ESKIMOS of the Bering Sea coast understood personal illness and wellness as the entry into and exit from the body of a spiritual essence. In the same way, they understood the end of both human and animal life as the departure from the body of its essential life force. The seal's *yua* ("its person") retracted to its bladder when the seal was killed, where it remained until it was placed back in the water and reincarnated. The human life force likewise separated from the physical body at death and began a journey underground to the land of the dead, where it, too, awaited rebirth. Though some part of the human dead remained behind in the land of the dead, where it was maintained as a separate entity, an essential aspect was believed reborn in the namesake. Death was simultaneously an ending and a new beginning.

The living and the dead existed in separate, but closely related, worlds, and the maintenance of both boundaries and passages between these worlds was critical for their mutual well-being. The dead could injure the living and the living could do harm to the dead if either acted inappropriately. The relationship between the living and the dead, like that between human and nonhuman persons, resembled that between host and guest, wherein care of the living namesake and careful human action in general supplied the dead. Just as people carefully regulated the entry and exit of animals into human space to insure the animals' willingness to return the following year, they rigorously circumscribed the passage between the world of the living and the world of the dead to insure continued human life in the present and continuity of life in the future.

ASPECTS OF THE HUMAN PERSON

The nineteenth-century Yup'ik conception of the person was complex and remains unclear. Yup'ik cosmology made no simple distinction between body and soul. On Nelson Island the word *yua* (from *yuk,* human being) applied to the "person" of an animal—its human aspect—that survived death and was destined for rebirth. Coastal orators also designated as *unguvii* (soul or life spirit, from *unguva* life) that aspect of the seals that rushed to their bladders at death to await rebirth. Human beings were also believed to have *unguva;* however, this was only one of many aspects of a person's being, and each might have a different destination after death.

Each human person was thought to be accompanied through life by a *tarneq* (possibly related to *taru* or *taruq,* rarely used words for "human being" or "person"; possessed form *tarnera*). This probably corresponds to the *tă-ghûn'-û-g'âk* referred to by Nelson (1899:422) and described as an invisible shade in the shape of the human body. A person's *tarnera* was both sentient and destined for future life, sometimes in the form of an animal and sometimes as a *tuunraq,* or shaman's helping spirit. By some accounts, its potential for rebirth was finite, as it could reincarnate no more than five times (Eskimo Heritage Project 1985:73). Although *tarneq* is translated variously as "spirit" or "soul," the term "shade" best captures its character as a shadowlike being in human form.

According to Nelson Island elders (November 1983 NI62) the *tarneq* corresponded to a person's visible ghost and was that part of the person which left the body at death: "When one sees a ghost, it is the *tarneq* of a person—the one that does not die."[1] Many people believed that a person's *tarnera* might be stolen or might leave one's body while the person slept, resulting in illness and ultimately in death if it did not return. Waking someone up suddenly was strictly forbidden, because if a person's *tarnera* was elsewhere at the time, it would be prevented from returning.

Mather (1985:105–108) and Morrow (1984:128) record that the terms *anerneq* (breath), *avneq* (felt presence, ghostly humming), *yuuciq* (life, lifeline), and *puqlii* (its warmth, heat) were also used to designate distinct aspects of the human person. Nelson Islanders also referred to a person's *umyuara* (one's mind), *unguvii* (one's life spirit), and *yuucian unguvii* (one's living spirit). Some people held that a person's "mind," "heat," and "breath" did not survive death. Others identified a person's *anerneq* or *yuucian unguvii* as capable of rebirth when a newborn received that person's name. But as with a person's *tarnaa,* all agreed that loss of either one's breath or heat brought death, just as their possession was essential to living. Recall the power of a woman's breath, a hunter's vision, and an elder's mind, both to help and to harm.

---

1. Just as a person's *tarnera* did not always take on ghostly form, not all ghosts were believed to be the visible images of humans. Other kinds of ghosts or apparitions included *alangru* (literally "thing that appears suddenly"), *alairtuq, carayak* (literally "terrible fearsome thing"), *iinraq* (evil spirit), *nepengyaq* (from *nepa* "noise," a spirit whose presence is indicated by noise at night and a cold mist), *uliguayuli* (ghost that captures children in a blanket), and *yuilriq* (ghost which walks in the air above the ground and has no liver) (Jacobson 1984:55, 57, 109, 160, 260, 386, 416).

Morrow (1984:128) helps to clarify the discrepancies between the different classes of spiritual essences, while admitting that the suppression by missionaries of nineteenth-century Yup'ik concepts of the person makes it unlikely that we can ever fully understand the significance of these distinctions. Also, as today, people in different parts of the region defined and used these concepts differently. What is clear is that there was no single correct term for a person's soul as distinct from the physical body. Rather, people believed that aspects of their being (one's mind, breath, heat, vision, voice, and visible image) possessed properties essential for life, both in the present and the future. Although the human person could not live without these aspects of being, they might exist separately from and independent of the human body.

As essential to life as one's thought, breath, heat, vision, voice, and visible image was the possession of a name *(ateq)*. A nameless person was a contradiction in terms. When a child received a name, that aspect of the dead destined for rebirth entered the child's body. With the name an essential aspect of the dead was transferred across the boundary between worlds. As the part recalls the whole, the dead were reborn through the gift of the name. The name of the deceased was not, however, always or even usually bestowed on a single person. More than one child might be named after the same person (depending on the extent of the deceased's kin group and personal reputation), and most children received more than one name. An *atellgun* (from *ateq* name, plus *-llgute-* fellow) was a person having both name and namesake in common with another (Fienup-Riordan 1983:149–58).

Essential aspects of a person, like the *tarneq*, separated from the human body at death and began to follow the path to the underworld. However, it appears that the name, like the *yua* of the seal, was destined for rebirth in human form. Nelson (1899:437) observed that the human hunter both propitiated and to some extent controlled the *yuit* of sea mammals by keeping them with their bladders and later returning them to their watery world. In this way he produced more game than if he let them wander freely or go to the land of the dead. The same belief extended to inanimate objects (furs, food, parkas, and so on) of which a small part could retain the essence of the entire article. Thus, a person could give away goods while retaining them in potentiality. By retaining the name of the deceased, a part of the dead was reborn at the same time a channel was created between the world of the living and the dead.

CARE OF THE HUMAN CORPSE

When a person died, relatives prepared the body as for a journey. Provisions included both food and clothing. Nelson Islanders referred to this provisioning for a long trip as *taquigurluki* (from *taquaq* provisions for an outing). Relatives threw bits of food into the fire or placed them at the feet of the corpse (*tuqumalria*, from *tuqu* death, literally "one who has died"), after which they transferred the remainder of the offering to another container for later consumption:

> With food, they sat up the dead one.
> They would put a gut parka on men
> and putting on mittens,
> sit them up
> like a person in readiness.
>
> They would have the hood on
> and their mittens,
> and they also put on sealskin wading boots.
>
> Then the people
> from out there
> would bring him food in wooden bowls,
> placing them in front of him.
>
> And taking a little
> they would place some in front of him.
>
> That was how they provided provisions for him.
>
> Then the foods
> were eaten by the people there when it was time.
> (Toksook Bay Elders, November 1983 NI62:7)

Mourners *(tuquilriit)* might also provision the dead relatives of other community members by giving offerings to the recently deceased. People considered the corpse a medium through which they could communicate with the dead: "Those who want to bring food to the dead fill [the corpse's] bowl and talk to it and use it as a medium to send food to whoever the person is thinking about, the one who had died before. They name the person according to how s/he is related to the dead one" (Billy Lincoln, Toksook Bay, April 1986 NI83:15).

Provisioning the dead continued for years after the burial. When people picked berries, they would bury a small piece of fish or tobacco on the tundra, or place a bit of *akutaq* in the fire, saying, "Eat, whoever passed away before us." Some people today continue to put part of every food they have underground when they go camping. Also when people accidentally drop food or water, they may say the dead caused them to spill to satisfy their hunger and thirst. Children are told not to pick up berries that they drop on the tundra, as the people who died want them as food. When intentionally dropping food for the dead, people must always say where the gift comes from. Otherwise the dead will not know who the gifts are for and will not claim them.

Aviuqaryaraq (the process of giving food offerings to the dead) not only provided for the deceased, but insured continued access to food for the living. According to Joshua Phillip of Tuluksak (July 1, 1988 BIA48), "Whenever they came across a burial, they would take a bit of their food, in little portions saying, 'While I am traveling I would like to travel safely and I would also like to catch a lot. I am trying to catch a lot, please place before me things to catch.' They would talk to that person in that manner. . . . They would place on those graves, to their deceased relatives, those things. . . . They say [they] *aviuqarluni* when they are doing that ritual, giving a food offering to that [dead] person."

After mourners had provisioned the dead person, they prepared the body for burial. On Nelson Island members of the deceased's gender dressed him or her in new clothing and adorned the body with personal jewelry. Relatives sometimes placed objects on the eyes of the corpse to keep them open so that they could "keep watch within the surface of the earth."[2] They might also sprinkle ashes on its face. Mourners then placed the corpse in a sitting position with knees flexed on a skin or blanket and wrapped it around five times with cord. Nelson (1899:481) reported that people bound corpses to prevent their reanimation by evil spirits, and this may have applied on Nelson Island as well:

> Then when it was time,
> when the thing [the corpse] was going to be in was finished,
> they would take the person's body down to the floor,
> laying it on something,
> they rolled it up in it.
>
> They would then tie [the corpse] up
> in fives
> crosswise.
> There would be five places where it was tied
> to its end.
> (Toksook Bay Elders, November 1983 NI62:7)

Mourners wailed continuously while they carried out these preparations, in marked contrast to the proscription against such noise during the period of mourning. They also kept a lamp burning beside the corpse, as they thought that, without light, the shade would be unable to find its way to the land of the dead (Fienup-Riordan 1983:175–76; Lantis 1946:227; Nelson 1899:310). Comparable to the light kept burning in the *qasgiq* during the Bladder Festival, the lamp burned constantly near the corpse until after the funeral.

Once mourners prepared the body, they removed it from the house, ideally on the same day that death occurred. Men pulled it through the central smoke hole or through a hole opened in the wall.[3] They were forbidden to

2. Compare this to the Siberian native practice of carefully covering the corpse's eyes. Whether this was done to protect the corpse from the entry of unwelcome spirits or to prevent the exit of some spiritual essence from the body is unclear.

3. Removing the corpse from the house through a special aperture was nearly universal in the Eskimo world. As Lantis (1947:19) points out, there is more consistent agreement on this point

use the entryway for this purpose, as that was the pathway for the living. People rigorously separated the two passageways, both to prevent the dead from returning and harming the living as well as to keep the living from inadvertently passing into the place of the dead:

Then when they were done with [the body]
when they had a window up there,
opening the window,
they would pull it up and take it out through the window
and not through the door.

Then when they took it out,
his relatives,
his wife
if he had a wife,
or his parents
would go out through the door.

Then when they took him away,
with people carrying him,
they would take him away slowly,
and his family would follow behind them.

But the people behind them and around him
would go ahead of him.

As they were going,
they would stop and stay for a while
before they reached the spot.
They would stop five times.

Only at the fifth time they put him in.
(Toksook Bay Elders, November 1983 NI62:7)

Along with the distinction between the pathways of the living and the dead, a congruence existed between the pathways out of this world employed by the human and animal dead. Just as men pulled the bladders through the smoke hole at the close of the Bladder Festival, so the human corpse took the same route following death. People carried both the bladders and the corpse in a ritual circuit around the skylight and placed them in each of its four corners and the center. Likewise, on their arrival at the ice hole and grave, respectively, participants circled the hole in the direction of the sun's course and placed the bladder or corpse in each of the four corners and the center prior to final disposal. As noted, the mourners also stopped five times on their journey from the village to the grave site. The repetition of the numbers four and five probably referred to the ritual "steps" separating the world of the living and the dead as well as the number of days—four for a man and

---

than on any other pertaining to funerals. See also Serov (1988:251) on the Chukchi practice of taking the deceased out through a special hole cut in the wall, which was later mended so that the soul of the deceased could not find its way back in to take the souls of the living.

five for a woman—the spirits of the dead were in transit between the world of the living and the land of the dead. Elders alternately likened these steps to those carved into the ladders of raised food caches, and to the snow steps shoveled in the entryways of sod houses. A similar stairway marked the daily stages in the shade's journey to the land of the dead. On the first day the *tarneq* arrived at the first step, where it waited one day, the second day it reached the second step, and so on for four or five days (see William Weinland, March 12, 1886, cited in Oswalt 1963:74).

On the way to the grave, the mourners were forbidden to carry the corpse over water, for example, from one side of a river to the other. In the same way that a menstruating woman might "cut" the path of the migrating fish the following season, the corpse had the power to block their annual return. Villagers had to retrieve the corpse of a drowned man, or its presence in the water might have a similar effect.

When they arrived at the grave site, the mourners placed the corpse in a shallow, sometimes circular, grave or directly on the ground and covered it with stones or pieces of wood intended to keep predators from bothering it. They might also place grave boxes of hewn planks directly on the ground or on raised posts.[4] Before covering the body, however, mourners carefully severed the cords that bound the corpse to enable the shade of the deceased to enter or leave the body at will (Nelson 1899:315). They then placed the dead person's worldly goods within or upon the grave unless the deceased had given them away before death:

> Then, after they placed [the dead person] in,
> when everything was done,
> [the person's] markers would be put on.
> They would be nailed with their possessions.
> If it was a man, he would have his possessions,
> and if it was a woman, she would be surrounded by her tools.
> (Toksook Bay Elders, November 1983 NI62:8)

Brentina Chanar (June 30, 1989) added detail to this general prescription: "They take what the deceased had, like their cups, kettle, cooking pots, bowls. They nail them to those *napartaat* [poles]. They would look so attractive when they stood erect like that. . . . They never kept them. And they scattered their clothes that they had around their coffins. They do not burn them at all. Around the grave they put *eliveq* [grave marker, possession of the deceased placed on the grave; related to *elivte-* to flatten a standing object]."[5]

A woman's grave goods might include pots, pans, ladles, kettles, and buckets, whereas a man's grave might have hunting equipment, tools, weapons,

4. Raised graves and coffin interment on a platform appear to have been introduced in the late nineteenth century (Gordon 1917:136; Himmelheber 1938:52; Lantis 1959:51; Nelson 1899:312).

5. Missionaries reported that Yup'ik parishioners would not accept secondhand clothing unless they were assured that the owners were living. Conversely, the worn-out clothes of well-thought-of (living) missionaries were in demand.

Coastal grave, early 1900s. Oregon Province Archives, Gonzaga University.

and even sleds. More recent burials have included rifles and metal tools, and many were marked by wooden crosses. According to Billy Lincoln, mourners would disassemble the kayak of the deceased and attach their possessions to a pole erected at the grave. In some cases this pole was topped by the carving of an animal or a human figure. Alternately, mourners might place an animal

Coastal graveyard, Quinhagak. G. B. Gordon, 1907; University Museum, Philadelphia.

"Tununak's burial grounds; nowhere else could be found the duplicate of Nelson I's burial grounds and methods." O. W. Geist, 1933; Anchorage Museum of History and Art.

skull or plant a paddle, blade up, by the grave. Commemorative drawings might be painted on the coffin.

People referred to the accompanying grave goods as *alailutet* (from the root *ala-* as in *alaite-* "to be visible" and *alair-* "to appear, come into view"), as they served as the visible memorial to the character and persona of the deceased as well as a marker for the burial place. Billy Lincoln (April 1986 NI83:17) recalled, "After the dead had been put into its coffin, they put its clothes in the coffin. And if it was a man, they took his kayak and tore it up to the size of a boot sole and gave it out to the people. And his oars and other things were kept by the people. And when there came to be kettles and cups, they used all his things as *alailutet*. So they erected a pole by the coffin with those things, including sleds and such."

Although mourners did not totally disassemble most grave goods, they sometimes rendered dysfunctional such containers as pottery bowls, wooden dishes, and tin cups and kettles by making a hole in their center. This perforation both truncated their usefulness in the world of the living and signified their owner's, and their own, passage to the land of the dead. Elsie Mather (1985:123–25) noted that grave goods could be taken for use by the living if the new owner supplied a replacement. Nels Alexie of Tuntutuliak

"Here may be seen one of the images as placed on the burial grounds near the grave of the one in whose honor and memory this image was carved in driftwood." O. W. Geist, 1933; Anchorage Museum of History and Art.

told the story of a man who placed an entire box of bullets on a grave in exchange for what he needed. That night he camped on the tundra, and when he woke up, he found a washtub, which had also been on the grave, beside his tent. He looked back at the grave and said *"Quyana!"* (Thanks). He assumed that the dead thought he had given too much for the first item and so gave him the washtub in addition (Martz 1992).

Butzin (Fienup-Riordan 1992:36) wrote that a man's *angyaq,* or large skin boat, was an exception and passed to the man's son. However, should a wife die owning a skin boat, it was destroyed. A person's food caches also were spared, as the idea was to destroy personal property closely associated with the deceased, not wealth as such. Only if people considered the deceased impoverished or potentially dangerous did they leave the grave empty of the goods necessary to provision them in the land of the dead. Garber (1934:207) added that people did not place weapons, tools, or implements on the graves of people considered insane lest they run amuck and bring unhappiness in the next world.

The relatives of the deceased might also put up a grave post to commemorate a person who had drowned or been lost on the ice (Nelson 1899:318; Ray

"Another view of Tununak burial grounds which are located directly in front of the village between the village and the beach." O. W. Geist, 1933; Anchorage Museum of History and Art.

1982:52). Billy Lincoln (April 1986 NI83:17–18) recalled such a grave post raised at Tununak in the early 1900s to commemorate a family killed by an avalanche:

> There were dolls with beautiful clothing on them, *alailutet* [visible grave markers]. The relatives made those dolls in remembrance of them. They were put on top of the board so the people could see them. . . . They were by the *qasgiq*. They were attractive in appearance. . . . There was only one platform but inside it, on its side, were hung those caricatures of people depicting the members of the family who had been trying to make a living, including the man and wife and their children. They put all of them inside that platform. At that time that was an *alailun* [singular]. They pretended that it was that family. . . . Their relatives did that pretending those dolls were those people in that avalanche.

Wooden memorials boasting elaborately clothed figurines also sometimes accompanied burials along the coast below Nelson Island.

> And there were a lot of *alailutet*, those wooden figures. They wore parkas. . . . They wore fur caps. They look just like real people! They had houses. They had shelters over them. And inside those, they were there standing. They look just like real people. They had parkas of those people that have died, that is the way those wooden people were that had been made.
>   Some of them were decorated with ivory things, up there. . . . They are so finely made! They are made with care and clothed with care. . . . It is said that

"A close up of one of the peculiar images," Tununak graveyard. O. W. Geist, 1933; Anchorage Museum of History and Art.

"This grave is absolutely intact just as left at time of burial, evidently a man's grave; it may also contain the remains of a woman, for with all the hunting equipment of the man, the woman's kitchen utensils are also placed on the post." A Jesuit priest photographed the same grave, still intact, in Tununak in 1942 (Fienup-Riordan 1983:226). O. W. Geist, 1933; Anchorage Museum of History and Art.

Kuskokwim grave board and effigy. G. B. Gordon, 1907; University Museum, Philadelphia.

Turn-of-the-nineteenth-century Kuskokwim graves. Clark H. Garber; Alaska and Polar Regions Department, University of Alaska Fairbanks.

those are the *alailutet* of those people who have died. There used to be so many of them, those that were made in the middle of the village, and they look just like real people. So some of them are scary, too. They look just like real people! (Mary Worm, Kongiganak, May 13, 1989)[6]

Before leaving the grave site, the relatives of the deceased threw morsels of food in a fire that they had kept burning by the grave since the beginning of the funeral. They then distributed the rest of the food and sprinkled fresh water beside the grave. In this way they provisioned the dead person for the journey ahead with food as well as water to quench the dead's perpetual thirst. They might also place wood shavings by the grave to enable the shade of the deceased to light a fire on arrival in the land of the dead.[7]

After they had attended to the corpse, the parents or spouse of the deceased would circle the grave "following the motion of the day," cut across

6. See also Gordon (1917:136), Himmelheber (1987:46), Porter (1893:105), and Ray (1982) on masks and human figures accompanying Kuskokwim and coastal burials.

7. Compare Hughes (1958:76–77) on the Siberian Yup'ik ceremonial feeding of the dead.

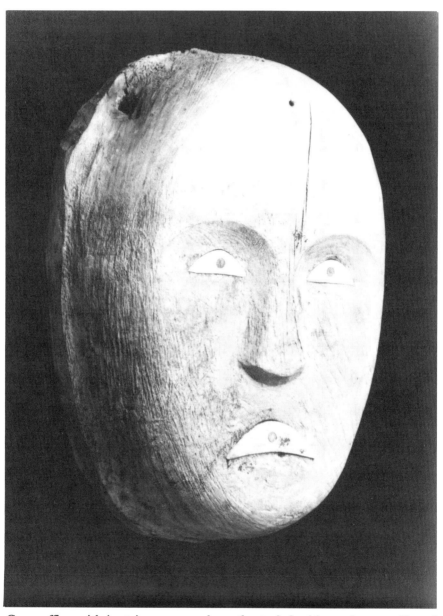

Grave effigy with inset ivory eyes and mouth attached with wooden pegs. Newark Museum.

their path, and remove their pants, which they would rip to pieces and leave at the grave site, telling the deceased, "Here, take these pants, let them be your parent" or "Let these be your spouse."

> Those parents when their child has died, when they are going to leave him/her, they would go around him/her like that [from east to west]. And after they do that, using a knife or a tool, they would cut across the path. Same thing if one's spouse has died. . . .
>
> After a person has put [the dead spouse] in a coffin, the living spouse would rip their pants, take them off and leave them right there [near the coffin]. S/he wears another pair of pants under those that s/he will tear. . . . That was their custom a long time ago, and when I briefly saw them they used to do that. They did the same thing when their children died. They would rip open their pants and leave them by their coffin. (Brentina Chanar, Toksook Bay, June 30, 1989)[8]

Following these acts the mourners returned to the village. The distance to and from the grave site was not far. The mourners took a direct path to the grave so as not to confuse the dead. On their return journey from the grave, the mourners alternately erased their tracks, cut across their trail with a knife, or spilled ashes across their path to prevent the shade of the deceased from following them home.

Graves at the mouth of the Yukon were often placed so close to the houses that they formed part of the village (Nelson 1899:424). Nelson Islanders buried their dead at the edge of the village within sight, and, according to Lantis (1946:229), Nunivak Islanders did the same. People most often placed graves on the landward side of a coastal or riverine settlement, depending on where high ground was available. Tununak's graveyard was between the village and the beach.

Once the *tarneq* had left the corpse, people viewed the body with neither anxiety nor disdain. In fact, under certain circumstances, people believed a dead body had the power to attract, rather than repel, animals. Some hunters used human body parts, including the genitals of either sex or the whole corpse of a dead child, as hunting charms to attract the seals and overpower them (Lantis 1946:229) or to watch for game and guide the spear in its flight (Nelson 1899:429).

According to Joe Friday of Chevak (August 1983 BIA 22), the grave itself had the power to attract or draw the living: "Not far after the people died at a particular site, people who traveled through this area would go and, without knowing it, they would come back to the same spot they started from. Two people had this same experience. One man left the area and while he traveled he came back to the same spot. When he noticed that it was the second time he came back without knowing it, he said out loud that he would destroy the graves if he comes back unintentionally to the same spot. On the third time

8. Compare Serov's (1988:251) description of Koryak mourners covering their tracks by placing a stone or drawing a line across the path to prevent the spirit of the deceased from following the funeral party back to the village.

he left he did not come back to the same spot after he made that threat." Just as the hunter and his wife drew the seals out of the sea, the dead drew humans out of land of the living.

MOURNING THE DEAD: MAKING THE TRAIL CLEAR

A person's journey to the land of the dead began even before death. According to Nelson (1899:489), as people lay dying they would think of their dead relatives who would soon come to guide them to the land of the dead. After death they could see nothing at first and existed in complete darkness. Gradually, however, they began to regain their senses until, by the time the funeral was completed, they had attained clairvoyance (Nelson 1899:424). Once their senses returned, they rose in the shape of their old selves and followed an underground trail to the land of the dead. This is the trail that their living relatives strove to make clear for them, both to aid their progress and discourage their immediate return. This same passage had to be kept clear through adherence to an elaborate set of rules so that, among other things, the *tarneq* could return on the occasion of the birth and feasting of its namesakes.

After burial the villagers, especially the relatives of the deceased, abstained (*eyagaluteng*) from a number of ordinary activities to allow the dead soul'to "follow the way s/he is to go without any problems" (Toksook Bay Elders, November 1993 NI62). These restrictions or *eyagyarat* ("traditional abstinence practices") also insured that the dead, who lingered for four or five days in the world of the living before their final departure, did no harm to the living. The quality of these restrictions makes it apparent that although people did not consider the corpse dangerous, they viewed the *tarneq* of the deceased as ominous. Until the *tarneq* had finally departed the world of the living, people had to take care. The period directly preceding and following a death was a dangerous time. A passageway between the worlds of the living and the dead had opened, and if people acted carelessly, they might inadvertently slip from one world into another or injure the shades of the dead moving unseen in the world of the living.[9]

In sum, the restrictions following a human death had the twofold purpose of clearing a pathway for the dead soul out of the world of the living and creating a boundary between the living and the dead. Until the corpse was placed in the grave, villagers restricted all their activity. As soon as they heard that someone had died, people extinguished all fires and ceased all work. They emptied water buckets to avoid contamination and kept them covered after they were refilled. No one in the household of the deceased could sleep, and no one in the village could cook food, until they had buried

9. In the 1920s Butzin noted that "the departed spirit was supposed to hover about for that length of time and any jar or the movement of a sharp tool might damage the 'exit' of the spirit. Sometimes they hunted for the departed spirits and found them. In such an event they 'pressed' the spirit into the earth" (Fienup-Riordan 1992:45).

the corpse. Elsie Tommy of Newtok (June 9, 1992) reported, "If s/he did not fast, s/he would block the way of the person who had died. His/her path to the place of the dead would be blocked."

Men did not chop wood in the village, and women did not sew or cut fish while the corpse lay unburied. According to Theresa Moses (August 1987 NI95A:1), "If there is a death in the family, one of them would visit around telling the people while the dead is not buried not to work at all. While a person is lying dead, the whole village could not do anything at all. They could not work with any tools, and even if it is a needle one could not poke it anyplace. But after the dead has been buried, the village could then use knives and could also sew." William Tyson from the lower Yukon (August 1, 1991) added, "When they made a coffin, I don't know how they made it. They tied everything up. Never nailed it. That was their superstition. Or they could go out in the river and make a coffin there, where you can saw, chopping, drive nails there. And after you put a body in there, you can't drive any nails in there."

The prohibitions against cutting, sewing, or use of sharp instruments for the first day following a human death were standard practice throughout western Alaska. Recall that the same prohibitions were in effect after killing a seal or while a seal head was in the house. In fact, the rules were not as strict following a human death as those following a young man's first seal hunt. Moreover, along the Kuskokwim the observances for both a human death and a belukha kill required rest for a set number of days by the immediate family of the deceased or the family of the successful hunter—five days for the death of a woman, four days for a man, and four days for a belukha whale (Kilbuck 1887:727–28).

Before village activity could resume after the burial, villagers ritually cleansed the community with the smoke of "land plants," such as wild celery or Labrador tea, just as they did during the closing days of the Bladder Festival.[10]

Then after burying [the corpse],
when they go back home,
when they arrive
when there was not anything for them to do,
all the houses
and the *qasgiq*
lighting up pieces of tundra,
opening the window,
the whole household would burn one for a while.
And after making smoke, they would stop,
and only after that would they handle tools.
(Toksook Bay Elders, November 1983 NI62:10)

10. Compare Serov (1988:251) on the purification of Koryak mourners by fumigation following a funeral.

According to Billy Lincoln (April 1986 NI83:16), villagers also purified the fire pits before relighting the fires and resuming normal daily activity: "Before they were buried, the villagers did not do anything. They did not work with any tools or a knife or anything. After they came home from burying the dead, they merely lighted something in the fire pit and opening the window let that smoke billow outside. They burn anything, even a handful of grass. After that, they can work with tools."

People took special precautions to purify and protect the living members of the community, especially the children, by ritually bounding them off from unclean influences. According to Brentina Chanar (June 30, 1989):

If someone had died in the village, they let their children come in the house, they *tarvarluki* [purify with smoke] upwards like this [towards the roof]. . . .

When someone dies from the village, they rub their children with a rock. They rub the body of every child with that rock. . . .

When someone had died, they take the rock out of the house. They take it away from the door and take it all around the house *ella maliggluku* [following the universe]. When they got to each corner of the house, they would drop it roughly, and when they brought it back into the house they did the same thing.

They purify the people in the house *[cayaircarluki]*; they make sure nothing will happen to them, and they did the same thing to a child. Because some people that died long ago used to be so terrifying.

The stone used for this private ritual was an *ipegcarissuun* (from *ipegcar-* to sharpen), the whetstone used to sharpen women's knives. As an alternative to rubbing their children with a rock, parents might rub them with seal oil to make them slippery and difficult for evil influences to catch hold of.

The restrictions on the activity of the immediate relatives of the deceased were more prolonged and elaborate than those placed on the rest of the community. The deceased's close relatives observed for a full five days the restrictions placed on the village immediately following a death. People referred to this five-day period as *kanaranluni* (mourning, literally "to be bent over [with sadness?]"). According to Theresa Moses (August 1987 NI95A:1): "The immediate family of the deceased are called *kanarat* [ones that are bent forward]. For these five days they could not do anything. They could not cut anything or sew at all. Also they could not hunt. They could not go into the wild before these five days had passed." Mourners could not handle tools, sew, or use an *uluaq*. Another Nelson Islander recalled, "For five days . . . they did not use whatever little tool was in their house."

Here the number of days corresponds to the steps separating the land of the living from the land of the dead and, presumably, the period during which the shade of the dead was in transit between the two. Nelson Islanders made it clear that the restrictions against cutting, chopping, and work in general prevented the trail of the deceased from being "cut," thereby causing the shade to miss its way. A direct parallel existed between the restrictions

during the five-day mourning period, the restrictions prior to the hunt when
it was also essential not to "cut" the seal's passage, and the restrictions on a
woman's activity following the birth of a child. As we shall see, rules also
prohibited cutting during the five days of the Bladder Festival when the seals'
souls were in transit.

> And the immediate family
> during that time,
> they try not to handle tools before making smoke
> because they are mindful of the one they had sent off.
>
> For that reason they try not to cut their way.
>
> They hope for [the dead] to go well.
> They want them to follow the way they are to go without any problems.
>
> Having that in mind that is what they did.
>
> But if someone mistakenly used a tool,
> those people who are departing,
> the ones who had been going along well,
> they will travel missing their paths.
>
> They suddenly lose their trail.
>
> They suddenly have no path to travel on.
>
> For that reason they *eyagtut* [abstain]
> during that time.
>
> They referred to those five days as *kanarayaraq* [mourning].
> (Toksook Bay Elders, November 1983 NI62:10)

When the five-day mourning period ended, the immediate family appeared belted and marked with ashes: "If the dead was a child of a family or a
husband or wife, the family would bundle up, tie their waist in a belt. A bag
of ashes in a piece of material would be hung on their belt and a fish or
salmon tail fin hung from the bag. The purpose of doing this was to complete the five-day mourning" (Gertrude Therchik, Toksook Bay, July 14,
1985 NI86A:3).

Both going belted and carrying ashes were said to inhibit *ellam iinga* (the
eye of the weather, the eye of awareness) from seeing them during the
mourning period and were directly comparable to the belt and ashes worn by
a woman following her first menstruation. While the encircling belt rendered
them invisible, the ashes blinded *ellam iinga* and prevented their being seen.
Lantis (1959:52) recorded the same practice of belting the bereaved to insure
invisibility on the lower Kuskokwim. After the death of a child, a man would
throw ashes to the four cardinal points when he went hunting on the sea so
that the ashes would get in *ellam iinga* and prevent it from seeing him and
bringing more misfortune. People might also rub ashes all over their bodies or
paint their faces with charcoal to protect themselves from spiritual invasion.

Death, like illness, may have been viewed in some instances as a punishment by *ella* for some infraction (see Lantis 1959:52). Certainly these practices reflect the idea that the Yupiit considered the bereaved susceptible to outside intrusion, perhaps permeable by virtue of proximity to death. They should be covered because they were particularly vulnerable during this period.

Close relatives of the deceased were a living passage to the world of the dead, just as the corpse was viewed as a conduit for the care and feeding of the human dead. They were therefore rigorously bound off from normal daily activity, both to insure that no unclean influence enter their body and that their essential spirit not unwittingly depart. As in the restrictions against tool use and domestic and subsistence activity in general, social invisibility was also prescribed in the event of a young man's first seal kill or a young woman's first menstruation. Elsie Mather (1985) recorded that along the coast below Nelson Island when news arrived that someone had died in another village, people would paint their hands with the drippings of their seal-oil lamp and make motions of encasing each other. The same principle was at work when fellow villagers of the deceased rubbed their homes, and sometimes their bodies, all around with a rock. Both actions protected them by creating a boundary between themselves and the shades of the dead (see also Morrow 1984). Here again the twofold goal of death duties is revealed: opening a passageway for the shades of the dead and bounding off the world of the living.

Following the initial five-day period of mourning, the immediate family continued to abstain from certain activities for a full year following the death. During that period, they went covered and belted to hide themselves from the sight of *ella*, to bound themselves off from a sentient, knowing, and responsive universe:

> Then when those [five] days were done
> if he has parents, his parents,
> his wife, if she is alive,
> or her companion, if he is alive
> after her death
> they would always be covered up.
>
> And they never went out without something tied around their
>   waist.
> Even if they are men,
> they always had a hood on and mittens. . . .
> It was connected to *ella* [the weather, world or universe]
> so that they not be seen by *ella*.
>
> They told about that, too—
> how it could make the world bad.
>
> Also,
> for the one they had sent off
> they did that.
> (Toksook Bay Elders, November 1983 NI62:9)

The same requirement of invisibility probably underlay the rule that the husband or wife of the deceased not go outside for twenty days following the death of a spouse. On Nunivak Island close relatives refrained from going up on an eminence and looking around for the first twenty days following a death (Lantis 1946:228). Nelson Islanders maintained that they must keep not only their person out of sight, but also their clothing: "The ones who are in mourning did not hang out their clothes. They refrained from hanging out their clothes because of *ella* [the weather or world]. When the weather saw them, the weather would be bad" (Toksook Bay Elders, November 1983 NI62:3–4).

During the year following the death, close relatives of the deceased could not wash, cut their hair, or change their clothing. They were restricted from contact with the doings—with the very air—of the everyday world. The surviving spouse could not remarry for one year following the death. According to Brentina Chanar (June 30, 1989), "If it is a male [who dies], the wife would *umcigqluku* [literally "to be plugged or airtight," as of a door caulked against cold air]; if a female dies, her husband *umcigqluku*. That person could not be married within one year of the death of his spouse. Only after one year has passed, then he or she can get a spouse."

Restrictions on sexual and commensal activity reinforced the social invisibility of the bereaved, who for twenty days must refrain from sexual intercourse and must be the last to eat. When they did eat, the food could not be fresh, and they must consume it tail first. By some accounts the mourners must not only begin with the end piece but must refrain from eating fish heads altogether, as these were considered the preferred food of the dead.

Immediate relatives of the deceased also abstained from harvesting activities. During the summer following the death of her spouse, a woman could not pick berries. A man must curtail his hunting and fishing activity.

Then, if there is a death in the winter
or in the spring,
his family, his dad,
or her companion
would not go seal hunting through the whole spring.
He was to stay at home.

He kept himself covered up.
Even while it was very calm he would have his hood on.

He would do that perhaps for twenty-two days.

Then when the ice was going out,
only then,
if he is able to fish again,
or when he can go gather greens or eggs,
like the other one,
only after smoking himself
he goes net fishing or goes hunting things.

But like the others,
they would not do things for a whole year,
they would abstain from doing things.
(Toksook Bay Elders, November 1983 NI62:9)

Before a man could resume harvesting activities, his equipment had to be carefully fumigated to remove the association and "smell" of death: "When the ones that are abstaining are thinking of fishing, they would light things of the earth over the net. They are wiping it away. They take away the smell of death when they do that" (Toksook Bay Elders, November 1983 NI62:4). As in the fumigation to prevent illness in general, this action "swept away whatever was bad." Again the universe *(ella)* was depicted as sentient and capable of both sight and smell.

Both the belting and covering of the bereaved, as well as the prohibition against harvesting activities, served to protect the relatives of the deceased. Other *inerquutet* were intended to insure the shade's safe arrival in the land of the dead. Just as noise was prohibited during the funeral, drumming was prohibited afterward lest the sound "wake up the dead." Whereas daily life contained numerous activities intended to wake up the minds of young adults, it was precisely these activities that were forbidden following a death. Not only did the bereaved seek to remain invisible and odorless to the spirits of the universe, but they also strove not to be heard.

They also had this custom,
because they only used drums in the winter
if one of the people died
they would disassemble the drum
to the point where it would not make noise.
They removed their skins.

That is what they did.
They were not to drum
after that time.

Then after some time had passed,
they resumed playing drums.

Then,
during the time after a person's death
when one of the ones [that deceased] left behind
handles a drum too soon,
they would say to [the offender] that s/he might wake the person up,
the one who died.
(Toksook Bay Elders, November 1983 NI62:1)

The orator followed immediately with a story recalling the consequences of ignoring this *inerquutet*. As in so many proscriptions, the rule was tied to a particular incident as proof of its veracity.

I know of a *qanemciq*
about Qussauyaq's dad,
the one they called Qaquilitaq.

That person's wife died.
Then at some time after did that one drum?

While they were using spirit powers,
drumming, he sang.

Then while they were drumming,
he noticed a cold draft in the *qasgiq*.

The draft began to have something strange about it.
While the people were there,
the *tuunrilria* [the one who is using spirit power] became aware
that the one who had died
had come into the *qasgiq*.

The one who was doing it took hold of it
and asked it why it was there.

When those things happen,
they usually ask them questions.
And they say that the person answers,
even when the *angalkuq* is far away in the universe.
It mentions the name of the *angalkuq*
that has ordered it.

When they name another,
saying that it was not real,
the one who is holding it,
when he says that he was not real,
it would mention his name.

And it would mention the one holding it,
that that person has ordered it to appear.

When they have nothing left to do,
they say that those things cry.
The dead ones would cry.
It would cry audibly.

Then after doing that,
it would mention the one who is holding it.
It would name the one who was doing it.

So when that one did that,
she said that because Qaquilitaq kept knocking on her,
she has come to him.

So while he was drumming,
because he was knocking on her,
she has come, she has entered.

So to prevent that happening,
when they have recently lost a relative,
the ones who are left behind
are not to try to drum.
(Toksook Bay Elders, November 1983 NI62:2–3)

Drumming was not the only proscribed noise following a human death. People discouraged crying and loud lamenting lest the dead wake. Nastasia Kassel of Kasigluk (May 25, 1988 YN27:9) recalled, "When people finally die . . . the whole village is silent. And they never let children be around those dead people. From the time they get sick, kids are never exposed to their presence. And they never let any children into the house where a member of the house had died."

The woman who returned from the dead advised the people concerning their mourning, telling them that the salty tears of the bereaved make the dead wet and uncomfortable. Their tears also added to the river of tears, making it more difficult for the dead to cross. According to Billy Lincoln (April 1986 NI83:15), "It is said that the woman who came back from the dead advised the people that if the ones who are still living are crying for the dead one, that dead one becomes very uncomfortable, maybe by being wet with tears. After they have died, those who are living were told to be neat in appearance and try to give the outward appearance of being happy even though their mind may be lonesome. If they do that, they help the one who is dead. If the living are happy, the dead one is also happy."

Here the bereaved had to act happy so that the dead would feel happy. In important ways the bereaved were connected to the dead, their mirror image in the world of the living and as such responsible for their condition. During the mourning period, the bereaved must be invisible, noiseless, odorless, inactive, and free from unhappy thoughts. In short, they had to act in ways that undercut or deemphasized their humanity and approximated as closely as possible the disembodied quality of the human shade. It is possible that human sight, smell, and sound had to be minimized because the senses of the deceased were heightened and could be easily disturbed. By some accounts, if the mourners were noisy, the dead would wake up and return to haunt them. Mourners carefully followed these restrictions both to insure an open pathway for the dead as well as to bound them off from the living.

Billy Lincoln (April 1986 NI83:12–15) related a final incident in support of the prohibition against noise following a human death. This story has been recorded in other parts of western Alaska (Mather 1985) and describes how a woman died and was buried along with her living child. The child's cries woke her from death, and she returned to haunt the living until a shaman was able to show her the path that the cries of her child had caused her to miss:

At that northern place called Qivgayarmiut, a woman died while she still had a little baby. So when she died—strange that no one wanted to keep the baby—they put the child inside her coffin and put her away.

In those days they put a coffin outside, on the ground, enclosing them with rough wood boards, and they did not bury them. So that baby was heard crying in the coffin. Eventually in time he stopped crying.

So one of those days (she had died during the summer), in fall time, that woman came to be seen packing her baby. After that, she would go outside.

Being afraid of her, they went to their winter camps. And at that place, they were going to have Elriq [the Great Feast for the Dead] that coming winter. They were the ones to host Elriq at that time.

So that winter people gathered at that place. They came from all over.

It happened that one of the people was a shaman from Qissunaq [original home of the residents of modern Chevak]. He was one of the strangers, and probably he was not the only stranger from that area.

So that winter, about the time Elriq was going to be celebrated, two young men went to Qivgayarmiut to get food because they had fished there that summer.

When they got there, they went up to the elevated food cache, and while they were busy there, someone said from beneath them, "Oh, well. Hoping that you may give food for my baby, I have come to you."

One of them peeked through the crack in the floor and saw that it was that woman!

So one of them took a pinch of food and let it drop down. When he did that, there came a big thud. When he peeked, he saw a big bundle of fish down there! That was the way they hit the ground.

When that woman took them, after expressing her gratitude, she went up to her coffin.

With haste, they got ready and departed for home as fast as they were able. Probably their winter village was not far, and they would get there before night.

While they were going along, they saw her again coming after them! That dead woman!

Because she was not far, they scratched a line behind them just in case. When she got to that line, she stopped momentarily and having gone back and forth at the line, she continued to keep coming after them.

So they kept doing that because she stopped momentarily when they did that, as they went along.

So finally, they reached the village. And because it was inevitable that she would soon arrive, the people gathered in the qasgiq. And her husband was also in the qasgiq, but he was on the side someplace.

By and by, she came by the door. She was burping as she came in. When the vapor came down during one of her burps, when she got to the lights, one of them suddenly went out. And when she did something again, the other went out also.

The only light was on the back wall. Because the shaman must have done something to it, that light did not go out even though she came to it.

Pretty soon, that woman came up through the underground entrance. Then she looked around and said, "Qamuralria's father, is he in here?"

She was sweeping the interior of the *qasgiq* with her gaze by the rim of her cap. When she got to a spot where her husband was hiding while lying behind those people in front, she would comment that it seems like it was him in there even though people said that he was not in the *qasgiq*.

And the shamans who were in the *qasgiq* who had come, when they put them down on the floor, they would spin in circles, step over the floor, and having gone through a complete circle, they would sit in their designated spot.

So those people tried to throw the shamans at her, but when she does something, dust would fall from the *qasgiq*. When they did that, she would threaten to do something to their village. And the window up above would fall down, and almost touching the floor, it would spring back up again. Dust was falling down.

When all the shamans had been used in vain, they threw that shaman from Qissunaq down to the floor! When they put him on the floor, he asked for mittens made of dog skin. And he donned a hat used for dancing. When he was all ready, he approached her who was standing through the door, and squatting beside her, he said to her, "I'm going to try to help you. So move over and make room for me, and let me go down by your interior side. You have made a mistake and have arrived at Qissunaq."

"I did not make a mistake," she answered. "Having followed those two who went to Qivgayaq, I arrived here."

"Because I am not from here, I am at fault that you have come," he said to her. "Let me help you. Make room for me on your interior side [in relation to the *qasgiq*]."

When she insisted that he place himself on the door side, he refused and told her that he wanted to be on the interior side.

Then the interior of the *qasgiq* became cold and lonely.

So putting his feet by her door side, he vibrated them and started to go down. When the floor was even with his seat, he came to sit on the floor directly facing her. Then he started knocking on the floor board on each side of him, and then he said to her, "You who are a dead person, you think you are the only one that is terrifying. Look at those two things that are going to get you!"

Soon while he was doing that, she began to cry out, begging that he leave her alone.

So while she was doing that, he started to go down again, and that woman started going down with him. And then they completely disappeared down through the floor. After they went down, the inside of the *qasgiq* slowly became peaceful. And so it became peaceful again.

Soon, while the people were waiting in the *qasgiq,* that shaman nonchalantly came into the *qasgiq* with small beads of sweat on his face.

It is said that shaman saved the village from certain doom. It is said that the woman was awakened by her baby from her death stage, when he was crying in the coffin.

THE LAND OF THE DEAD

Just as following the rules for proper conduct in the world of the living was the prerequisite for a good life, so careful action on the part of the mourners insured the shade's successful passage from the land of the living to the land of the dead. As in the story of the haunting woman, inappropriate action in the world of the living could jeopardize the departure of the shade for the land of the dead. On each of the five days following the burial, while the bereaved remained noiseless, invisible, odorless, and inactive in the land of the living, the dead person's shade came one step closer to the land of the dead.

Although people believed that the spirits of those who died a natural death descended gradually to the underworld after death, all human shades did not share this fate. The shades of shamans and those who died violently—including death by suicide according to some people—were said to go up to the skyland to a land of plenty. The shades of evil or spiritually powerful people might return directly to the land of the living, where they would reanimate either a human or animal body. To insure against such an immediate return, the joints of potentially dangerous people as well as animals might be cut so that they would "die dead, forever."

Following a natural death, however, the shades of both humans and animals gradually descended to underground villages of their own, which Hawkes (1914:29) reported were grouped according to the localities from which they came. There they remained dependent on the gifts of the living, who gave them small morsels of food, which they received as whole stores. As we shall see, people celebrated both the Bladder Festival as well as Elriq (the Great Feast for the Dead) to supply the needs of the animal and human dead.

Nelson (1899:424) noted that the shade gradually became conscious after death. When people died, they could not see or hear anything at first. When mourners placed the body in the grave box, however, the *tarneq* regained consciousness. It then rose as its old self and followed the trail that extended from its grave to the land of the dead. Along this trail were the villages of other animals, whose *yuit* (persons) appeared in semihuman form.

If no mishap such as the cries of a child or the sharp edge of a knife cut across their trail, the shades of people who had lived life carefully would find their way to the land of the dead, referred to, on Nelson Island, as Pamalirugmiut (from *pamani*, "that place back there obscured from view"). Mather (1985:115) notes that in this place delicious, two-headed (therefore tailless) whitefish were the preferred fare of the shades of the dead.

If they had erred in life, their descent would not be easy. Punishments were meted out according to the way a person had lived. Although Lantis (1959:52) contended that the idea of punishment after death originated with Christianity, detailed descriptions of the perils of the afterlife occur in Yup'ik oral tradition. For example, if people were careless with water during life, their shades would travel to a place where bowls full of water were forever beyond their reach. If they picked their teeth with grass while alive, thus showing their lack of respect for this valued item, their bodies would be impaled by grass after death (see Nelson 1899:488).

If people were cruel to dogs during life, after death they would find themselves perennially licked by them (Mather 1985). Nelson (1899:488) also noted a village of dog shades where a human shade who entered one of the houses was summarily chased away with a piece of wood, providing a lesson as to how dogs felt when they were roughly treated in the human world. According to H. M. W. Edmonds (Ray 1966:70), the village of the dogs was the first place a shade reached on the trail to the land of the dead. The inhabitants would rush out and tear to bits the shades of people who had mistreated them in life. Apparently, a special relationship existed between dogs and the shades of the dead. People were advised to let the dogs devour the food that was presented to the dead at Elriq, saying that the dead had come as dogs and were trying to eat. The feeding of the dead through the dogs during Elriq lends support to the view that the children who were deemed "dogs" in the ceremonies preceding the Bladder Festival also represented the spirits of the dead who, through them, came to partake in the feast.[11]

THE GIRL WHO RETURNED FROM THE DEAD

As we have seen, people learned in part about the care of the bladders and the Bladder Festival from the boy who went to live in the underwater home of the seals. Conversely, a young woman who died and returned to the land of the living communicated to humankind an understanding of the underground land of the dead and the ceremonies that should attend them.

The story of the girl who returned from the dead is well-known in western Alaska, and a number of versions have been recorded (Anderson 1940:106; Hawkes 1914:29–30; Mather 1985:108–15; Nelson 1899:488–90). Billy Lincoln, born at Kaialuigmiut, told the story as follows:

I heard this story from a person from the Yukon area. This young girl died and so, as far as she was aware, she went on a journey and arrived at this village. And since her grandmother was at that village, they came to stay together.

So they stayed at that beautiful and wonderful village.

When the time came and they were asked, they would go to this certain village to participate. It was there that her father would give her parkas.

So when her father gave something to her namesake, he meant it for her (the dead one). One of those times when they were told to go they went.

After having been to that village, they went home when the time came. While they were going home, her grandmother said to her, "Oh my, I have forgotten to take along those things that I have been given. After I placed them on the elevated cache, I forgot to take them again."

So the grandmother asked her to get them. But before she went back to get them, she told her that if she comes upon the fallen evergreen tree, even though she could go under it or go around it, she distinctly told her to try to go over it.

11. Today on Nelson Island people believe a dog that cries like a human child portends death, and they will kill it to avert disaster.

So when she backtracked, she came upon that fallen tree. It had not been there when they had been going home. One could go under it or around it.

Following her grandmother's advice, she tried to go over it. But while she was trying to do that she tripped.

The fact that she tripped was the only thing she remembered. Eventually she became conscious. She found herself in a place that was bleak and dark. She saw that she was in this village, and when she was conscious, she was by the elevated food cache.

And even when she wanted to go with her previous companions, she did not know which way they went. So she went into the cache and cried sitting against the wall.

While she was crying, one of the young men came out from the *qasgiq* to urinate. This was in the days when they went outside to urinate during the night.

While he was urinating, the noise of his water hitting the ground seemed to be accompanied by some other noise. When he finished, he listened and heard the sound of weeping from the direction of the food cache.

When he got curious, he sidled toward the food cache. And he ascertained that the weeping sound was coming from inside the food cache.

When he went in, he found this girl who had died four or more years ago. And he asked her, "What the heck! How and why did you arrive?"

"Well, I found myself in this lonely place somehow!"

When he approached her and tried to take hold of her, he could not get ahold of her with his arms. It was like grabbing thin air.

But after he rubbed his arms with food matter, he finally did take hold of her.

Even though she was reluctant, he took her into the *qasgiq* still holding her.

But when that man leaned on the floor boards to go up, he would sink down as if nothing was holding him.

But there was an elder inside who had something to solve that problem of them sinking. He rubbed the girl and the floor with drippings/soot from the seal-oil lamp, and that is when they were able to stand on the floor.

They all saw that this person was the same one who had died some years ago. She was wearing the same parkas that her father had given to her namesake during Elriq. And when her parkas were taken off from her, she had on the same amount of parkas that had been given to her namesake!

She was like any other living human being. But her namesake, after she had come home, died very soon. They changed places!

So she lived to a ripe old age. When she became an old woman, she pined for the place and people where she had been. She longed for that place where she used to be. They used to call it Pamalirugmiut [the place back there obscured from view].

So at night when they were going to eat, she would say, "Those people from Pamaliruk are going to eat a certain kind of food." (When I first heard it, she said they were going to eat *qamiiqulget* [the ones with heads], but she called them some food with something big about them.)

She used to be lonely thinking about that beautiful and happy village where she used to be. (Billy Lincoln, Toksook Bay, April 1986 NI83:10–12)

Mary Mike of St. Marys (October 1, 1992) told an abbreviated version of the same story in which the boy deliberately blocked the pathway between the living and the dead, causing the girl to remain in the human world:

There was a couple whose daughter had already died, and she was their only daughter. They had already named someone else after her. They had also made the namesake a young caribou parka, that girl there, the one who had been named after their daughter.

So they were ready to go [to celebrate Elriq]. With them there was a young boy who was not married yet. Back in those days when the *angalkut* lived with them, that boy refused to be an *angalkuq*. When they asked him to try and join the others, he would refuse. He had been directed to be an *angalkuq*. He did not want to reveal himself to other people.

So then when they were about to leave in the morning . . . when the young boy went out, the gifts they were bringing to their hosts were ready next to their storage sheds. Then as he was there, down below the shed, a young girl wearing a caribou garment came running over this way, behind those people who were leaving. She had nice clothing. She then entered the shed. When she entered, that young boy followed her. After all, he was destined to be an *angalkuq*. He ran after her and blocked the entranceway as she was trying to escape. He recognized her. She was the daughter of that couple. Then that girl said to him that she was going to go visit her relatives for a while, and she asked him not to delay her. He totally blocked the doorway and told her not to go. He asked her to stay a while.

So when it was clear she could not leave, she suddenly entered the world of the living humans.

Oh, she was bringing back her dish at that time. She had forgotten her bowl down there and had returned to get it. And ultimately she had the young boy catch up with her.

When he brought her over to her parents, her poor mother began crying when she saw their daughter. Then the boy told her not to cry. He told them that since he recognized her, he had totally blocked her way back and returned her.

However, that girl kept thinking about her home. She wouldn't forget her former place. She would say she liked that Pamalirugmiut, the place of the dead.

Apparently, these people who continually die, everything we give to their namesakes would go directly to them. And we used to give food offerings, anything like a little food. A little bit like that would come to her or him as a whole. The gift would multiply. But their water is bad. The only thing they yearn for is water. You know, when someone wants to receive the name of the deceased, when we give them water, they get well. That is because [the dead] have bad water. I don't know why they have bad water.

That is the one who returned *[tauna utertelleq]*. She accidently returned home, that person allowed her to return. Since he knew her, he apparently watched her very carefully. She came home, but she was not happy. She could not shake off the experience of that place back there where she stayed, the place where she stayed when she was dead.

That is how long it is.

Just as the tale of the boy who went to live with the seals helps explain the relationship between seals and humans in their closely related worlds, the story of the girl who returned from Pamaliruk provides a vivid image of the relationship between the living and the dead. Different versions of the story emphasize different details (Morrow and Mather 1992). Billy Lincoln's account tells of the relationship between the girl who returned from the dead and the girl's namesake who dies following her return. Mary Mike mentions this relationship only in passing. But she speaks at length on the dead's desire for fresh water, perhaps because the source of their water—the river of tears—is salt.

The two versions also differ in the explanation each gives for the girl's return and the obstacles she encounters. In Billy Lincoln's version, the girl is sent back along the trail to the human world by her grandmother, and she encounters a fallen evergreen tree blocking her path. In Mary Mike's account, the young shaman blocks the entrance to the shed, so preventing the girl from returning to the land of the dead. In another version told by Martha Mann of Kongiganak (Morrow and Mather 1992:7–11), the girl's path is blocked by what appears to be a pair of inner cones of fishtraps, and her grandmother tells her she should fall on them to reenter the human world and retrieve her gift. A fishtrap cone is a one-way passage that fish can enter but cannot exit. The implication is that the girl is able to travel the path between worlds in the proper direction but, like a fish, would encounter difficulty if she tried to retrace her steps. The girl successfully surmounts this difficulty and retrieves her gift, but when she tries to return, her pathway has disappeared. It was "pressed shut" when another woman in the village had a miscarriage, causing the girl to lose her path. Although accounts differ markedly in the manner in which the girl's path is blocked, all describe her traveling between the world of the living and the dead on a path, the condition of which is subject to change. Barriers are to be expected, and the passage between worlds is impossible without careful action on the part of both the living and the dead.

THE RELATIONSHIP BETWEEN THE LIVING NAMESAKE AND THE DEAD

The Yup'ik concept of soul was complex and did not correspond to a simple mind/body distinction. The human person comprised a number of spiritual components. At death at least one of these, in some accounts the *tarneq*, left the human body and went to live in the land of the dead. From then on its physical link with the human world was the namesake who reincarnated some essential part of the deceased.

At birth a child was named in a ceremony designated *kangiliryaraq* (literally "to provide with a beginning," from *kangiq* meaning, beginning, source). At this time the essence of the dead destined for rebirth entered the newborn. Parents usually named a child for a recently deceased relative or community member. The person naming the child *merrluku* (from *merte-* sprinkle water), dropping water at the "four corners" of the child's head, but not on the head itself—an act reminiscent of the ritual placement of the bladders and human corpse in the four corners of the ice hole and grave, respectively. While doing so, they would say that the spirit of the one whose name the child was receiving had come. To this day people believe that some part of the dead enters someone named after them and bestows something of themselves. The name carries an essential aspect of the dead across the boundary between worlds. As the part recalls the whole, the gift of the name constitutes the rebirth of the dead.

Sometimes a child became ill after someone died, and people attributed this to the child's desire to acquire the name of the deceased. The child was said to *kangingyugluni,* literally "to want to get a (new) beginning." Alternately a shade might want to enter a particular child and would hover over the child, making the child sick until the child was properly named, at which point the resident shade would come to the surface and the child would recover. If a couple had several children die at an early age, they might deduce that the infants' namesakes were requesting different parents. One remedy was to name a subsequent child Atrilnguq ("No Name") to avoid having discontented namesakes. Alternately the child might be adopted to kin to satisfy the shade's request (Morrow and Pete 1993:5). Parents also avoided punishing small children out of respect for the elder that may have taken up residence in the child. If they treated the child harshly, the shade would forsake the child, causing illness or death.

Not only children were named and renamed to avoid death and cure illness. Sometimes when a person died, the members of his or her family changed their own names to avoid detection by the deceased's *tarnera.* According to Brentina Chanar (January 25, 1991), "They used to change names at the time when I was a very small girl [1912–20]. And if their father or their mother died, they changed their names. And if a sibling died, they changed the names of some. Martina's late mother was Nusiang. And when her older brother Ayaprun died they named her Cimiralria [the one who changes]. . . . That is the way they always used to change the names of some people."

People with the name of the deceased might also have their name changed. Brentina Chanar continued: "And if a person with the same name dies, they changed the names of the one person with the same name. They never change their names anymore. But when Nancua's father's son died, his name was Ayaprun. He had a boat accident when he went hunting. And because of that, he took away the names of everyone who had the name Ayaprun and changed their names. Just the way he told people to do." In both cases the goal of renaming the living was protection from the *tarneq* of the dead. The reverse procedure is reported in a Siberian Yup'ik tale in which a boy took the name of his dead brother so that the spirits would think him dead and not harm him (Serov 1988:249). In this case taking a new name was considered dangerous, as it was equivalent to killing the bearer of the old name and being born again.

The Yupiit placed great importance on the fit between the child and the name. Illness and even death could result if the match was not acceptable. Not only did the shade seek out a particular child, but the child desired a particular name. A newborn cried because it wanted its name and would not be complete without it.

Although some part of the dead was reborn, some part also remained behind. Moreover, as demonstrated in the story of the girl who returned from the dead, the human shade and living namesake, while closely related, could not exist as separate entities in the human world at the same time. A gift to the spirit of the dead, reborn in the living namesake, supplied the human shade. Each "lived" through the other. Gifts given within the human world perpetuated not only a transfer between the living and the dead, but a continual affirmation of their separation and the boundary between them. That aspect of the spirit of the dead that entered the namesake at birth was the conduit for the transfer between these separate worlds. Death was less an interruption than a medium of continuance, an opening through which a spiritual essence was transferred and reestablished (see Block and Parry 1982).

As noted, the relatives of the deceased person for whom the child was named presented the child with gifts of food and water (compare Nelson 1899:424–25). According to Billy Lincoln (April 1986, NI83:15), "They give food to the namesakes remembering one's dead baby, father, or mother. They fill a bowl with good food and also include water in it. That is the way they give food. They also talk with him. And then the one being given things drinks the water. And the rest of the food in the bowl is buried in the ground, *aviuqarrluki* [making a food offering to the dead]. It is said that the food goes to the ones they are thinking about when they do that." Mary Worm of Kongiganak (May 13, 1989) continued, "When people die, they say what they call *kangiliryaraq* [to provide with a beginning]; they give them names. It is said that their namesakes, when they get clothes, [the dead] also get clothes. When these people with the same names are given those things, the things do not go to any place else. But it all goes to that person who has died."

The child was sometimes placed on a skin or mat during the presentation. This protective covering acted as a boundary between the world of the living and the dead and insured that when the spirit of the dead entered the infant, the child would not fall through the earth into the underworld below. Relatives of the deceased later might give the child clothes or other small gifts. These gifts supplied both the needs of the namesake in the human world and the needs of the shades in the land of the dead. Relatives of the deceased both referred to and addressed the child with relational terms appropriate to the dead namesake, rigorously avoiding use of the proper name. Moreover, people said that the actions of children, especially very young ones, mirrored those of their namesakes.

The child's behavior and abilities, more than its appearance, made it apparent who the child was. This was especially true during the first years of life. For instance, my third child was born with a lung condition, and for the first week of his life was very ill. My friend subsequently gave him the name of her brother, who had been sickly all his life and had recently passed away. Sometime later she called me on the phone and asked right away after the baby's health. Assuming she was checking up on my mothering, I assured her that her "brother" was fine. In fact, he had a bad cold. When we met my friend the next day, she warmly greeted her baby brother, and he responded by coughing in her face. Tears came to her eyes, and she exclaimed that now she really knew him.

Yup'ik names were sexually undifferentiated—neither male nor female—and were gendered by reference to the person they were inherited from. Parents often dressed their young children according to the gender of the one for whom they had been named. As the child grew, however, parents usually emphasized this gendered treatment based on the name only during special ceremonies such as Elriq.

By the Yup'ik view of the world, procreation was not the addition of new persons to the inventory of the universe, but rather the substitution of one for another. Some spiritual essence passed with the name, and in an important way the dead were believed to live again through their namesakes. Out of respect for the namesake, however, the name was then never used in direct address or indirect reference. Thus, at birth, a person entered into a relationship with the dead based on shared name and a relationship with the living through terminological skewing. Later, when people had their own offspring, they would enter into a relationship with the living child through shared name (teknonomy), while simultaneously entering into a relationship with the dead by way of terminological skewing in reference to the child. By means of this system, a man became father to his father and offspring of his child. Alternate generations were thus equated. More than a relationship between the living and the dead, there was a cycling between them, and a consequent collapse of the system into two generations (Fienup-Riordan 1983:153–58).

With the birth of their first child, a couple became subject to elaborate gift-giving requirements in their child's name. Besides the relation through the name and the classificatory cycling between generations, at the birth of a child parents were bound to honor requests for special favors by nominal relatives. Relatives of the deceased might also give small feasts in honor of both their dead relative and the child. Sophie Lee of Emmonak recalled, "I really wanted to put up something—a little party for that baby because she was named after my mother. We all want to bring little gifts to the *qasgiq*, to the dancers. So me and my sister made *akutaq*. In the evening we brought it over and passed it around in the *qasgiq*. These people know what we meant.

We meant that we were so happy to have that baby. We named her after my mother. So we have to do something to show the people that we're glad to have that baby" (Kamerling and Elder 1989).

A child's first culturally significant accomplishments—such as first bird harvested, first dance, first berry gathered, or first fish caught—also provided the occasion for elaborate distributions. These distributions could occur during annual ceremonies or as a separate event accompanied by gifts of food to the elders of the community. Moreover, at all the major ceremonies, people distributed the most valuable gifts in the name of the young children who were, by name, their ancestors incarnate. Also, when guests gathered in the *qasgiq* to receive their shares in the distributions, the hosts gave out gifts to the eldest first, down to the youngest. At the very head of the receiving line were parents with babes in arms who received special gifts in the name of their offspring.

The annual feast for the dead, known in some areas as Merr'aq or Merr'aryaraq ("process of providing a human with *meq* [fresh water]"), reaffirmed the original relationship between the living child and the dead namesake established at the time of naming. At this time relatives gave gifts to the living namesakes to provision the deceased. Donors sprinkled pinches of food and small amounts of water in the fire pit or on the ground, being careful to recall who had gathered the food and helped in its preparation. As in the food thrown from the cache to forestall the haunting woman, or placed beside a grave, people believed the dead received these morsels as whole stores. People always included fresh water to supply the needs of the "thirsty" dead. Conversely, Nelson (1899:313) observed men offering the contents of their urine buckets to the shade of a shaman to discourage its return.

Just as the living left the deceased's possessions at the grave to provide tools for them in the land of the dead, so they fed the namesake so that the dead might eat and drink. Observers have often remarked on the importance of children in Eskimo society and have attributed it to the need for someone to provide for a person in old age. From the Yup'ik point of view, a namesake was just as important to provide for a person after death. The relationship between grandchild and grandparent took on special importance in this regard. Not only did grandchildren—especially a grandson—provide material support for the living elder, they also acted as a conduit for food, water, and clothing to the grandparent who had already died.

THE RELATIONSHIP BETWEEN DEATH AND LIFE

The foregoing has described the rules surrounding the treatment of the dead to "make their trail clear" out of the world of the living into the land of the dead. These rules simultaneously identified the dead with their close relatives and bound them off from contact with the community at large. During the five days immediately following death, the dead were gradually sent out of the world of the living following a path toward the land of the dead. During the same period, the mourners were initially separated from and subsequently reintegrated into the human world. The restrictions placed on close relatives were directly associated with the passage of the deceased into the land of the dead. The surviving relatives could do nothing that the dead could not do. They could not eat fresh food or fish heads until the dead had arrived and eaten in the land of the dead. They could not be seen until the dead had regained their sight. They could not make noise until the dead had completed their journey. In sum, they were required to act dead until the departed had passed into their new abode.

Bounding off the dead and their kin during burial and mourning displays striking parallels with the bounding off of women during birth and first menstruation. Mourners and menstruating women alike were belted and covered; they refrained from eating fresh meat, did no work, and abstained from social and sexual intercourse. Both remained odorless, inaudible, immobile, and invisible to the eye of *ella*. The five days of mourning, like the five-day menstrual seclusion as well as the five-day period following childbirth, were periods of danger. Breaking rules would be disastrous, alternately blocking the path of the deceased into the land of the dead or blocking the passage of the animals into the human world.

Oosten (1976:71) describes a comparable association between women and the dead among the Netsilik and Iglulik Eskimos. He concludes that both women and the dead were considered "unclean" because of their association with natural processes and, therefore, had to be kept separate from the preeminent cultural process—hunting animals. Although the Yup'ik Eskimos also made this separation, what was opposed at one level was related at another.

The Yupiit portrayed sexuality, specifically female sexuality, as a potential cause of death in some contexts as opposed to the activities of eating and sharing food, which they viewed as sources of life. As some Yup'ik people say to this day, "A woman is death to a man" and "Our food is our life." Unregulated intercourse between the sexes brought death, as it squandered the finite human resources of sight, breath, and touch, rendering the hunter and his wife powerless to attract animals. Sharing the hunter's catch and communal feasting, on the other hand, created life, as they added to a person's strength and power to attract animals. Sexuality—the relationship between men and women—was associated with death and opposed to the source of human fertility—the relationship between humans and animals. On one level, then, female reproduction was presented as incompatible with hunting animals and the relationship between the sexes incompatible with the relationship between human and nonhuman persons (Bloch and Parry 1982:18–19).

This hierarchical opposition between biological/individual reproduction (birth, maturation, and death) and cosmological reproduction is concretized in gender symbolism: "Sexuality is set up in opposition to fertility as women are opposed to men" (Bloch and Parry 1982:19). This opposition is eloquently expressed in the differences between the story of the boy who lived with the seals and the girl who returned from the land of the dead. Reflected in the everyday world, the women's house was the site of biological reproduction and production. The men's house was the focus of spiritual reproduction. Sexual intercourse, childbirth, and death took place in the women's world, whereas the ceremonial rebirth of both human and nonhuman persons occurred in the men's house.

At the same time sexuality and death were opposed to spiritual rebirth, there was also a parallel between the rituals surrounding a human death and the celebration of the rebirth of animals. People had drawn the seals into the human world, hosted them during the Bladder Festival, and sent them away to return the following season. So the *tarneq* was invited to return to the land of the living during Elriq (the Great Feast for the Dead), where it was feasted and hosted and sent away satisfied. Just as people took the bladders up through the *qasgiq* smoke hole and put them down through the hole in the ice, so they moved the corpse out through the smoke hole and down to the grave, where it began its journey to the underground land of the dead.

For the five days following a human death, the mourners not so much acted death as played the part of the gestating fetus. Moreover, their mourning was not finally completed until after the naming and subsequent gifting of a newborn child. Through the ruled behavior surrounding death, childbirth, and naming, the Yup'ik people transformed the biological opposition between life and death into a cosmological cycling between birth and rebirth. Whereas sexuality and death were opposed to fertility and life on one level, birth and death were ultimately subsumed as part of a larger cosmological process of reproduction (see also Bloch and Parry 1982:15).

Yup'ik people dealt with death in two phases. Immediately following the burial, they rigorously bound off the dead and their relatives from the living. This initial separation was followed by the birth of a namesake through whom a legitimate passage was formed for the reentry of an essential aspect of the dead. As the name came to reside in a living namesake, the world of the dead gave back to the world of the living some part of what had been lost.

The rebirth of the dead in the living namesake not only denied individual extinction but reasserted the reproductive character of death itself (Bloch and Parry 1982:5). Just as in other life-cycle rituals implying a passage from one group to another, an exclusion at one level resulted in a new integration (Wagner 1977). Crossing the biological boundary between life and death resulted in a cosmological passage between worlds. Moreover, the pathway metaphor was explicit in descriptions of the shade's journey to and from the land of the dead.

Comparable rules circumscribed the emergence of newborn children from their mothers, mature men and women from their childhood, the dead from the world of the living, and the seals from the sea. The passages of children, menstruating girls, young hunters, deceased humans, sea mammals, and land animals were all surrounded by restrictions "to make their trail clear." Taken individually, these passages were a one-way movement between opposing worlds—the land of the dead versus the land of the living, the women waiting in the land, drawing the seals from the sea. Yet following a human death, the name returned to reanimate the newborn child, just as following the seal's death, its *yua* was returned to live again in the sea. Instead of a static opposition between life and death, men and women, sea and land, pure and impure, their relationship was one of perpetual cycling, transformation, and hierarchical encompassment. Both the opposition and the relationship are captured in the comparison between the boy who went to live with the seals and the girl who returned from the dead. Although opposed at one level, both tales recount the same cycle of departure and return.

The coastal Yupiit considered nonhuman persons to be capable of perpetual regeneration if given the proper treatment and respect. Similarly, the gift of a name following a human death insured human life in perpetuity. Death as a final exit had no place in this system of cosmological reproduction, and the symbolism of rebirth permeated the rituals surrounding it. Mourners were covered and belted not because they were "unclean," but because, like sexually mature woman, they were fertile and in the process of reproducing life. Their carefully controlled actions insured that the dead safely arrive in their new underground home. The life of the namesake as well as the entire human community was put in jeopardy if the dead failed to accomplish their journey and subsequent separation. Birth into the land of the dead was ultimately the source of continuing life in the form of living namesakes. Rather than a grand finale, the death of an individual was an instance of cosmological reproduction.

CHAPTER 8

YUP'IK SPATIAL ORIENTATION
The Ringed Center

YUP'IK ESKIMOS INSCRIBED their ideas about the human and animal worlds onto the physical world, which they viewed as the concrete manifestation of their cosmology. Differences between men and women framed activities in everyday life and concepts about the nature of the space in which these activities occurred. A major component of their annual ceremonial cycle was to effectively transform these relations so as to remake their world and their relationship to it.

As we have seen, a sexual division of labor circumscribed everyday activity and dictated where it took place. Men concentrated on the provision of fish and game, while their mothers, wives, and daughters processed their catch. The moment the hunter reached home, he lost jurisdiction over his catch. Women worked mainly in the house to prepare the food and clothing that the family required. Along with processing the kill, women were also largely responsible for its distribution.

Into the 1940s residential division in the larger winter villages reflected this division of tasks. Men and boys over the age of five lived and worked together communally in a central dwelling *(qasgiq)*. Women lived and worked in smaller sod houses *(enet)*, sometimes connected to the *qasgiq* by passageways and sometimes not. The residential division of the sexes that characterized winter village life had important cosmological as well as social ramifications. In a variety of contexts the women's house or domestic apartment was comparable to a womb in which biological, social, and spiritual production were accomplished (chapter 5). In this space women worked to transform the raw materials supplied by their men into food and clothing for the people. When pregnant, a woman's activity within and exit from the house was likened to that of the fetus within her own body. Certain contexts

251

equated both the sod house and her womb with the moon, the home of the *tuunrat*, the spirit keepers of the land animals. The cutting of a door in the side of the women's house marked the arrival of spring itself. Finally, the women's house appeared in certain contexts as a symbolic womb, productive of animals as well as people. Women's activity and inactivity were directly tied to a man's ability to succeed in the hunt.

Though the sod house was the focus of women's private reproductive activity, the central men's house was the social and ceremonial center of the community and was treated with respect. According to Stebbins Elders (Eskimo Heritage Project 1985:66), "They never had dogs tied around it because it was the men's house. It was highly respected, like a church. The whole area around it was kept clear and neat. We always tried to get wood to heat it with. There wasn't even any running or jumping allowed near it." As in the treatment of bones, archaeological evidence from historic sites does not entirely bear out this observation. Yet keeping the area around the *qasgiq* clean was the stated ideal. Custom also required that anyone who disturbed the peace of the *qasgiq* through noise or argument must furnish wood for a sweat bath or food for the occupants.

People gave the men's houses in the larger communities proper names. According to Billy Lincoln of Toksook Bay (January 15, 1991), if a village had two men's houses, they had independent names such as Qasgirpak (big *qasgiq*), Qukatvalleq (the middle one), and Qasgicuar (little *qasgiq*). Unlike the indirect use of personal names, people used these names in direct reference. The names themselves, however, often referred to the structure's position in relation to its surroundings, for example, Qukatvalleq (the middle one). Billy Lincoln continued: "At Kaialivik, I know only those two former men's houses. One was named Qukatvalleq and the other was named Qasgirpak." Joshua Phillip of Tuluksak (July 9, 1988 BIA58:17–18) reported the same practice on the middle Kuskokwim: "Our forefathers gave proper names to their *qasgit*. It was to give a blessing and sacrament to the *qasgiq*. The village Nunapiarmiut had two men's houses. . . . [T]he *qasgiq* that was at the upper part of the village was called Kiaqliq [the one upriver]. And the one down below was called Uaqliq [the one downriver]. However, if there is one *qasgiq* in the village the residents will pick a name for it. Every *qasgiq* in the village had a proper ceremony to receive a name. It will not be used until this is done."

The inhabitants of the *qasgiq* regularly purified their abode by vigorously sweeping the floor and emptying the urine and water buckets, accompanying the procedure with noise and drumming to drive off evil spirits (see Lantis 1946:196). A *qasgiq* might also receive gifts in its name, such as a new gut window or clay lamp during ceremonial distributions. In the 1920s Butzin reported, "Last winter a man from Tsitsing [Cicing] donated windows to all the kashiges from Tsitsing to Akiatsoak [Akiachak], a distance of over one hundred and fifty miles" (Fienup-Riordan 1992:40). Just as the sod house

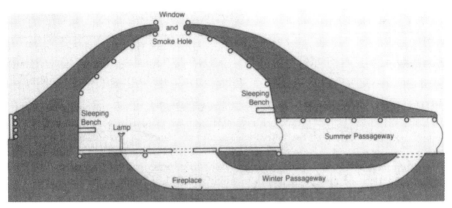

Drawing of a qasgiq, *after E. W. Nelson (1899).*

was viewed as comparable to the woman's body, in numerous ways—deferential treatment, naming, purification, and gifting—men treated the *qasgiq* as a respected person.

Along with its social importance, the men's house was the site of the spiritual reproduction of the community during the winter ceremonial season. The coastal Yupiit performed five major ceremonies during this period, at least three of which focused on the creative reformation of the relationship between the human community and the spirit world on which they relied. In all three of these ceremonies (the Bladder Festival, the Feast for the Dead, and the masked dances of Kelek) people invited members of the nonhuman world into their community, formally hosted them, then sent them back. This ritual movement effectively recreated the relationship between the human and spirit worlds and placed each in the proper position to begin the year again.

The spatial organization of the winter village reflected the sexual division of labor as well as the distinction between public ceremonial center and private productive periphery. The men's house was the spiritual window of the community, surrounded by the individual women's houses. The spiritual rebirth and vision of an otherworldly reality accomplished there were the counterparts of the physical birth, female productivity, and seasonal rebirth symbolized by exit from the women's sod house. Largely, although not exclusively, it was in the men's house that visions of the supernatural were realized in material and dramatic form. Physical birth and spiritual rebirth were not regarded as opposing each other. Rather, the Yup'ik Eskimos were deeply committed to a cyclical cosmology and embodied their fundamental belief in the spiritual constancy underlying temporal flux in a multitude of forms.

Younger members of both sexes regularly traveled the paths between public ceremonial center and private productive periphery. Young women and

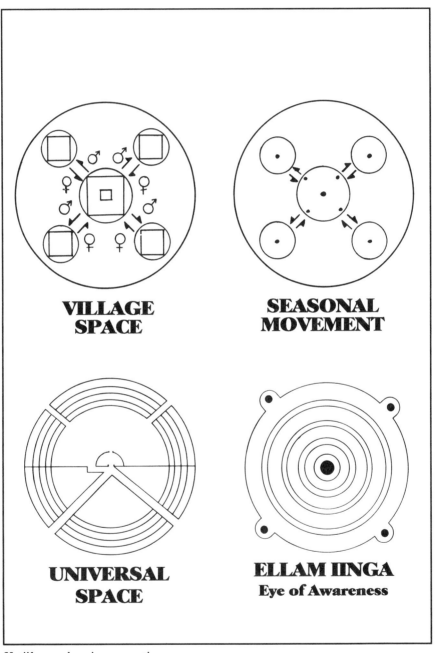

VILLAGE SPACE

SEASONAL MOVEMENT

UNIVERSAL SPACE

ELLAM IINGA
Eye of Awareness

Yup'ik cosmology in cross section.

girls dutifully brought cooked food to their male relatives in the *qasgiq*, often receiving instruction in exchange. Billy Black of Kongiganak (May 13, 1989) remembered: "These females, according to their ways, when they come to the *qasgiq* to bring food, they would let them sit down on the floor just in front of the men, and then someone from around there would tell her about how to live and how to take care of her husband, how she should live her life." Likewise, young men worked to sweep the porches and gather water for their mothers and sisters. In the evening a husband might visit his wife for social or sexual intercourse. Older men and women, however, rarely breached the residential separation and left to the younger generation the task of going between. As we shall see, winter ceremonies radically reversed this social separation.

The space within the men's house further reflected the image of a ringed center. The performance of a number of important ceremonies in the men's house dramatically reinforced its image as the spiritual center of the community, and its fire pit and smoke hole as passageways between the human and nonhuman worlds. Residents arranged themselves in ranked fashion around a central fire pit in which the spirits of the dead, both human and nonhuman, came to reside during specific ceremonies. Each man occupied a special position on one of the four benches built along the interior walls of the men's house. The seating arrangement reflected the hierarchical relations between categories of men. Married men sat along the entryway wall, the oldest man placing himself beside the entrance. Unmarried men of lesser age and worth ranged themselves along the back wall. Thus the men's house framed a number of internal distinctions, including that between young and old, married and unmarried, and host and guest. Billy Lincoln (January 15, 1991) remembered:

> They never sat randomly. In the *qasgiq*, each male had his very own spot to sit in. Starting from the side of the door, the oldest men sat. And toward the interior, each male became younger and younger, that is what they did. The elders sat on the door side of the wall. So each one had his own place to sit, and no one would ever sit in it. But when they were outside, other people did sit in that spot. But eventually when the owner of that spot came in, the person got up and made room for him because that was his designated spot to sit.
>
> Unwed young men sat along the *egkuq* [far wall facing the door]. . . .
>
> And the small boys sat on the floor because the *qasgiq* used to be crowded then, just down from where their fathers sat, all of them did that. . . .
>
> When those elders die, the one who was married and had children, he dies in the house, and the one who sat next to him assumes that spot.

The occupants of the men's house in the Chevak area arranged themselves somewhat differently. There older men occupied the corners while young boys sat in the middle of the benches to tend the lamps.

> From the corners of the entranceway wall called *ualirneq* are seated the men until they are seated to the youngest in the middle side walls of the *qaygiq*

Interior of qasgiq *at Tununak, still used for dances in the 1970s.*

[men's house]. The side walls are called the *nakirneq*. In the middle of the side wall, the seal-oil lamp is situated. On the two ends of the lamp, the two youngest boys are seated. The young boys are called *ayakutat* or *ayagyugat* [adolescents, teenagers].

On the farthest wall called *egkuq*, the young unmarried men called the *nekevyuut* are seated. The older young men are seated on the corners and they get younger to the center. In the center of the wall is located another lamp, and on each side of the lamp, the youngest *nekevyuut* are seated. The corners in the *qaygiq* are called *kangiraq*.[1]

The seating arrangements are learned by all men, and each sitting and sleeping area is respected by all men. . . . The personal belongings of the men are placed around their sleeping and sitting areas. (Pingayak 1986:24)

One of the most important ceremonies performed in the *qasgiq*, the Bladder Festival, helped to insure the rebirth of the *yuit*, or "persons," of the animals thought to be located in their bladders. During the closing ceremonies of the Bladder Festival, the shaman would climb out through the skylight to enter the sea, visit the seal spirits, and request their return. The men removed the inflated bladders through the *qasgiq* smoke hole and took them to an ice hole. There they deflated the bladders and sent them back to their underwater *qasgiq*, requesting the seals return the following year. In addition to serving as a passage permitting movement and communication between

---

1. Barnum (1901:304) describes the Kănnĕrăt as "the corners where the house spirits are supposed to be."

the worlds of the hunter and the hunted, the central smoke hole also served as a pathway between the worlds of the living and the dead. This image of the ringed center is repeated again and again in Yup'ik cosmology and ritual action, always with the connotation of vision as well as movement between worlds.

MOVEMENT IN THE WORLD AT LARGE

As soon as the ice began to break up in spring, residents of the large winter villages dispersed to the mountains and the coast, then to the river mouths for summer fishing, and later in the fall to the tundra sloughs and streams for trapping and fall freshwater fishing. As freeze-up approached, families returned to the winter village, hauling the stores harvested from the tundra and the sea. As in the daily cycle of movement between the men's and women's houses, the annual cycle of movement between the permanent winter village and small, dispersed seasonal camps was a loosely bound movement from public ceremonial center to private, production-oriented periphery.

The regional confederations identified in western Alaska each centered on one or more of these winter settlements (Fienup-Riordan 1984:63–93; Pratt 1984:45–61; Shinkwin and Pete 1984:95–112). In turn, these confederations centered on the use of a loosely bound territory in which seasonal migrations occurred around a relatively fixed point. The crossing of these boundaries for intervillage festivals was carefully controlled. In the intervillage Messenger Feast (Kevgiq), for example, the movement of the guests toward their hosts was accompanied by the constant attentions of messengers from the host village, whose primary function was to act as go-betweens during their approach.

Village space, as well as the landscape over which villagers ranged in their annual migrations, can be seen as a nucleated circle characterized by regulated movement from center to periphery. Nelson Islanders also sometimes represented the world as an island space surrounded by water. In the origin myth of Nelson Island, Raven created land from a block of ice on which his wife was being carried out to sea (Fienup-Riordan 1983:372–73). In a Chevak version of the same story, Raven created land by throwing ashes on the surface of the ocean to save his daughter:

When [Raven] was going to create this place—Scammon Bay, Nelson Island, and Nunivak Island—at that time the shoreline was up there at the tree line. . . . The ocean had its shore at that tree line. . . .

But when he first made the land here, after he arrived from seal hunting he was tired. And while his daughter was getting the seal he caught, ice broke up and she drifted away. While she drifted, he had fallen asleep because he was tired. And then he woke up.

When his daughter was in the ocean and since there was no other way he could get her, taking ashes from the campfire pit outside, he flung it and spread it by sending it like that. He covered the ocean.

And he covered this area all the way down to Nelson Island and Nunivak Island. He covered them with ashes.

When we put ash on water, it stays, as you know.

And so he let his daughter come on shore on top of that.

And that ash stayed and after one year, green stuff grew on it. After that, that's why we have stories that are related to . . . that time when the land was thin.

When the land was thin, men used to always go out hunting with a staff. . . .

And then debris came by the south wind. Plants died and land began to get thick after it was thin. . . .

And those mountains up there, according to the elders, used to be icebergs, pieces of tall ice. The way ice rests in shallow places. So that is what that Scammon Bay mountain was. . . . That is why water comes out from the side of the mountains. (John Pingayak, Chevak, December 14, 1987)

In another genesis myth, recorded by Nelson (1899:454), the Raven father fashioned woman out of bits of earth, using grass for her hair. Cecelia Martz told the story of Tengmiarpak (literally "big bird"), who soared high into the sky with feet full of mud that dried and crumbled to the earth, forming the Kilbuck and Kuskokwim mountains (Polechia 1992:36).

The story of the origin of land at the mouth of the Yukon River places the power of creation in the hands of a woman. Joe Ayagerak, Sr., of Chevak tells the story of a man who is paddling down the river in his kayak. He comes to an iceberg and ties his kayak to it to stop and eat his food. Meanwhile his wife at home starts to worry about his not coming home. She takes some dirt from the ground, holds it in a small pocket that she made by folding the skirt of her parka, and spreads out the dirt by hand. The land begins to form, and plants, mostly grasses and willows, start growing there. Soon her husband returns safely. This story relates to a specific piece of land near the village of St. Marys, and the plants and the mountain can still be found on this location (Madsen 1990:108).

The story of the origin of Nunivak Island recorded by Curtis (1930:73) also places a woman in the role of creator. According to this narrative, two brothers are lost at sea. "Schlumyoa" *(ellam yua,* "the person of the universe") hears the cries of the youngest brother and appears dressed in a woman's white, fish-skin parka. She scatters something on each side of their kayaks, which becomes land, and the ice becomes a mountain. She then transforms the youngest brother into a wife for his older sibling. Again, woman is created out of man, although this time a female agent accomplishes the feat. Lantis (1950) has suggested that apparent contradictions in ideas concerning the genesis of the world may originate from the meeting of two ancient traditions in western Alaska—the female Cella of the eastern Arctic and the myths of the Raven father characteristic of the Athapascan interior. At the same time, they may also reflect the regular alternation between the creative powers of men and women prevalent throughout Yup'ik activity and oral tradition.

YUP'IK COSMOLOGY IN CROSS SECTION

The Yup'ik conception of the universe also displays the cosmological motif of circles within a circle apparent in the structure of daily life and movement in the world at large. The Yupiit believed that the world was originally thin and permeable—*nunam mamkitellrani* (thin earth)—hardening since its creation by Raven (Nelson 1899:426) and making intercourse between the human and spirit worlds more difficult. This "hardening" is cited today as the reason why people do not see ghosts and extraordinary persons such as *ircenrrat* as often as in times past. The thickened earth prevents their passage into the human world. According to Joe Ayagerak, Sr. (Madsen 1990:108), "When the earth was thin, supernatural beings were real close. You had to be careful. When I was young and the earth was thinner my parents would tell me not to comment or shout out if I heard a strange noise, maybe a knocking from beneath the ground. Saying something would catch the attention of that one [making the noise] and it would bother me."[2] These encounters still take place today. The more a person knows about the appearance and habits of such supernatural creatures, the more safely one can travel on the tundra.

In the beginning of time, if a person journeyed far enough in any direction, that person would eventually arrive at a point where the earth folded back up into the skyland, home of the spirits of land animals. Lantis (1946:197) designates this place "łamqa'pa'ɣali'xa," probably from *ella* (universe) and *qapiar-* (to skin a seal starting from the head and pulling the skin back over the body), literally "the universe after it has been 'skinned' or folded back." Edmonds (Ray 1966:84) recorded an account of a man who reached the horizon and became caught in the crack between the sky and the sea. Dramatic reversals of the normal seasonal cycle characterized the space between earth and sky—men wearing parkas in the heat of summer and, alternately, fish-skin clothing in the snow.

Nelson (1899:497–99) recorded the journey of Doll to the edge of the earth-plain, where the sky came down to the earth and walled in the light. There, far to the east, Doll saw a gut-skin cover fastened over a hole in the sky wall and bulging inward. Opening the hole, he looked inside and saw a world similar to earth. Doll then circled the earth-plain, passing and opening holes in the east, southeast, south, west, northwest, and north before returning to the center of the flat earth. This ritual circuit marked the origin of the winds. Doll's journey, as well as his words of propitiation to each of the cardinal points, are repeated at various stages during the annual ceremonial cycle, a reenactment of creation. Cecelia Foxie (May 30, 1993) from Kotlik

2. The layers observed when digging into the ground (as in archaeological excavations) demonstrate to many Yupiit today that the earth is getting thicker all the time. People also cite the need to use heavy equipment in the construction of village airstrips as proof that the earth is thickening. Conversely, in 1981 I listened to elders debate the merits and drawbacks of oil development on the Bering Sea coast. Several cited the danger of drilling equipment breaking through the earth's surface and doing irreparable damage.

described performing a comparable ritual circuit following her first menses. She faced each direction in turn, wet her fingers in her mouth, lifted them up, pulled the wind from that direction down to the bottom of her feet, and stomped on the ground. After she did this to all the winds, she removed her hood and resumed normal activities.

Lantis (1960:121) reported a Nunivak shaman's description of his circuit of the *qasgiq* to stop the winds, during which he put dry grass crosswise on the bench: "I had a big ice dipper full of grass. I went clockwise to south, west, north, northeast, and southeast. . . . The old man told me to pound in the corners of the kazigie as hard as I could. They said Nunivak was like this. One should pound to drive it down solidly into the earth." Lantis (1960:127) notes that the man did not offer the traditional explanation of stuffing the mouth of the wind with grass, although this probably was the basis of his action. Still today in western Alaska, women sometimes climb to a high point and perform a simple ceremony to produce good weather. Turning to each of the cardinal points in turn, they touch their two index fingers to their mouth, blow on the tips, and then turn their fingers outward and perform a tearing motion, moving them apart. By this act, they make holes in the sky, letting in the good weather.

The skyland could also be reached by moving upward through the holes in the heavens—the stars. People believed shamans regularly entered the skyland through the star holes to request that *pitarkat* (prey, literally "things to be caught") come to the earth below. A story told by Thomas Chikigak of Alakanuk (August 11, 1987) described a shaman's journey to the skyland in search of food for his people. Sighting a rabbit sitting on its haunches beside a star hole, the shaman pushed the animal down into the world below, thus insuring an abundant supply.

> In wintertime that shaman was going through a ceremony when he was in the process of getting animals to be used here on the earth.
> He had on snowshoes made by the Yup'ik people. He went flying. He was getting something to be used by the people, and he was on his way home.
> While he was going home somewhere in the sky he saw a rabbit. It was sitting by the edge of the hole. It was by the hole of the star. The rabbit was sitting still on its haunches ready to fall.
> The ground where the people were was visible under him. He was holding what he had gone to fetch. While he was traveling he wished to get that rabbit.
> He thought, "People from my home are in need of it because it is something to eat and its skin could be used as clothing."
> Because it was on his path, and it was near the edge of the hole, he kicked with his snowshoe and let it fall off the edge.
> He saw it fall, and he saw it hit the ground.
> When he got home and was in the *qasgiq*, he told of his journey. That was before I started going to the *qasgiq*.
> So he told of his journey while he was traveling up in the sky when he saw a

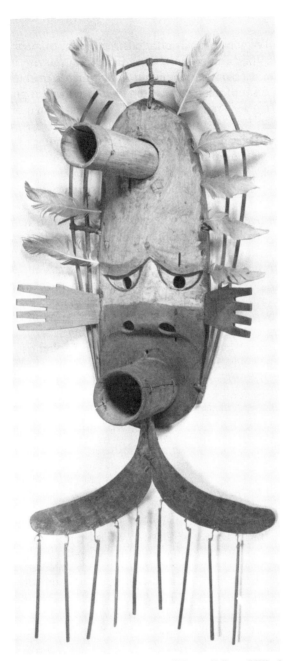

Kuskokwim mask representing "Tomanik," or "Wind Maker." The white tube is for winter and the black for summer. Notice how the mask turned on its head shows an opposing face. A. H. Twitchell, 1910; National Museum of the American Indian.

rabbit resting by the hole, having wished then to get it for the people back home in want of something to eat.

He wished it for the people, and he also had thought about his sons. He had nudged it with his snowshoes while it was sitting on its haunches by the hole.

In this way he had kicked with the snowshoes on his right foot letting it fall through the hole.

So, if he is not lying, during the coming spring, during the course of lengthening days, rabbits will be increasing in number.

Rabbits will be caught.

So he went through his sighting ceremony for a month/moon, and then there came another month. When the next month was just beginning, the number of the rabbits began to increase. Those who hunted began to see more and more rabbit tracks.

Just about the time of March rabbits could be seen. More and more came, and they were no longer scarce. There were rabbits then.[3]

In another story recorded by Nelson (1899:494–97), a shaman sitting on a hill had a vision in which the skyland came down upon him. He climbed through three successive star holes, each of which provided access to another level of reality. From this vantage point he looked through the star holes and viewed the earth, just as the sea mammals viewed activity in the human world by looking through the gut skylight of their underwater abode. The three globes hanging from the ceremonial Petugtaq wand collected by Nelson (1899:359) may refer to this three-tiered model of the universe. Other accounts describe four and five levels above the human world, each looking like our world but far away (Lantis 1946:197, 1960:121).[4]

Ellam yua, the person of the universe, watched the world from this celestial vantage point: "*Ellam yua . . .* I understand it to be one person. That was the person who watched all the people at that time" (Herman Neck, Kasigluk, June 1988 YN28:10). *Ellam yua* not only watched the world with boundless sight but, according to many accounts, observed transgressions and meted out punishment. This view of an ever-watchful universe motivated many small personal ritual acts in daily life, for example, the proscription against children taking their toys outside during winter lest *ella* see them and turn the weather stormy. To produce good weather, a person might turn a worm inside out, impale it on a stick, and place it on the open tundra. *Ella* would see it and bring out the sun to dry the worm. When a woman pulled down her pants to urinate on the open tundra, she risked shocking the weather into changing itself, for better or worse. *Ellam yua* possessed all the human senses—sight, taste, smell, hearing, and touch—and people alternately curtailed and accentuated their actions to influence it to advantage.

---

3. According to Camille Joseph (Alakanuk, August 9, 1987), this "ultimate ancestor" brought home other kinds of animals as well.

4. Northwest Siberian peoples conceived the cosmos as a series of five, seven, or nine vertically superimposed worlds (Serov 1988:242).

Just as *ellam yua* observed the human world, humans performed numerous acts, small and large, intended to influence *ella*. Coastal Yupiit practiced personal rituals each morning on rising where they exited the house, faced the direction of the day, and took three, four, or five breaths. Along the Kuskokwim, men routinely exited the *qasgiq* each morning and took a deep breath facing each of the four directions. Lantis (1947:35) reported that Nunivak men climbed to the top of the *qasgiq* and sang a little song saluting *ella* the first thing each morning.

As the star holes allowed access from earth to the skyland, lakes and water holes allowed *ellam yua* access to the human world. Nastasia Kassel (May 25, 1988 YN27:21–22) reported, "They say that big lake which is across from us is open all the way up to the heavens! This is the way they talked about it. People regard it with utmost reverence! And they kept it clean! That *nanvarpak* [big lake] across there is radiant because it is open to the heavens." On Nunivak people taught that sometimes a man traveling sees a board hanging down from the sky by two ropes. Like the girl returning from the dead who encountered a tree blocking her path, he must not try to run around it or jump over it but should crawl under it: "Then Lam-chuakh *[Ellam yua]* will take him up and give him power to get lots of seals" (Lantis 1960:116). Stories still told in western Alaska that refer to *nunam taqra* ("the land's vein," sometimes translated "the artery of the world") and *nunam yualua* ("the land's sinew or thread") may relate to comparable connecting links between levels of the universe.

Recent descriptions of *ellam yua* have a Christian ring, reminiscent of a heavenly father and almighty, all-seeing creator. Although *ella* is probably an ancient Yup'ik concept, the idea of a "person of the universe" may be more recent. Still, *ellam yua* differs in significant respects from its Christian counterpart. Rather than a deity in human form, *ellam yua* was a genderless, sentient force. *Ella* is a key concept in Yup'ik cosmology and epitomizes their transformational and interconnected view of the world. According to the context, *ella* can mean "outside," "weather," "sky," "universe," or "awareness."

Ella is not the only natural element referred to as personlike. According to oral tradition, the sun is a transformed woman who fled to the skyland followed by her brother, who became the moon and continues to pursue her (Nelson 1899:481–82; Lantis 1946:268).[5] To this day people metaphorically refer to them as persons. They describe an eclipse as *akerta nalauq* (the sun dies or withers) or *iraluq nalauq* (the moon dies or withers), using the verb

---

5. Variations of this tale are told all across the Arctic. Nelson Island oral tradition attributes the origin of the sun and the moon to the lust of one of five brothers for their younger sister. Although at first unaware of the identity of her lover, one night the sister marks him with soot from her lamp. The next day she confronts her brothers in the *qasgiq*, identifying the culprit by the mark of soot. Thereupon she flees from the *qasgiq* and up into the sky, followed by her brother, who comes dragging his pants and carrying his empty bowl. There she transforms into the sun and her brother becomes the moon.

base *nala-*, a term for the death of plants or animals. People say *akerta waniw' piqaarluni* ("after the sun rises [or catches game]") as the sun begins to come up and *akerta takuyartuq* ("the sun is looking back [over its shoulder]") in the evening when the sun gets bigger as it approaches the horizon. *Akerta aliimatengqertuq* ("the sun has mittens") describes the sun in wintertime when oval sun spots appear underneath it, *akerta aqumgaluni* ("the sun sits down") the winter solstice, *akerta asguruarluni* ("the sun has a parka ruff around it") when it is surrounded by rings; and *akertem ayarua* ("the sun's walking stick") designates a sun column caused by ice crystals in the air. A meteor is *agyam anaa* (star dung). In the summer the rain "wakes up" the fish, and winds push and pull birds and fish in their migrations. Of a warm, mild winter that "can't get cold," people will say *arnacaluq uksuurtuq* (literally "the female has become winter," using the term for female animal, rather than human female).

Not only was the earth encompassed by a canopy from above. Below the earth's thin surface resided the spirits of the dead, both animal and human, each in separate villages according to their social and biological affiliation. No single entrance to the underworld ("da'laxpax" very dark place [Lantis 1946:197]) existed. Shamans made their own path, and people could sink through the ground or enter through any hole or opening in the earth. Similar to the skyland's four or five levels, four or five "steps" separated the world of the living and the underworld land of the dead. The numbers four and five recur in ceremonial transformation and probably refer to both the five cardinal points on the earth-plain and the five steps required to move from one spatial domain to another.

The underworld land of the dead held no negative value nor the upper world a positive one in Yup'ik ideology. In contrast to the polar opposition between heaven and hell in the Christian schema, people did not state a preference for one over the other as a destination in the afterlife.

A Nunivak woman who was a shaman described seeing three levels on returning from her first journey to get seals for the people: "I found two trails when I went. I went under the sea on the right one, and came back on the left trail. When I returned toward my own village, I saw three villages, on three levels. I went to the middle village. . . . A woman shaman taught me what to do. But without being taught, I knew about the hole in the ice that was like an entrance-way and about the trails under the ice. When I went to the hole in the ice, there was no water under the ice. It was just like a world" (Lantis 1960:134). The shaman's reference to three levels recalls the three doors leading from the world of the *ircenrrat*, the middle of which leads back to the human world while the other two lead to disaster (see also Lantis 1960:116). Note also the three different positions in which seals observe oceangoing hunters (above the water, immersed in water, or on the water's surface) as well as the three different net positions observed by salmon traveling up river. Here, too, only the middle way was acceptable.

Yup'ik cosmology can be schematically depicted as successive circles, each one simultaneously closed and enclosing. This cosmological circle is a recurrent theme in both social and ceremonial activity and paraphernalia. As described elsewhere (Fienup-Riordan 1987), the circle-and-dot motif so common in Yup'ik iconography is designated *ellam iinga*, literally the "eye of the universe or awareness." The use of this decorative motif is associated with both spiritual vision and the creation of a pathway between the human and spirit worlds. The central dot accompanied by four outlying dots has been identified as a means of both depicting and effecting the five-step movement between the world of the living and the dead. The relationships described in the preceding pages also may be a part of what was represented. Although both the smoke hole and the ice hole were rectangular rather than round, this does not diminish their significance as spiritual eyes. One variant of the circle-and-dot motif is a circle with a small projection at each corner, within which was carved a dot surrounded by concentric circles. The reference to square or rectangular holes and the quadrangle functioning like a circle and dot may form a logical symbolic complex with this added sacred dimension.

In cross section, the spirit world can be seen to enclose the human world. The Yupiit annually enacted their ceremonial cycle in part to travel the distance between domains that daily life kept rigorously separated. The image of circling the center was more than a static idea, it was an activity. If successful, ritual circuits *ella maliggluku* ("following the universe," east to west) had the power to recreate the world anew. To perform this creative transformation, the normal relationships between humans and animals, men and women, and the human and spirit worlds were alternately exaggerated, reversed, and inverted.

CHAPTER 9

NAKACIUQ
The Bladder Festival

THE KNOWLEDGE THAT the eye of *ella* was watching and that human activity was visible to the spirit world controlled daily Yup'ik life. Comparable visibility of animals (their appearance, disappearance, and eventual reappearance) was a central problem during the annual cycle and one which Yup'ik ritual activity directly addressed. Ritualized movement in ceremonies reversed the rules and the rigorous separation between domains that daily life required. These ceremonies powerfully recreated the passages between worlds as well as the ability to see into, and in some measure control, them and evoke their presence in the future. The spirits of both the human and animal dead, which had disappeared during preceding seasons, were drawn back into view to be feasted and hosted and sent away again supplied for the coming year.

Both public and private ceremonies revolved around the appearance and disappearance of animals and the power of humans to control their periodicity. The Yup'ik people effected this control through a series of dramatic reversals of the culturally constituted relations of daily life—the relationship between humans and animals, male and female, land and sea, attraction and predation, naked and clothed, noise and silence, light and dark, restricted vision and powerful supernatural sight. The ceremonies turned inside out established oppositions and hierarchical relations. Ritual acts made fluid the boundaries between the human and spirit worlds and realized dramatic passages between them.

During spring, summer, and fall the Yup'ik Eskimos dispersed over the landscape, preoccupied with a variety of harvesting activities. After freeze-up they gathered in winter villages, where they enjoyed a "round of pleasure," which marked winter as the ceremonial season. They performed five major

ceremonies during this period, three of which focused on the creative reformation of the relationship between the human community and the spirit
world on which they relied. In these three ceremonies—the Bladder Festival,
the Feast for the Dead, and the masked dances known as Kelek—members
of the spirit world were invited into the human community, formally hosted,
and finally returned to their own domains. This ritual movement effectively
recreated the relationship between the human and spirit worlds and placed
each in the proper position to begin the year again.

All the major ceremonies were legends as well as rites. The ritual hosting
of spirit guests, who in the course of the ceremonies moved from their abodes
outside the human community to its ceremonial center and back again,
elicited their participation in the future by reenacting an original encounter
in the past. Both Lantis (1946:182) and Curtis (1930:56–57) described the
Bladder Festival on Nunivak Island as the reenactment of a *quliraq*, in which
spirits visited a couple and instructed them in the rites. This was also true of
segments of the Nelson Island Bladder Festival, the Great Feast for the
Dead, and Kelek.

THE BLADDER FESTIVAL AND RELATED CEREMONIES

The way that people do things
and the way of helping others,
and the way of creating friendship
the Bladder Festival is like an opening for those things to occur.

And through those events
the people being scattered
through that too they are gathered.
(Toksook Bay Elders, November 3, 1983 NI57)

The celebration of the Bladder Festival or Nakaciuq (from *nakacuk* bladder, literally "something done with bladders") marked the opening of the
winter ceremonial season. At the time of the winter solstice, when the sun
"sat down" on the horizon,[1] families inflated the bladders of seals killed that
year and brought them into the men's house. They believed the bladders
contained the animals' souls and treated them as honored guests during their
stay. They first hung the bladders above the entrance of the men's house, then
along the back wall. The bladders' position prior to being ceremonially
feasted and taken out through the gut skylight was comparable to the posi-

1. John Pingayak (1986:6) described how men tabulated the approach of the winter solstice
in the Chevak area: "In the middle of the day, every day the men would measure the height of
the sun. One of the men would extend their open hand toward the horizon of the sun. The
four fingers are put horizontally between the horizon and the sun. By closing one eye they
determine when the winter solstice starts. If the sun lands between the index and the middle
finger, this indicates winter solstice or the 'sitting of the sun.'"

Nelson (1899:279), on the other hand, placed the Bladder Festival in December, "the exact
date depending on the phase of the moon."

tion of honor occupied by the elders, who were nearing their time of departure from this world. Rather than a final exit, in both cases people viewed their position as but one step in the cyclical movement between birth and rebirth characteristic of both humans and animals.

Nakaciuq or *nakaciuryaraq* (the process of doing something with bladders) functioned primarily to reverse the separation of body and soul effected at the time of the seal's death and to insure the animal's rebirth in the coming harvest season. As described, a hunter worked to "draw" the seals through proper thought and deed. If he succeeded, he returned to the village with his catch and immediately gave it over to his wife or mother. The woman then greeted the seal by giving it fresh water. Some people said that if a man caught a seal, it was because it was coming for fresh water. If his wife neglected to supply the needs of her animal guest, it would not come again. In the Chevak area the hunter's wife might also make a small incision on the seal's forehead to "cut" the bond between body and soul and allow its soul to escape. After this, she was free to butcher the animal. Although she might cook the meat and blubber, she carefully preserved the seal's bladder as it was believed to contain the seal's *unguvii* (its life).

After butchering, the hunter's wife inflated the bladder and hung it to dry. Then she packed the inflated bladders out of sight in fish-skin sacks:

> At spring camp, after they throw away the bones, they *petuk* [tie up] the bladders.
>   They tie them at the ends. After they tie them, they pack them away as something precious into a big bag.
>   They made sacks for them from pink salmon skin, pike skin, burbot skin. Those were the materials they used. They made sacks out of those skins.
>   They put them in those sacks. Like that, while still inflated, they kept them so they could take care of them during the Bladder Festival. (Dennis Panruk, Chefornak December 17, 1987)

As winter solstice approached, the people performed a series of ceremonies that effectively reunited seal body and soul. As in many other parts of western Alaska, a number of discrete but closely related ceremonies preceded Nakaciuq on Nelson Island, including Qaariitaaq, Qengarpak, and Aaniq. Nakaciruaq (literally "pretend Bladder Festival") also sometimes followed the Bladder Festival.

TIMING

The timing of the Bladder Festival varied slightly from place to place and from year to year. Nelson (1899:379, 392) wrote that the Bladder Festival at St. Michael occurred between December 10 and 20. Preliminary ceremonies began in mid-November as people gathered in the winter village. The people of Andreafski held their Bladder Festival in January. Lantis (1946:182) said that it could be held in either November or December on Nunivak, Hawkes (1914:26) placed it in December, and Curtis (1930:56) in January. In all cases people celebrated the Bladder Festival during the shortest days of winter, when there was little or no hunting.

Accounts vary substantially in both the ideal length of time the Nelson Island Bladder Festival required as well as the amount of time it actually took. Billy Lincoln described a fifteen-day ceremony starting in early December, while more general accounts report a five- to ten-day feast. According to Billy Lincoln, during the first four days and nights they held Qaariitaaq. On the fifth day they had Qengarpak (sometimes referred to as the last day of Qaariitaaq), usually followed by Aaniq on the fifth night. The next day they gathered wild celery and that night inflated the bladders in the *qasgiq*. For the next five days the bladders remained in the *qasgiq*, except when the men were going to bathe and moved the bladders to the porch. On the fifth day following their entrance into the men's house, men moved the bladders to the rear wall, where they remained for a final five-day period before being taken out and returned through the ice. The division of Nakaciuq proper into two five-day periods probably relates to the five steps leading to and from the land of the dead. Curtis (1930:56) connects the five days of the Nunivak Bladder Festival with the five outstretched fingers of a supernatural hand that appeared above the entrance hole and ordered people to celebrate the feast.

PRELIMINARY ACTIVITIES

Soon after the people living on and around Nelson Island had gathered in winter villages, they began a series of acts ritually important to the Bladder Festival finale. First the men carefully cleaned the *qasgiq*, paying special attention to the fire pit in which members of the spirit world would await the festivities. Then they collected the bladders of sea mammals taken before freeze-up. The people would not be getting any more seals until the following spring, and the women brought the bladders to their owners in the *qasgiq*. They also brought along bladders of mice, muskrats, and other small mammals killed by young boys, accompanied by big bowls of *akutaq*.

After the bladders had been presented, they were deflated and combined with the bladders of seals caught the previous spring. The men then packed the bladders away without any paraphernalia:

In the fall, when the Bladder Festival is just beginning, first they start by deflating the bladders.[2]

In the fall, from the ones they caught with harpoons, the young bearded seals' bladders, when they do not have seals to go after in the winter, they deflate those.

They bring them. The women bring the bladders along with a bowl into the *qasgiq*, and they give it to whoever the bladders belong to.

Then, when they are done eating, the men with bladders grouped together, the ones with bladders, the ones trying to make a life, are grouped together,

2. Butzin (Fienup-Riordan 1992:41) designates "Itlsiarak" (Elciyaraq, process of deflating [the bladders]) as a distinct ceremony along the Kuskokwim.

putting together the bladders of related ones. But only one person is in charge
of them, one of the teenagers is in charge of them.

They deflate them. All the people in the *qasgiq* participate in the deflating of
the bladders.

Then after deflating them they bring them out [of the *qasgiq*]. (Billy Lincoln, Toksook Bay, July 10, 1985 NI77A:1)

On Nunivak men wrapped deflated bladders in sealskin and placed them
on top of the women's houses. Women wearing seal-gut parkas would then
gather up the bladders and return them to their husbands in the men's house
(Lantis 1946:183). Both the wrapping of the bladders as well as the women's
protective attire probably related to the maintenance of boundaries between
the spiritually potent bladders and their human handlers. Nelson Island
women also wore seal-gut parkas while handling the bladders.

On Nelson Island inflated bladders were moved from the women's house
to the men's house, where the men deflated them and took them out again.
On Nunivak deflated bladders moved from the men's house to the women's
house and back again. In both cases the bladders that the women had inflated
were deflated by the men as they traveled the distance between private,
invisible village periphery to public, visible village center.

In the *qasgiq* the men began composing new songs prior to the Bladder
Festival. According to Billy Lincoln (July 10, 1985 NI77A:2), "When they
are going to have Qaariitaaq, in the evening they turn off the lamps and sing
songs. Whoever wanted to would make a song but only a slow song. He
himself sings it. Then when they have no more songs they quit and have
Qaariitaaq." The people performed these same songs at other ceremonies,
and they would not compose new songs until the next Bladder Festival
(Koranda 1968:30).

Perhaps men composed these songs in the dark to hide them from the
spirits whom they would honor later in the ceremony. Their future power to
"draw" the spirits derived in part from the secrecy of their composition. Just
as the gut garments protected the women when they handled the bladders, so
the lack of light and noise protected the men from the spirits about whom
they thought and sang. Gut skin, silence, and invisibility established a protective boundary that the noisy, naked participants of Qaariitaaq and the
brightly lit *qasgiq* during the Bladder Festival proper would subsequently
transcend.

QAARIITAAQ

Then after so many days, they had Qaariitaaq.

That is the beginning of the Bladder Festival.

For four nights they had Qaariitaaq; the young boys go visiting, going into
houses holding the bowls.

The ones receiving them, those in the houses, had small amounts of food
they kept ready to give out. They pass out food to those who enter.

They visit all the houses. That is how they did it. (Billy Lincoln, July 10, 1985 NI77A:3)

On Nelson Island the ceremony Qaariitaaq preceded the Bladder Festival proper. The literature refers to it variously as Tu-tu'-úk or "going around" (the first night of the Ai-ya'-g'ûk, or Asking Festival) (Nelson 1899:359; Hawkes 1914:22–23; Ray 1966:87) and as Itertaaq (going in and out of houses) (Morrow 1984:118). Hawkes describes the event as "purely social in character." The women worked in their houses sewing new clothing during the four days of Qaariitaaq while their husbands in the men's house carved new wooden bowls for each family member. As they worked, they ideally focused their minds on the spirits of the animals, both the seals they hunted and the animals that acted as their helpers in the hunt.

The people fasted during daylight, and the space between the houses was deserted. Women did not serve their husbands in the men's house, and men did not visit their wives in their homes. In the evening, however, vigorous interaction between the two domains prevailed. In the men's house the men painted the bodies of the village boys. After dark the group of painted children took their bowls and went to the edge of the village, where they sang a song and howled like dogs. The men then led the boys (and immature girls in some accounts) sunlike *ella maliggluku* ("following the universe") around the village, entering each woman's house in turn. Every house was brightly lit, and the hostesses wore their best. The women also fumigated their houses with the smoke of wild celery or *ayut* (Labrador tea).

A great deal of commotion, including howling, grunting, and stamping feet, accompanied the children's entry into the house. John Kilbuck reported that along the Kuskokwim three times in succession the boys shut their mouths tight and made a murmuring sound, which rose in intensity until it exploded into a yell (Fienup-Riordan 1991:344). Contemporary elders remember making this "empaa" sound, putting their lips together and pushing the air out with force. Perhaps this was associated with the "powerful breath" later used to inflate the bladders.

At each entranceway the men and boys backed through the entrance hole and circled the room in a sunlike direction. They held out their bowls, and the women first gave them fresh water followed by choice food, including *anlleret* (cottongrass tubers known as "mouse nuts"), *iitaq* (cottongrass stems), *piirrarrluk* (small dried fish), bite-sized pieces of walrus skin, and *akutaq*. The bowls that the women "fed" each night received food for the last time, as during the day the men were busy carving their replacements. Some of what the boys received they gobbled on the spot, carrying the remainder back to the men's house where the men distributed it. At a Qaariitaaq witnessed by Edmonds at St. Michael, the men returned to the *qasgiq* and held the bowls upward to each of the four corners and the center as an invocation to the elements (Ray 1966:89). This action following the men's ritual circuit dramatically recalls the image of the universe as a four-cornered circle or dome.

Qaariitaaq reversed the normal course of daily events in a number of ways. Instead of quiet, carefully covered women entering the communal men's house headfirst to take food to their men during the day, noisy, naked men and boys entered the individual sod houses backwards to take food from the women at night (Oldham 1987). Through this ritual circuit, the children (by some accounts representing members of the spirit world, specifically the shades of the dead) opened the community to the seal spirits. Butzin reports that the children were received in the houses "with kindest hospitality for these masqueraders represented their dead" (Fienup-Riordan 1992:41). Subsequent to Qaariitaaq, the people invited the seals into the human world to participate in the Bladder Festival. During the four days of Qaariitaaq the participants perhaps represented the approaching spirits whom they would ultimately embody on the fifth night.

Numerous tales demonstrate the ways in which painting had the power to create and transform the recipient of the designs. One well-known story concerns the original painting/designing of the animals by Raven and Loon when the earth was new. Qaariitaaq entailed the annual redesigning of clothing and utensils by women and men as well as the bestowal of totemic designs on the bodies of their joint production—their children. In Hawkes's (1914:23) description of the Asking Feast, two boys named Raven and Hawk painted marks on the participants' bodies. As the men painted the children on Nelson Island, perhaps they reenacted an original act of creation.

During Qaariitaaq, two men worked together to paint the faces of the village children, including the toddlers. Like Raven and Loon, they employed a combination of charcoal *(kangipluk)* and white clay *(urasquq)*. After the clay had dried on the children's bodies, the men drew figures on their bodies in charcoal and lamp soot. Originally the entire body of each participant may have been painted, as were the bodies of the first animals. After the men had decorated the children, the two men led the children around the village.

The lamp is strongly associated with the soul in Eskimo oral tradition (see Nelson 1899:464–65), and painting the children with lamp soot both protected and transformed them. One story often told in association with Qaariitaaq recounts the fate of a group of unpainted children who broke through the earth's surface and lost their way underground (Morrow 1984:122). The people in the houses could hear them crying in the underground passage but could do nothing to help them emerge. The children gradually wandered away from underneath the village. Days later some of them returned home through a door in the cliff below Umkumiut. They did this by closing their eyes and taking five steps necessary to reenter the human world (see also Pingayak 1986:7).[3]

3. Compare the Siberian Yup'ik practice of painting the faces of sick people with black

Men cautioned the children not to proceed in haste during their house-to-house circuit, even if they fell behind, lest the ground vanish beneath them and they become *aciirutellret*, literally "those that go underneath." They were advised to walk backward if they found themselves in an unfamiliar house, or in the presence of a ghost, to avoid going underground. The women kept their houses well lit during the processional lest the children miss them and go underground instead. Finally parents told their children not to remove the paint from their faces after the ceremony, as the spirit Qaariitaaq would come and lick off the paint while they slept. The gradual disappearance of the designs in the night constituted proof that the spirit had indeed been present.

The behavior as well as the appearance of the painted children supports the view of them as ancestral spirits incarnate. People believed that members of the spirit world were impervious to cold and often appeared surrounded by a chilly vapor. The painted men and boys also could be naked in freezing weather without harm, proof of the transforming power of the rite. Edmonds (Ray 1966:87) remarked that no one with clothing was allowed outside the houses during Qaariitaaq, or the comparable body parts of the Qaariitaaq participants would freeze.

After the men decorated the children on four successive nights, on the fourth day of the ceremony the men painted their totemic marks on their newly made bowls. The designs applied to the bowls during Qaariitaaq often depicted a particular animal, bird, or fish with whom the man maintained a special relationship, perhaps the bird or animal form in which the seals perceived the hunter. On Nelson Island a man inherited his designs from his father, a woman her special clothing designs from her mother. In both cases an individual's designs usually related to a special instance of interaction between a particular ancestor and a particular animal or spirit.

These individual designs were not identical to the designs painted on the bodies of either the children or the bladders during the ceremony. Yet like the painting of the children, decorating the bowls and sewing individual designs into newly made clothing served to identify the objects of human production (whether child, bowl, or hunting parka) with the specific totem of their human creators at the same time they imbued them with the power of the animal represented. Once completed, the men treated their finished bowls to a sweat bath to set the designs, after which they sent their bowls home to their wives.

As the children had to be ritually marked before they could receive gifts of food during Qaariitaaq, so the bowls had to be painted before they could be filled. A child was equivalent to a vessel that must never be sent away empty: "They consider a child's hands tiny, and they were to be given a little . . . towards the satisfaction of their hunger" (Toksook Bay Elders, November 5,

---

graphite to deceive the black-faced spirits of sickness into believing that the sick man was not a human whose soul could be stolen but another spirit (Serov 1988:245).

Mask representing Qaariitaaq as an androgynous person, with a downturned mouth under its beard. Napaskiak, A. H. Twitchell, 1910; National Museum of the American Indian.

1983 NI58). Children and bowls were literally "designed" by men and subsequently filled by women.

QENGARPAK

On the fifth day following the beginning of Qaariitaaq on Nelson Island, the people celebrated Qengarpak (from *qengaq* nose, plus *-pak* big; "Proboscis Festival"). Painted children had ritually prepared the human community during the four previous evenings for entry by members of the spirit world. Their daily circuit, repeated for four nights, perhaps represented the spirits' gradual approach or, alternately, the movement of the human participants toward their spirit counterparts. On the fifth day (corresponding to the five steps separating the human and spirit worlds), the men and boys perhaps came to fully embody the spirits that they had merely represented on the previous nights. The men again painted their faces with a combination of white clay, lamp soot, and the char from burned wood. Participants also wore small wooden face masks in the shape of noses, pretend eyes, and special painted marks around their mouths, and further disguised themselves by dressing in other peoples' clothing (Mather 1985). Nelson Islanders said that these nose masks represented animal spirits (see also Eskimo Heritage Project 1985):

> First, they had Qaariitaaq for four days and nights and on the fifth day they had a feast.
> They used wooden noses. . . . They smeared their faces with soot making them pretend to be something. And some had on big wooden noses. . . .
> So looking like that, they went from house to house, permitting themselves to be given a piece of food.
> So, they would laugh at us, when we went in with painted faces.
> The people in the *qasgiq* would be continually singing while they were gone. (Billy Lincoln, July 10, 1985 NI77A:4)

We know little about the performance of Qengarpak other than that it marked the transition between the four ritual circuits of Qaariitaaq and the arrival of the spirits on the fifth night: "On the fifth day they used big noses, and the fifth night they had Aaniq" (Billy Lincoln, July 10, 1985 NI77A:3).

AANIQ

The ceremony Aaniq (literally "to provide a mother [for someone]") was held directly after Qaariitaaq and Qengarpak, and it introduced the Bladder Festival proper. During Aaniq two men, dressed in gut-skin parkas and referred to as "mothers" (*aanak* dual), led a group of boys termed their "dogs" on a ritual circuit of the village. The men returned the bowls used during the previous year to the houses. At the same time, they collected the newly made bowls filled with *akutaq* from the women, a dramatic reversal of the usual pattern of women bringing cooked meat to their men in the men's house.

This first feeding of the bowls and their presentation to the two *aanak* was said to have originated with the boy who went to live with the seals. On his return the boy taught the people the importance of performing a ritual "removal motion" with their hand after eating from a bowl to insure that the container not stick to their face and block their vision. At the same time he instructed them in the care of newly made bowls, which were likewise endowed with a spiritual essence that must be generously hosted so that they would willingly give up their contents during the year to come.

The men carefully prepared the two "mothers" in the *qasgiq* before they visited the houses. According to Frances Usugan of Toksook Bay (July 6, 1985 NI65:1), "Before the *aanak* came to the men's house, a grass mat was placed near the doorway, along with a bowl of food that they most preferred. A *qikuq* [lamp] would also be lit in front of where the two *aanak* would sit. When they came in they would sit down facing each other. Then they would give them their bowls."

The two *aanak* were accompanied on their ritual circuit by a group of boys (and sometimes girls) of all ages deemed their "dogs":

> The two men prepared for Aaniq in the *qasgiq*. They had boys with them considered as their dogs. When the time came for them to go out, they donned gut rain parkas. So they went to the houses.
>
> The one going before the other [the leader] walked backwards. That person sang that particular song used at that time. [Aaniq] had its own song. So the one going before the other sang while shaking the rain parka. He started off the song with "Yaa! Yaa!" and he kept mentioning "*Aani*" [his mother].
>
> When the song finished, the leader went through the tunnel entrance. And when he emerged, he sat on the edge facing the door. He sat there away from the people, his legs dangling in the doorway.
>
> When he assumed that position, the people in that house gave him a bowl filled with food. They told him that that food was for a particular man who is at the *qasgiq*, and they named him.
>
> That was the way each wife sent food to her husband who was at the *qasgiq*. They *aaniurluki* [mother] their husbands.
>
> As they took those bowls out of the house, children grabbed some of the food in the bowls. They tried to grab for delicious food and eat. (Billy Lincoln, July 10, 1985 NI77A:5–6)

During Aaniq the "dogs" were said to seize and eat the food, in part to insure that it would be available in the future. Compare this to the story of the shaman who dramatically "ate" a baby to produce a new one (Frances Usugan, November 5, 1983 NI58). The dogs' activity, in fact their very presence, may also relate to the village of the dogs, which by some accounts was the first place one arrived at following the five steps into the underworld (Mather 1985). These dog-shades, the Yup'ik counterpart to Cerberus, were particularly ferocious and tore at and tormented those persons who had treated them unkindly in life. The ritual feeding of children pretending to be dogs may have been an attempt to placate these dog-spirits.

Theresa Moses (August 1987 NI95A:6) added detail to the reception and behavior of the "mothers" and their "dogs" (including herself) in the sod houses. She described the two *aanak* as men who had become parents and had reached their prime.

> Before the two males came into the house they got a mat ready for them inside and placed it right by the door. They spread the mats carefully, and they got two bowls ready for them.
>
> And when those two males entered they were two fathers wearing clothes not belonging to them. They were regally dressed in the clothes of young men having a lot of designs and ornaments.
>
> And when they came in, as soon as they sat by the door they were each given a bowl. Then they [the *aanak*] said, "Our dogs keep trying to eat our food."
>
> Those two had helpers who were waiting outside the door. And when they went out following them we [the children or "dogs"] proceeded rolling on the floor.
>
> We started off rolling. And when we got to the end of it and when it ended probably the day after we *tarvarluta* [fumigated ourselves, letting the smoke go under our clothing] with wild celery and other plants.
>
> It is said that they cleansed themselves taking away any of their sickness.

By some accounts a third man, designated *cauyarturalria* (from *cauyaq* drum) the "drummer of the *aanak*," followed the two male "mothers," beating a drum and singing unintelligible songs. Although both men were considered "mothers," one pretended to be a woman and the other a man, and the drummer was considered their child. When the women were presenting bowls of food to the *aanak*, but before the "dogs" began to grab at them, they fed this "child." Without looking, the *aanak* threw a pinch of the contents of each bowl over their shoulders toward their "child's" mouth:

> Outside or in the porch were their dogs who were actually young boys.
>
> Near the door in the porch was also a singer. The singer would sing, "I am doing *aaniq*, give to me."
>
> The two would then take a piece of food from their bowls and toss it over their shoulders out to the porch. (Frances Usugan, July 6, 1985 NI65:2)

The *aanak* tried to hit the open mouth of the child, who would then swallow the morsel. If the snow or food thrown at the child's mouth disappeared without hitting it, it meant that someone would die in that particular household. If they hit the child's open mouth, it meant successful hunting during the coming year. Butzin reported a similar practice along the Kuskokwim (Fienup-Riordan 1992:42).

This designation of the husband and wife dyad as "mothers" supports the view that in Aaniq the physical reproductive capacity of women was taken over, reversed, and in some way transformed by the men into cosmological reproduction. Likewise the normal, nurturing parental role was inverted by the backward feeding of their "child" and the unruly and highly inappropriate behavior of the children. Men understood the mischievousness of the boys in the context of Aaniq and did not scold them.

The final stage of Aaniq, the presentation of the bowls of food in the men's house, was designated *nalugyaraq* (literally "pulling up"), the same term used to describe the act of putting the bladders down under the ice:

> And so they take the food to the porch of the *qasgiq*. Men inside were singing songs. Some of the bowls did not contain much due to people taking from it. And the good ones are empty.
>
> When the other person takes the bowl into the *qasgiq* he would give it a shove when he places it on the floor saying, "This is so-and-so's Aaniq offering."
>
> And if the bowl is empty, he would say, "Whose *Aaniuteq* is this? The dogs have eaten it all!" They said this when most of the contents of the bowl were gone. (Billy Lincoln, July 10, 1985 NI77A:6–7)

When the two *aanak* presented the food bowls in the *qasgiq*, they repeated the identification of the bowls with their owners that had taken place in the women's house. According to Curtis (1930:60), also on this night the spirits of the men who had originated the family symbols that marked the bowls were present in the *qasgiq*. Perhaps the gift-giver's name had to be stated so that these spirits could identify and claim the gifts intended for their use. The *aanak* also spilled fresh water and dropped crumbs of food onto the floor of the *qasgiq*, another indication that the dead were present among them.

This dramatic reversal of male and female roles marked the transition from the "inward" movement of Qaariitaaq, in which humans impersonating and/or animated by spirits cleared the path between the village and the spirit world, and the outward thrust of the Bladder Festival, which ended by sending the spirits of the seals back to their underwater home (see also Oldham 1987). Men made new dishes during Qaariitaaq that would be fully initiated during the Bladder Festival. At Aaniq the women filled them for the first time, and the two *aanak* subsequently took them to feed the men in the *qasgiq*. In Qaariitaaq, old empty bowls had been brought from the *qasgiq* to the houses, where women filled them and gave them to unrecognizable men and boys disguised as spirits. In contrast, during Aaniq the men brought new full bowls from the houses and presented them in the *qasgiq* in the name of specific men.

The five days of Qaariitaaq and Qengarpak followed by the feeding of unruly and ferocious "dogs," which constituted a key feature of Aaniq, may have signified the gradual descent and arrival of the participants into the land of the dead. Such a reading of the ceremonial sequence would explain the increasing need to disguise Qaariitaaq participants as they completed their passage between worlds. The feeding of the dogs simultaneously constituted the end of Qaariitaaq and the opening of the Bladder Festival proper. Perhaps before the path could be cleared for the *yuit* of the seals to enter the human world, the spirits of the ancestors also had to be invoked.

Along the Kuskokwim, Butzin described the final acts of Qaariitaaq:

> On the fifth day there was to be no cutting or chopping of anything before sunrise. At sunrise the pater familias took two stones and placed one on top of

the other, then he lifted the other one up and down as if to strike counting, one, two, three, four, and five, now retaining the stone aloft and moving in a circular motion as if painting the interior of the igloo and the air thereof. This was to make everything therein as enduring as stone. Then he returned the stone to the mate and imitated a chopping and cutting over it. Now all work could go on again. The karetak [Qaariitaaq] was over. Should anyone break the taboo of this last morning he was hated. (Fienup-Riordan 1992:42)

Lantis (1960:7, 22) noted that before the beginning of the Bladder Festival proper on Nunivak a specially clean man stood up in the *qasgiq*, took a rock into each corner, and motioned as if to touch the corner with it. Then he repeated his circuit, dropping the stone on the floor in each corner and the center as hard as he could. This action with the stone "nailed the earth down, kept it in place," and "was a positive ritual act, to keep things right with Nunivak." Such circular motions, forming an invisible boundary around a person or object, were ubiquitous in Yup'ik ritual activity, simultaneously creating a boundary against evil influences and a symbolic passage between levels of reality. Note that in Butzin's account the action occurred on the fifth day and was repeated five times, corresponding to the five steps separating the world of the living from the world of the dead.

The five steps might also have functioned to take the participants to the edge of the world, where it was believed everything appeared in reverse. At the very least, the human community dramatically transformed itself into the antithesis of daily life. Such an interpretation is supported by the fact that Aaniq was an occasion that virtually turned the relations of the everyday world on their head—men walked backward, entered houses back first, threw food over their shoulders, and came to the women's house to be fed rather than allowing the women to serve them in the *qasgiq*. Moreover, during Aaniq men were designated "mothers," children acted unruly, private personal names were said out loud, old men dressed as young men, and children were served before their elders.

THE GATHERING OF WILD CELERY

On Nelson Island the Bladder Festival proper began the morning following the ritual reversals of Aaniq, when two young men were sent to the tundra in search of wild celery *(ikiituut)*.[4] The youths were fed fat-rich food to insure an equally rich harvest the next year. Villagers then spread the skin of a young bearded seal *(amirkaq)* in the middle of the *qasgiq*. The young men rolled on top of the skin in unison four times, stood up, and clothed them-

4. Hooper Bay and Chevak specified five runners (Pingayak 1986; Hawkes 1914:27). According to Lantis (1946:184), although Nunivak Islanders formally required five runners, all young men actually participated. Koranda (1966:19) reports that on the evening before the men went out for the plants, they sang a "wild parsnip song" while five young men held their arms high above their heads and performed an exhausting dance.

selves in gut parkas and mittens. The celery gatherers on Nunivak Island also wore masks bearing totemic marks (Lantis 1946:184).

The young men then circled the village *ella maliggluku*, "following the universe," before departing for the tundra. This circling occurred repeatedly during the Bladder Festival, always with the connotation of clearing a path between the spirit world and the human community at the same time a ritual boundary was reaffirmed:

> The next day after Aaniq they prepared two young men. They sat at the far end of the *qasgiq* all ready to get leaves of wild celery out from the wilderness.
> And then the next day when they woke up, they went out and departed taking along small sleds using braided grass as tarps.
> When they came back, their sled would be inundated with celery plants. (Billy Lincoln, July 10, 1985 NI77A:7)

To show their respect, the men left small bits of food at the plant's base each time they picked a stalk of wild celery. On their return they lowered their harvest through the *qasgiq* smoke hole. According to Billy Lincoln (July 10, 1985 NI77A:4), "They bring those wild celeries to the *qasgiq*. They place them over the doorway, making a bed for them, spreading them out. They take a sweat bath for them to dry them."

Participants in the Bladder Festival treated the wild celery plants as sentient in a number of ways. Men ritually fed the celeries' spirits when they gathered the plant. When they brought the celery stalks into the *qasgiq*, they carefully placed them on the platform over the door. Hospitality required that the men give sweat baths in their honor: "For [the wild celery] the men *maqi*." Moreover, when the men first brought the celery plants into the men's house, they placed them on the platform over the door. Later, the men attached celery stalks to a stake placed by the fire pit and connected them to the bladders before removing them from the *qasgiq*. Thus, the stalks of wild celery gradually moved closer and closer to the bladders until, near the end, they were attached to them.

Oswalt (1957:31) reported that along the Kuskokwim, people believed the roots of wild celery "represent each man's partner from the underworld and appear to represent spirits of the dead." If so, the Nelson Island ceremonial sequence may have enacted a relationship between the ancestral spirits and the *yuit* of the seals. Just as the *yuit* of the seals were drawn to and hosted by human hunters, so were the human ancestral spirits who also received gifts later in the ceremony. Although nowhere explicitly stated, it is possible that the opening of the boundary between the human and spirit worlds accomplished during Qaariitaaq, and culminating in the feeding of the "dogs" during Aaniq, allowed the ancestral spirits to enter the human world, where they came to reside in the wild celery. Bringing the celery plants out of the wilderness into the human community enabled them to participate in the Bladder Festival.

INGULAQ

Following the gathering of wild celery, the bladders were carefully covered with a skin or something woven, such as an *issran* (loose-weave grass basket), and returned to the men's house. There men put them in water to soak and soften before inflating them. They brought in all the seal bladders, including those of adult and young bearded seals, spotted seals, and hair seals. There the bladders were housed for ten days, during which time the people feasted and entertained them as honored guests. Tim Agartak (Nightmute, June 1987 NI98:7) noted that people feared walrus bladders and so did not include them.

Residents celebrated the bladders' entry into the men's house with a feast and a special variety of dancing known as *ingulaq*. According to Theresa Moses (October 26, 1987 NI99:1), the slow, stylized motions of the dance imitated the mating dance of loons: "They say that when the loons are going to dance, they fly in circles, and when they land on the water, they sing to themselves and dance. . . . They say that every living thing dances. . . . Those loons dance *ingulaq* dances. Some people dance according to how they have watched loons dance. They move their arms like wings. They dance just the way the loons danced. And some people dance by pinching their hems."

People also sometimes performed *ingulaq* as a separate ceremony:

Sometime around wintertime in the fall time they *ingulaq*, and they used to bring in food also. . . . In the fall when it first ices up, they have that event.

They fill [bowls] with all kinds of food, and they bring them in. Then they dance slow dances holding on to the hems of their *qaspeq*. They *ingulaq*. They dance.

And pretty soon they had Qaariitaaq, Aaniq, Nakaciuq. (Theresa Moses, August 1987 NI95A:6)

Ingulaq sometimes was held as a separate event in the late summer or early fall to celebrate the building or refurbishing of a *qasgiq*.[5] Given the importance of the *qasgiq* as the locus of spiritual rebirth, it is not surprising that its maintenance required such elaborate display and was necessary to open the ceremonial season. According to Eddie Alexie of Togiak (March 10, 1988), "When the blackberries and salmonberries ripen, they have *ingulaq*. So at that time, they have *ingulaq* around here also. I have seen that done. So they have *ingulaq* when the time comes. They dance. They bring salmonberries into the *qasgiq*. Women who can, they *ingulaq*. They make them dance taking turns."[6]

The performance of *ingulaq* dances by the women during Nakaciuq

5. See Brentina Chanar (Toksook Bay, June 16, 1989) for the *ingulaq* song *"Angualnguunga"* ("I'm Tired of Rowing").

6. Moravian missionary John Kilbuck referred to *ingulaq* along the Kuskokwim as a "berry festival" (Fienup-Riordan 1991:66–67). Butzin described *ingulaq* as "a call dance" in preparation for which boys caught songbirds and ptarmigan, removing their insides but leaving the skins intact: "These were stretched and shaped with sticks. They were then taken into the kashige together with the akutak (native ice cream) and small gifts" (Fienup-Riordan 1992:41).

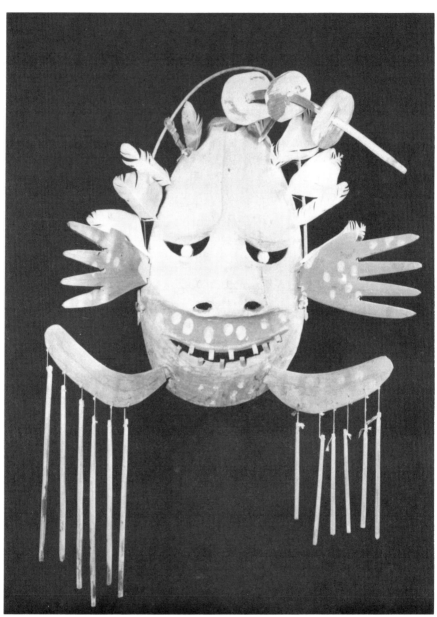

Wooden mask representing "Walaunuk," or bubbles as they rise through the water. Bubbles were of consequence because they related to the spiritually potent breath of both humans and animals as well as the bubbles expelled from the deflated bladders at the close of the Bladder Festival. A. H. Twitchell, 1910; National Museum of the American Indian.

accompanied the bladders' entry into the *qasgiq*. The men subsequently inflated them, filling them with their breath *(anerneq)*, a spiritually charged aspect of the human person. Thus, as Oosten notes (1990:8), the hunter adds a crucial element in the seals' regeneration. Billy Lincoln (April 1985 NI83:4) recalled:

> That night [after gathering wild celery] they had *ingulaq*. The women wore rain parkas and brought in the bladders. The [hunter] who would take care of [the bladders] received them. They were in an *issran* [grass bag].
> And then those women *ingulaq*, sometimes three or two of them. They *ingulaq* with slow songs. And they also included food or *akutaq* with those bladders.
> That night when they were having *ingulaq*, they inflated the bladders.
> The bladders were inflated by each individual man who had caught the game except for the one who had not been married.
> After they were inflated, they were hung up on the rafters separately according to one's catch.

On Nelson Island the performance of *ingulaq* by a young woman on this occasion constituted the announcement of her marriage. The young bride appeared with lowered eyes and bedecked in the furs and finery procured for her by her newly acquired mate. Only men who had been married could fill the bladders with their breath and take care of them during the ceremony. This formal announcement of the renewed potential for human procreation is particularly meaningful given the Bladder Festival's focus on the reproduction of animals during the year to come. The marriage dance performed on this occasion by women followed by the inflation of the bladders by married men provided a strong image of the complementarity between the reproduction of both human and nonhuman persons.

ATTENTION TO THE BLADDERS IN THE *QASGIQ*

The community strictly enforced a number of rules while the bladders hung in the *qasgiq*. For example, the men's house could never be without people and the lamp must be constantly lit or the bladders might become offended and return to their home, taking the village with them. Each in his accustomed seat in the *qasgiq*, the men would sing to the spirits, accompanied by drumming. This quiet chanting continued to hold the reluctant spirits. According to Billy Lincoln (April 1986 NI83:4), "While the bladders are hanging in the *qasgiq*, they keep singing. One of the men keeps singing old songs including songs that were sung during the time of warfare. They did that for five days."

Drumming and singing were important activities during the entire ceremonial season. The constant singing performed during the Bladder Festival served to "draw" or "wake up with noise" the spirit participants in the event. At this point in the ceremony people "brought into the light" the new songs composed in the dark prior to Qaariitaaq, along with older traditional songs to summon the spirit-guests. Many traditional tales recall the power of singing and drumming to effect the action or transformation of a person or spirit. Billy Lincoln (July 10, 1985 NI77) told the story of a shaman who chanted in the *qasgiq,* sending his *tuunraq* (spirit helper) to battle on his behalf against a rival shaman. Frances Usugan recalled the story of a spurned wife who returned to her faithless husband and sang him a song describing the sad events his neglect had produced. As she sang, she placed a bowl on the floor and twirled it, and her husband and his entire village spun round and round and were swept away. Likewise, during the opening days of the Bladder Festival people believed the men's constant singing in the lighted *qasgiq* commanded the attention of the spirits of the animals.

While constant singing drew the seals, loud noises were believed to scare them. Lantis (1946:308) recorded a Nunivak story in which a man making a new dish accidentally made a loud noise: "A little seal appeared from the entrance and the men involuntarily in a kind of sleepwalking got down from the platforms and went out and down toward the hole in the ice. The man who made the noise closed the entrance, and no more went out. Men lay dead all the way from the kazigi to the ice."

A variation of this story is told in the Chevak area. A small ringed seal called an *ikuyguuq* hops from the ocean to the *qasgiq* and back to the sea, followed by all the people in the *qasgiq.*

> The length of their lives are determined where the people died. Those who are going to live a short life would die before they reach the doorway, while others would die along the way to the ocean. Those that were going to live a long life crawl on their backs, the elbows making the body move across the snow covered ground until they dive into the freezing waters of the Arctic. . . .
>
> Ikuyguuq happens during the bladder festival celebrations [as well as at other times]. The walrus bladders are the most sensitive of all the bladders. They get easily startled when people make sudden noises during the bladder festival celebrations. People often blame the walrus bladders for being responsible for bringing the Ikuyguuq to the people. When the walrus bladders are displeased with the people who treated them disrespectfully and startled them during the Bladder festival celebrations. (Pingayak 1986:16–17)

John Pingayak (1986:18) also related how the *ikuyguuq* approached the village of Qissunaq when the man who was left to guard the bladders fell asleep: "During the time the small seal was on its way to the *qaygiq,* the seal bladders were trying to get away. The guard had fallen asleep and when he woke up, the bladders were swaying back and forth. The lamp light went out and noises of all kinds of animals could be heard. The man summoned all the men in the other *qaygiq* and they tried all they can to calm the bladders down. Many people say that the bladders would have gone away if they were too late." Both stories emphasize the necessity of careful treatment of the bladders during their stay in the *qasgiq.* Not only might the bladders get away, but the *ikuyguuq* might come and draw the hunters into the sea, dramatically reversing the normal hunting process, during which men bring seals out of the ocean to dry land.

The men took sweat baths regularly during the five days of the Bladder Festival to "shake off" unclean essences (Mather 1985). They removed the bladders to the porch of the men's house whenever they bathed.

> When they are going to bathe, the one who is in charge of them, after he washes his hands, and after he does this over a burning lamp [passes his hand through the smoke], he would then take the bladders to the porch out there. He does this while they are taking a sweat bath.
>
> Then when they are done with the sweat bath, like that, after washing his hands, he fetches them and brings them in and hangs them in their hanging place. They have wood for a hanger.
>
> That is what they do. (Billy Lincoln, July 10, 1985 NI77A:5)

Another important rule in effect while the bladders resided in the men's house was the prohibition against the use of sharp implements of any kind. People believed that cutting something during the Bladder Festival would be like cutting off one's future catch. They also feared that the use of sharp implements might pierce or injure the invisible spirits that they believed were present during the ceremony. Not only were sewing, cutting, and chopping prohibited, but during the days that the bladders were hanging in the men's house all work in the village came to a halt. This rule remained in effect for four days following the disposal of the bladders in case the spirits might linger.

Men and women circumscribed their sexual activity during the Bladder Festival. Pubescent girls could not enter the *qasgiq,* and women in general were excluded from the men's house except during special periods. Brentina Chanar (January 16, 1991) reported one notable exception: "During Na-kaciuq, we [young girls serving the men] try to be the first ones to go through the *qasgiq* door. When they were preparing the bladders, I was the errand runner for my older sister. And when I opened the door during Nakaciuq, those who were awake yelled, 'Qua! Qua!' And then the boys would wake up. That is how they wake people up during Nakaciuq. And when they 'Qua, Qua' me, I used to be so glad, and I wasn't embarrassed at all because I had been the first one in!"

Although both men and women were required to be sexually continent during the Bladder Festival proper on Nelson Island, in the 1920s Butzin reported significant sexual activity during its Kuskokwim counterpart: "The men having secured the most mukluk, deer or other of the larger animals are honored. Wives of less successful men [are] often pantless during those nights that might entice their successful men to sexual intercourse with them and thereby secure for their own husbands in their hunts success" (Fienup-Riordan 1992:43). The parallel between people's sexuality and their ability to attract animals was an important theme in Yup'ik moral discourse. The husband and wife worked together to "draw" the seals from the sea. In this case the successful hunter transferred his prowess to a less successful man through intercourse with the unsuccessful hunter's wife. The woman acts as both conduit and active partner in the transfer (Phyllis Morrow, personal communication).

Men regularly purified both the bladders and the human participants with the aromatic smoke of wild celery, which was said to please them (Nelson 1899:393). They also offered the bladders food and water periodically throughout their stay. Some even gave the bladders small model weapons with which their *yuit* might "capture" or "hunt" the food in the bowls offered them, and so supply themselves. According to Morrow (1984:121), men sometimes hung the tips of hunting tools with the bladders to allow them to hunt in the dishes of food that were presented to them.

The restriction on human activity while the bladders were present, as well as the care and "feeding" of the bladders themselves, were comparable to the restrictions surrounding the treatment of the human dead. While the shade of the deceased lingered in the world of the living, the human community rigorously circumscribed its activity. Both men and women limited productive and reproductive activity during the period in which they hosted the *yuit* of the seals in the human world.

GATHERING THE BLADDERS

After the bladders had hung in the men's house beside their individual "owners" for five days, the men gathered them together and hung them in bundles tied to the heads of sealing harpoons or ice augers, which they then pressed into the back wall of the *qasgiq* (compare Nelson 1899:381). There the bladders remained for the third and final five-day period, during which the men did not bathe and continued to circumscribe their activity.

> When the five days have been used, they gather them up. Along the inner wall they tied the ice augers together depending on the length of the wall. That night when the time came, they tied seal twine around the ice augers making knots on it.
>
> And when it is time, the men who have prepared their bladders rush to that apparatus and hang the sticks with bladders in the knots.
>
> They are attractive when they all hang together. . . .
>
> These bladders that they were holding, where they are tied right here they tie them like that. They would shove it in so those bladders would hang along the wall.
>
> That is when people cannot do anything while they are there like that along that wall. They do not bathe for five days. This is during the wintertime. Nevertheless the interior of the *qasgiq* does not get cold. (Billy Lincoln, July 10, 1985 NI77:9–10)

While the bladders were hanging on the far wall, the men covered any noise they made that might disturb their sensitive guests. According to Billy

Lincoln (April 1986 NI83:5), "If they had someone who had something to do, they pounded on the drum even though they were not singing. So if anyone in the *qasgiq* makes a noise to signify that he had his own thing to do, they kept pounding the drum. They kept covering him."

The gradual movement of the seal spirits into the human world corresponds to increasing care lest loud noise or unclean acts offend or repel them. Some people referred to this five-day period as the time during which the bladders were "seated" *(aqumlluki)*, evocative of both the seating of guests in the place of honor as well as the young girl's "sitting down" during her menstrual seclusion. The seals originally were seated for only three days; but on his return, the boy who lived with the seals extended the period to a full five days.

KANGACIQAQ

> *That one then*
> *to this event they are celebrating*
> *it is like a middle.*
>
> *They cannot do without* kangaciqaq.

> —*Toksook Bay Elders, November 3, 1983*

After the men hung the bladders along the back wall of the *qasgiq,* an old man carefully planted a ceremonial pole in front of the oil lamp to the right side of the entryway (compare Nelson 1899:380). This pole was known as the *kangaciqaq* and consisted of four stalks of the wild celery that had been gathered at the beginning of the Bladder Festival. After the men brought the celery stalks into the *qasgiq* and thoroughly dried them during their baths, they erected the *kangaciqaq.*

> And there is this person who will be a caretaker of the *kangaciqaq.* This is a piece of wood that is long.
> When one goes into the men's house it is on the right side, beyond the floor boards, standing erect. They tie celery plants on it, but it stays right at that place.
> Whatever the people did that caretaker of the *kangaciqaq* takes constant care of it.
> That is when people could not do anything at that point, absolutely nothing. (Billy Lincoln, July 10, 1985 NI77A:10)

> Also this one, the thing that was made to guard the *kangaciqaq* is embedded between the floor boards to the left side of the entryway. It is tied with pieces of wild celery. (Billy Lincoln, July 10, 1985 NI77A:6)

The men treated the *kangaciqaq* as a sentient person during its residence in the *qasgiq:* "[While the *kangaciqaq* is being made] four bush sticks are tied together. Two young men sit and throw them at each other. One would fling it on the floor, and the other who is across from him would catch it. During one of its ricochets, it comes to hang on one of the celery plants on the *kangaciqaq*. Saying that the *kangaciqaq* had caught it, they would stop" (Billy Lincoln, April 1986 NI83:5).

When the old man first stood the *kangaciqaq* in the *qasgiq*, he poured a dipper of oil over its top. If the oil dripped onto the floor, the year would be a bad one, but if the floor remained clean, it was an indication that the *kangaciqaq* had accepted the gift and that the coming year would be bountiful. Subsequently, whenever people brought food into the *qasgiq*, they placed a small amount from the top of each bowl on the top of the *kangaciqaq*. Only after they had fed the *kangaciqaq* did they eat. Even so, people could not eat the contents of their own bowls but only what others gave them.

The day after erecting the *kangaciqaq*, the people entertained their "guests" by competing in various shows of strength, attack maneuvers, and jumping games *(qeckaraluteng)* in which they ran and jumped over each other. Young men took turns climbing a rope up to the skylight, pretending to be spiders. More than mere entertainment, the hunter's prowess affected the bladders' ability to return to their underwater homes. According to Butzin, "The ease with which they may return will depend on the ability of their hunters in the games that follow the dance. If, for instance, the man who shot a caribou can jump the highest, the bladder he secured will not have to go around mountains but will jump over them" (Fienup-Riordan 1992:43).

NAYANGAQ

Just as the women's performance of *ingulaq* marked the bladders' entry into the *qasgiq*, young men entertained the bladders daily with the performance of *nayangaq*. According to Billy Lincoln (April 1986 NI83:6), "Each night while the *kangaciqaq* was standing in the men's house, the men would *nayangaq*, performing their individual dances in which they depicted their particular helping spirits. Before they danced, they decorated themselves with *qaraliit* [designs] and hanging things."

Teenaged boys' dances, performed from a sitting position, imitated the movements of birds or other animals. They made noises following the directions of the person who asked them to dance. It was easy to see what the boys were imitating from the refrain of their songs, which consisted of motions performed without an accompanying drumbeat.

> And at night, every night, they have what is called *nayangaq*. They dance. These young people who are sitting against the far wall go down in front of them and dance, sitting down pretending to be some animal, so thus, he *nayangaq*.
> They imitate a certain animal. When the time came whatever animal he is pretending to be he imitates its noise.
> They imitate all kinds of animals—loon, hawk, raven, arctic fox. They make noise accordingly. They dance pretending to be some animal.
> Those that dance like that are very entertaining! (Billy Lincoln, July 10, 1985 NI77A:11)

As in the games of skill, the performance of *nayangaq* was more than simply entertainment. During the performance, boys depicted if not embodied the animal helping spirits whose aid they required both to hunt and host the seals.

OPENING BETWEEN THE WORLDS

On the fifth and final day that the bladders hung against the back wall of the *qasgiq*, men carefully cut a square hole in the ice close to the village. Lantis (1946:185) recorded that villagers made five ice holes at the close of the Bladder Festival on Nunivak. In villages located along the coast, men sometimes made holes in the nearshore ice, but, more often, they opened the passageway to the seals' world in a nearby lake or slough. Whether or not the people returned the bladders directly to their ocean home, they believed the animals found their way there whatever their route.

After the men opened the ice hole, they carefully tended it so that it did not freeze over. The opening constituted the creation of a direct pathway between the seal and human worlds to which the whole ceremony had been building. Special performances took place in the village that night, including the seal spirits' dramatic appearance in the human world and, sometimes, the shaman's journey down under the ice. The boundaries between the worlds were at their weakest, and the passageway between them finally was fully revealed.

On their return to the village from the hole in the ice, the men planted paddles in front of the *qasgiq*, signifying a formal call to the bladders to depart the human domain. The gesture recalls the hunter out on the ice raising his paddle to call a companion: "He will not put the oar down until the other one acknowledges his call" (Dennis Panruk, Chefornak, December 17, 1987). Similarly, the gesture solicited the attention of the seal spirits (compare Nelson 1899:384). The paddles planted by the grave during a funeral, and stakes planted at the beginning of Elriq, replicate this formal announcement, just as the fallen tree in the path of the girl that returned from the dead inverts it.

On the last night before the bladders' departure, participants performed special acts to encourage the seal spirits to return to their underwater home. Men might dip their spear tips into the ice hole and then use the spears to stir the bladders to remind them of their watery home. Koranda (1968:29) added that the bladders could not be kept too long in the human world or their spirits would become angry and bring sickness and death to the people.

Also on the last night, teenagers performed special dances *(yaryarraarluteng)* and put on large and small wooden visors. According to Billy Lincoln (July 10, 1985 NI77:11), "When they finish with *yaryar*, those young people don big caps. They also don small caps. They *yaryar* and make noise like 'Ah.'"

During a Bladder Festival that Nelson (1899:384) observed, men arranged hunting hats on the floor around a walrus skull, which they had placed in the

Model qasgiq, or men's house, with bird and bladder suspended from the center. Phoebe Hearst Museum of Anthropology, University of California at Berkeley.

center of the *qasgiq,* surrounded by buckets of water to represent the sea. The *qasgiq* entryway became the seals' hole leading under the ice. No one was allowed to leave the men's house during this part of the ceremony, presumably because the exit hole had become the entrance to the sea. Nelson observed young men in this setting imitating the calls of the eider duck. Subsequently, one young man imitated the motions of a loon and another the motions of a murre diving and swimming underwater. Shortly thereafter various other dancers began similar bird movements. Thus, in the presence of the bladders, hunters acted like birds, the form in which the seals would see them. The loon and the murre danced side by side, recalling the women's loon dance at the opening of the Bladder Festival and the hunter's appearance as a murre during the hunt. Production as well as procreation required a combination of male and female elements.

Hawkes (1914:27) also described a pantomime performed on the last night of the Bladder Festival by naked men who were pushed into the tunnel entrance to signify the bladders returning to the sea. According to Lantis (1946:185), on the last evening before the bladders were returned under the ice, the exit hole likewise constituted a passageway into the seals' underwater home. At that time the shaman journeyed to the seals. He did this by putting a figure of a seal in the exit hole to lead him under the water.[7]

Lantis (1946:185–86) also described the dramatic appearance of men impersonating seal spirits. These "spirits" emerged from the exit hole of the men's house at the close of the Nunivak Bladder Festival and pretended to eat the women and children. The loud singing of the old men purportedly drew them. Whereas people increasingly curtailed the noises of the workaday world as the Bladder Festival progressed, they replaced these sounds with ritual chants, perhaps including the *yaryar* referred to previously, to call the spirits.

Also on the night before the bladders were returned through the ice hole, women lay down by the door of the men's house and threw grass toward the bladders. By this act they were said to be making beds for the bladders on their return home (Toksook Bay Elders, November 3, 1983 NI57). Similarly Lantis (1946:185) noted that on Nunivak men, women, and children wearing gut parkas threw grass toward the bladders, saying that they were putting a mat on them so they would not get cold. In both cases people provisioned the bladders as if they were human persons.

Finally, on the last night of the Bladder Festival the entire village, and guests invited from nearby villages, gathered in the men's house. Parents celebrated their children's accomplishments through gift-giving. The young girls who had come of age gave away their wooden dolls. A village-wide distribution began. Families gave out tons of frozen fish, hundreds of dried

---

7. Compare Edmonds's account (Ray 1966:38) in which a shaman journeyed to the seals' underwater home on the last day of the Bladder Festival; see also Kasaiyuli (1981:80–82).

fish, and sealskin pokes full of seal oil. Donors would say that the gifts they were presenting had been given to them. Giving gifts in someone else's name, particularly a deceased kinsman's, was part of a number of ceremonial distributions, and it enabled the spirits to identify their gifts. This gifting in the name of the dead during the Bladder Festival led Butzin to say that the Bladder Festival was given in their memory. He described the simultaneous hosting of the shades of the dead and of the bladders dramatized in a ceremonial circuit performed during a Kuskokwim Bladder Festival.

> A luftak [*lavtak* processed bearded seal skin used for boot soles] and caribou hide are brought in and placed before a lamp, now two young men, who are well and strong and most successful in the hunt, strip and bathe with cold water, using a grass towel for wiping. Then they sit down side by side, one on the luftak and one on the caribou hide. Two other men stretch out with heads toward the wall and feet toward the center of the room [the sleeping position of a pregnant woman].
>
> Then a woman comes in bearing a dish of akutak. This she carries twice around the room; on the first round she stops in front of the two naked men on the skins, but they do not receive the dish. Then she jumps over the legs of the men stretched out on the floor and after another round sits down in front of the two sitters with the dish of akutak placed between her legs and one leg pointed to each sitter. These take a bite of the akutak and throw it over their heads—a libation for the dead. Then they receive the dish and divide the contents for the two divisions of the village. . . . The woman then got up and went out acting as if she were carrying the dish out again.
>
> The medicine man watched the akutak and the kantaks [*qantaq* bowl or dish] very carefully lest the "shade" of any person might be unprotected from evil spirits. The kantaks of akutak of any who had a death, or miscarriage or still birth or any misfortune whatsoever, might possibly cause an unsettling of the "shades" of people. Therefore the shamans had to shepherd the "shades" carefully for safekeeping until the danger of the dish or the akutak was over. (Fienup-Riordan 1992:42)

This example shows just one of many ways in which a sense of generational cycling and continuity undercut Yup'ik individuality. In western Alaska today, social ties between the living are both created and maintained through the relationship between the living and the dead. Feasting and gift-giving during the Bladder Festival, honoring both the *yuit* of the seals and the shades of the human dead, were no exceptions.

NALUGYARAQ

The final act of the Bladder Festival was the performance of *nalugyaraq* (from *nalug-* to hoist or raise, literally "the process of pulling up"). Pairs of young men took the inflated bladders, along with bunches of wild celery, out through the central smoke hole and down to holes in the ice. There men deflated the bladders and returned them to their underwater home, where the people hoped they would boast of their good treatment and subsequently allow the villagers to take them the following season. Whereas the women had effected a private, individual separation of seal body and soul after the animal's death, here a communal, public act effected its rebirth.

The morning following the opening of the holes in the ice, the men began preparations to *naluk* (raise up) the bladders. First they gathered together in the *qasgiq*. Then they ran to the pole to which they had tied all the bladders and yanked off the ones bearing their ownership marks. According to Billy Lincoln (July 10, 1985 NI77:7), "When it was time they would run to the pole in haste, and the owner would yank his bladders off, there. With the seal spears, two of them, making a space to hold them they tie [the bladders] onto their tips. They had these seal spears as handles."

Next the men prepared the *kangaciqaq*. They attached dried grass to the wild celery that had been gathered previously and tied the whole to a wooden shaft or spear. Billy Lincoln (July 10, 1985 NI77:12) continued, "And that person who is the *kangaciqaliurta*, the caretaker of the *kangaciqaq*, ties and connects the strands of grass. After they put grass they put dried celery plants in the middle collecting them together. And they also use dried grass. They tie them. That thing is so long, that *kangaciqaq*."

Then, wearing seal-gut parkas, the men removed the gut covering from the *qasgiq* smoke hole. The *kangaciqaliurta* climbed to the top of the men's house and pulled the burning *kangaciqaq* through the open skylight. Some accounts describe the *kangaciqaliurta* as a young boy fully clothed in a fur parka and boots and mittens prepared like "one who is going out." Brentina Chanar observed a *kangaciqaliurta* wearing a gut parka tied tightly around the face while Billy Lincoln saw him dressed in woman's clothing:

> Soon up there, there reflects a light from below.
> And when the time comes they raise that *kangaciqaq* handle first. The ones up there take hold of it, and they light it from below.
> So it is all ablaze! They pull it up, they raise it up. And that *kangaciqaq* is really burning then!
> That caretaker hoists it on his shoulder. It is really burning.
> They raise those spears backwards, and the owners take their bladders outside. When they take them out, he strikes them against the *kangaciqaq*, shakes them off and shoulders them. That *kangaciqaq* would spew cinders.
> They are entertaining when they do that! Right under that blazing fire!
> (Billy Lincoln, July 10, 1985 NI77:13)

After each man had taken his bladders through the fire, the entire group ran down to the hole in the ice. The one holding the *kangaciqaq* was in the middle of the group, with the others running around him. The runners retrieved any pieces of celery stalk that fell from the *kangaciqaq* during this journey. Billy Lincoln (April 1986 NI83:6) observed, "When all have done that, they would depart together. The fire would be in the middle of them. They all go together toward that hole in the lake. Those who followed would occasionally go up to the *kangaciqaq* and thrash it with their bladders and

sparks [cinders] would fly! After they thrash them, they would shake them and carry them. They were very attractive when they departed."
If the people had chosen the proper person to carry the *kangaciqaq*, the sparks would not burn his clothing. Conversely, a wicked person would be burned even if he was not near the fire (Tim Agartak, Nightmute, June 1987 NI98:7).

The fire,
on the body of that young boy,
even though it might be snowy,
even if sparks land on him,
his *atkuk* [parka] does not catch fire.
It will not burn.

If by chance
some part of the *atkuk* burns
that young boy has no way of remaining alive
through the winter.
(Toksook Bay Elders, November 3, 1983 NI57:11)

Because of both the importance and the danger of the job of *kangaci-qaliurta*, the shaman helped choose the carrier. When they had completed *nalugyaraq* and returned to the *qasgiq*, the men carefully examined the clothes of the *kangaciqaliurta* inside and out. According to Elsie Tommy of Newtok (June 9, 1992), "If the people in that village were not going to experience some personal disaster in the coming days, the person's seal-gut parka would not be deformed. However, if an adversity among the people was imminent his seal-gut parka would be deformed." The people were filled with gratitude if they found no marks. When the men returned, however, they had burned holes in the soles of their boots from treading on the cinders of the *kangaciqaq*.

If the procession with the *kangaciqaq* started at dawn, daylight would break before the fire went out. The arrival of daylight when the fire was no longer red insured a good spring; if the fire was red, they would have a bad spring with little game available. Compare this to Nelson's (1899:381) description of the end of the Bladder Festival at St. Michael, in which the people made a fire of wild celery on the beach, then circled it. After each man submerged his bladders, he would leap through the fire. This completed, the women and children would stamp out the fire and all would circle the village, the men and women sometimes in opposite directions.

After the procession on Nelson Island reached the hole in the ice, the runners circled it once *ella maliggluku* ("following the universe") and then immediately took the *kangaciqaq* up to the land and erected it. As Billy Lincoln (July 10, 1985 NI77A:8) described it, "They went to that lake, and it had a hole for them to use. Then when they arrived at that place going down, they would circle it, . . . and when they encircled it the one with the *kangaci-qaq* would go up to the edge of the lake. He would then stick the *kangaciqaq* into the ground. It would be standing upright there." The other men would also go up to the edge of the lake, where they would sit down and start piercing their bladders, starting with the big ones: "They would burst and spread the biggest one and burst the other and put them in that big one. So they break and rip up the bladders!" (Billy Lincoln, April 1985 NI83:6).

After bursting the bladders, the men tore them into small pieces. When they burst, the bladders "cracked like gunfire." As they worked, the men imitated the sounds of birds, perhaps presenting themselves to the bladders as the small seabirds that had also "burped" out air when they sighted the living seals in the hunt. The men then packed the pieces into a large bladder, remarking on their abundance, and took them down to the ice hole tied to the end of a spear.

Hunters in some areas deflated the bladders rather than pierced them. The terms for "deflate" *(ellelluni)* and for "burp" *(elciarluni)* have the same base *(elte-* to let out air), recalling the connection between the air burped by the hunter/bird when he kills the seal, the breath used to inflate the bladders, and the air let out of the bladders when he returns the seal to the sea.

Before sinking the bladders, they attached tiny woven pack baskets *(issra-tet)*, small spearheads, tiny paddles, and other miniature implements. These models replicated all the tools needed for ocean hunting. The tools were for the seals' use, given to help them provide for themselves so that they would be able to return. People said that if the bladder's tiny pack basket became full, so would the large pack baskets of the hunter's family.

After the men had fully prepared the bladders, they shoved them under the ice along with their accoutrements. Hunters sometimes used the reverse end of their *negcikcuar* (small hook) to push down the bladders, the same implement that they held upright to announce a successful seal hunt. Each individual hunter in turn sank his bladders. If the water was shallow, the men shoved them into the mud bottom. They never saw the bladders again, neither floating on the surface of the lake nor in the debris washed up on the shoreline. Their disappearance constituted proof that they had returned to their underwater home.

Finally, as the last act of *nalugyaraq* on Nelson Island, men poured fresh water into each of the four corners and the center of the ice hole. According to Paul John (February 7, 1977 NI3:22), "After they plant them down into the mud, they pour a little bit of water, in the four corners of the window [waterhole]. In the four corners of the waterhole, there are places to pour water on them. They pour water in those corners, after they have submerged those bladders."

The boy who returned from the seals initiated this last act. Here again, the five dippers full of water probably relate to the five-point anointing of the dead seal with water and the five steps separating the human world in which the bladders had been hosted, and the seal world to which they returned. The five dippers of water poured into the corners and center of the hole simultaneously recall and reverse the lifting of the food bowls toward the four corners and center of the *qasgiq* as an "invitation to the elements" at the close of Aaniq. In the first instance men lifted full bowls upward, while in *nalugyaraq* they emptied the dippers downward (see Ray 1966:89). This act concluded *nalugyaraq*.

> So they went back, and through the whole day they stayed without doing anything.
> Only the next day, they did something then.
> So for that length of time, they do that one. It ends, whatever events occur.
> Their way of having a Bladder Festival ends. When they lift them that way they quit working with bladders until the next year.
> Then that one has ended. I saw the ones that did that. (Billy Lincoln, July 10, 1985 NI77A:9)

After the hunters had pushed the bladders under the ice, they left the *kangaciqaq* standing by the hole. Throughout the winter, people deposited food at its base whenever they held a feast in the village. Parents warned children to stay away from it and never to eat the food they had left there. In the spring it floated away and, like the bladders, no one ever found it. Eddie Alexie of Togiak (March 10, 1988) added that the bladders allowed the *kangaciqaq* to follow them "because it was their parent."

On their return to the *qasgiq*, the people fashioned grass "ladders" for the bladders, perhaps to help them reach their destination: "And then the night after that they did something else like lie down by the door and throw grass. They do say something while they are doing that. These bladders probably make ladders for them when they get to where they land" (Billy Lincoln, April 1986 NI83:6). A sweat bath in the men's house followed *nalugyaraq*, as well as a continuation of the restriction against work for another four days (compare Nelson 1899:381). As following a human death, no wood could be chopped on the day after *nalugyaraq*.

NAKACIRUAQ

Nelson Islanders sometimes followed the Bladder Festival with Nakaciruaq (literally "pretend Bladder Festival"), in which young boys and girls paired off as husband and wife and together took care of the tiny bladders of the boy's catch:

> After they have Nakaciuq they have Nakaciruaq.
> The bladders of a young boy's catch, the bladders of minks or other small animals, they pretend to provide one of the boys with a bladder. They pretend a young boy and a young girl are mated.
> In those days they had Nakaciruaq as a custom.
> They had the young boys and young girls have a pretend Bladder Festival.
> But when they were going to do that, these ones first held a dance.
> They did things, they tried to coax people to give them things. They called it *cingarturluteng* [asking for special favors, usually from a grandchild].

Cingarturluteng the grandchild of his *iluraq* [male cross-cousin of a male], and also to his grandchild, he requests that he would like to acquire something. It was part of their custom.

And the other did not mind those who did that because it was a custom.

They would say that they wanted something, a tool, that they want to acquire a plane. . . .

So they would give a little something to the one who is requesting a favor.

They would not mind him doing that because that was what they did.

To their advantage they were such givers. . . . When they were going to have a pretend Bladder Festival that is what they did. (Billy Lincoln, July 10, 1985 NI77A:10)

Older relatives had the right to "kiss" their grandchildren and request particularly valuable gifts from the child's parents in a number of ritual contexts, including Kevgiq as well as the Bladder Festival. Parents could not refuse gifts asked in the name of their offspring.

ELLA MALIGGLUKU: FOLLOWING THE UNIVERSE

The primary focus of the Bladder Festival on Nelson Island was the renewal of life. The ceremony focused not only on the return of the seals but also on maintaining continuity in the relationship between living humans and the shades of their dead, as well as helping spirits and other natural elements that participants "fed" and otherwise honored. An elaborate series of events took place over a number of days around the winter solstice. Just as the sun "sat down" on the horizon, the *yuit* of the seals were "seated" in the place of honor in the *qasgiq,* the ceremonial center of the human world.[8] At the point at which the sun reversed its downward movement and once again began to brighten the sky, the seals' souls were sent out of the human world so that they, too, might return with the new season.

The image of a cosmic cycle (alternately celestial, lunar, and seasonal) dominated at numerous points throughout this ritual renewal. Especially important was the performance of ritual circuits *ella maliggluku* ("following the universe," clockwise from east to west) and, less frequently, *ella asgurluku* ("going against the universe," counterclockwise from west to east). To this day December, the month of solstice, is designated Uivik (from *uive-* to circle or revolve). Although the full significance of these processions and encircling actions is irretrievable, people likely performed them as part of a common effort to produce or control the cosmological cycle on which they were modeled. As noted, the five ritual circuits performed during Qaariitaaq and Qengarpak, and culminating in Aaniq, likely served to open the passage

8. Although Billy Lincoln sets the number of days during which Nelson Islanders celebrated the Bladder Festival at fifteen, the timing varied so that the day the bladders were sent back corresponded with the solstice. Given the general nature of the accounts, it is unlikely that we can reconstruct how Nelson Islanders determined the actual timing of the event. Note Nelson (1899:379): "The bladder festival . . . occurs annually at St. Michael, commencing between the 10th and 20th of December, the exact date depending on the phase of the moon."

between the human and nonhuman worlds at the same time they protected the human participants from merging with their spirit counterparts. As the painted men and children left the village center to circle its perimeter and return again to the center, they enacted and perhaps produced the step-by-step entry of spirits, both human and nonhuman, into the human world.

The young men made another ritual circuit of the village before they went to the tundra to collect the wild celery for the Bladder Festival proper. At various points during the bladders' residence in the *qasgiq*, people in turn made offerings to each of the cardinal points. After they hosted the bladders in the *qasgiq*, they made additional circuits both within the *qasgiq* and without to clear the path for the bladders' departure. At the same time, the *qasgiq* and its inhabitants were protected from going along with them. Men circled both the smoke hole and ice holes before the bladders departed, and after they had placed the bladders under the ice, participants circled the village a final time. Nelson (1899:381) recorded that the Bladder Festival formally closed with a sweat bath, after which the naked men circled the inside of the *qasgiq* from left to right four times. Ritual circuits both "following the universe" and "going against the universe" during all these acts alternately served to clear the paths between worlds and create boundaries between them. They also may have served to define events through time by literally bounding off discrete sequences within the ceremonial process.

The nineteenth-century Yupiit did not believe that the new year followed the old one automatically. Rather, human and nonhuman persons actively participated in the annual regeneration of the seasons. To engage in such activity, however, was not without its dangers. As a result, participants working to clear the passages between worlds carefully protected themselves against fusion with the spirit world. They did this by painting their bodies with soot, clay, and urine; by covering themselves with gut parkas and wearing encircling belts; by placing mats and skins between themselves and the "thin earth" on which they sat; by disguising themselves with the clothes or the identity of a person of another sex, age, or status (Morrow 1984). At the same time, through songs sung in the *qasgiq*, the painting of personal designs, and imitative animal calls, hunters explicitly identified themselves with their ancestors and familiar helping spirits.

The many reversals enacted during the Bladder Festival were part of this elaborate attempt to remake the world. This was apparently a male-dominated task, as hunters performed the majority of ritual circuits and sent the bladders back under the ice. At critical moments in the Bladder Festival, however, androgynous spirits, male "mothers," husband/wife dyads, boys dressed as women, and even young girls accomplished acts of regeneration. Far from a male-dominated spiritual regeneration standing in opposition to "unclean" female physical reproductivity, cosmological reproduction required the full participation of both men and women, husband and wife.

CHAPTER 10

ELRIQ AND KELEK
Living Spirits and the Shades of the Dead

THE FEAST FOR THE DEAD

In the yearly Feast for the Dead and the ten-year Great Feast for the Dead (Elriq) living relatives provided for the shades of the human dead through the feeding and clothing of the namesakes with whom they were identified.[1] People believed some essential aspect of the human person was reborn in the succeeding generation, similar to their beliefs about the seals. Procreation was not creation, only a stage in an endless cycle of birth and rebirth. The name-giver was as important in the union of human body and soul as the hunter's wife had been in the separation of seal body and soul. On the occasion of a human birth, the name-giver ritually named the newborn child while giving the child a drink of fresh water to satisfy the human shade believed to be suffering from thirst like its animal counterpart.

The annual Feast for the Dead, known on Nelson Island and the lower Bering Sea coast as Merr'aq (from mer- "to drink"), was the public occasion on which the spirits of the human dead were invited back into the human community to receive the food and clothing they required to maintain them in the underworld land of the dead. The timing of Merr'aq on Nelson Island

1. Although contemporary Nelson Island elders provide confirmation of the general form and meaning of the annual and great Feasts for the Dead, their accounts are not detailed. The vigorous suppression of the Feast for the Dead beginning in the 1920s in the Nelson Island area probably accounts for this paucity of information. Although a handful of older residents witnessed the ceremony, no living feast-givers remain. Said Brentina Chanar, born in 1912, "I did not catch up to Elriq. But our mothers caught up to it. They used to say that they used to go to Elriq to some places, but I do not know it. I only know it by saying it. But I do not know anything about it."

The best ethnohistoric description of Elriq is contained in Nelson (1899:363–79), with valuable additional information provided by Mather (1985:105–58) and Morrow (1984:127–31).

299

varied. Orators indicated that it usually occurred just after the Bladder Festival, although this was not always the case.[2]

Merr'aq was held for those who had died that year and for those whom Elriq had not as yet celebrated. The rite began when men placed stakes at the graveside, inviting the spirits to enter the village as in the ceremonies prior to the Bladder Festival. According to Nelson (1899:363), men decorated these stakes with carvings, indicating the gender of the deceased, as well as totemic marks specific to them. This practice called particular shades out of their underworld home. As in the Bladder Festival, people ritually cleansed and fumigated the village with the smoke of Labrador tea and wild celery in preparation for the arrival of the dead. Again, participants took great care during the ceremonial period to limit any human activity (such as sewing or chopping wood) that might injure or "cut" the dead during their journey to and from the center of the human world.

After men had placed the stakes by the graves, the dead came to await the feast. Just as men had lighted the seals' passage from their underwater home, so they kept a lamp lighted in the qasgiq during the entire feast to guide the human shades on their journey. Men then sang songs of invitation in the qasgiq, and the human shades moved to the fire pit under the floor. There they were believed to wait to enter the namesakes during the feast, just as the spirits of the seals had waited to enter the bladders during the Bladder Festival.

As the feast-givers served food, the namesakes ate from each dish and then threw portions of their food into the fire pit, where the dead received them as whole stores. They also received fresh water, which they sprinkled on the floor so that the dead might drink. According to Nelson (1899:364), the dead entered and possessed the bodies of their namesakes to obtain these offerings, the receipt of which supplied them for the coming year. If the living made no offerings, the dead would leave empty-handed and suffer pitifully from hunger and thirst during the following year.

As the daylong ceremony progressed, the dead moved gradually closer and closer to the center of the human world, where they were feasted and finally sent away with a ritual stamping on the floor. This movement parallels the Bladder Festival in which the hunters and their wives gradually drew the seals into the human world to be feasted and hosted at its center before their departure. Both ceremonies reversed the normal relations between living and dead human and nonhuman persons, and those on whom the living world depended for their well-being entered the human world to be hosted in their turn.

Elriq, or the Great Feast for the Dead, was a much more elaborate event.

2. Nelson (1899:363) noted that on the lower Yukon River the annual Feast for the Dead was held twice—once after the Bladder Festival as well as a second time before the beginning of salmon fishing in the spring.

Stakes planted at the graveside to call the dead. A. Hartmann, 1884; Moravian Archives.

Different villages on Nelson Island sequentially hosted Elriq. Although families might attend Elriq annually, they held it in their own village only once every five to ten years. Just as the spirits of the dead cycled between the land of the living and the land of the dead, so the location of the feast moved in a regular circuit in the land of the living.

Perhaps the most elaborate distributions of the nineteenth-century ceremonial cycle occurred during Elriq. It required years to acquire and prepare the tremendous supply of goods necessary to play the part of host. Such a distribution left a successful feast-giver materially impoverished but rich in fame. The event attracted hundreds of people from both Nelson Island and the upper and lower coast. Guests came from as far as the mouth of the Yukon and Kuskokwim rivers, and distant visitors received particularly valuable gifts. Elriq was, however, primarily an intraregional celebration.

As with Merr'aq, the timing of Elriq varied. Nelson Islanders indicate that it usually occurred in late February or March at the close of the winter ceremonial season. Whereas people initially invited the recently deceased into the human community at the opening of the annual ceremonial round, they reserved their final departure for the season's close.

Elriq was the ceremony after which relatives no longer honored deceased loved ones through formal distributions. Thus, the relatives of the departed concluded their obligations to give to the community and living namesakes in the name of the dead just as the namesake began to mature and provide food and gifts for the community on the occasion of their first fruits celebrations. Although the dead were not explicitly honored after Elriq, they continued to be honored in the celebration of the acts of their namesakes.

A close relative of the deceased on Nelson Island hosted Elriq, aided by his or her relatives. In other parts of the delta, the individual (called *elriq*) who hosted Elriq patrilineally inherited the right to do so (Morrow 1984:128). Writing in the 1920s, Butzin confirmed that along the Kuskokwim, Elriq "was partaken in by a traditional group. A sort of 'priesthood.' Tradition confirmed who would be in line to become an illeritulle *[elrituli]* (Illere performer). . . . The Illeritullit gave to their dead. He calls for his dead—sometimes the dead whom his father before him gave gifts to" (Fienup-Riordan 1992:44).

Elriq opened with the singing of *qiatait* ("crying songs" from *qia-* "to cry") accompanied by slow, steady drumming. According to Toksook Bay elders (November 5, 1983 NI58), the performance included recently composed songs as well as ancestral songs that people performed at Elriq year after year. Like the songs sung during the Bladder Festival to draw the souls of the seals into the human community, men sang the Elriq songs at the graveside to "wake up the dead" by name and draw them out of their underworld abode. The reverse proscription applied during mourning. Relatives made no noise lest they disturb the dead and cause them to lose their way. After the dead awoke, people kept a constant light in the *qasgiq* to guide their step-by-step approach.

After the human hosts had performed the "crying songs" and called the dead to the feast, the host village likewise called out to and then received their human guests. Each guest gave a gift on arrival, after which all were fed. The hosts also provided for the living dogs of the guests both prior to and during Elriq, just as they fed fictive "dogs" in the ceremonies preceding the Bladder Festival and the *yuit* of dogs on the way to the land of the dead.

The next day the hosts provided a second feast. Participants danced dressed in complete sets of new clothing made according to the sex of the deceased. The hosts again danced on the third day, but this time they wore old clothes and gut raincoats, which likely served a protective function comparable to that of the gut parkas worn during the Bladder Festival. The dancers cast down their eyes in humility during the second performance (Nelson 1899:368), in marked contrast to the powerful supernatural vision of the approaching shades. The hosts then formally invited the dead to enter the *qasgiq* and attend the feast. The namesakes came forward and ate from each dish. They also sprinkled water and dropped small portions of food from each container on the floor over the fire pit, thereby feeding the shades of the dead as well.

The major distributions took place on the fourth and fifth days of the ceremony, when first the women and then the men ritually clothed the living namesakes according to the sex of their deceased relatives. Donors lowered these sets of new clothing down through the smoke hole for distribution. A number of individuals might bear the name of the deceased, and during the ceremony all would be clothed according to the sex of their departed namesake. As Yup'ik names are not gendered, following Elriq it was not unusual to see young men dressed as women and, alternately, young women dressed as men (compare John Kilbuck in Fienup-Riordan 1988:40).

The namesakes could ask for special gifts from the host, including anything from a small wooden bowl to a sled or a kayak. Food, water, and clothing always were included. According to Butzin (Fienup-Riordan 1992:44), the host might also give "fur on the hoof" (the promise of meat or fish in the future). People considered such a gift particularly prestigious as it demonstrated the donor's confidence in fulfilling the promise. Butzin added that the host as he distributed would not claim ownership, but would state that the gifts had been given him or that he had stolen them. Billy Lincoln (July 10, 1985 NI77) explained that the host explicitly named the people who provided the gifts for distribution. As in Aaniq, the visiting shades would not accept the gifts unless their origin was clear.

Like the girl who returned from the land of the dead wearing the parkas used to dress her namesake, the dead received the gifts the host gave the namesake. Articles were offered in sets of four, five, nineteen, and twenty (four sets of five) to cloth the namesakes completely and, through them, the dead incarnate. The Yup'ik word for "twenty" (*yuinaq* from *yuk* person, plus

+*nginaq* merely, referring to the fact that a person has twenty digits and no more) translates as "a complete person" (Morrow 1984:130–31). The numbers four and five refer to the number of days after burial before a male and female shade finally departed, stepping down into the underworld land of the dead. Celebrants often pulled these gifts into the men's house through the central smoke hole, reversing the route used to remove the human body at death. Just as the Bladder Festival had reversed the separation of seal body and soul that occurred when a seal was killed, the Great Feast for the Dead effectively reversed the human mortuary process.

After they had fully clothed the namesake, the feast-givers called to the dead to return to their grave boxes and go back to the land of the dead. According to Nelson (1899:377), this dismissal was accompanied by directions for the shades to circle either the grave or the entire village one or more times before entering. This ritual circuit at the close of the ceremony parallels the ritual circuits that opened and closed the Bladder Festival. Like their counterparts in related ceremonies, these circuits alternately served to open the pathways the shades took out of the human world and bound off their entryway so that members of the human world could not follow them.

KELEK

The Bladder Festival's primary purpose was to draw and please the souls of the seals killed the previous year, and that of Elriq to supply the shades of the human dead. The Yup'ik people performed Kelek (from *keleg-* "to invite to one's house") to interact with and influence the spirits of animals and other entities of the natural world to elicit successful hunting in the year to come. Whereas both the Bladder Festival and the Feast for the Dead supplied the needs of the dead (both human and nonhuman), people performed Kelek primarily to please the spirits of game yet to be taken to supply the needs of the living.

Like the Bladder Festival and Elriq, Kelek primarily concerned traversing the boundaries between worlds. It was also referred to as Itruka'ar (from *iter-* to enter or come into a habitation) on the Kuskokwim and lower Yukon (Morrow 1984:136) and the "Masquerade," "Inviting-In Feast," or "A-gai'-yu-nûk" (Agayuneq) in the literature (Hawkes 1913:1, 1914:40–41; Kilbuck in Fienup-Riordan 1988:23; Nelson 1899:358, 421–22). Kelek was the final feast of the winter ceremonial season on Nelson Island and, like Elriq, was an intervillage event that rotated between related communities. This complex ritual involved singing songs of supplication to the spirits or "persons" *(yuit)* of the game, accompanied by the performance of masked dances under the direction of the shaman. Moravian missionary John Kilbuck summed up the significance of the ceremony: "The Masquerade—closes the festal season—and it is in the nature of a petition to the regent spirits for a bountiful supply of the animals and fishes upon which the Eskimo depends for life and happiness.—This festival was probably instituted by the shamans—certain it is that they jealously keep up and attend to all the details of its yearly celebration" (Fienup-Riordan 1988:23).

Both the Bladder Festival and the Feast for the Dead originated in legendary encounters between human and nonhuman persons. When the boy returned from the underwater home of the seals and the girl from the land of the dead, each recounted detailed instructions about how the seals and the dead desired to be treated during the annual ceremonies held in their honor. Kelek was also a legend as well as a rite. Nelson (1899:494–97) recorded the lower Yukon story of a shaman who journeyed up through the star holes to visit the *inuit* (Iñupiaq for *yuit*) of the skyland in their heavenly *qasgiq*. From its roof hung wooden hoops decorated to represent the different levels of the universe. Beside each person the shaman saw a small wooden image representing a different mammal, bird, or fish. The occupants of the skyhouse were the *inuit* controlling the fish, birds, and land animals.

The shaman later returned to earth, falling headfirst through the exit hole in the heavenly floor. When he awoke, he told the people to hold a festival during which they should decorate their *qasgiq* like the skyhouse he had visited. The people offered food and drink to the *inuit* of the skyland and sang songs at the festival in their honor to insure the return of the animals. If satisfied with these offerings, the sky people caused the images beside them to grow, endowed them with life, and sent them down to earth to replenish the supply.

THE SHAMAN: THE ONE WHO COULD SEE

Kelek originated on the lower Yukon in the supernatural encounter of a shaman, and during its annual reenactment the shaman played a critical role as the intermediary between the human and spirit worlds. According to oral tradition, Kelek was "of the *angalkut* (shamans)" (Morrow 1984:136). Just as the shamans advised their fellows to perform certain rites following their visit to the skyland, during Kelek they were called on to direct the dramatic representation of these *yuit* as well as enactments of what was hoped from them in the future. The shamans' actions during Kelek reflected their role as mediators between worlds. Their power emanated from their ability to look into places and times not accessible to ordinary humans. With this supernatural vision went the ability to travel to the skyland, the undersea home of the seals, and the underground land of the dead, where they could communicate with and pacify the forces of nature. This they did with the aid of their helping spirits *(tuunrat),* who were invisible to all but the clairvoyant shaman.

People called on the shaman in times of personal and community crisis, such as illness and famine, believed to result from transgressions of the rules for living. The *alerquutet* and *inerquutet* defined clear boundaries between men and women, land and sea, and the living and the dead, and people crossed these boundaries at their peril. During the ritual process, however,

"Eskimo medicine man," Nushagak, 1890s. Thwaits Collection, Special Collections Division, University of Washington Libraries.

the mediating activity of the shaman dramatically transcended these boundaries so scrupulously maintained during daily life.

Ordinarily, a rigorous separation between the sexes circumscribed daily
life. The shaman, however, held an ambiguous position. For example, both
men and women could wield shamanic power (Hawkes 1914:11; Weyer
1932:421–22). Although male shamans are mentioned more often in oral
accounts, this by no means supports the view of male spiritual leadership
dominating female productive activity. On the contrary, in important respects and specific ceremonial contexts, shamans presented themselves as
male mothers.

Although a shaman might be a man, he was not a hunter. Shamans were
notorious for their lack of hunting prowess, and oral tradition often depicts
them as physically weak and apparently defenseless. Accounts describe them
as routinely sleeping in the sod houses among the women and children rather
than in the *qasgiq* (see Kolmakov in Liapunova and Fedorova 1979:78). Also
the shaman was perceived as possessing spiritual power comparable in at least
one respect to that of women—the shaman empowered the male hunter.
Recall that the seasonal rebirth of the game was marked by the opening of
the women's house and the release of land animals from the moon. By some
accounts the shaman effected the latter by journeying to the moon at night to
influence the land animals in their decision to visit earth. In one especially
vivid account, Tim Agartak (Nightmute, July 18, 1985 NI73) depicted the
shaman as going to the moon, where he copulated with a spirit to release the
game and insure a rich harvest season for the coming year. Here human
sexuality directly prefigured natural abundance. Oral accounts also represent
the moon as a transformed man yearning to consummate sexually his love for
his sister or aunt (see chapter 8).

Ceremonial masks, said to represent the beings that lived in the moon and
controlled the supply of game, were sometimes presented as hermaphrodites
(Kaplan 1984:2). Some rituals ambiguously represented the sexual activity of
the shaman. For example, a Nelson Island woman who stole a beaded hat
was purportedly cursed by a shaman, causing her to walk in a squatting
position. A second shaman cured her by sleeping at the foot of her bed. Their
spiritual intercourse produced a child, and when the baby was able to stand
erect, the woman too was able to stand.

In a number of ways the supernatural reproduction accomplished by the
shaman both drew upon as well as inverted the natural birth process. In one
contemporary account, a Nelson Island man recalled his encounter with a
shaman in the early 1940s. He said that the shaman had told him that if he
did not believe in spirits to feel them for himself between the shaman's legs.
When he did as the shaman said, he felt a head sticking out from the ground.
The head was shaking, had hair, and was very cold. The shaman then told
the man to push it down. When he did so, the shaman started trembling all
over and yelling out in pain, and his mouth became very dry. The shaman

later told the man that the spirit had "almost been born." Here the emergence of the cold, hairy spirit from between the legs of the shaman and the pains associated with its disappearance both dramatically draw upon and invert elements of the natural birth process.

Finally, during his travels between worlds, the shaman's movement was wrapped in images of biological reproduction. Prior to departure on a "spirit journey," the shaman was carefully covered and sometimes tied in a fetal position in the *qasgiq*. His simultaneous exit from the human world and entry into the spirit world were represented as movement through a restricted passage, either an entryway, ice hole, or star hole. As during birth, a helper stood in attendance during the shaman's journey. Following his return, the shaman gave away the clothing that he had worn during his travels and rested for five days, actions comparable to those of a girl following her first menstruation or a woman following childbirth.

Joe Friday of Chevak gave this account of the journey of the shaman Kangciurluq, who traveled through the ocean floor to bring ice floes—and the seals associated with them—to the Qissunaq area.

Preparation for travel was made for Kangciurluq on a cold mid-winter day. All the people were gathered into a *qaygiq* [*qasgiq* men's house]. A few hundred feet away from the *qaygiq* a hole was made into a lake and covered with snow. The hole in the lake is called *anluaq* [a breathing hole]. It was made so a person can go in and stand up without lacking room.

There were two women watching the door, one a shaman's wife and the other, a close relative. Kangciurluq brought along Joe Friday to act as a witness for the people. The shaman considers a person witnessing him [to be] an assistant even though that person does not do anything but watch every move that the shaman made.

The snow was being blown all around the village, making it hard to see, even for a few feet. So an older man was asked to come along just in case Joe Friday got lost while he was on his way to inform the people of the shaman's activities.

On their way to the *anluaq*, Kangciurluq walked with his head down holding on to two walking sticks. When they got to the *anluaq*, Kangciurluq jumped in. Joe was watching every move that the shaman made. After a few seconds, Kangciurluq wiggled his body and each wiggle would bring him deeper into the lake. His seal-gut raincoat was blown up around his body. He wiggled again one more time and he went in deeper. Joe heard an uttering of words in Cup'ik [dialect of Central Yup'ik spoken in the Hooper Bay/Chevak area], but could not make out what he was saying. Joe Friday went closer to Kangciurluq's face and heard him say, "Make sure you tell the people everything I have done." His words came from deep inside his chest but they were understandable. After telling Joe to tell the people of everything he did, he went into a deep trance.

Joe hurriedly went to the *qaygiq*, after the shaman went into the deep trance. As he entered the *qaygiq*, the men jumped up from their seating places and asked him what the shaman had done. Joe told them of how the shaman jumped into the lake and mimicked the way he had wiggled. The men excitedly stated, "Yes, he has gone!" The men started to sing and drum the special songs taught to them by Kangciurluq.

After singing for quite a while, the people started to think that Kangciurluq was frozen by now because it was extremely cold outside. The men sang and sang the special songs until finally Kangciurluq's head appeared through the entranceway and two men helped him up. His body was not frozen but dripping wet from the trip he took.

Kangciurluq started going around to each person and gave them an item of clothing that he wore on his trip. The first item that came off was a wooden pendant carved in the image of an animal that he had pursued. He was worn-out from his trip and he let the people take one item off of him. The clothing he gave to the people consisted of mittens, a muskrat parka, *piluguuk* [two skin boots], and five [gut] raincoats.

After all his clothes were taken, he started beating his drum. He crouched down and uttered, *"Abuba!"* He rested for five days in the men's *qaygiq,* and he went out only when the men came to have their fire baths. (Pingayak 1986)

The shaman's spiritual journey was not only clothed in images of birth and female reproduction, but also those of death. As noted, the number five replicates the menstrual and postpartum seclusions as well as the number of steps separating the world of the living and the world of the dead. The binding of the shaman at the opening of a seance recalls the bound corpse as strongly as the unborn fetus. Likewise, shamanic initiations and cataleptic trances often involved the symbolic death of the shaman, after which he might travel to the land of the dead before returning to the land of the living (Nelson 1899:434).

Conversely, the powerful shaman was almost impossible to kill. One Nelson Island account recalls a particularly malevolent shaman whom his fellow villagers tried to destroy in a number of ways. They finally succeeded in their efforts by capturing his eyes, putting them in a box, and then cutting the shaman's body to pieces. Although the shaman was able to put himself back together, he could not find his powerful, all-seeing eyes. In this blind state, he journeyed to the Nushagak area where he was reborn from the womb of a barren woman. Nelson Islanders knew this was so because they had heard the child sing the shaman's songs.

The shaman derived power from his paradoxical position as a person who had experienced death but could not die. Yet Yup'ik cosmology did not present the contrast between birth and death as an opposition. Rather, the Yupiit clothed death in images of birth, thereby transforming it into a new beginning rather then a final exit. By employing these contrasting images, the shaman transcended the apparent opposition between life and death, which was reconceptualized as a cyclical movement between birth and rebirth.

Not only did the shaman transcend the boundaries separating the sexes and those between life and death, he or she also regularly traversed the boundaries between worlds, including the underwater home of the seals, the skyland, and the land of the dead. These travels served to expel evil spirits, uncover transgressions, and change the weather. One of the most important motivations of such travels was to request the *yuit* of the animals to give themselves to human hunters: "The trips that the shamans made are to the areas where the spirits of the animals are. . . . All living things and animals caught for food have spirit places where they will never die. During spring seasons, the shamans bring the spirits of the animals and fishes to the people so that starvation will not plague their villages. When the shamans get what they are pursuing, they take a long time to come home. Also other forces made by the other area's shamans might hold them back from coming home" (Pingayak 1986).

Shamans did not universally intend these encounters to benefit people. For example, the shaman Paningcan used his power in a negative way following the death of his son: "On some nights, when his sorrow was too great for him, he would go out beyond the village of Qissunaq and grieve for his son. He would open his body towards the sea and the area around him would light up. He was scaring the animals of the sea, making them hard to catch and hard to find. The action he was using is referred to as *ullirtaaq* [to open or cut so as to expose the inside]" (Pingayak 1986).

Just as the shaman visited the seal world at the close of the Bladder Festival, during Kelek the shaman journeyed to the moon to request animals. Paul John (February 1977 NI31:1) described such a journey:

In those days,
some of the *angalkut* [shamans] said
they went to the moon.
The people,
when they were going to the moon
at night,
[the *angalkuq*] would tell the people.
When they were going to convene in the *qasgiq*
because they believed in the *angalkut*,
and when one of the *angalkut* was going to go to the moon,
all the men went to the *qasgiq*.
And all the boys went to the *qasgiq*,
they were all in the *qasgiq* like this.

And out in the houses were the women,
only women
with little boys who were not old enough to be in the *qasgiq*.

Then when [the shaman] was going to go,
he would have someone warn them not to go outside,
until he came back [or the shaman would not find his way back].

That was what the *angalkuq* did.

Nelson (1899:430) also described the manlike being that people believed inhabited the moon and controlled the animals. In times of food shortage, the shaman would go up, get one of the animals, and turn it loose so that the species would become plentiful once more. This occurred in the story of the shaman who went to the skyland, saw a rabbit sitting by a star hole, pushed it through, and so supplied his people with meat for the coming season (chapter 8).

As in the ceremonial drawing of the souls of the seals during the opening of the Bladder Festival, songs facilitated this movement. Paul John continued:

Then, that *angalkuq* had songs.
They apparently sang songs
when they were going to go out,
when they were going to go.

They apparently told the people
when the song was to this point,
when the song has been sung five times,
they would arrive.

A shaman might also employ a spirit guide or *anelrayuli* (literally, "one who's good at exiting") to help them locate and control animals.

Apparently, after they made something to use as a guide
like the one who is going to the ocean,
he would first make a carving of a bearded seal.
This is him making a guide.

Also, one who is going just to the outside
would make an animal.
He would make it go ahead of him.

Then when his guide was coming back
from the porch out there,
it would bounce in from out there,
and when it landed on the board near the back wall,
one of the men would rush to it and find,
taking it.
Because they used to have little mouths,
the one who had gone to the ocean,
the shaman's guide's mouth
would be filled with the fur of ocean animals!
(Paul John, February 1977 NI31:1–2)

Just as song facilitated travel to the moon, *qaniqun* (chants or incantations) and prescribed ritual actions accompanied the use of such a "guide" to travel to the ocean. These chants were taught in private at night and had to be completely memorized to be effective. John Pingayak (1986) describes the return of such a guide in the Chevak area: "Aparrliq would become very serious and concerned when [the guide] approached the Hooper Bay point

. . . [and] he would get ready to meet it. He would put on a seal-gut raincoat and tie a belt around his waist. He went to one corner of the *qaygiq*, ran toward the underground doorway and jumped in. He didn't even touch the sides around the entrance way. He looked like he jumped into the water. When he returned he started laughing and said, 'What we were scared of was a tiny smelt coming back!'"

Billy Lincoln acted as a shaman's helper in Tununak on Nelson Island around 1925, and he described in detail what he observed. Especially noteworthy is the shaman's use of women's clothing when he journeyed with his guide to the ocean.

I was a helper two times at that time.

At that particular time, all that whole day, just as he was supposed to, he made his bed at the *qasgiq* bench. He played the drum all day long as he was going to go to the ocean.

And then we [six helpers, five boys (including Billy Lincoln) and one girl][3] brought him clothing that he was going to wear—female boots and parka. After we put female boots on him, we let him put on a female parka. And we helped him put on five pairs of raincoats.

At that time before he prepared, he went down to the floor and took out a miniature wooden animal. It was his *ciuliqagta* [leader] if he went on a *tuunraq* [spirit] journey. It was to go before him, the one who would pave the way for him. And one of the females outside was braiding using a sinew that was five double-arms long. And here was this *qaltaucuar* [small wooden bucket], just as big as that but longer—a small bucket with a handle. He put that miniature wooden animal inside that bucket. And because that *qaltaucuar* had a wooden bottom, he drilled it with a wood drill and made a small hole in it. They punched a hole in it with a nail. They just punctured a very small hole.

And when he was about to, he wedges the end of the braided sinew on the throat of the miniature animal. He does not tie it. And then he wraps that around, taking care not to tangle it.

And when he goes down, he puts on raincoat before he puts on other clothes, and he puts it inside his clothes after he sits down. So he goes through the usual routine motions—that is what they call *qaniqluni* [performing incantations without drumming]. And while he did that, they told me to unravel that sinew taking care not to get it tangled while it was going out. And this female is holding the end of it by pinching it with her fingers, and the very end of it has a small knot. And so that string of sinew keeps going, slowly but surely. And when this wrapped sinew is all gone, that female, your *anaanaq* [mother's sister, maternal aunt] Kuimulria keeps holding the end. She was a small girl before her first period at that time. While she was pinching it like this, I pinched on top of her pinched fingers because they told us not to accidently let go of it. And then it kept going down, and he had it covered inside his stomach under his raincoat. And when it got to that bucket, it went down, and then it got to the bottom of the container. When it got to its bottom, then we let it go. When

3. Lantis (1960:117) reported a shaman journey witnessed by four young men and one young woman.

he took away that small bucket, that miniature wooden animal was gone, the one that was inside it.

After he did that, having prepared, he left on a journey; we took him down to that hole in the river ice. So that was the animal that was going to make way for him, that miniature wooden weasel.

So he *tuunrirluni* [used spirit power] all night long. And another *angalkuq* would tell about where he was. He would say that he was this far. And then he would say that he had turned around and that he would be arriving back soon, that his *tumkiurtii* [his guide] was going to arrive while we are sitting and those in the *qasgiq* are singing songs.

Pretty soon something thuds loudly against the *egkuq* [bench]. After that thud, that miniature wooden weasel hit the floor and rolled. When they suddenly stopped singing, having told me to, I stood up right away, went to it, and took it, and they told me to show it close to the light. There were three lights [lamps] in the *qasgiq*, those Yup'ik ones that used seal oil. When I looked at that wooden weasel, its snout was very worn out, and some seal fur was stuck to it. And after showing it around, and that sinew that went with it was rolled as in a tight ball, and it had collected on its back as if it was toting it. So I hung it up on the ceiling.

And so the people sang again. And when they stopped singing, they all started to look up to the window. When I looked up, up on the sealgut window, I saw footprints bouncing along with the bouncing sealgut. And while that was happening, when those people in the *qasgiq* yelled, those footprints disappeared.

And not too long, as the night progressed, the top of the head began to come up through the door on the floor where people came up when coming inside. When they told us to pull him up, we went to him. And when we pulled him up, he was such a small person, and he was dragging his raincoats which were really wet! . . .

Just the ones on the outside [were wet]. And then they told us to take him to the corner and to fluff his body like this. When we did that, he got a little bigger. We kept doing that in all the corners. And then on the fifth time, we took him down to the middle of the floor. When we did that to him, he was back to his normal size.

We did that to him on the four corners and the fifth time down there.

And then we started to take off his clothes. His second pair of raincoats was also wet. But the third was just a little bit drier. Each raincoat was drier than the ones just outside it. When we saw the last pair of raincoats, it was not wet at all. And his parkas were not wet at all, but only the hem.

So that was how he was, and thus he came back. So that was the end of his journey at that time. . . .

He didn't say anything. . . .

At that time, he went to get the seals that they would catch that spring, whatever they told him to get at that time.

So I watched the *angalkuq* do that twice. That was the only kind of *tuunraq* that I saw. But those *tuunrat* before that I heard about, the ones that did the same thing as the person [that I saw]. But I used to watch that particular *angalkuq*. (Billy Lincoln, January 15, 1991)

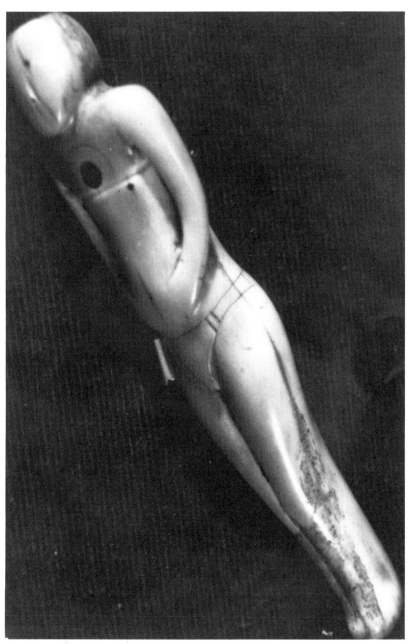

Shaman doll. Milotte Collection, Alaska and Polar Regions Department, University of Alaska Fairbanks.

Not only did the shaman use a guide to travel to the animal world—a guide might also see into and lead them to the land of the dead. In 1946 Theodore Hunter, Sr., of Hooper Bay gave this description of a shaman's ivory doll:

That ivory doll mean Fortune Teller. Medicine man hang that doll on the wall behind his bed. That doll sometimes they find it has a tear in his eye that mean it going to be bad or sad is coming to them, one of the family going to die. Also when the doll make noise happy voice, those family going to have luck or happy or joyful come to them when they believe those things. . . .

The hole (in the chest) is just like a secret treasure. Kind of spool is cover. The groove (around the chest) is for the . . . string and owner of this doll tie a string same way. The doll lead him when he going somewhere in magic way. Stained mark (on feet and lower legs) while they on their way they reach deadly river and he carry his master. That he got stained by. (Milotte 1946)

MASKED DANCES: MAKING THE
UNSEEN SEEN

Shamans routinely left the human world to interact with the spirits or sent out their magical "guide" to do so. They disappeared from human view to see, and thereby know and in some measure control, the unseen members of the spirit world. Kelek reversed this pattern, as it was the ceremonial invitation of these spirits into the human world where they were made visible. Although

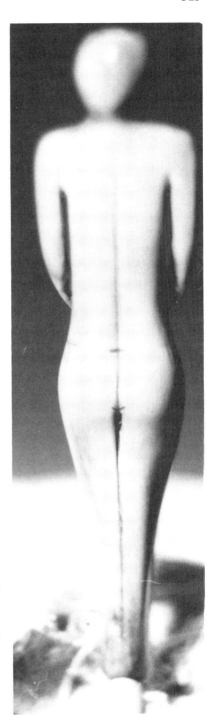

Rear view of shaman doll. Milotte Collection, Alaska and Polar Regions Department, University of Alaska Fairbanks.

shamans sometimes journeyed to the moon or made use of a "guide" as part of Kelek, the focus of the ceremony was on the masked dances in which animal spirits and shamanic spirit-helpers made themselves visible in the human world in dramatic form. Whereas the shaman crossed a boundary passing into another realm during a spirit journey, Kelek redefined the boundary between human and spirit worlds and incorporated both in the same space and time.

In preparation for Kelek, the shaman directed the construction of the elaborate masks, *agayuut* (from *agayu-* to participate in a ceremony) or *kegginaqut* (from *kegginaq* face, blade of a knife), through which the spirits revealed themselves at the same time as dangerous and potentially beneficial. People believed that the use of masks in enactments of past spiritual encounters had the power to evoke them in the future. They created ritually powerful masks especially for use during Kelek, which represented the *yuit* of the animals, the totemic animals of individual hunters, and the *tuunrat* (shaman's spirit helpers). These masks often concretized a shamanic vision, making it visible and knowable to the human audience. Carvers made them according to specific instructions by the shaman, and they were used only once. These powerful masks were dangerous and had to be carefully handled at all times. Prior to the dramatic performances in which they played so large a part, the masks were hidden under the benches of the men's house wrapped in grass mats. They must be protected from human gaze, lest the animals be offended (Ray 1966:84). They were destroyed after the ceremony, either burned or placed out on the tundra to rot (Hawkes 1914:41).

In contrast to the careful concealment of masks both before and after Kelek, participants believed that during the performance they endowed the performer with supernatural vision. According to Hawkes (1914:17), "When the actor puts on the mask, he is supposed to become imbued with the spirit of the being represented." The use of masks during Kelek provided a concrete image of the contrast between restricted vision and powerful supernatural sight. Like the all-seeing eye of *ella*, the large, hooped masks functioned as eyes into a world beyond the mundane. Their use in masked performances made the unseen seen.

Throughout Yup'ik cosmology, vision was an act constituting knowledge, and witnessing was a potentially creative act. According to Joe Beaver of Goodnews Bay (June 1988 YN31:17), "A speaker will not scold you for looking at him too much. But looking all the time while someone is teaching that is how one must keep listening." Watching a person's face, masked or otherwise, was particularly revealing: "And they keep saying this: The mind of each individual is known by the middle of the face. And I also know that. I know how a person thinks even though s/he may pretend to be happy, it is easy to see!" (Nastasia Kassel, Kasigluk, May 25, 1988 YN27:23). In the case of the animal spirit masks used during Kelek, attention to the center of the face was particularly important. There, embedded in the carving of the supernatural being, a small, human form often represented the *yua*, or

Mask representing "Negakfok" (negeqvaq), the north wind, looking sad because of the approach of spring. A. H. Twitchell, 1910; National Museum of the American Indian.

Wooden mask representing "Isanuk" (asveq), the Walrus. This is the spirit that drives the walrus, sea lions, and seals toward the shore so that the hunter can get them. A. H. Twitchell, 1910; National Museum of the American Indian.

Kuskokwim mask representing young Avanak, son of Avanak. This spirit is sent by his father to help and do errands for young medicine men. A. H. Twitchell, 1910; National Museum of the American Indian.

"thinking part" of the creature, which at death became its shade (Nelson 1899:394). Alternately the carved face of the mask was raised up to reveal the face of the performer representing the "person" of the animal.

Kelek not only involved serious dances but also the performance of comic masked dances and the use of "practice masks" by the young dancers performing for the first time (Morrow 1984:137). People did not fear these masks, and they did not bury or burn them following the performance.

Dancers performed less serious dances during Kelek, but the dramatic performances employing spirit masks were at its core. Significantly, the singing of songs of supplication to the spirits or "persons" of the animals accompanied these masked performances. People referred to this singing as *agayuliluteng*, a term that later came to refer to prayer. According to Nelson (1899:421–22), "Curiously enough, the great mask festival (A-gaí-yu-nûk) [Agayuneq] of the Eskimo south of the Yukon mouth has supplied terms by which the natives speak of the Greek [Russian Orthodox] church and its services among themselves. When they saw the Russian priests in embroidered robes performing the complicated offices of the church, it was believed that they were witnessing the white man's method of celebrating a mask festival similar to their own."

As in the Bladder Festival and the Great Feast for the Dead, participants composed and performed songs during Kelek to draw the *yuit* of the fish and game as well as *tuunrat* (spirit helpers) into the human world. Some songs depicted hoped-for future events, which their creators intended their performance to produce. Others described past encounters in which the *tuunrat* had provided aid. For example, Theresa Moses of Toksook Bay told the story of two young men lost in the ocean and eventually brought to land through the intervention of a spirit helper that appeared to them as a woman with long hair. On returning to their home, the older brother made a mask depicting the woman in remembrance of their encounter.

Just as the singing of special songs accompanied the use of masks, carefully performed dance motions *(arulaluteng)* accompanied the songs. According to Theresa Moses (October 26, 1987 NI99:2), "*Arulat* are the dances that they perform holding on to dance fans. They call that *ciuqiluteng* [doing the first or ancestral one] and it takes the form of *agayuliluteng* [singing or praying]." These dances were precisely choreographed, and the dancers danced according to the words of the song. In the same way that the masked performer became enlivened with the spirit of the being represented, if properly performed, the song had the power to realize that which the motions of the dance depicted.

These dance motions were more than the mere imitation of the motions of animals. When the performers danced during Kelek, they actually performed the animals' dances. Just as married women danced the loon's mating dance during Ingulaq, so the performers during Kelek danced the dances of the animals whose presence they hoped to elicit in the year to come. According

Masked dancers performing in Qissunaq for the film Alaskan Eskimo *in 1946. Milotte Collection, Alaska and Polar Regions Department, University of Alaska Fairbanks.*

to Theresa Moses (October 26, 1987 NI99:1–2), "They say that every living thing dances. And my former sister-in-law told me that one morning when she was going to church, she saw a mouse. Because it was going to dance, it kept going out of its hole. It stood up and danced. I think everything dances, even ducks and geese. . . . And it is a fact that everything has dance connected to it. . . . And that is what the Yupiit did, they danced for everything." The Unalakleet chief quoted by Hawkes (1913:3) gave an eloquent estimation of the value of these dances within Yup'ik culture: "'To stop the Eskimo singing and dancing,' he said, 'was like cutting the tongue out of a bird.'"

During Kelek participants viewed the masked dances in the context of an all-encompassing dramatic display. Along with masks, they also employed huge wooden hoops, suspended effigies, and dramatic staging to recount past events as well as depict a bounteous hoped-for future.

> Long ago they made the dance house a happy and exciting place. They hung a hoop from the ceiling and hung feathers from it which they called snowflakes. From the center of the sky they hung the pretend hawk, held together with string. When the song ended, the hawk would fall and break into pieces. It was breathtaking to see, like a movie. It lifted one's spirits. They shook this pretend universe in rhythm as they sang, and the whole dance house moved with excitement. At the same time masked dancers would call out in the voices of animals they represented . . . like bearded seals, foxes, ravens, and seagulls. It was something to behold. (Ivan Hamilton, Emmonak, in Kamerling and Elder 1989)

As in both the Bladder Festival and the Feast for the Dead, the boundaries between worlds were temporarily breached. The spirits entered into the center of the human community, into the bodies of the masked dancers themselves, and the unseen was partially revealed.

As described, the control over the appearance and disappearance of animals was a central problem in Yup'ik cosmology, and at different points in the annual ceremonial cycle participants made spirits visible in the present to insure their ability to retain them in the future. Given the power associated with sight and sound, the dramatic presence of the spirit world within the human world during Kelek was likely viewed as an act of empowerment that afforded the human participants some measure of control over the spirits represented. Moreover, during Kelek the boundaries of the human world were extended until a visible essence of the spirit world was contained within it. Through the dances men and women contrived to "hold" the spirits they had drawn for the year to come. As in the closing acts of the Bladder Festival and the Feast for the Dead, an encircling action and a feeding of the spirits now contained within the human world brought the ceremony to a close.

> Then the shaman donned an *inua* mask and began running around the entrance hole in ever lessening circles. He finally tumbled over and lay in a trance, the while he was communing with the spirit guests . . . in the fire-place below. After a time he came to and informed the hunters that the *inua* had been pleased with the dances and promised their further protection for a successful season.
>
> After appropriate offerings of meat and drink and tobacco had been made to them through the cracks in the floor, the celebration broke up, and the Unalaklit started home. (Hawkes 1913:17)

As in the Bladder Festival and the Great Feast for the Dead, Kelek embodied yet another instance of the cyclical nature of Yup'ik cosmology whereby the past was reborn in the future through appropriate action in the present. Moreover, this was accomplished in the process of a comparable movement of the spirits from the edge of the human community to its center and finally back out of the human world. In each of these three ceremonies, the normal relationships between humans and animals, the living and the dead, and the human and spirit worlds were inverted. In the Bladder Festival, the seals that had been hunted and killed were royally hosted and returned to the sea. During the Feast for the Dead, the human dead returned to the land of the living. And during Kelek, unseen spirits became visible within the center of the human world. In each case, although a normal, everyday relationship was transformed, the contrast was maintained. This was least true in Kelek, where humans "became" the spirits they represented in the dance, and the *yuit* of the animals were depicted in human form. This is not surprising given the focus of Kelek on shamanic activity. Just as the shaman had transcended the limits of gender, space, and time, so the ceremony most strongly associated with shamanic activity likewise transcended the fundamental contrasts of everyday life in an effort to remake them.

CHAPTER 11

KEVGIQ AND PETUGTAQ
Ambiguity and Renewal

KEVGIQ: THE MESSENGER FEAST

> *They used to do that a long time ago. They have Kevgiq with songs. You know they used to beg from others. They invited other villages. They competed against each other. . . . They give everything away so that they receive something in their turn.*

> —Brentina Chanar, Toksook Bay, August 1987

THE PRIMARY FOCUS of the Yup'ik ceremonial cycle was on the relationship between human and nonhuman persons, both living and dead. However, people also placed attention on the renewal and renegotiation of relationships between each other. Many dark winter nights, men and women gathered in the *qasgiq* to draw the spirits from another world and alternately play upon and invert relationships between members of the human community.

Perhaps the most important celebration of Yup'ik intercommunity relations was Kevgiq (from *kevgak* [dual], the name for the two messengers who went to invite the guest village) or *kevgiryaraq* (literally "the way of sending messengers"). The literature often refers to Kevgiq as the Messenger Feast or the Trading Festival (Curtis 1930:67; Dall 1870:151; Lantis 1946:188–92, 1947:67–72; Mather 1985:159–85; Morrow 1984:131–35; Nelson 1899:361–63), and it was as important among the Iñupiat of northern Alaska as among their Yup'ik neighbors (Spencer 1959:210–28). Although its timing varied from village to village and year to year, elders on Nelson Island indicated that it was usually held after the Bladder Festival. Daniel, born on Nunivak around 1860, recalled attending a Messenger Feast to which Nelson Islanders were invited at the beginning of summer (Lantis 1960:16), and John Kilbuck observed what was probably the reception of Kevgiq guests at Quinhagak in August 1897 (Fienup-Riordan 1988:385–86). Kevgiq did not take place annually in each community but was nonetheless a regular intervillage activity, and it continues in modified form to this day (Eskimo Heritage Project 1985; Fienup-Riordan 1986b:191–202; Wooley 1989).

A mutual hosting between villages characterized Kevgiq, whereby one village would go over to another to dance and receive gifts. The guest village might be either a near or distant neighbor. Although contemporary versions

324

of both intra- and interregional Kevgiq are still held on Nelson Island, residents have not celebrated its traditional counterpart complete with wooden messenger sticks since the early 1930s. According to Theresa Moses (October 10, 1987 NI99:2), "They invited people from far villages and danced. I saw them do that three times, and I did not pay close attention then when I watched. And after that, they stopped doing that."

THE ORIGIN OF KEVGIQ

Just as stories describe the origins of the Bladder Festival and the Feast for the Dead, so a story recounts the origin of Kevgiq. According to Nelson Island oral tradition, intervillage dancing in general, and Kevgiq in particular, began where interregional bow-and-arrow warfare left off.

One of the elders was making a drum and *enirarautet* ["pointers"], three of them.
Then they sent out one person, not caring whether or not he got killed.
There were two of them. . . .
So they went to their enemy taking those things that the elder had made, and that elder told them exactly what to say. Nothing written but only spoken.
So when they arrived at their enemy they waited across from their village and waited for the night fall. There must have been two of them if not three of them. They were across the river.
When the people subsided from walking around they went across to the *qasgiq*. So they appeared holding a drum and pointers. When the enemy saw them they said to them, "Let us stop fighting each other, but let us use these that we should use during the winters. Having established villages not far from each other like this, let us stop fighting one another, but using these let us be antagonists!"
So the [messengers] repeated everything that they had been told to say.
"During the wintertime, if we are going to use these [dances] during spring, let us hunt and try to catch game. Let us try that instead of trying to harm people. After seeing what we have caught, if our catch is large enough to take into the *qasgiq*, let us invite each other. Let us use these things, and if we use them to compete with each other, we will then have a festive occasion!"
When they finished giving their message, the elders replied, "It is certain that we start doing it like that instead of tormenting and harming each other."
And the two [messengers] also said, "Let us not be on guard against one another but try to get food that really matters. Let us try to catch some game so that when winter comes we will invite each other. We should do just that."
The elders agreed with them. "We will surely have fun if we do that, competing with one another instead of killing each other, but having friendly competition only."
Having agreed with them and having assured them that they would not fight anymore, they let them go home.
So when winter came, they invited the other village. Then they had a festive time.
The former enemies commented, "This is good. Instead of trying to kill a human being this is the way to do it. It is time to stop fighting."

So from then on, warfare was terminated. But they competed with each other with Kevgiq. That was the reason for the end of warfare. (Brentina Chanar, August 1987 NI94:5–6)

Beginning where war left off, Kevgiq on Nelson Island was also referred to as Curukaq (from *curug-* "to go over to physically attack"). Moreover, participants couched both the invitation to attend Kevgiq as well as the acceptance in images of conflict. These references became more and more explicit as the feast progressed, with the hosts referred to as *inglut* (enemies) of the guests, the guests referred to as *curukat* (attackers), and their arrival followed by a mock battle over the *qasgiq*. Stebbins people,[1] for example, initiated Kevgiq with a "fight" consisting of a race in which the best runners from St. Michael and Stebbins competed to see who could be the first to arrive at St. Michael: "The Stebbins runners had to run all around and touch every part of the St. Michael *qasgiq* and touch the door before going into it. If they missed one part of the outside wall, they would lose. . . . When they fought over a *qasgiq* the village that won [the race] sat down and let the losers dance first" (Eskimo Heritage Project 1985:63, 68).

In other ceremonies, participants drew the spirits of living and dead animals and humans into the human community from outside its normal boundaries, while in Kevgiq they invited human guests from outside the host community to enter. Kevgiq obviated the rigorous separation between worlds that characterized daily life, and participants interacted on common ground. A comparable ambivalence figured in each ceremonial passage. Whereas during the Bladder Festival and the Feast for the Dead the human hosts covered themselves with paint and soot to protect themselves from spiritual entry, Kevgiq clothed the invitation to share food and exchange gifts in explicit images of intergroup hostility. When men and women from distant communities shared a feast, they simultaneously exaggerated and suspended the suspicion that normally kept them at a distance and crossed the boundary between war and peace.

THE COMPOSITION OF "SONGS OF SOLICITATION"

A host village on Nelson Island initiated Kevgiq by presenting their guests with a long list of wants. The guests subsequently reciprocated with a list of their own. The elders of the host village composed a *taitnauraaq* ("asking song" or "song of solicitation," from *tai-* "to come to the area of the speaker"), directed at each male head of the invited families. Like the songs composed prior to the Bladder Festival and those for Kelek, the participants

---

1. People from Nelson Island originally settled near Stebbins when they migrated from Nelson Island to Norton Sound in the early 1900s, in part to be nearer to the trading post at St. Michael (Shinkwin and Pete 1984:101). The early-twentieth-century "potlatch" that contemporary Stebbins elders described probably combined elements from Kevgiq as it had been celebrated both on Nelson Island and around Norton Sound.

both composed and practiced the asking songs after dark with no light in the *qasgiq* (see also Curtis 1930:69).

These "songs of solicitation" always contrived to ask for things that the guests could supply only with difficulty. One song might ask for walrus meat if few walrus had been taken the previous spring. Another might request reindeer skins from coastal people who could acquire them only through trade or with the help of relatives. Ideally, community members pooled their resources to meet the demands made on them. They "gathered their minds together and made them one." If the guests could meet all of the requests made of them, their village acquired the reputation of a place in which people worked together (Eskimo Heritage Project 1985:48–49, 62).

After they had completed the songs, the dance leaders of the host village composed a list of those they wished to attend the feast and the gifts they wanted them to bring. Messengers in the past had to memorize this list carefully and in the proper order, whereas today they may write it down (Eskimo Heritage Project 1985:48). If the list of wants proved too demanding, the perspective guests could decline the invitation, though not without a loss of face tantamount to a humiliating defeat.

> Negtemiut [Nightmute] was invited by Qungurmiut. After having been invited and having accepted the invitation they decided not to come. They felt that what was asked of them was too much; they did not want to give. Their leader was called Tuunraq.
>
> He was your uncle Simeon's father. He made them renege on their acceptance because he did not want to give away his stove.
>
> But not long after that two runners came from Kanerlulegmiut—Iquilnguq's father, Maniigaq, and Issurill'er.
>
> So we made preparations for them.
>
> Qussaviaq's father made a song ridiculing Negtemiut for having reneged. (Brentina Chanar, August 1987 NI94B:3–4)

SENDING OUT THE MESSENGERS

Once the dance leaders had completed the asking songs, they chose two young men as messengers and sent them to invite the guest village. According to Himmelheber (1987:40) these young messengers were preceded by two old men who were secretly sent to the invited village at night to make known their village's requests. Only after they learned the gift capacity of their guests did they send the real messengers with the invitation. Morrow (1984:132) notes that young men were employed as messengers in other ritual contexts. After a death young boys, also called *kevgat* (messengers or helpers [plural]), cut wood for the mourning villagers and replaced all of their drinking water with fresh water. In ordinary usage young people who lend assistance to the elderly are referred to as *kevgat*.

The host and guest villages vied with each other to have their gifts and asking songs in readiness. When everything was prepared, they gathered in the *qasgiq* to dispatch the two messengers. They dressed each in a complete set of new clothing suitable for traveling. They also provided them with small gifts, such as grass socks or gloves, and fat-rich foods, such as *akutaq* and poke fish, to warm them on their journey. They then formally presented them with the *ayaruq* (messenger stick or staff) made of new wood with an ivory point and decorated with bands of red ocher. Stebbins elders reported that the width of the bands indicated the quantity of goods the host village had to offer. Without this stick, the "messenger was nothing" (Eskimo Heritage Project 1985:50–52).

Curtis's (1930:67) description of Kevgiq noted that the feast-giver of the host village initiated the event when he planted the staff in the center of the *qasgiq* before the messenger was sent. He then instructed the messenger concerning the proper order of the requests and what gifts were required of each guest. The messenger subsequently presented this staff in the *qasgiq* of the guest village and returned bearing one in return. Both staffs were destroyed after use.

The planting of the messenger staff at the occasion of the invitation followed by the movement of the messengers out of the center of their community and back again replicates the placement of invitational stakes outside of the *qasgiq* and at graves during the opening of the Bladder Festival and the Feast for the Dead. In all three cases, the planting of a staff by a "messenger" initiated the movement of the guests, whether human or non-human, living or dead, toward the center of the community hosting the feast. The planting of the staff formally marked the passageway and the commencement of intercourse between communities normally kept apart. Lantis (1946:188) noted that before the messengers left on Nunivak, a shaman "made a path" for them, insuring good weather for their journey by dancing and blowing vigorously to get rid of bad weather.

According to Stebbins elders, the two messengers slept in the *qasgiq* the night before they left. The next morning, rested and well fed, they started on their errand. If they met messengers from another village on the trail, the opposing pairs would "fight" each other, pushing and trying to turn each other back. The first person to lose balance and fall back a step lost this circumscribed, but intense, contest. The winners went on to complete their errand, while the losers returned slowly to their home village (Eskimo Heritage Project 1985:53).

If the guest village was more than a day's journey, the messengers might receive hospitality overnight in a camp or village along the way, but on no condition could they bring the messenger stick indoors. Rather, it was left concealed outside the village to be picked up the next morning. The messengers could not speak until after their hosts fed them. By their silence their message was known before it was told (Romig 1923:2).

When they arrived at their destination, the messengers concealed themselves outside the guest village until sunset, just like an attacking war party.

Only at nightfall would they enter the village *qasgiq* to make their errand known. According to Brentina Chanar (August 1987 NI94B:1), "When they are going to have Kevgiq, they have two runners that they send out to the villages with a gaff for a staff. They go into the *qasgiq* at night at the village they are inviting. When they come in, the people exclaim, 'Quaaq! Quaaq!' [The people being invited] are very thankful."[2]

The invited village greeted the arrival of the messengers with feast food and small gifts comparable to those that the home village had given the messengers at their departure. Brentina Chanar continued:

> Not ignoring them at all, they ready the drums. So they get the drums ready and when they tell us we all go to the *qasgiq*.
>
> They say that those two runners *qeceglutek* [jump]. They dance by jumping around.
>
> They really go all out preparing the two runners. They seat them in the corner of the *qasgiq*, and whoever has things brings things to them, all kinds of things like food. I have seen them when they give them socks and hats.
>
> So like that they keep giving to those two. Soon they have lots of things.
>
> Your father [Cyril Chanar] and someone else were runners from Negtemiut when we were living at Qungurmiut during the first ice before it was safe.
>
> So that was the way they let them dance. And then the day after that, they left for home. . . .
>
> They got runners who could run fast. They let them leave at night, those two fast runners. And at night, they arrived. But they spent a night at the [guest] village and came back [to the host village] the next day.
>
> They tell that village that they are inviting them. They have three things to say to them, calling it *qaluurarlutek* [dipping the net]. This one is approaching his cousin in case he might want to give him something.

Brentina Chanar (June 16, 1989) recalled the variety of songs used for *qecgutet*, to welcome the two *kevgak* and accompany their jump dance: "*Qecegluteng* [They jump?]. Some of them used their own individual motions. Some pretend that their stomach is full. Some pretend to *paangeq* [use double-bladed oars]. This song was about those two brothers. This happened during one spring. When his brother towed his younger brother in the ocean, he was lost having ice go out on him. When the south wind came up on them. That was the *apalluq* of this song."

According to Anatole Bogeyaktuk of Stebbins (Eskimo Heritage Project 1985:54), the messenger ran into the *qasgiq* at the guest village, jumped into the air, and landed on the floor in a crouching position. Holding the messenger stick in both hands in front of him, he kept his face hidden. From this position, he named the principal feast-giver from the host village and his "teasing" cousin in the guest village, to whom he gave the messenger stick.

Although the entire village was invited to the feast, particular cross-

---

2. This is the same exclamation uttered when the first young girl entered the *qasgiq* early in the morning during the Bladder Festival.

cousins formally exchanged the invitation, most often in the name of their children. On Nelson Island the feast-giver's child was called *kinguneq* (the one behind). The feast-giver directed his invitation to the child of his male cross-cousin. A joking relationship existed between cross-cousins in daily life, and the aggressive teasing that characterized this relationship suffused Kevgiq with its distinguishing feature—ritual ambiguity. Morrow (1984:132) notes that typically two feast-givers, each with a *kinguneq*, invited their cross-cousins' children (referred to as *aqvak'ngat*, "the ones being fetched"). On Nelson Island the *aqvak'ngat* were sometimes children who were themselves cross-sex cross-cousins. During Kevgiq these children and their parents were the recipients of special gifts—sometimes given in embarrassing amounts.

> Those are who we call *aqvagut,* the people who are inviting other villages. They used to have that between cross-cousins when I used to see them do that. He said that this person has come to his cross-cousin even though his cross-cousin would not host him. So they called him his cross-cousin. Those who were cross-cousins used to do that. . . .
>
> It sure was a long time ago when your *qulicungaq* [older brother, Frank Sam] was a small boy and before he got younger siblings. He and Uliggaq [Susan Angaiak] were *aqvak'ngak* [dual] [because they were cross-cousins]. They were *inglut* [enemies] to each other. But then their enemies there gave them things like parkas. They let them put on parkas with tassels. They tried to give [things to] all the members of that family. They gave their parents cloth parka covers and their fathers shirts. When they did not have lots of material things, they really gave that other one a lot of things. They made mukluks and just gave him all the clothing. . . .
>
> Uliggaq and Allgiq, your older brother, because they were cross-cousins, they let them *ullauguq* [go to each other]. They let him say to Uliggaq, when they used to call him [Allgiq] Ayaprun, that he had come to her, even though she will not hear him.
>
> So those were the *aqvak'ngak*. (Brentina Chanar, June 16, 1989)

Stebbins elders noted that since the demise of the *qasgiq,* contemporary messengers might deliver their message to the people gathered in the local bingo hall. Although in the past women were not present to receive the messengers, today their presence is tolerated: "They won't let the women get in the way. To them it will be like there are no women there, but these women now, they can scold the Messenger when they are playing bingo because he slowed or stopped the game" (Eskimo Heritage Project 1985:57–58). After the messengers returned home, "They tell their home village, and the village is also thankful" (Brentina Chanar, August 1987 NI94B:2).

Following the acceptance of the invitation, the hosts sent two additional messengers called *paiqak* (greeters or meeters, from *pairte-* to meet or encounter) to the guest village to communicate the specific requests contained in the formal "songs of solicitation." This second envoy was designated *paiqerluteng.*

It takes a while before the event. After the [first] runners have been sent, others are sent out who are called *paiqak* [the (two) greeters] when they want more information about certain things. . . .

Those *paiqat* are those who go to that place after those two *kevgak* [messengers] had come already. They go there to tell about those things that they want again. They call that *qalurraq* [dipping or bailing]. And after they have arrived, those leaders mention that this is what this certain individual wishes to have. So he mentioned what is needed by everyone and mentions everything. They sent their request to all the people in that village. You know they used to have *taitnaur* [another dance where one wishes for something to come, from *tai-* to come]. So people get those things that are wanted by those who request things.

In those days, they did not know how to write and how those people never forgot. But they merely talk about those requests. They did that to all the villages.

So when they *kassuuskuneng* [finally meet together], they show those things that they have tried to get for their *inglut* [enemies]. They used songs to show them and give to them. (Brentina Chanar, August 1987 NI94B:2; June 16, 1989)

Both hosts and guests made their requests in the name of the children. Brentina Chanar continued, "When they used to have Kevgiq, they made sure that all their children got something. All of them. And if your family did that, they would call out [by name] your eldest child first and say that they wanted this certain thing. And then they also asked that their younger sibling help him also. And then they try to get what is asked. And they would also want your youngest child there to help them. That is how they would do that."

These indirect requests in the name of children carried weight that a direct request would not and obligated parents in special ways in this as well as other ritual contexts. To be asked for something in the name of a child may itself have been an indirect way of asking for something in the name of the dead person for whom the child was named. It may have been a request to the specific shade as well as to shades in general to help the living meet the demands made upon them. Although contemporary descriptions of Kevgiq do not focus on the relationship between the human and spirit worlds, members of each community also probably invoked helping spirits to help them supply the required gifts. During Kevgiq the living and dead of one community (including both human and nonhuman members) worked together to supply the living and dead of another. Kevgiq negotiated boundaries differently drawn.

THE RECEPTION OF THE GUESTS

The acceptance of the invitation to attend Kevgiq and the delivery of requests preceded a period of preparation in which both villages worked to meet the demands that would be made on them during the feast. This preparation might take months, and an invitation extended in November might not be realized until February or March. Time was necessary for hosts and guests alike to call in old debts and secure through trade what they did not already possess. Weather was also a factor. Extenuating circumstances, such as a death in one of the communities, might postpone the celebration indefinitely.

Finally, when all was in readiness, the hosts sent a third set of messengers to fetch the guests: "When all preparations are completed and the dance songs completed then they get the invited village" (Brentina Chanar, August 1987 NI94B:3). Before the guests set out, however, these messengers "captured" two of them and took them to the host village as hostages or "prisoners." On their way back to their home village, two additional greeters met the messengers, and together they returned to the host village to warn them of the approaching "attackers." This errand completed, the messengers set out once more to meet the guests.

Hosts and guests continued to send messages back and forth during this formal and often lengthy approach. Guests would challenge their hosts, asking for special foods they knew would be hard for their hosts to provide. Conversely, even if the hosts had a plentiful supply of whatever was requested, they would deny they had any, offering lengthy apologies for their ineptitude. Teasing and innuendo marked these exchanges, and failure to meet their guests' demands embarrassed the hosts and opened them up to ridicule (see also Eskimo Heritage Project 1985:57–58).

Finally, when the guests were in view, the messengers went to meet them one last time, performing arm motions that mimicked dipping with a dip net or bailing a boat. Throughout this reception they continued unabated the teasing and friendly "fighting" characteristic of the relationship between host and guest.

> So while they travel, there would come a person. That person is called *qaluarluq* [the dipper]. And so they *qaluraq* [dip/bail].
> And they did that to their *iluq* [male cross-cousin of a male] who was at the host village; they answered them. When they did, they added more challenges!
> So they did that.
> So they answered them as if it were for real.
> So that messenger took off.
> So when that messenger arrived at his village, he told them that he was given those messages to relay from the oncoming party.
> If their mind was jolted, they would send out another messenger, running all the while. . . . The advancing party sent out teasing messages to the invited village, like one is teasing one's cousin. (Toksook Bay Elders, November 3, 1983 NI57:8–9)

The *qaluarluq* often sang quite elaborate requests: "They say that they tell stories, thus they *qaluraq.* . . . They are really enthused with each other. They want boats, kayaks, seal skins, guns, tents, these are the biggest things that they used to ask for. They wanted stoves. And then they make it, put fire in it, put wood in it, put kindling in it. So that one particular song for that thing would mention all those things. That song is so fun and exciting. The way they do it with a song is so enjoyable to listen to!" (Brentina Chanar, June 16, 1989).

In the last stage of their approach, the two "greeters" circled the guests in an encompassing action reminiscent of that used in other ceremonies to bound off the spirits of both the living and the dead before their entry into the human world.

> Then the two greeters are sent out. They run around the oncoming dogsleds and then they come back running. . . .
> The villagers being greeted not being scattered all approach the [host] village together.
> The greeter comes back to the village and, having been told something more to say to the oncoming villagers, runs back and conveys the messages, whatever they want him to say.
> That time is very exciting when the invited villagers are approaching. Around them are the runners, circling them. Runners are never tired. People with athletic constitutions were used as runners/greeters. (Brentina Chanar, August 1987 NI94B:3)

Curtis (1930:71) observed that on Nunivak the hosts circled the oncoming guests in a counterclockwise direction. This ritual circuit parallels Rasmussen's (1927:129) "magic circle" as a means of controlling the bad influence of strangers.[3] As in the gift requests in the name of the children, this ritual precaution points to the presence of nonhuman as well as human participants in the event. Agnes Waskie of Emmonak makes explicit the connection between the arrival of strangers and the spirits of the dead: "Remembering their dead ones, people go to the kashim . . . and give gifts to every one there. At that time, they think their dead ones are there with them. That's what the people say. They also say that when strangers come, the spirits of the dead come with them. For that reason we try to bring good gifts to the kashim" (Kamerling and Elder 1989).

Like warriors of old, the guests timed their arrival to coincide with night-fall. Eddie Alexie (March 10, 1988) described a particularly dramatic approach at a Kevgiq held in the Togiak area in the early 1900s: "So when they are approaching the attacking village, they do not arrive during the day. So at night, when the attacking village and the host village are meeting, when the attacking village is on the last stretch to the host village during the night, some of the sleds would shoot guns. They pretend that they are warring against each other. They are very fascinating to see! The discharge of the guns throws sparks! So when they arrive, they are all warmly received." After

---

3. Recall also Billy Lincoln's *ircenrrat* story in chapter 2 in which the *ircenrrat* are invited to attend Kevgiq and are circled by their hosts.

the guests arrived, the men of the host village performed *arulaq*, a men's Iñupiat-style dance done in a standing position.

After the hosts had received the guests and entertained them outside, everyone entered the *qasgiq*, where the hosts served an elaborate feast, including the special foods the guests had requested during their approach. While they were ostensibly enjoying the generosity of their hosts, the hosts began to sing *nernerrlugcetaat*—ridicule songs or "songs of indigestion" (from *nere*- "to eat," plus *-nerrlugte*- "to have trouble with one's V-ing"). The immediate goal of this performance was to make it impossible for the guests to enjoy the feast. The teasing also exposed the rules that members of the guest village had broken or acts they had performed that their hosts had found laughable or irritating. Although expressed indirectly, the audience clearly understood the references to past indiscretions.

> The *nernerrlugcetaat* [songs of indigestion] that they make are so entertaining.
> You know when we used to have Kevgiq we had songs of indigestion.
> The people always wanted to hear that song. . . .
> The guests [were the objects for the songs of indigestion]. They used two able individuals to do that. They exaggerated the opposition's past incidents or deeds. (Brentina Chanar, August 1987 NI94B:4; see Brentina Chanar, June 16, 1989, for an example of a "song of indigestion")

The primary feast-givers were also often the primary objects of ridicule: "They give them indigestion then with those two songs. So those two songs are about those individuals whom they suspect will give out the most material things. [They are] about those people who have a lot of material things. They sing about those two that people are going to get really excited about. . . . But some of them make a mistake in suspecting which ones will have a lot of things!" (Brentina Chanar, June 16, 1989).

The host's goal during the performance of the "songs of indigestion" was to embarrass and inflame members of the guest village. According to Theresa Moses (October 10, 1987 NI99:5), "And when they arrive, they give them indigestion *[nernerrlugcetaarluki]*. When they do that, they let their strangers hear of what they feel bad about." The challenge to the guests was to remain calm and controlled during this onslaught. Even during the most damaging accusations, the accused ideally listened passively and remained in good temper. Although women were normally immune from these merciless attacks, a man's slightest failing could be transformed by his cross-cousin into biting satire at the guest's expense.

Any man who transgressed the rules for living was the potential object of ridicule during Kevgiq. Each man paid close attention to his cross-cousins' misdeeds (both real and imagined), using them as the subject for songs at the offenders' expense. People traveling between the villages during the months before Kevgiq reported any blunders or unusual actions their opponents were unlucky enough to perform as possible subjects for new songs. Particularly eloquent and enjoyable "songs of indigestion" from years past might also be repeated. At the least, the performance of these songs made the object of their verse uncomfortable and at most "shamed the offender and made him change his ways." Nothing was too private to be exposed in the singer's effort to "tease [his cross-cousins] really hard" and embarrass him in front of everyone: "While the offender stands and faces the people he has to show great self control. He could be asked in a song to bring out what he has stolen so everyone will laugh at him and cause him great embarrassment and shame. It is the law that the offender can't get angry, no matter what is being said about him. He has to bear the teasing until he no longer can stand to hear of his shameful deeds" (Eskimo Heritage Project 1985:14–15, 45).

During the performance of these "songs of indigestion," the "accused" would sometimes try to cover his embarrassment by performing a comical dance for the people. If an offender was immobilized with shame, his female relatives might pull him onto the dance floor, where they would try to amuse the audience and take their attention away from the offending song (Eskimo Heritage Project 1985:15). "Songs of indigestion" remain an important component of contemporary Kevgiq. Both same- and cross-sex cross-cousins still challenge each other with songs. Today both men and women compose and perform songs at their cross-cousins' expense during these exchanges.

The dynamics of the performance of "songs of indigestion" are reminiscent of Central Eskimo song duels, in which two opponents faced each other and sang about the other's faults until the response of the audience declared a "winner." As pointed out by Eckert and Newmark (1980:198), song duels did not eliminate the causes of conflict. Rather, the event reconciled, within a ritual framework, the contradictory forces and ambiguity between inter- and intragroup cooperation and competition—central features of Yup'ik life. Similarly, the performance of "songs of indigestion" during Kevgiq allowed for the "framed expression of grievances in an ironic context."

As in the Central Arctic, any resolution of conflict that aimed to keep the offender and the offended in the community involved the contradiction between working out the conflict and avoiding the placement of guilt (Eckert and Newmark 1980:198). The singing of "songs of indigestion" along with the elaborate teasing that permeated Kevgiq created a safe context and an ambiguous genre for the airing and defusing of conflict. The performance of *nernerrlugcetaat* during Kevgiq took the conflict out of the everyday and isolated it in ritual. Realizing the conflict as a ritual event introduced sufficient ambiguity into the confrontation to allow (ideally) all involved to part on good terms. The setting and timing of the performance, festive occasion, comic context, audience participation, and use of a stylized song genre all separated and differentiated the event from normal interaction.

Finally, because the joking relationship between cross-cousins was covered by the metamessage "this is only teasing," the insults delivered in *nernerrlug-cetaat* were simultaneously ironic and required an ironic response (Eckert and Newmark 1980:204). To react negatively to a ridicule song was to bring the event into the real world and acknowledge the possible truth of the accusation. Thus, the smiling response of the accused was imperative. The ambiguity of the event had to be maintained at all costs lest the conflict explode into the real world. Instead of a means to resolve conflict, the performance of "songs of indigestion" maintained the ambiguity so essential to community life.

THE PRESENTATION OF GIFTS

Following the songs, the host village danced and presented extravagant gifts. Although one man might be prominent in this distribution, no one monopolized it. When the hosts redistributed the goods at the close of the dance, they gave widows, orphans, and elders first choice and amply provided for them: "First of all they would call on a woman who had lost her mate, or a child with no parents. Those two, deeming them special, almost in the way an elder was regarded, they used to give them things first. Then when these were all given, only then would they give things to older men, only after the orphans were given something" (Toksook Bay Elders, November 3, 1983 NI57:14).

In the evening following these initial exchanges, the first performance of the formal "asking songs" took place.

> And at night when they finish performing the songs of indigestion they have a dance. They beg for things from them. That is when they "attack."
>
> The people who have arrived ask for things. They sing songs such as "This person should give this . . . whatever." That is the way they did it. After the [hosts] sing songs of indigestion to them then the [guests] sing songs of solicitation . . . because this one person had asked the other person about a thing. He had asked for a gun from him or they wanted a boat from him or fabric, and this one was asked for a kayak.
>
> That was the way they did it. (Theresa Moses, August 1987 NI95A:8)

As in the requests communicated by the messengers, the "asking songs" made a point of requesting things that were difficult to find, causing concern in their opponents. Stebbins elders noted that through the "asking songs" people tried to "wake up a person to be a good hunter." By choosing something that was hard to get, they required their opponents to work diligently so that they could demonstrate their ability to perform difficult tasks and draw elusive animals (Eskimo Heritage Project 1985:22). Again, the strength of the relationship between human and nonhuman persons was an unstated but essential referent.

On the first night of Kevgiq, the guests danced and gave gifts, while the hosts sang their requests. On the night following, they reversed roles and changed sides *(mumigarulluteng)*. The dance was initiated when the three "pointers" (*enirarautet,* from *enir-* to point), dressed in beaded headdresses fringed in fur, took their places in front of the singers and drummers. The central pointer was the song starter, designated *meng'esta* (from *menge-* to sing a song with drumming preliminary to dancing; from the root *eme-* to quiet down, to sooth) or *kita'arta* (from the exclamation *kita* "here, take it, there it is"). To one side sat the *apallirturta* ("one who performs the *apalluq* [verse]") or *agniurta* (from *agna* "the one across there"), who called out the first words of each verse, while on the opposite side sat the *eriniurta*, "the one who shouts out what is to follow" (see Morrow 1984:133). Only men could take the part of pointers in intervillage Kevgiq, although men and women alternated as pointers in its intravillage counterpart, Kevgiruaq (mock or pretend Kevgiq).

Each of the three pointers held a dance baton or *apallircuun* (literally "device for making the verse"), also referred to as *enirarautet*, a two- to three-feet-long wooden wand that the pointers moved in time to the drumbeat. It was decorated with feather shafts stripped of their barbs and topped with down or rabbit fur. Carvers also sometimes appended small wooden figurines. Nelson Island dance wands were straight, but in other areas wands were sometimes made with a wooden crosspiece at one end. At Stebbins the wands held by the two outside pointers had crosspieces. The central wand was straight with a wolf or fox tail attached to it, referring to the story of a man who was killed when wolves encircled him and beat him with their tails (Eskimo Heritage Project 1985:76, 78; see Billy Lincoln's *ircenrrat* story, chapter 2).

Like the messenger stick, the *apallircuun* or *enirarautet* was stained red from a mixture of *uiteraq* (red clay or ocher) and seal oil. Like the huge wooden dance "trays" used during Kevgiq on Nunivak Island (Lantis 1946:191–92), these wands were proprietary and commemorated extraordinary hunting feats and personal experiences. Holding the dance wands, the pointers recalled remarkable encounters between human and nonhuman persons. Often the wands represented the same stories year after year. Wands also sometimes depicted notable recent events.

> Those *enirarautet* depict real life things that have happened as their designs. They have all kinds of designs. When we first were going to have a Kevgiq at Toksook having moved there the first time [in 1964], our *enirarautet* had miniature designs of houses that were being moved. Those that were pretending to move. Miniature kayaks and boats. That is what we had when we sang, when we moved by putting houses on the rafts and moved them down to Toksook.
>
> We put those designs on our *enirarautet*. . . . While they sang those songs they said, "All those many houses, across there at Toksook River, are all coming over!"
>
> And then its reply was "Even though there is a south wind, bring them all up on land!"
>
> And then they hit the drum hard with gusto! (Brentina Chanar, June 16, 1989)

Billy Lincoln holding dance wand, St. Marys, 1982. James H. Barker.

Boys dancing at Toksook Bay, 1975. Note the drumskin designs depicting the move from Nightmute. James H. Barker.

Like the masks used during Kelek, people never handled or displayed the dance wands after their use in Kevgiq, and they burned them following the feast. Participants handled them carefully and respectfully during Kevgiq. Damage to the stick required the person responsible to pay compensation. Stebbins elders report that the dance wands represented traveler's sticks or ice testers, without which hunters would never journey onto the ice. Also, like winter travelers, the pointers usually wore gloves. It was customary for the pointers to wear new clothing, and the dancers presented them with new gloves and other small presents when they performed. The people gave these gifts to show their thankfulness for being "awakened" by the dance. They presented them before or after, never during, a dance (Eskimo Heritage Project 1985:72, 79).

The three pointers stood up and danced a "stick dance" at the beginning of the performance of the asking songs. Standing in place with eyes lowered and knees bent, each placing one hand on his hip and holding the dance wand in the free hand, they alternately moved the wand in and out and from side to side. Their postures represented a traveler proceeding on a long journey, and the standing dance signified the formal request for gifts that had likewise "traveled the path" from one village to another.

After the pointers took their seats, gift presentations commenced. The central pointer led by singing the words of the asking songs. According to Stebbins elders, "The singers behind the Pointers then repeat the first verse of the song as they keep time to the beat of the music with their bodies. Then as they got warm the Pointers begin to strip between the dances. This represents walkers getting warm as they walk with their stick. Wearing their shirts while they dance equals walking cold" (Eskimo Heritage Project 1985:80).

As the pointers began to sing the first asking song, the wife of the man from whom they were requesting the goods stood up and performed her individual "story dance". The motions of these *yurapiit* (from *yuraq* dance, literally "real dances") sometimes depicted a particular event, such as an encounter between warriors, and their performance enhanced the people's comprehension of their history. Alternately, the dance might portray such an activity as the sewing of a fancy parka, beginning with the preparation of the skins and ending with the modeling of the finished garment. Stebbins elders describe the significance of these dances: "Wives dance to try to make the men become more patriotic, more aware, see and feel things intensely in a new way so their enthusiasm and vigor reaches great heights. They try to sharpen all aspects of their lives, past and present" (Eskimo Heritage Project 1985:83–84).

Each woman inherited her story dance from her mother and mother's mother before her. Unlike the *yurait*, or verse/chorus dances performed on other occasions, she neither wore gloves nor held fans while she danced. Although performed to the rhythm of the drum, her dance recounted a

Author trying to perform the mouse-food-hunting story dance, Nightmute, 1977.

story independent in meaning from the song being sung. Theresa Moses (October 10, 1987 NI99:4) recalls the following details about the story dances:

> When a woman stands up to dance, she dances her own designated dance. Your mother has her own individual dance about warfare. It is just like having one's own individual designs. Each woman dances her own dance. They use their

ancestral dances. Your mother dances what her mother danced. My dance is taking care of seal gut and also going smelt fishing. . . . Some have one, and one who has more than one has more than one. But most of the people do the mouse-food hunting dance. And some pretend to make *akutaq*, and some pretend to be infested with lice. Whatever one has experienced, they try to enact them. Each individual has individualized motions.

The women would continue the dance from beginning to end, with or without the accompaniment of the drum. Men would not dance while a woman was performing. Just as people considered it inappropriate to interrupt a storyteller, so they were not to disturb a woman while she told her story with every motion she made.

When they have Kevgiq,
when they invite another village to their village,
the one who is doing the inviting,
his wife dances.

When she dances,
the ones who are endeavoring to live,
her relatives, her sisters and brothers,
she will dance the ones that have been passed down to her.

And the ones watching her dance
even though she has not spoken,
they recognize her story through her motions.

They recognize who she is,
they recognize her story
through her dance.
(Toksook Bay Elders, November 3, 1983 NI57:14)

As his wife continued her performance, the hunter brought the required gifts into the *qasgiq*, holding them high above his head for the audience to admire. Then, throwing the goods aside, he performed a "kayak dance," in which he simultaneously stomped one foot on the floor and pretended to paddle a kayak with exaggerated arm movements. The wife continued to dance, and her husband brought more and more goods into the *qasgiq*, hauling the larger gifts in through the central *qasgiq* window.

The *curukat*, or "attackers," danced first, giving out what they had brought; they attacked *(curukaraluteng)* the inviting village. The host village danced the following night and gave extravagantly—sleds, kayaks, guns, pots, pans, traps, and tents. The hosts also distributed smaller gifts in abundance. They gave both raw goods and tools, and intense competition developed to see who could give the most. When someone presented a particularly valuable gift, the pointers stood up to show their thankfulness. Hosts not only gave out these gifts, but were also obligated to give away any piece of personal property a guest requested.

Those giving the least presented their gifts first, while the ones with the most came last. Each person tried to give more than had been requested. Dancers entered in the order of the value of the gifts they were presenting, from least to most. As each dancer came onto the dance floor, the pointers would begin to sing that person's song. Dancers demonstrated appropriate modesty by presenting their gifts in their ancestors' names rather than their own. In the past the providers' names were not mentioned, in marked contrast to the explicit use of personal names accompanying food and gift distributions during both the Bladder Festival and Elriq.

If the dancer did not bring in the requested gifts, the central pointer could bring up the dancer's bad acts, trying to embarrass the dancer and make the people laugh. As in the performance of the "songs of indigestion," a dancer should not show anger regardless of what was said. While dancers performed, their teasing cousins could also call out to them, encouraging them to dance faster and pestering them to bring in more gifts. Conversely, a dancer could heap embarrassment on a rival by giving an exceedingly generous number of gifts. The three "pointers" would stand in response to such generosity and move their dance wands emphatically to show their appreciation. In the end, the dancer who gave the most was designated *kasmilraq* (from *kasme-* "to push," referring to pushing forward through gifts) and "won" the dance for his village. No formal announcement had to be made, as the quantity of gifts spoke for itself.

Parents gave particularly large and extravagant gifts in honor of the first catch or first dance of their child or grandchild. This was referred to as *ineqsuyugluteng* ("doing something because a child is cute or lovable," from *ineqe-* "to coo to a child using special words made up for that child"). Again the gifts honored the child's namesake as well as the child: "Those that first come into the *qasgiq* bring things in. They invited villages and distribute a lot of things that they have collected all through the preceding summer. Things and food. That is what they call *ineqsuyugluteng* . . . [when they] celebrated the first catches of their grandchildren. They display a catch which has been a first catch by a specific grandchild. And some mark them into the *akutaq* as caricatures" (Theresa Moses, October 10, 1987 NI99:2).

Children who danced for the first time were specially treated. Dressed in new clothing from head to toe, they stood on a valuable skin or grass mat at the center of the dance floor while they shyly went through the motions of their dance. Their mothers and other close relatives joined them on the floor, showing their support of the young person. The skin on which they stood served a protective as well as an honorific function, bounding the initiant off within the world and placing them at its ceremonial center. The boundary between the world of the living and the world of the dead may also have been part of what was represented.

Stebbins elders described a formal ending of their "Potlatch" (combining elements of Kevgiq and other ceremonies) in which they "tricked" spirit guests into leaving:

We close the Potlatch with a different style of dancing, with three or four Hand Motion songs. We do this to keep the spirits of dead people and animals from floating around.

They make songs and make motions that mean to step on the Potlatch, or end it. They might sing and take a month to make songs and make the motions that mean they are stepping on the Potlatch to end it.

Men dance and sing for two nights and the women do the drumming, they change roles and let the women drum to trick the spirits and make them leave.

They would tell everyone, "This is the end of the Potlatch. At this time the pointers end the Potlatch by singing the motion songs to settle it. . . .

At this time they make masks and show them to their teasing cousins and say, "This is what my grandfather has used and I'm using it. Shaman walrus mask, teasing cousins, I would show you. This is what my Grandfather has used and I have used them." Showing the masks puts the Potlatch down, stops it from moving, as the Potlatch travels by mask and dance. (Eskimo Heritage Project 1985:109–10)

Although Nelson Islanders describe no comparable conclusion to Kevgiq, they sometimes followed it with Kevgiruaq (literally "pretend Kevgiq"), in which the men and women of a single village took turns hosting each other on alternate nights. Here too, perhaps, the people changed roles and let the women drum "to trick the spirits and make them leave" after their participation in Kevgiq. Although similar to Kevgiq in many of the dances as well as the elaborate gifting that took place, Kevgiruaq was an informal, more humorous affair, and teasing played a large part. Brentina Chanar (June 16, 1989) gave a lively account of the manner in which the invitation to Kevgiruaq was recently delivered.

At that one particular time when we had Kevgiruaq, and Stephanie was a *kevgaq* [messenger], she went to the men at the time they were gathered together. She said to them that she had come to them without being bashful at all because she knows that they know that they were easy to please. She has now come to them without any reservations and not being bashful because she knew they would be thankful right away!

Those men who were there, started to laugh! . . .

At that time, your *acagpak* ["big father's sister," Anna Kungurkaq] had said that the men were not too enthusiastic. So she told them if they were lazy, it would be okay just the same.

And those men said, "We will never be lazy!"

The structure of Kevgiq was the unstated referent throughout Kevgiruaq. Men and women alternately played the part of host and guest. Each sex took on a name as a separate group. For example, at Nightmute in the 1940s, the men were designated Uaqlirrarmiut (downriver people) and the women Kiaqlirrarmiunek (upriver people). When people moved to Toksook Bay, they called the men Qairuarmiut (people from the pretend waves) and the women Peñacuarmiut (people from the small cliff): "Because where they sang was located on the high ground, that is why they were called Qairuarmiut. And because us women were way down there, they called us Peñacuarmiut" (Brentina Chanar, July 7, 1989).

On the men's night, the men sang asking songs and the women danced, and on the women's night they reversed roles: "When they danced, men donned women's clothes starting from a long time ago, when they dance what they call Kevgiruaq" (Brentina Chanar, January 25, 1991). Men and women also performed as pointers on this occasion. Nelson Islanders held their most recent Kevgiruaq in Toksook Bay in 1979 (Fienup-Riordan 1983:321–44). Unlike Kevgiq, participants distributed primarily "raw" rather than prepared products. Gifts included bolts of cloth, rolls of twine, cases of toilet paper, boxes of tea, bags of sugar, and packages of cured tobacco. Women redistributed these goods several months later as part of the annual spring *uqiquq* distributions in honor of the hunters' first seals of the season.

In their description of the "stepping on" or ending of the Potlatch, Stebbins elders may also be referring to the masked dances performed during Kelek. Kevgiq, with its emphasis on intercommunity relations, was often followed by Kelek, which focused on the relationship between the human and spirit worlds. Although Mather's sources mentioned only the use of masks in connection with Kelek (Morrow 1984:137), Lantis (1946:188) and Curtis (1930:69) include masked dancing as a feature of Kevgiq. Nelson Islanders reported the performance of "humorous" masked dances during Kevgiq.

The functions that Kevgiq served were as numerous and rich as the gifts. The literature emphasizes Kevgiq's effective redistribution of wealth. Although this redistribution was certainly a significant feature of the event, it was far from its only effect. In fact, Kevgiq celebrated opposite principles— equality and hierarchy (Jean Briggs, personal communication). At the same time people redistributed huge quantities of goods, they confirmed status distinctions both within and between groups. Moreover, if gift-givers displayed wealth without proper circumspection, participants would ridicule them. Thus, Kevgiq displayed a fundamental tension between pride and humility, giving and receiving. It also provided social control through public confession and recalling people's misdeeds. Ambiguity and contradiction greeted the Kevgiq participant at every turn.

The Eskimo Heritage Project (1985:22–28) added a range of functions. By allowing an outlet to people's aggressive emotions, Kevgiq helped to keep the peace. The event encouraged the passing on of expert knowledge as it gave people an incentive to work hard to provide the requested gifts. Kevgiq kept people busy, which some viewed as an end in itself. The performance of story dances dramatically portrayed and passed on knowledge of history and tradition. The festivities provided security in times of food shortage by extending kin ties within and beyond the village and regional group. At the same time, Kevgiq insured safe travel between villages and provided the opportunity to arrange marriages beyond the community. It expressed social differences and celebrated and recognized a young person's coming-of-age.

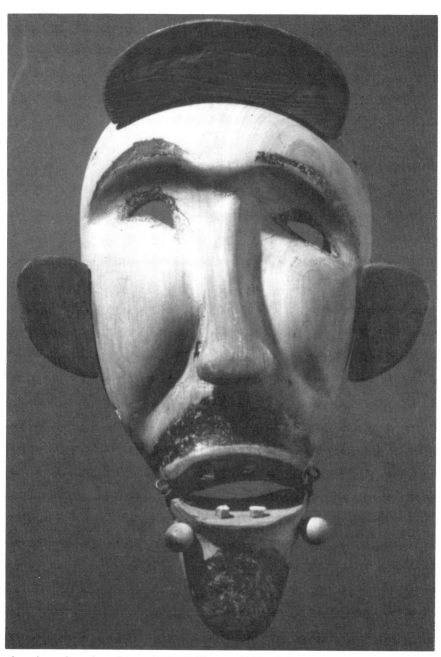

A comic mask made and worn by Cyril Chanar of Toksook Bay to mildly ridicule his iluraq *(male cross-cousin). The chin is movable, wired through a hook in the upper lip. University of Alaska Museum.*

Last but not least, Kevgiq stands out as a particularly elaborate display and distribution of the bounty of the harvest, providing a clear statement to the spirits of the fish and game that people had done right by them and that the hunters were once again ready to receive them. Just as hoarding food was unacceptable, so also was failure to use up one's stores from the past year. Animals would not return to people who were stingy with their catch. People had to make full use of past harvests to host animals in the future. Not only were generous gifting and ample feasting during Kevgiq required for good relations in the human world, they were essential demonstrations to the animals that people were worthy of their generosity: "Good things come to us when we share with other people. It is believed that the things you give will return in larger amounts. Like my father might catch a seal. We share the meat and oil and we find that later the seal itself might not come to us, but we receive something big. Like fishing for us might be better. That's the way we live" (Lala Charles, Emmonak, in Kamerling and Elder 1989).

Considerable rivalry undoubtedly existed as to the quality and quantity of the gifts given during Kevgiq. As a result, a calculated ambiguity circumscribed the event, playing out the movement of persons across the boundary between friend and foe. Just as the performance of "songs of indigestion" enacted the ambiguity between conflict and cooperation, festivity and hostility, so Kevgiq as a whole both expressed and maintained the ambiguous relationship between human communities, simultaneously involving cooperation and competition. As has been said of the song duel, "The ambiguity . . . is not a form of uncertainty, but a form of richness—a dual certainty. The participants are joking and attacking; singing a contest and seriously arguing; friends and adversaries. The function of the duel is to reconcile these pairs and perhaps to demonstrate the constant potential to flip from one term of an opposition to the other. . . . Yet conflict itself was never resolved. . . . Rather, a stable ambiguity was restored" (Eckert and Newmark 1980:209).

Kevgiq involved a circularity comparable to that of the Bladder Festival, the Feast for the Dead, and the masked dances of Kelek: "An individual gives away all his worldly belongings. He gives away his boat and kayak. Even when he does that, all those things get replaced before the coming of summer. They say that they obtain the same things that they give away" (Theresa Moses, October 10, 1987 NI99:2). In the Bladder Festival, the Feast for the Dead, and Kelek, human and animal souls were believed to be reborn contingent on proper treatment during the ceremonies. People also insured their continued ability to produce the necessities of life when they gave them away during Kevgiq. Conversely, stingy people not only lost face, they jeopardized their future ability to produce the wealth they refused to share. As one elder said, "People who were greedy and want to hold on to their possessions are treated like dirt" (Eskimo Heritage Project 1985:39). The more you gave, the more came back to you in the years ahead.

PETUGTAQ: "THEY CALL TO THEIR COUSINS"

Another important annual event throughout western Alaska was the "commercial play" known as Petugtaq (literally, "something tied on") or *petugtaryaraq* ("the way of tying something on") referring to the stick to which participants attached small models of the gifts requested. The literature usually describes Petugtaq, often designated as the Asking Festival, as an exchange of gifts between the men and women of one village (Lantis 1946:187; Morrow 1984:115; Nelson 1899:359). For instance, the men might begin the play by making tiny replicas of things that they desired, such as grass socks, bird-skin caps, mittens, and *akutaq*. They would then hang these replicas on the *qasgiq* wall or on a stick, which messengers took to the women of the village. Each woman then chose one of the images and prepared the item requested. When all was in readiness, the women brought their gifts to the *qasgiq* and presented them to the men who were duty bound to provide a suitable return.

Much variation existed within this general framework. Whereas in some areas Petugtaq was held either during or just after the Bladder Festival (Lantis 1946:187; Nelson 1899:359), Nelson Islanders placed it in the early fall. In some places Petugtaq requests and gift returns followed in a single day. In other places, and possibly at other times in the same place, Petugtaq involved two separate events—the first formal requests from the men to the women followed by a return and the second formal requests from the women to the men followed by a return. Some Nelson Island elders did not make a distinction between Petugtaq and Kevgiruaq, and it is difficult to say how closely related these events were.

By most accounts the fun of Petugtaq derived from the pairing of both biologically and socially unlikely couples in the exchange, as no one knew who had made a specific request until the actual distribution. People considered the pairing of cross-cousins particularly delightful in this context: "The men often do not want their mothers, grandmothers, wives, aunts or sisters to pick their carved images of what they want as gifts. They preferred their cousins, because the Cup'ik people find it humorous and challenging in providing gifts for one another that are hard to find. The cousins tease each other, lavishing the other with gifts and challenging him or her to return it with better ones until one can't return them anymore" (Pingayak 1986; see also Burch 1975:188–89 on Iñupiat cross-cousin teasing).

Central Yup'ik designated cross-sex cross-cousins as *nuliacungaq* ("dear little wife") and *uicungaq* ("dear little husband"). Marriage between cross-cousins was not prescribed, though teasing, complete with sexual innuendo, characterized the relationship between them, as distinct from the much more serious and respectful relationship between siblings and parallel cousins. As in the men's impersonation of women just prior to the Bladder Festival, the pairing of cross-cousins during Petugtaq derived its transformative and ca-

John Milo, of Pilot Station, dressed in a woman's qaspeq *and decorated with ptarmigan tail feathers at the 1993 St. Marys Potlatch.*

thartic power from its reversal and exaggeration of the proper day-to-day relationship between husband and wife.

Though the primary focus of Petugtaq was on the teasing and competition between cross-cousins, the pairing of husband and wife also had a comic "edge" in this extraordinary context:

In the fall, before they have Kevgiq, the *qasgiq* people [men] sent *petugtat* ["things tied on"] to all the houses within a village.

This person wants this. This one wants to eat this, and this person (when guns used to have cases) wants a gun case, *piinrek* [dried grass insoles (dual)], things to use for steam baths, just any kind of small things.

And so this parent from this house takes those things for their children to make that are easy to get. And those *petugtat* are taken to all the houses in the village, and pretty soon every item is taken.

So after getting those things like food in the bowl or other things that they

John Milo and his iluraq *Sebastian Cowboy of St. Marys (dressed in* qaspeq *and wig) pretending to get married, St. Marys, 1993.*

want, they bring them into the *qasgiq* when they were going to dance [that night]. And if they show that particular thing, the one who had asked for that particular thing tells that person to give it to him.

Some people end up making things for one's own father or uncle. When people accidently make something for someone so closely related to them, that causes a lot of laughter. . . .

And one time when those *petugtat* came into the house where your Aunt Frances and I were staying, she and I each took those things that represented a gun case. And when we went to the *qasgiq*, I had taken the gun case wanted by Kumi's father [Frances's husband]. And your Aunt Frances had taken your father's gun case!

So she and I accidently took those, getting things that belonged to our husbands! When we did that, after laughing about it, Kumi's father said, "Since we are the ones that you should make such things for, go right ahead and make us some!" (Brentina Chanar, June 16, 1989)

Petugtaq in the Chevak area was quite elaborate, involving gift requests by the women as well as the men and ending in a dance reminiscent of Kevgiruaq. First the men carved small wooden images of the things they wanted and hung them on the *qasgiq* wall facing the entryway. The women then came into the *qasgiq* and chose an image.

After the women have finished the gifts, they return to the *qaygiq [qasgiq]*. There are usually two young men directing the women to the man that the woman made a gift for. The woman would give the gift to the man and then tell him what she would like to get in return. This is referred to as *akngirqelluki* [from *akngirte-* to get hurt].

The men start practicing Eskimo dance songs that they will be singing for the women to dance to. The women disguise themselves like the men. Some would wear humorous masks and others would paint their faces with black soot. They all wore old clothing so they can look unrecognizable. They would dance all night and everyone would have an enjoyable evening.

The next day the women take over the *qaygiq*. The women carve out miniature wooden objects of what they want as gifts and hang them on the furthest wall of the *qaygiq*. The men start coming in and pick out what they can afford or make. All the wooden objects would be taken. Some of the women's wants would be hard to get but the men would try to get what they wanted.

The women start practicing Eskimo dance songs. When they are done, the men are gathered into the *qaygiq*. The men would bring the gifts that the women wanted. Then the men dress up in the porch as women but with humorous masks or painted faces of black soot. Their roles reverse during the Eskimo dances, the women sing and drum, and the men danced. Everyone would have a lot of fun, especially the cousins exchanging humorous remarks to one another. (Pingayak 1986)

People usually exchanged relatively small gifts, the idea being to have fun rather than to play for great amounts. The potential value of these small Petugtaq gifts is captured in Eddie Alexie's vivid recollection:

They have Petugtaq during fall. They Petugtaq and the men try to "retaliate" against the women.

I have observed them while they have Petugtaq, at the time when I was a young boy.

Then one time, that nephew of mine, that man . . . it happened that one of the women broke an eye of her needle. And because she really valued that needle, she hung it up on a Petugtaq stick indicating that she wanted it to have an eye, that is the way she had it hung. That happened in my very presence.

So people took those *petugtat* [tie-ons].

And no one took that needle. No one took that needle for a long while.

And then that man, my nephew who was just about to get grown up said, "Give me that needle."

So he took that needle.

So the time passed.

So one day, after I had gone out, when I came back in, he was bent [working] down by the light. He was kneeling. At that time, before I went out, one of them said, "After you have exposed it to the fire, I think you may be able to work on it."

And so after that, I did not think about him doing that.

And then when I did come in, that person who had taken that needle was staying like that, kneeling down.

"That is all," he said. "Well, this one has become an eye anyway. It has a hole now but I have almost made it too far to one side! . . . But since it is an eye, it is like this now."

So taking it along, he went out. It was so that he would include it with a bowl of food so that it would be given to its owner.

That is all. A man who made an eye of a needle. How impossible. I cannot begin to think that I can do that! An eye for the needle!

So that person made me see that during *Petugtaq.*

Well, that woman was very grateful for what he had done. (Eddie Alexie, Togiak, March 10, 1988)

During the fall following Petugtaq, villagers gathered together to practice dancing, and some men continued to make special gift requests to their female grandchildren and cross-cousins:

And then after they *petugtaq,* they do what they called *qayagauq* [call repeatedly]. They *qayagauq* to one's grandchild or to one's cross-cousin. One wants this, one wants to eat this for dinner. . . .

Only the men *qayagauq.* They would use a young man as an errand boy, and [the man requesting] would let [the boy] go to a house like his grandchild saying that he wants to have food for dinner.

So that night . . . we would all go to the *qasgiq.* So they are about to dance. And those bowls that we "called," we give them to those who had requested them.

So that is called *qayagaurluteng.* Men "call" to their grandchildren and to their cross-cousins.

Only the men do that. Us women never do that.

But when the man returns that bowl to a person that he has "called," he returns it with something in it. He repays her. . . .

Even though it may not be the very same thing, he fills it with something that he values. . . .

He does not "call" to a male, but to a young female, his grandchild or his other relative, to someone that he loves and is fond of, anyone he has fun teasing. (Brentina Chanar, June 16, 1989)

Brentina Chanar distinguishes between *qayagauq* requests from people in one's own community and *cingartuq* (from *cingar-* to kiss or snuffle a child), in which older people "kiss" their grandchildren in other villages, requesting something that the child's parents were obligated to supply. Although other accounts associate "kissing" requests with the intravillage Bladder Festival, Brentina Chanar identified them with Kevgiq: "At the time they are having Kevgiq, they do what they call *cingartuq.* And their 'enemy' *cingartuq* toward them likewise."

Another winter entertainment playing on the normal, respectful, relationship between husband and wife was a wife-guessing game called *pinirtaaguqu'urluteng* (literally, "seeing which one is stronger," from *pinir-* to be strong physically):

Their wives are covered with a canvas. . . . They do not let their husbands know where they are while they are covered. So they are covered while they are crouched down.

So their husbands try to guess where their wives are just like the ones that are trying to win. So each husband would go to his covered one, claiming that it is his wife. So when all the husbands have made their choice, then the women get up to show who they are.

Some of the men would make a mistake!

One time the former father of Terkuaq . . . because he was a teasing sort, he had sneaked a peek while his wife and the other wives were being covered, so he knew just exactly where his wife was being covered.

So then all [the husbands] came in. This must have been in the *qasgiq* then.

Then after he looked around briefly, he remarked, "Okay, that one down there, I seem to recognize the spine!"

And so he went down to her while she was crouching like this, and he patted her and said again, "I really think that this is really her, our mother! It cannot be anyone else! Her spine is just like it should be!"

It was that he had peeked! (Brentina Chanar, June 16, 1989)

Nelson Islanders also described an activity in the *qasgiq* called *quuyurniqalria* (literally, "the one who smiles"). This was a competition in which cross-cousins sat across from each other, staring with a straight face and trying to make their opponent smile:

One time the late father of Nupiigaq and the late Nasaaller were going to be antagonists in *quuyurniqalriarcuulluteng*. So then that Nasaaller came in with his eyes anchored back [with sticks] so they were wide open.

So his antagonist was stone-faced, not smiling at all.

And then, his antagonist who was trying to make him smile burst out laughing! When he laughed out, that An'ngaqumtalleq burst out laughing too.

So that is how they used to compete. They try to make the others smile. (Brentina Chanar, June 6, 1989).

Dennis Panruk of Chefornak (December 17, 1987) summed up the character of these fall festivities: "And then when the fall comes, because those people used to celebrate events, they call on others to come, they call to their cousins, they have Petugtaq, then make models of tools for the *maqi* [sweat bath], so they pretend and have events."

Petugtaq shared features with Kevgiq and Kevgiruaq both in Chevak and on Nelson Island. In Chevak the two young men acting as "messengers" to guide the women recall the two messengers that acted as go-betweens for the two villages in Kevgiq. On Nelson Island, the men and women were desig-

nated as distinct "peoples" during Petugtaq—Qairuarmiut and Peñacuarmiut respectively—as they had been in Kevgiruaq.

Just as Kevgiq involved cross-sex and cross-cousin competition and teasing
between communities, both Kevgiruaq and Petugtaq involved teasing and
friendly competition between men and women of a single community. While
generous gifting during Kevgiq insured ample stores in the future, appropriate provision of requests during Petugtaq demonstrated to both the human
and nonhuman audience the participants' ability and goodwill. The abbreviated descriptions doubtless leave out much of the richness of these events.
From what we know, the events allowed participants to see themselves and
their fellows as if in a fun-house mirror—both reflected and distorted. They
are remembered chiefly for their character as "humorous and challenging"—
simultaneously exaggerating relationships (especially between cross-cousins)
and standing the day-to-day world on its head. They both tested and pushed
to the extreme the normal boundaries between different communities and
people, displaying their fame and foibles for the edification of members of
both the human and nonhuman worlds.

CHAPTER 12

FOLLOWING THE UNIVERSE

They made the path clear. . . . They followed the direction of the universe. . . .
They did this so that the animals would come to them.

—*Billy Lincoln, Toksook Bay, January 30, 1991*

YUP'IK COSMOLOGY is a perpetual cycling between birth and rebirth, humans and animals, and the living and the dead. The relationship between humans and animals reflects a cycle of reciprocity in which animals give their bodies in exchange for careful treatment and respect. The preceding pages detail the statements of Yup'ik narrators and the metaphors they use to describe the ruled boundaries and ceremonial passages through which this cosmological cycle was created and maintained. Accounts have not focused on action observed—innumerable exchanges of gifts and services that continue to shape life in western Alaska today. Rather, they describe the ideal rules that forged the shifting and permeable boundaries between worlds and the ritual acts that created the pathways between them.

Comparable rules circumscribed the emergence of children from their mothers, mature men and women from their childhood, the dead from the world of the living, and the seals from the sea. The passages of children, menstruating girls, young hunters, deceased humans, sea mammals, and land animals were all surrounded by restrictions "to make their way clear." These passages provided for a one-way movement between opposing worlds—movement from the land of the living to the land of the dead, women waiting in the land, drawing the seals from the sea. Yet following a human death, something essential returned to reanimate the newborn namesake, just as, following the seal's death, its bones and bladder were returned to live again in the sea. Instead of a static opposition between life and death, men and women, sea and land, metaphors of interaction and encompassment defined their relationship.

The image of the frowning seal found on nineteenth-century Yup'ik hunting equipment and ceremonial paraphernalia is a fine example of such inter-

dependencies. This image has puzzled ethnographers and led some to speculate that the Yup'ik Eskimos considered seals to be "female" beings, which
male hunters subsequently attracted and overpowered. But like hermaphrodite
masks (Kaplan 1984:2), the frowning seal may be meaningful insofar as it
transcended the boundaries separating male from female in the same way
that wolf/whale transformation masks combined the power of land and sea.
As in much of Yup'ik iconography, the ambiguous character and the "combined" quality of persons was the starting point, and their separation in daily
life was an ongoing and constant process.

The Yupiit were preoccupied with maintaining continuity in the relationships between human and nonhuman persons through time and space. A
major focus of activity was on the capacity of acts of differentiation—
cutting, binding, covering, circling—to create the possibility of future relation. All creatures were considered analogically related "persons" until differentiated through action. Following Wagner (1977), when relationship
occurred, it was the consequence of contrived difference flowing from an
original interdiction. One all-consuming focus of ritual acts then became a
project of differentiation—the creation and maintenance of boundaries and
passages between persons and the worlds in which they lived. Only when
difference had been established could relationship take place.

The Yupiit paid particular attention to the senses of human and nonhuman persons in their rules for living. All persons, both living and dead, could
see, hear, smell, taste, touch, and "think strong thoughts." Humans could
initiate communication with the nonhuman world by appealing to these
shared senses through speech, sight, touch, taste, smell, and sound. Men
singing and drumming in the *qasgiq* drew members of the spirit world. The
shaman and his helpers made visible the unseen through dramatic use of
masks. The healer allowed disease to "walk out" of the human body through
a laying on of hands. Boys prepared a path for the seals by shoveling snow
and clearing passages with the thought of the seals foremost in their minds.
The successful hunter held his hunting staff vertically or planted his paddle
blade upward outside the *qasgiq* as an act of invitation into the human world.
Women drew land animals and seals into the human world with promises of
oil and water to satisfy their hunger and quench their thirst.

The thoughtless use of one's senses also could block passages and create
obstacles, and the proper boundaries between persons were carefully maintained. A man avoided looking at a woman's face or breathing her "bad air"
at all costs, to insure his "strong vision" and "powerful breath" during the
hunt. Menstruating women went about belted and hooded to bound them off
from the "eye of *ella*." Sleeping late opened a person's body to the entry of
illness. A person must also perform the proper removal motion after drinking from a bucket and eat with care, wasting nothing and disposing of bones
in the proper place. Children especially must refrain from loud or inappropriate noise.

"Woman looking into the future" through the ellanguaq *(pretend universe). Doll made by Rosalie Paniyak, Chevak, 1987. James H. Barker.*

Many ritual acts separated people and kept them apart, while other actions brought them together. The major ceremonies employed these acts to draw animal spirits and the shades of the human dead along the path into the human world while maintaining the differences between them. It was in this context that the acts of circling *ella maliggluku* ("following the universe") or, alternately, *ella asgurluku* ("going against the universe," from *asgur-* to go against a natural force such as water current or wind) took on special importance. The path one cleared was not straight but circled back on itself. To follow a circular path had the power either to create and maintain the boundaries between persons or states of being, or to initiate movement and travel across the distance between them, depending on the context and direction in which people performed it.

Inuit people all across the Arctic practiced the act of circling in the direction of the universe ("with the sun" from east to west). Robert Petersen (1966–67:262) recorded the comparable expression *sila maligdlugo*, translated "according to the world order" among the Inuit: "The idea . . . seems to be transposed to cover the cycle of life and everything connected with it, particularly the division and interchange between life and death." *Sila agssordlugo*, which Petersen translates "contrary to world order," denotes a direction of movement opposed to the course of the sun.

People performed circling actions again and again during both formal and informal Yup'ik ceremonial activity. For example, Nelson (1899:381–89) recorded celebrants moving in a circle within the *qasgiq* at various points during the Bladder Festival as well as circling the ice hole at the ceremony's close. On the sixth day of the Bladder Festival, after returning from the ice, "men form a circle around the room, each bent over and having his hands on the nape of the one in front of him; everyone is completely nude. Two nude boys are placed in the middle of the ring while the men circle four times around the room from left to right (with the sun)" (Nelson 1899:381). Nelson (1899:383, 384) also refers to a circle of helmets around the walrus skull in the men's house during the Bladder Festival and, later, to a man circling once around the room with a wooden dish of food high over his head as an offering to the shades and "tunghat" (*tuunrat* or shaman's helping spirits) in the skyland. Later, during the same feast, the shaman "lighted a parsnip-stalk torch and passed it about the room, holding it close to the floor. He then circled with it about each of the dancers, who removed their fur coats and the torch was passed about their bodies and inside and about their fur coats" to purify them and remove any evil influence (Nelson 1899:388). More than one hundred years later, Nelson Islanders recalled comparable ritual circuits during Qaariitaaq, Aaniq, and the Bladder Festival proper.

The action of circling in the direction of the day was also an important part of the treatment of the human dead. On the fourth day of the Feast for the Dead at Razbinsky in January 1881, Nelson (1899:372) observed, "As the dance concluded the central drummer, an old man, arose, and, holding the drum and stick overhead, called out, 'Turn now as light (of day) goes,' and, with a loud, hissing noise, he turned slowly a quarter of a circle with the sun, from left to right, and stopped; after a short pause he turned another quarter of a circle and stopped again, and so on until the circle was completed. . . . When the circle was completed the dancers stamped their feet and slapped their thighs to make themselves clean, and all went outside." After clothing the namesake on the fifth day, the feast-giver called out in a loud voice, bidding the shade of his relative to return to its grave, "'Go back to your grave on Clear creek and there circle around it once and then enter your grave box.' Others told the shade to circle about its grave three times and enter it. Others told the shade to circle about the village where it was buried and then enter the grave. The dead who were buried beside this village were told to go out and circle about the place or kashim and return to their graves" (Nelson 1899:377).

The Canadian Inuit likewise employed sunlike circles in the care of their dead. In his description of Baffin Island Inuit, Julian Bilby (1923:166) wrote:

> At burial they march single file seven times round the cairn following the direction of the sun, i.e., from east to west, chanting directions to the departed: "My life, pray let it be put right, through that which is pleasant alone (Illoo-prakoole kissearne). Through space following (Nakrook mallilugo). Following that which gives light (Kamattevoot milliglo).
>
> For unpopular or badly conducted men, people walk round the cairn in the reverse direction, i.e. from west to east, with a different refrain. The idea being to direct the spirit away from the light and into the outer darkness, their refrain begins with the words to the effect "Evil will always have evil." All this is called the custom of the Kingarngtooktok.

Franz Boas (1888:614) reported that among the Central Eskimos, on the third day after death, the relatives visited the grave and circled it three times "in the same direction as the sun is moving, at the same time talking to the deceased and promising that they will bring him something to eat." The Siberian Yup'ik Eskimos of St. Lawrence Island engaged in a comparable practice: "On five days following burial, at sunrise and sunset, they must go up together to the grave and go once around it in the same direction as that of the sun's circuit of the heavens" (Moore 1923:371–75).

Private ritual circuits were also abundant among the Yup'ik Eskimos of western Alaska, including the act of circling the house "following the day" after someone in the village died, following childbirth, or at the conclusion of a young girl's menstrual seclusion. The very winds were created when a mythic Doll circled the earth-plain, passing and opening holes in the east, southeast, south, west, northwest, and north before returning to the center of the flat earth (Nelson 1899:497). A common curing technique among the Siberian as well as the Central Alaska Yup'ik Eskimos was to encircle a joint or body part with a string to prevent the disease from progressing.

Moreover, shamans circled around their patients during healing ceremonies.

References to acts of encircling by women as well as men abound in the literature describing Inuit as well as Yup'ik ritual activity. Knud Rasmussen (1927:129; 1931:60) observed the efficacy of the "magic circle" performed by Netsilik women to protect their community from the entry of unclean influences: "It is the custom on the coming of strangers, for the women who have borne children, to step a circle round the sledge with its team; undesirable spirit entities are then 'bound' within the magic circle and can do no harm."

According to Hawkes (1914:9), shamans were noted for the dizzy circles which they ran around the *qasgiq* entrance hole. Peter Freuchen (1931:162) described how a person who wished to obtain concentration (and thus knowledge) went to a lonely place and rubbed a stone in a circle on a rock for hours and days on end. The Viking saga of Eric the Red describes the appearance of Skraelings "in skin canoes" with paddles in their hands who "revolved in the same direction in which the sun moves" (Hawkes 1916:1). Thus, moving in a sunwise circle was among the first acts Euro-Americans observed Eskimos performing, and the Inuit may well have intended it to contain the power of these pale-faced creatures from another world.

The turn-of-the-century Yupiit did not believe that years followed each other one after the other in necessary succession. Rather, people bore responsibility for the cycle of the seasons and participated in its annual renewal. Such activity, however, was dangerous if participants did not follow the rules and take proper precautions. Men and women engaged in opening the boundaries between worlds protected themselves from merging with the spirit world by covering their bodies with gut parkas or by painting themselves with soot, clay, and urine. Or they might place grass mats or skins between themselves and the thin earth lest they slip through. Both men and women wore encircling belts to protect themselves from the entrance of unclean influences as well as to hold in their life force. At the same time, through ritual circuits performed during the major ceremonies, people alternately opened the boundary and traveled the distance between worlds and protected themselves from merging with their nonhuman counterparts.

The act of circling was also performed during the ritual of the hunt throughout the Eskimo world. Collins reported that the successful crew on St. Lawrence Island paddled sunwise around the dead whale (Lantis 1947:49). When the Nunivak hunter launched his kayak, he walked around it east to west clockwise, set sail, paddled in a circle clockwise three times, and only then went out to sea (Lantis 1947:39). Voblov reports that during the Siberian Eskimo ceremony of the tusks following walrus hunting in June, the celebrant left the house and solemnly circled it, "moving with the sun" to the place where a pole had been planted. Later he returned home, cut pieces of food, placed these in a dipper, took a rattle, and circled his house from east to west. Lifting the dipper in the direction of the sunrise, he called out and returned to the house again according to the direction of the sun's movement: "During the ceremony the celebrant had invited unto himself the mightiest of spirits—the spirit of the sun, giver of warmth, light and life" (Hughes 1958:73–75).

Celebrants circled around a pole in the center of the *iaranga* (skin tent) in various rituals among the Siberian Eskimos, including the ceremony of the tusks (Hughes 1958:79–80; Serov 1988:254). This pole was said to mark the passage between three layers of vertically superimposed worlds (Mikhailova 1990:5). The significance of the central pole in Siberian Yup'ik ceremony recalls the importance of vertical stakes in Central Yup'ik ritual activity, including the raised hunting hook following the successful hunt, the stakes planted at the grave at the opening of the Feast for the Dead, the messenger stick used to extend an invitation to the guest village, and the *kangaciqaq* (pole topped with wild celery) honored throughout the Bladder Festival and planted by the hole in the ice when the bladders were sent back to the sea. These vertical poles served to mark a point of passage between worlds for both the Siberian and Central Alaska Yup'ik Eskimos.

A vertical pole did more than mark a point of passage, as it often provided the focus for encircling actions. For example, in the Siberian Yup'ik "Winding Around" ceremony at the end of January, participants sang and twisted around the pole in a half circle to the right and then to the left (Hughes 1958:84). Nelson (1899:381) also recorded celebrants moving in opposite directions at the same time at one point during the Bladder Festival. Similarly Voblov (Hughes 1958:84) described movement against the direction of the sun's course during a Siberian Yup'ik ceremony. During the "Kamygtak" rite in January, "The celebrant . . . moves around the outside of the house against the direction of the sun, comes to a stop halfway, and shouts: 'Right now we will hold a great ceremony. . . . [Spirits] come onto us.' He then returns to the house, takes his drum and, beating it, goes around in a circle inside the house. . . . Having made a few turns around the house, the celebrant then makes his way toward the entrance and more intensely beats the drum, concluding in that way the cleaning out of evil spirits from the bed platform." Boas (1888:611) reported that among the Central Eskimos, those who were born in abnormal presentations wore women's dresses and circled "in a direction opposite to the movement of the sun" during the Sedna Feast.

The paucity of recorded occurrences of this reverse movement, as well as the many instances where descriptions do not specify the direction of the encircling action, make it difficult to speculate on its meaning. Though the full significance of these processions and reverse processions is irretrievable, people probably performed them as part of a common effort to effect the cosmological cycle on which they were modeled. The Yupiit annually performed a multitude of ceremonies, in part to extend the boundaries between domains kept rigorously separated during daily life and to evoke a response from the spirit and animal worlds. The act of circling the center might be taken as a metaphor for the ritual process as a whole, the focus of which was traveling the distance between worlds while simultaneously reestablishing the relationship and affirming the differences between them.

MAKING THE PATH CLEAR

> *Now, if a person truly has confidence and pride in his/her life, s/he will not make too many mistakes and will travel on the smooth path. . . . If one was asked to approach those people with rank and does not lose one's style and manner, one's mind will be clear to articulate and inquire.*

> —*Paul John, Toksook Bay, November 5, 1991*

Life on the coast of the Bering Sea has changed dramatically over the last fifty years. People no longer practice the Bladder Festival, the Feast for the Dead, Kelek, or Petugtaq and have not held such ceremonies for decades. Kevgiq and an occasional Kevgiruaq still take place, but modified in important respects from their late nineteenth-century counterparts. Older men and women still recall past rules for living, although they practice them less and less.

There was little interest in recording the Yup'ik past and apparently little regret at its passing when I began work in western Alaska in the mid-1970s. The ceremonies that were still such an important part of life at the turn of the century had been abandoned, and myriad rules and ritual acts—including "following the universe"—had come to be viewed as "the devil's work" and were only infrequently talked about. By 1980 Yup'ik people were becoming more and more aware of the fragility of their past—and how much of it they had already let go. Few elders remembered the days before the missionaries. Many Yup'ik children were ignorant of pre-Christian "superstitions" and repeatedly demonstrated their lack of understanding of past rules of interpersonal action, circumspection, attention, and survival. As the older generation got out of the habit of talking, children lost the habit of listening. A boundary grew up between them, according to one elder: "My high school children come home to our one room house. They are here, but a partition exists between us. They are losing our language and way of life, yet there really is no alternative lifestyle other than subsistence for many years to come. They now have needs and wants based on the white man's way" (Kawagley 1989:17).

What followed in the wake of this recognition has been a dramatic cultural renaissance in western Alaska. This has taken many forms—political action, elders' conferences, oral history projects, cultural heritage programs, multivillage dance festivals, the development of bilingual material for the schools based on interviews with knowledgeable elders. Today many older men and women are anxious to discourse on "tradition" as an avenue to cultural identity. With the increase in problems associated with rapid culture change (dramatic increases in the rates of suicide, homicide, alcoholism, and

Toksook Bay dancers Martina John, Frances Usugan, and Paul Agimuk at St. Marys, 1982. James H. Barker.

domestic violence) has come the conviction that Yup'ik children need a firm grounding in the values of the past to survive in the future. Ulrick Nayamin, commenting on the importance of the Chevak Cultural Heritage Program, leaves no doubt about the value he places on the past: "In the past it was a big mistake to stop the dances—a lot of things died in this process. Restarting the dances is only one thing. . . . You only saw a small portion of what they used to do in those days. . . . By learning the dances, you young people will have weight so that nobody can brush you off the top of this earth. You will be the exciting ones because you have something of your own—your culture!" (Madsen 1990:48–49).

Elders actively seek to affect their children's future by recounting the past. Just as the Yupiit viewed a person's sight, touch, and consciousness (mind) as possessing the power to alter the future, so telling a story in part reproduces the relationships it narrates. When elders speak, the narrated world regains a measure of reality. The Yupiit view oratory, like sight and breath, as having transformative power. According to Eddie Bell (1990:13) of Hooper Bay, "We must gather together and speak so there will be an awakening." Just as they believed that saying a person's name might call the spirit of the namesake from the land of the dead, to tell a story is more than recitation, it is an act of re-creation. To talk about an ordered universe can help to make it so. As eloquently stated by Marie Meade (1990:230), a Yup'ik language teacher and translator from Nunapitchuk:

> Today, many indigenous people of the North feel like they're losing something. . . . We are having a difficult time accessing and obtaining information, a problem the Yup'ik people never had in the recent past. We are acting like we've lost our breath and are gasping around. . . . In the oral presentation the message is kinetic. It's alive and moving. . . . The storyteller and the listener can always elaborate and find new meaning. The listener can influence how you tell a story. The oral system is giving and taking. . . . The giving is very generous, but taking is limited. It depends on how well you can listen.

When Yup'ik elders talk about their history, they evoke a harmonious view of Yup'ik life in the past. This is in part because they are describing an ideal view—how people were supposed to behave rather than how in fact they acted. Because they are influenced by modern perceptions of the past, their words cannot be taken as timeless facts but as selective recollections. This partiality, however, does not reduce their value.

Yup'ik orators repeatedly employed the metaphor "clearing the path" when talking about their view of the world and what they hoped listeners would remember and apply to their own lives. Anthropologists often speak of ruled "boundaries" and ceremonial "passages" among the people with whom they work. In this case, however, the metaphor is indigenous. The Yupiit themselves talk of "traveling on a smooth path," "making a way," and "cutting off one's future catch" when presenting their view of the world. Describing her

Young people dancing traditional dances at Stebbins. James H. Barker.

student teaching experience at Bethel Regional High School, Theresa John of Toksook Bay retained her father's metaphor: "It's important to teach our future leaders proper knowledge and build solid trails so that they too can successfully lead their young peers."

This book began as an effort to make connections—to "figure out" Yup'ik cosmology. It concludes that the project of differentiation was also at the core of Yup'ik life. Connection could not be taken for granted, and human effort was required to "clear the path," making relation possible. With these paths in place, multiple acts of relation—gifts given, names passed on, the return of seals the following year—were once again possible between human and nonhuman persons. The elaborate flow of goods and services that continues to texture Yup'ik life is the necessary result and consequence.

Yup'ik people viewed the world as originally undifferentiated, but they invoked an elaborate set of rules to create and maintain differences. Ironically these same rules are now invoked to differentiate between the native and nonnative worlds. The idea that Yup'ik people "make their path clear" by living according to ancestral rules is one that residents of western Alaska use to define themselves in opposition to the careless, unregulated actions of nonnatives: The Yupiit live an ordered life. They "follow a path," whereas many outsiders live without respect. Just as Euro-Americans have alternately viewed Eskimos as an idealized or diminished image of themselves, many Yupiit construct their identity in opposition to a generalized nonnative.

Yup'ik people today strive for simultaneous recognition of their shared humanity and their special place in history. On the one hand, they work for recognition of their similarity with members of the human race in the 1990s. Just as every American needs a job, a house, an education, a doctor when they are sick, so do they. At the same time, many Yupiit actively seek recognition as different—possessing sovereign rights to their land, a special subsistence economy, their own language, a unique view of the world. For contemporary Yupiit, their relationship with animals is still central, although differently defined. Harvesting retains important cultural and economic functions, and the desire to retain control over their lands and waterways is the focus of political action and debate. And traditional rules for living still have relevance:

> During this time now, some of the ways of life have changed, but even though some of it has changed, the ways in which a person's life can be good cannot change, the ways which we have learned in us, who are called Yupiit. And the way we live together apparently should not be lost since our ancestors have lived this way from the ancient time.
>
> In our way of expressing, traditionally, the Yupiit have an adage saying that there are no other humans in the world.
>
> And that still holds true during this time now. . . .
>
> They would say that someone may try to become a *Kass'aq* [white person], but they would say that was impossible. (Paul John, November 6, 1991)

Today, Yup'ik orators create and maintain a boundary between themselves and others, in part by making detailed statements about a unique past. Over and over again they cite a special past as justification for present action. Yup'ik oratory, dance distributions, harvesting acts—all are used to define what is Yup'ik and what is not as a source of personal identity and power. The orations quoted in this book are thus embedded in issues of cultural survival. The interviews recalling information about the past are part of the Yup'ik effort to control both the education of their children and the outside view of themselves. The interviews presented them with a chance to speak— not to record timeless memories, but as part of a larger struggle for self-determination. Contemporary accounts of the past explain the nature of the world to Yup'ik participants as well as provide an opportunity for Yupiit to state their own identity in opposition to the non-Yup'ik way of being in the world.

Yup'ik statements about their past concern their future. We should not, however, underestimate the value of these statements as windows into the past. What we are told may be partial, but it is not false. As described, the Yupiit place high value on repeating only what a person knows from experience. Orators claim to speak only for themselves. All stress things were done differently in other places and that they can tell only about what they had observed or experienced (Mather 1986; Morrow 1990).

Orators placed tremendous emphasis on living according to the rules "to make one's path clear." They gave voice to the variation in how these rules were played out. In fact, local variation was a point of pride, and abandonment of these differences today was remarked. For example, a Stebbins elder ruminated on the way in which people from other villages can use each other's dances: "Nowadays the dance customs have become very mixed-up. When the people of Kotlik come over and do their own style of story dancing, when they leave we can use their dances. The people have no more prohibitions, and customs are now used as playthings, for fun. . . . They bring their songs and dances over to us and give them to us as gifts" (Eskimo Heritage Project 1985:87). Although each group and each person had elaborate mechanisms for dealing with the nonhuman world, these varied widely both in form and application. This brings to mind Jean Malaurie's (1982:xv) statement regarding the Greenlandic Inuit: "Eskimos combine the most firmly asserted individuality that coexists with the most restrictive group laws."

Nevertheless, one is struck by the close fit between what individual elders reported in the 1980s and what ethnographers and explorers recorded in the late nineteenth century. We can use what we are told today to understand better the significance of what Nelson and others observed a century ago. For example, we know from Nelson's (1899:382–84) description of the Bladder Festival that it was a complex ceremony with a central focus but many separate parts. He recorded in tremendous detail the activity of participants,

Nelson Island elders with their grandchildren, Toksook Bay, 1977. Clockwise (ella malig-gluku), *Anna Kungurkaq, Magdeline Sunny, and Brentina Chanar.*

including their imitations of myriad birds. His words would remain incomprehensible but for contemporary accounts detailing the meaning of birds in relation to seal hunting, specifically the transformation of the seal hunter into a little seabird in the eyes of the seals he seeks.

No Yup'ik elder would sit down and organize discourse, let alone a book, in the way I have done here; but they eloquently, and generously, answered my questions, as the texts show. Taken out of the original context of the interviews, these severed bits of dialogue lose something. Yet put in the context of complementary statements by other orators, they gain something as well, helping the reader to understand how Yup'ik people talk about their world. As I am not Yup'ik, this is not a perfect solution. But just as I was inspired by the success of the Yup'ik author, Elsie Mather, in interviewing elders, Yup'ik readers may be inspired both to expand on and to correct what I have recorded. No one elder tells it all, wraps it up. No one can clear the path for you. Rather, they give an example, tell what they know, and I have tried to do the same.

REFERENCES

Alexie, Oscar, and Helen Morris, eds.
    1985   *The Elders' Conference of 1984.* Bethel, Alaska: Orutsararmiut Native Council.

Anderson, Eva G.
    1940   *Dog Team Doctor.* Caldwell, Idaho: Caxton.

Angaiak, Susan
    1991   "Letter to the Editor." *Tundra Drums* (Bethel, Alaska). May 16, p. 2.

Balikci, Asen
    1989   "Anthropology, Film and the Arctic Peoples: The First Forman Lecture." *Anthropology Today* 5(2):4–10.

Barnum, Francis, S. J.
    1901   *Grammatical Fundamentals of the Inuit Language as Spoken by the Eskimo of the Western Coast of Alaska.* Boston: Athenaeum Press.

Bell, Eddie
    1990   "Letter to the Editor." *Tundra Drums* (Bethel, Alaska). August 2, p. 13.

Biersack, Aletta
    1984   "Paiela 'Women-Men': The Reflexive Foundations of Gender Ideology." *American Ethnologist* 10:118–38.

Bilby, Julian W.
    1923   *Among Unknown Eskimos: Twelve Years in Baffin Island.* Philadelphia: J. B. Lippincott.

Birket-Smith, Kaj
    1936   *Eskimos.* Translated from Danish by W. E. Calvert. London: Methuen.

Black, Lydia T.
    1991   *Glory Remembered: Wooden Headgear of Alaska's Sea Hunters.* Juneau: Alaska State Museum.

Bloch, Maurice, and Jonathan Parry
    1982   *Death and the Regeneration of Life.* Cambridge: Cambridge University Press.

Boas, Franz
    1888   "The Central Eskimos." *Sixth Annual Report of the Bureau of Ethnology to the Secretary of the Smithsonian Institution 1884–85.* Washington, D.C.

1901–7   *The Eskimo of Baffin Land and Hudson Bay, I–II.* Bulletin of the American Museum of Natural History 15.

Bogoras, Waldemar
1904–9   *The Chukchee.* Vol. II of Memoirs of the American Museum of Natural History. Edited by Franz Boas. Reprint. New York: Johnson Reprint, 1975.

Borre, Kristen
1991   "Seal Blood, Inuit Blood, and Diet: A Biocultural Model of Physiology and Cultural Identity." Medical Anthropology Quarterly 5 (1):48–61.

Briggs, Jean
1991   "Mazes of Meaning: The Exploration of Individuality in Culture and of Culture through Individual Constructs." In *The Psychoanalytic Study of Society,* vol. 16, edited by L. Bryce Boyer and Simon Grolnick. Hillsdale, N.J.: Analytic.

Brightman, Robert A.
1983   "Animal and Human in Rock Cree Religion and Subsistence." Ph.D. diss., Department of Anthropology, University of Chicago.

Burch, Ernest, Jr.
1971   "The Nonempirical Environment of the Arctic Alaskan Eskimos." *Southwestern Journal of Anthropology* 27(2):148–65.
1975   *Eskimo Kinsmen: Changing Family Relationships in Northwest Alaska.* American Ethnological Society, Monograph 59. San Francisco: West Publishing.

Curtis, Edward S.
1930   *The North American Indian, Being a Series of Volumes Picturing and Describing the Indians of the United States, the Dominion of Canada, and Alaska,* vol. 20. Reprint. New York: Johnson Reprint, 1970.

Dall, William Healy
1870   *Alaska and Its Resources.* Reprint. New York: Arno Press, 1970.

Dixon, M., and S. Kirchner
1982   "'Poking,' an Eskimo Medicinal Practice in Northwest Alaska." *Études/Inuit/Studies* 6(2):109–25.

Dumond, Don E.
1977   *The Eskimos and Aleuts.* London: Thames and Hudson.

Eckert, Penelope, and Russell Newmark
1980   "Central Eskimo Song Duels: A Contextual Analysis of Ritual Ambiguity." *Ethnology* 19:191–212.

Eskimo Doll Project
1981   Interview with Joe Friday in Chevak, Alaska. Oral History Program, Polar Regions Department, Rasmusen Library, University of Alaska, Fairbanks.

Eskimo Heritage Project
1985   "The Stebbins Potlatch." Manuscript edited by Mary Alexander Wondzell, introduction by Anatole Bogeyaktuk and Charlie Steve. Nome, Alaska: Kawerak.

Evans-Pritcard, E. E.
1940   *The Nuer.* Oxford: Oxford University Press.

Fienup-Riordan, Ann
1983   *The Nelson Island Eskimo.* Anchorage: Alaska Pacific University Press.
1984   "Regional Groups on the Yukon-Kuskokwim Delta." In *The Central Yupik Eskimos,* edited by Ernest Burch, Jr. Supplementary issue of *Études/Inuit/Studies* 8:63–93.
1986a   "The Real People: The Concept of Personhood among the Yup'ik Eskimos of Western Alaska." *Études/Inuit/Studies* 10(1–2):261–70.

1986b   *When Our Bad Season Comes: A Cultural Account of Subsistence Harvesting and Harvest Disruption on the Yukon Delta.* Aurora Monograph Series 1. Anchorage: Alaska Anthropological Association.

1987   "The Mask: The Eye of the Dance." *Arctic Anthropology* 24(2):40–55.

1988   (ed.) *The Yup'ik Eskimos as Described in the Travel Journals and Ethnographic Accounts of John and Edith Kilbuck, 1885–1900.* Kingston, Ontario: Limestone.

1989   The Yupiit Nation: Eskimo Law and Order. Manuscript prepared for the Alaska Humanities Forum. Anchorage, Alaska.

1990   *Eskimo Essays: Yup'ik Lives and How We See Them.* New Brunswick, N.J.: Rutgers University Press.

1991   *The Real People and the Children of Thunder.* Norman: University of Oklahoma Press.

1992   (ed.) "Social Status Among the Yup'ik Eskimos of the Lower Kuskokwim as Told to Reverend Arthur Butzin by Alaskuk." *Anthropological Papers of the University of Alaska* 24(1–2):33–49.

Fitzhugh, William W.
1988a   "Eskimos: Hunters of the Frozen Coasts." In *Crossroads of Continents: Cultures of Siberia and Alaska,* edited by William W. Fitzhugh and Aron Crowell. Washington, D.C.: Smithsonian Institution Press.

1988b   "Persistence and Change in Art and Ideology in Western Alaskan Eskimo Cultures." In *The Late Prehistoric Development of Alaska's Native Peoples,* edited by Robert D. Shaw, Roger K. Harritt, and Don E. Dumand. Aurora Monograph Series, no. 4. Anchorage: Alaska Anthropological Association.

Fitzhugh, William W., and Aron Crowell
1988   *Crossroads of Continents: Cultures of Siberia and Alaska.* Washington, D.C.: Smithsonian Institution Press.

Fitzhugh, William W., and Susan A. Kaplan
1982   *Inua: Spirit World of the Bering Sea Eskimo.* Washington, D.C.: Smithsonian Institution Press.

Fortes, Meyer
1969   *The Web of Kinship among the Tallensi.* London: Oxford University Press.

Freuchen, Peter
1931   *Eskimo.* New York: Grossett and Dunlap.

Friday, Joe
1985   Interview by Louise Leonard, February 19. Lansburg Productions, San Francisco.

Garber, Clark McKinley
1934   "Some Mortuary Customs of the Western Alaska Eskimo." *Scientific Monthly* 39(3):203–20.

Gordon, G. B.
1917   *In the Alaskan Wilderness.* Philadelphia: John C. Winston.

Graburn, Nelson
1969   "Eskimo Law in the Light of Self and Group Interest." *Law and Society Review* 4(1):45–60.

Hallowell, A. Irving
1960   "Ojibwa Ontology, Behavior, and World View." In *Culture in History: Essays in Honor of Paul Radin,* edited by Stanley Diamond. New York: Columbia University Press.

Hawkes, Ernest William
1913   *The "Inviting-In" Feast of the Alaskan Eskimo.* Canada Geological Survey. Memoir 45. Anthropological Series No. 3.

1914   *The Dance Festivals of the Alaskan Eskimo.* University of Pennsylvania, Anthropological Publications 6(2).

1916   *The Labrador Eskimo.* Washington, D.C.: Government Printing Office.

Himmelheber, Hans
1938   *Eskimokünstler.* Eisenach: Erich Röth-Verlag.
1987   *Eskimo Artists.* Zurich: Museum Rietberg.

Hoebel, E. Adamson
1964   *The Law of Primitive Man: A Study in Comparative Legal Dynamics.* Cambridge: Harvard University Press.

Honigmann, John J., and Irma Honigmann
1965   *Eskimo Townsmen.* Ottawa: Canadian Research Center for Anthropology, Saint Paul University.

Hughes, Charles
1958   "Translation of I. K. Voblov's 'Eskimo Ceremonies'." *Anthropological Papers of the University of Alaska* 7(2):71–90.

Ivanov, Sergei V.
1930   "Aleut Hunting Headgear and its Ornamentation." *Proceedings of the Twenty-third International Congress of Americanists.* Reprinted in *Glory Remembered,* 1991. Juneau: Alaska State Museum.

Jacobson, Steven A.
1984   *Yup'ik Eskimo Dictionary.* Fairbanks: Alaska Native Language Center, University of Alaska.

Jenness, Diamond
1922   *The Life of the Copper Eskimos,* vol. 12. Report of the Canadian Arctic Expedition, 1913–18. Ottawa.

Kamerling, Leonard, and Sarah Elder
1989   *Uksuum Cauyai: The Drums of Winter.* Alaska Native Heritage Film Project, Fairbanks, Alaska.

Kaplan, Susan A.
1984   "Note." In *The Central Yup'ik Eskimos,* edited by Ernest S. Burch, Jr. Supplementary issue of *Études/Inuit/Studies* 8:2.

Kasaiyuli, John
1981   "Life in the Men's House and the Seal Bladder Festival." In *Yupik Lore: Oral Traditions of an Eskimo People,* edited by Edward A. Tennant and Joseph N. Bitar. Bethel, Alaska: Lower Kuskokwim School District Bilingual/Bicultural Department.

Kawagley, Oscar
1989   Yup'ik Ways of Knowing. Manuscript. University of British Columbia, Vancouver.

Keesing, Roger
1987   *"Ta'a geni:* Woman's Perspectives on Kwaio Society." In *Dealing with Inequality: Analyzing Gender Relations in Melanesia and Beyond,* edited by Marilyn Strathern. Cambridge: Cambridge University Press.

Kilbuck, John Henry
1887   "Letter to Weinland. July 26, 1887." *The Moravian* 32(46):727–28.
1916   "Report of the United States Public School at Akiak, on the Kuskokwim River, in Western Alaska." In *Report of the Work of the Bureau of Education for the Natives of Alaska. 1914–1915.* U.S. Bureau of Education, Department of the Interior, Bulletin no. 47. Washington, D.C.: Government Printing Office.

Koranda, Lorraine Donoghue
1966   *Alaskan Eskimo Songs and Stories.* Seattle: University of Washington Press.

1968   "Three Songs for the Bladder Festival, Hooper Bay." *Anthropological Papers of the University of Alaska* 14(1):27–31.

Krupnik, Igor
1990   "Pratiques ethnoculturelles dans des sociétés contemporaines et traditionelles." In *Hunting, Sexes and Symbolism*, edited by Ann Fienup-Riordan. *Études/Inuit/Studies* 14:159–68.

Lantis, Margaret
1946   "The Social Culture of the Nunivak Eskimo." *Transactions of the American Philosophical Society* (Philadelphia) 35:153–323.
1947   *Alaskan Eskimo Ceremonialism.* American Ethnological Society, Monograph 11. Seattle: University of Washington Press.
1950   "The Religion of the Eskimos." In *Forgotten Religions*, edited by Vergilius Ferm. Philadelphia: Philosophical Library.
1959   "Folk Medicine and Hygiene, Lower Kuskokwim and Nunivak-Nelson Island Area." *Anthropological Papers of the University of Alaska* 8(1):1–75.
1960   *Eskimo Childhood and Interpersonal Relations: Nunivak Biographies and Genealogies.* American Ethnological Society, Monograph 53. Seattle: University of Washington Press.

Lenz, Mary
1986   "Alaska Native Teens Are Nation's Highest Risk Suicide Group." *Tundra Drums* (Bethel, Alaska). March 6, p. 4, 5.

Liapunova, R. G., and S. G. Fedorova, ed.
1979   "Verbal [statement] by [F. L.] Kolmakov—Customs and Manners of the Kuskowimtsy and Aglekhmiutsy." In *Russkaia Amerika v neopublikovannykh zapiskakh K. T. Khlebnikova*, p. 78. Leningrad: Nauka.

Llorente, Segundo
1990   *Memoirs of a Yukon Priest.* Washington, D.C.: Georgetown University Press.

Madsen, Mette
1990   "'To Have Weight So That Nobody Can Brush You Off the Top of This Earth': On the Cultural Construction of a Cultural Identity in Chevak, Alaska." Field report, Afdeling For Etnografi of Socialantropologi, Århus Universitet, Moesgard.

Malaurie, Jean
1982   *The Last Kings of Thule.* Translated by Adrienne Foulke. Chicago: University of Chicago Press.

Martz, Cecelia
1992   Yup'ik Spirituality. Teleconference course, University of Alaska, Kuskokwim Campus, Bethel, Alaska.

Mather, Elsie P.
1985   *Cauyarnariuq* [A Time for Drumming]. Alaska Historical Commission Studies in History, no. 184. Bethel, Alaska: Lower Kuskokwim School District Bilingual/Bicultural Department.
1986   "Preserving Our Culture Through Literacy." In *Report of the 1986 Bilingual Multicultural Education Conference.* Juneau, Alaska: Department of Education.

McClellan, Catherine
1985   Keynote address. Twelfth Annual Meeting of the Alaska Anthropological Association, Anchorage, Alaska.

Meade, Marie
1990   "Sewing to Maintain the Past, Present, and Future." In *Hunting, Sexes and Symbolism*, edited by Ann Fienup-Riordan. *Études/Inuit/Studies* 14(1–2):229–39.

Michael, Henry N., ed.
  1967   *Lieutenant Zagoskin's Travels in Russian America, 1842–1844.* Arctic Institute of
           North America. Anthropology of the North, Translations from Russian Sources,
           No. 7. Toronto, Ontario: University of Toronto Press.

Mikhailova, Elena
  1990   "Ritual Objects of the Asiatic Eskimo's Fall-Winter Festivals." Manuscript.
           Institute of Ethnography, USSR Academy of Sciences.

Milotte, Alfred
  1946   Journal. Milotte Collection, Archives, Alaska and Polar Regions Department,
           University of Alaska Fairbanks.

Miyaoka, Osahito, and Elsie Mather
  1979   *Yup'ik Eskimo Orthography.* Bethel, Alaska: Kuskokwim Community College.

Miyaoka, Osahito, Elsie Mather, and Marie Meade
  1991   *Survey of Yup'ik Grammar.* Anchorage: University of Alaska Anchorage.

Moore, Riley
  1923   "Social Life of the Eskimo of St. Lawrence Island." *American Anthropologist*
           25(3):339–75.

Morrow, Phyllis
  1984   "It Is Time for Drumming: A Summary of Recent Research on Yup'ik Ceremo-
           nialism." In *The Central Yupik Eskimos,* edited by Ernest S. Burch, Jr. Supple-
           mentary issue of *Études/Inuit/Studies* 8:113–40.
  1990   "Symbolic Actions, Indirect Expressions: Limits to Interpretations of Yupik
           Society." In *Hunting, Sexes and Symbolism,* edited by Ann Fienup-Riordan.
           Études/Inuit/Studies 14:141–58.

Morrow, Phyllis, and Elsie Mather
  1992   "The Thickness of the Earth." Draft manuscript. Fairbanks, Alaska.

Morrow, Phyllis, and Mary Pete
  1993   "Cultural Adoption on Trial: Cases from Southwestern Alaska." *Law and An-
           thropology* 7.

Morrow, Phyllis, and Toby Alice Volkman
  1975   "The Loon with the Ivory Eyes: A Study in Symbolic Anthropology." *Journal of
           American Folklore* 88(348):143–50.

Nelson, Edward William
  1899   *The Eskimo about Bering Strait.* Bureau of American Ethnology Annual Report
           for 1896–97, vol. 18, pt. 1. Washington, D.C.: Smithsonian Institution Press.
           (Reprinted 1983.)

Nooter, Gert
  1976   *Leadership and Headship: Changing Authority Patterns in an East Greenland
           Hunting Community.* Leiden: E. J. Brill.

Oldham, Kellie
  1987   "Gender and Spatial Relations in Yupiit Culture." Manuscript. Department of
           Anthropology, University of Chicago.

Oosten, Jaarich G.
  1976   *The Theoretical Structure of the Religion of the Netsilik and Iglulik.* Meppel: Krips
           Repro.
  1990   "Cosmological Cycles and the Constituents of the Person." Paper presented at
           the Eighth Inuit Studies Conference, Fairbanks, Alaska.

Ostermann, Hother H., and Erik Holtved, eds.
  1952   *The Alaska Eskimos, as Described in the Posthumous Notes of Dr. Knud Rasmussen.*
           Report of the Fifth Thule Expedition, vol. 10, no. 3. Copenhagen: Gyldendal.

Oswalt, Wendell H.
  1957   "A Western Eskimo Ethnobotany." *Anthropological Papers of the University of Alaska* 6(1):17–36.
  1963   *Mission of Change in Alaska: Eskimos and Moravians on the Kuskokwim.* San Marino, Calif.: The Huntington Library.
  1973   "The Kuskowagamiut." In *This Land Was Theirs.* New York: John Wiley and Sons.
  1979   *Eskimos and Explorers.* Novato, Calif.: Chandler & Sharp.
  1990   *Bashful No Longer. An Alaskan Eskimo Ethnohistory, 1778–1988.* Norman: University of Oklahoma Press.

Petersen, Robert
  1966–67 "Burial-Forms and Death Cult among the Eskimos." *Folk.* 8–9:259–80.

Pingayak, John F.
  1986   "Cupik Eskimos." Cup'ik Cultural Heritage Project. Chevak, Alaska: Kashunamiut School District.

Pleasant, Charlie
  1981   "The Man Who Turned into a Wolverine." In *Yupik Lore: Oral Traditions of an Eskimo People,* edited by Edward A. Tennant and Joseph N. Bitar. Bethel, Alaska: Lower Kuskokwim School District Bilingual/Bicultural Department.

Polechia, Paul
  1992   "Rivers, Rafters and Raptors." *Tundra Drums* (Bethel, Alaska). August 13.

Porter, R. P.
  1893   *Report on Population and Resources of Alaska at the Eleventh Census: 1890.* Washington, D.C.: Government Printing Office.

Pratt, Kenneth L.
  1984   "Classification of Eskimo Groupings in the Yukon-Kuskokwim Region: A Critical Analysis." In *The Central Yupik Eskimos,* edited by Ernest S. Burch, Jr. Supplementary issue of *Études/Inuit/Studies* 8:45–61.
  1993   "Legendary Birds in the Physical Landscape of the Yup'ik Eskimos." *Anthropology and Humanism* 18 (1): 13–20.

Pratt, Kenneth L., and Robert D. Shaw
  1992   "A Petroglyphic Sculpture from Nunivak Island, Alaska." *Anthropological Papers of the University of Alaska* 24(1–2):3–14

Rainey, Froelich G.
  1941   "The Inupiat Culture at Point Hope, Alaska." *American Anthropologist* 43:364–75.

Rasmussen, Knud
  1927   *Across Arctic America: Narrative of the Fifth Thule Expedition.* New York: Putnam.
  1929   "Intellectual Culture of the Iglulik Eskimos." *Report of the Fifth Thule Expedition, 1921–1924,* vol. 7, no. 1. Copenhagen: Gyldendalske Boghandel, Nordisk Forlag.
  1931   "The Netsilik Eskimos: Social Life and Spiritual Culture." *Report of the Fifth Thule Expedition, 1921–1924,* vol. 8, no. 1–2. Copenhagen: Gyldendalske Boghandel, Nordisk Forlag.
  1938   "Knud Rasmussen's Posthumous Notes on the Life and Doings of the East Greenlanders in Olden Times." Edited by H. Ostermann. Meddr Grønland 109(1).

Ray, Dorothy Jean
  1966   "The Eskimo of St. Michael and Vicinity, as Related by H. M. W. Edmonds." *Anthropological Papers of the University of Alaska* 13(2).

1982   "Mortuary Art of the Alaskan Eskimos." *American Indian Art Magazine* 7(2):50–57.

Reed, Irene, Osahito Miyaoka, Steven Jacobson, Pascal Afcan, and Michael Krauss
1977   *Yup'ik Eskimo Grammar.* Fairbanks, Alaska: Alaska Native Language Center, University of Alaska.

Romig, Joseph Herman, MD.
1923   "The 'Potlatch' of Alaska Natives." *The Pathfinder of Alaska* (Valdez) 5(2):1–3.

Saladin d'Anglure, Bernard
1984   "L'ideologie de Malthus et la Demographie Mythique des Inuit d'Igloolik." In *Malthus Hier et Aujourd'hui.* Congres International de Demographie Historique. A Fauve-Chamoux (ed). CNRS, Paris.
1986   "Du Foetus au Chamane, la Construction d'un 'Troisième Sexe' Inuit." *Études/Inuit/Studies* 10(1–2):25–113.

Schneider, David
1984   *A Critique of the Study of Kinship.* Ann Arbor: University of Michigan Press.

Serov, Sergei Ia.
1988   "Guardians and Spirit-Masters of Siberia." In *Crossroads of Continents: Cultures of Siberia and Alaska,* edited by William W. Fitzhugh and Aron Crowell. Washington, D.C.: Smithsonian Institution Press.

Shaw, Robert D.
1982   "The Expansion and Survival of the Norton Tradition on the Yukon-Kuskokwim Delta." *Arctic Anthropology* 19:59–73.

Shinkwin, Anne D., and Mary Pete
1984   "Yup'ik Eskimo Societies: A Case Study." In *The Central Yupik Eskimos,* edited by Ernest S. Burch, Jr. Supplementary issue of *Études/Inuit/Studies* 8:95–112.

Snow, Joyce
1984   "Eskimo Illness Beliefs and Cross-cultural Doctor-Patient Communication." Manuscript, Anthropology Department, Harvard University, Cambridge, Mass.

Søby, R.
1969–70 "The Eskimo Animal Cult." *Folk* 11–12:43–78.

Sonne, Birgette
1988   *Agayut: Eskimo Masks from the Fifth Thule Expedition* (Knud Rasmussens Samlinger fra Nunivak, Alaska). Report of the Fifth Thule Expedition 10(4). Copenhagen: Gyldendal.

Spencer, Robert
1959   *The North Alaskan Eskimo: A Study in Ecology and Society.* Bureau of American Ethnology Bulletin 171. Washington, D.C. (Reprinted 1969).

Strathern, Marilyn
1986   "Dual Models and Multiple Persons: Gender in Melanesia." Paper presented at the Eighty-fifth Annual Meeting of the American Anthropological Association, Philadelphia, Pa.
1987   (ed.) *Dealing with Inequality: Analyzing Gender Relations in Melanesia and Beyond.* Cambridge: Cambridge University Press.
1988   *The Gender of the Gift: Problems of Women and Problems of Society in Melanesia.* Berkeley: University of California Press.

Turner, Edith
1990   "'Working on the Body': The Medical and Spiritual Implications of Iñupiaq Healing." Manuscript, Anthropology Department, University of Virginia, Charlottesville.

Wagner, Roy
   1977   "Analogic Kinship: A Daribi Example." *American Ethnologist* 4(4):623–42.

Weyer, Edward Moffat, Jr.
   1932   *The Eskimos: Their Environment and Folkways.* New Haven, Conn.: Yale University Press.

Whymper, F.
   1868   *Journey in Alaska.* New York: Harper and Brothers.

Wolfe, Robert
   1989   "'The Fish are not to be Played With': Yup'ik views of Sport Fishing and Subsistence-Recreation Conflicts along the Togiak River." Paper presented at the Sixteenth Annual Meeting of the Alaska Anthropological Association, Anchorage, Alaska.

Wolfe, Virginia
   1927   *To the Lighthouse.* New York: Harcourt, Brace and World.

Woodbury, Anthony C.
   1984a   "Eskimo and Aleut Languages." In *Arctic,* vol. 5, *Handbook of North American Indians,* edited by David Damas. Washington, D.C.: Smithsonian Institution Press.
   1984b   *Cev'armiut Qanemciit Qulirait-llu: Eskimo Narratives and Tales from Chevak, Alaska.* Fairbanks, Alaska: Alaska Native Language Center, University of Alaska.

Wooley, Chris
   1989   "Kivgiq: A Celebration of Who We Are." Paper presented to the Sixteenth Annual Meeting of the Alaska Anthropological Association, Anchorage, Alaska.

INDEX

Aaniq, 275–79, 296, 297, 303, 358. *See also* Bladder Festival

Abstinence (*eyagluni*): in mourning, 228–38; by women, 95

Adoption, 42, 148

Agartak, Clara, 61, 96, 112, 119, 121

Agartak, Tim, 51, 77, 107, 108, 281, 294

Agiirrnguat (extraordinary person), 83–85, 86, 87

Aglenrrat (girls having their first menses), 98. *See also* Menstruation

Akiachak, 80

Akulurak, 31

Akutaq ("Eskimo ice cream"), 3, 5, 25, 28, 62, 246; at Bladder Festival, 269, 271, 281 n; for the dead, 214; at Petugtaq, 348

Alakanuk, 40

Alangruq (ghost), 86

Alaska Native Claims Settlement Act, 39, 42

Alaska Native Language Center, 10 n

Albrite, Evon, 55, 176

Alcoholism, 40, 42, 362

Alerquutet (instructions), 9, 52–58, 104, 193, 203, 209, 305. *See also* Inerquutet

Aleutians, 30

Alexie, Eddie, 67, 79, 119, 146, 156, 281, 296, 333, 351

Alexie, Nels, 220

Amikuk (extraordinary person), 80–82, 86

Amllit (creatures), 86

Amulet. See *Iinruq*

Analogy, 119, 127, 128, 182, 188, 196, 198, 203, 356

Androgyny, 274, 298

Angaiak, Susan, 209

Angalkuq, 235–36, 242. *See also* Shaman

An'guqtar (Raven's daughter), 165

Angyaq (skin boat), 34, 128, 221

Angyaruaq, 65

Apparitions, 194, 212 n

Archaeology, 10, 38, 259 n; evidence from, 252

Arctic, 10, 18; Canadian, 47; coast, 10, 14

Arularaq (creature), 86

Ashes, 8, 9, 117, 119, 125, 153; eating small amounts of, 122, 163; at funeral, 215 227, 231; land created from, 257

Asia, 10

Asiatic Eskimo. *See* Siberian Yup'ik

Asking Festival, 271, 272, 348. *See also* Petugtaq

Ateq. See Name

Athapaskan Indians, 6, 10, 258. *See also* Cree

Avneq (felt presence), 212

Awareness (*ella*), 51, 57, 59, 62, 143, 145; seals', 128, 130

Ayagerak, Joe, Sr., 90, 92, 93 n, 94, 98, 112, 117, 126, 127, 200, 258, 259

Barnum, Francis, S.J., 256

Bear, 25, 51, 57, 61, 89, 113–15; head, 106, 117

Beaver, Joe, 144, 316
Beaver, Mary, 90
Bell, Eddie, 364
Bell, Kurt, 55, 129
Belt, 9, 149, 298, 360; curing, 201; during mourning, 231, 232, 234; women's use of, 94, 98, 161, 163, 164, 165, 193
Belukha. *See* Whales
Bentwood hat. *See* Hunting: hats
Bering Land Bridge, 10
Bering Sea, 29; mythology, 107
Berlin, Wassilie, 72
Berries, 23, 25, 58; picking, 162, 165; proscribed, 126
Bethel, 14, 31, 39
Bilby, Julian, 359
Bird, 17, 18; *amikuk* acting like, 201–202; dances imitating, 288–89, 291, 295; eggs, 111; giant, 85; helper, 134; hunter as, 9, 127–42; hunting, 17, 26, 42; images, 111, 128, 134, 137–38, 141; rules for treatment of, 124–42; skins, 66, 132, 142; soporific breath of, 128–30, 141. *See also* Egg gathering; Geese; Raven; Sea birds; *Tengmiarpiit*
Birket-Smith, Kaj, 132
Black, Billy, 154, 255
Blackfish, 119, 120, 122; as people, 123
Bladder Festival, 3, 4, 5, 6, 97, 106, 108, 116, 134, 137, 138, 139, 140, 141, 173–74, 239, 240, 249, 253, 256, 303, 304, 322–23, 329, 358, 362, 367. *See also* Nakaciuq
Blood: healing power of, 196; menstrual, 165–66, 188; seal, 198. *See also* Poking
Boas, Franz, 359, 361
Boat-launching ceremonies, 92 n
Bogeyaktuk, Anatole, 329
Bogoras, Waldemar, 137, 140
Bones, 86; care of, 62, 107–12, 117, 185; near *qasgiq*, 252
Borre, Kristen, 198
Boyscout, David, 97, 126, 127
Boy who lived with the seals (legend), 3, 5–7, 61, 62, 90–91, 93, 97, 106, 123, 127, 129, 138, 157, 168, 240, 243, 249, 250, 275, 295, 305, 371
Breast feeding, 182–83
Breath (*anerneq*), 51, 167, 212, 295; animals', 114; power of, 9, 141, 282–83, 356; restricted, 9, 168; shamans', 204, 208; *See also* Bird: soporific breath of
Briggs, Jean, 145
Brightman, Robert, 50 n, 62
Burch, Tiger, 177 n

Burial, 8, 106; rules accompanying, 215–38
Butzin, Arthur, 147, 149, 161, 165, 180, 221, 228 n, 252, 269 n, 272, 277, 278, 281 n, 285, 288, 292, 302, 303

Caarrluk (dirt), 64, 150, 192
Cakcaaq, 78, 83, 85
Calista Corporation, 39
Canada, 10; Arctic, 18, 47, 106, 198
Cape Romanzof, 14
Carayak (monster), 63, 144, 212 n
Caribou, 67, 75, 113, 114, 117, 155; head, 106, 117
Carter, Sam, 54, 57
Catholic mission, 31, 39, 117, 202. *See also* Missionaries; St. Mary's Catholic Mission
Cella, 258
Central Eskimos, 361; song duel, 335–36, 347
Central Yup'ik. *See* Yup'ik: language
Ceremony, 9, 36; cycle, 49, 255, 259, 265, 302, 322; exchanges, 47; season for, 253, 266
Challenge feast, 84. *See also* Curukat
Chanar, Brentina, 52, 57, 63, 64, 65, 75, 77, 78, 83, 92, 95, 105, 108, 112, 113, 115, 116, 120, 122, 126, 127, 161, 162, 164, 181, 183, 184, 185, 186, 202–203, 205, 208, 209, 217, 227, 233, 244, 281 n, 285, 299, 324, 326, 327, 329, 330, 331, 333, 334, 337, 344, 345, 350, 352, 353
Chanar, Cyril, 64, 134, 329, 346
Chevak, 122, 132, 341; Cultural Heritage Program, 364; elders of, 202; *qasgiq* in, 255. *See also* Qissunaq
Chikigak, Thomas, 77, 79, 105, 108, 113, 116, 121, 124, 260
Childbirth, 180–82
Children: care of, 143–145; instruction of, 145–58; as wealth, 177
Christianity, 239, 263, 264. *See also* Missionaries
Chukchi, 137, 140, 216 n
Cingarturluteng (asking special favors), 296–97, 352
Cingssiik (extraordinary person), 78–79
Circling, 279, 294, 333; to cure, 201, 360; graves, 8, 216, 225, 227, 304; sunwise (east to west), 92 n, 105, 181, 193, 259–60, 265, 358–62. *See also* Ella asgurluku; Ella maliggluku
Citaat (old-style coffins), 85
Collins, Henry B., Jr., 134, 360
Conception, 178
Confession, 209, 210

Consensus, 55
Corpse, care of, 213–38, 309
Cosmological: cycle, 49, 361; reproduction, 159, 248–50, 277, 298
Crane, 17, 18, 26
Cree (Athapaskans), 50 n
Cross-cousin, 54, 149, 297; teasing, 329–30, 332, 334–35, 346, 348–54
Crow Village, 10
Curing. *See* Healing
Curtis, Edward S., 92 n, 134, 258, 267, 268, 269, 278, 328, 333, 345
Curukat (invited villagers), 84, 346. *See also* Kevgiq
Cutting, 354; across path, 8, 9, 95, 120, 227; avoidance of, 8, 119, 200–201, 230, 233, 278, 285; of joints, 239

Dance: child's first, 343; fans, 136; imitating birds, 137, 139; marriage, 174–75; revival of, 364–67; story, 340–42; verse/chorus, 340. *See also* Ingulaq
Dead: food offerings to, 214–15, 245; journey to the land of, 238–243; living identified with, 143; relationship to namesake, 243–47; rules surrounding the treatment of, 211–38. *See also* Death; Elriq; Feast for the Dead; Merr'aq
Death, 55; foretelling, 76; rituals surrounding, 6, 8, 92. *See also* Dead
Dirt, 9, 152, 196, 258; pleasing smell of, 91, 96. *See also* Caarluk
Disease, 9, 58, 78, 272 n, 289; concepts of, 189–95; epidemic, 29, 31, 38, 39, 153, 190, 191. *See also* Illness
Dispute settlement, 37, 55
Distribution: of catch, 62, 98–105, 184–86; dance, 291–92, 336–48, 367. *See also* Kevgiq; Ritual: distribution
Division of labor, 251–52
Dog, 59, 111, 120, 196, 252, 271; children during Aaniq acting like, 275–79; food for, 113, 303; husband, 238; story of, 128; village of, 240, 276
Doll, 126, 162–63, 291; journey of, 259, 359
Domestic violence, 40, 42
Drozda, Robert, 128
Drum, 28, 72, 73, 97, 134; during Bladder Festival, 277, 283; during Elriq, 302; for Kevgiq, 325, 337, 339; restricted use of, 234–36; use by women, 344, 351. *See also* Dance; Shaman
Ducks, 17, 18, 25, 26

Eckert, Penelope, and Russell Newmark, 335
Edmonds, H. M. W., 240, 259, 271, 273, 291 n
Education, 37, 39
Egacuayiit (extraordinary people), 76–78
Egg gathering, 17, 18, 23, 138; rules surrounding, 125–26, 162. *See also* Bird
Eider duck, 128–29, 132, 138, 139, 140, 141, 291; ceremony, 137, 139; "people," 128
Elaayiq River, 80
Ella (weather, world, universe), 144, 151, 165, 232, 233; concept of, 263; sentient, 234. *See also* Awareness
Ella asgurluku (going against the universe), 297, 358
Ella maliggluku (following the universe), 230, 265, 271, 294, 297–98, 355, 358–62. *See also* Circling
Ellam iinga (eye of the universe), 126, 201, 231, 248, 265, 266, 316, 356
Ellam yua (person of the universe), 54, 89, 190, 201, 258, 262–63
Ellanguaq (pretend universe), 357
Elriq (Great Feast for the Dead), 4, 5, 6, 8, 237, 239, 240, 241, 242, 249, 253, 289, 299–304
Epidemic. *See* Disease
Equipment. *See* Hunting
Eskimo: "ice cream" (*see* akutaq); image, 46–47
Extraordinary persons. *See* Persons: extraordinary

Family: extended, 33, 34, 37, 42; nuclear, 38, 42
Famine, 28, 119, 121, 122
Fans. *See* Dance: fans
Feast for the Dead, 299–304, 322–23, 358, 362. *See also* Elriq; Merr'aq
First catch, young man's, 184; celebration of, 247, 302, 343
Fish: anadromous, 120; care of, 118–24, 165. *See also* Blackfish; Herring; Salmon
Fishing, 18, 23, 26; commercial, 22, 23, 40, 42; trap (*taluyaq*), 25–26, 76, 77, 115, 117, 123, 124
"Fishtrap-caught animals" (otter, mink), 115–17, 118–19, 123
Fitzhugh, William W., 75 n
Food: care of, 172–73; restrictions on, 198. *See also* Menstruation; Pregnancy; Ritual: distribution
Fox, 17, 28, 30, 70, 107, 116, 117; *ircenrrat* as, 63

Fox, Father John, 132, 133
Freuchen, Peter, 360
Friday, Joe, 80, 82, 126, 167, 227, 308
Frye, Matthew, 53, 155
Fumigation. *See* Tarvaryaraq

Gamulek (extraordinary person), 82, 87
Garber, Clark, 220, 225
Geese, 17, 18, 23, 26, 73; arrival of, 163; pro-
    scribed, 126, 179; ritual use of skin, 138. *See
    also* Bird
Gender, 49; determination of, 178–79; rela-
    tionship between, 159–88; residential sep-
    aration of, 160
Ghost. *See* Alangruq
Girl who returned from the dead (legend), 3,
    4–5, 8, 240–43, 245, 249, 250, 263, 289,
    303, 305
Gold Rush, 82
Goodnews Bay, 106
Gordon, G. B., 225 n
Grass, 25, 27, 95, 239; mat, 183, 204, 276, 277,
    343, 360; ritual use of, 106, 139, 260, 291,
    293, 296
Grave, 217; board, 224–26; boxes, 76, 239,
    304; circling, 8, 227; goods, 217–22; loca-
    tion, 227; post, 222–23; stakes at, 8, 289,
    300, 301, 361. *See also* Dead
Great Feast for the Dead. *See* Elriq
Greenland, 10, 106, 367
Gut parka. *See* Parka: seal gut

Hair: cutting, 200; women's, 94, 95
Hallowell, A. Irving, 48 n
Hamilton, Ivan, 322
Hands, 9, 86, 120, 125, 141, 143; dirt covering,
    152; in healing, 205–208; supernatural, 269;
    thumbless, 161. *See also* Itqiirpak
Hare, 17
Haunting woman (story), 237–38
Hawkes, Ernest William, 239, 268, 271, 272,
    291, 316, 321, 360
Head, 106–107, 114, 117, 139, 140
Healing, 9, 195–210, 359
Herring, 18, 20, 21, 25, 110, 120, 121
Hierarchy, social, 47, 62
Himmelheber, Hans, 50, 58, 59, 161, 225 n,
    327
Hobbes, Thomas, 46, 47, 55
Hughes, Charles, 193 n, 225 n
Human shade (*tarneq*), 51, 143, 232, 236,
    300–304, 359; at Bladder Festival, 272,
    273, 286, 292; causing illness, 192; jour-
    ney of, 8, 217, 231, 238–43; thirst of, 6.
    See also Elriq
Hunter, Theodore, 315
Hunter as bird. *See* Bird: hunter as
Hunting: charms, 134, 227; equipment for,
    91, 92; hats, 91, 129–32, 137, 138–39, 289–
    91. *See also* Seals: hunting

Ice conditions, 17
Igkurak, Kenneth, 53
Iglulik Eskimos, 248
Iinruq (amulet), 130, 201–202
Ikogmiut, 30
Illness, 54, 122, 150, 152, 158; from desire to
    acquire a new name, 244–45. *See also* Dis-
    ease
Individualism, 46, 47. *See also* Hobbes, Thomas
Inerquutet (prohibitions; singular, *inerquun*)
    9, 52–58, 67, 90, 93, 115, 126, 164, 179,
    203, 209, 234. *See also* Alerquutet
Ingluilnguq (creature), 86
Ingulaq (dance), 137–38, 174–75, 281, 320–
    21. *See also* Dance
Ingun (terms of endearment), 144
Inogo (animal helper), 130, 134, 137. *See also*
    Iinruq
Instruction, 57. *See also* Education
Inuit, 10, 29, 358, 359; conceptions of bodily
    composition, 198; socialization, 145
Iñupiaq, 10
Iñupiat, 14, 209, 260, 324; dancing, 334
Ircenrrat (extraordinary persons), 63–76, 86,
    87, 123, 128, 259, 264, 333 n; as foxes, 63,
    115; as wolves, 63, 115
Issiisaayuq (the shaman), 30
Issran (grass carrying bag), 108, 110, 281,
    283, 295
Itqiirpak (giant hand), 85, 146–47

Jacob, Lame, 59
Jacobson, Steven, 10 n
Jesuit priest, 55
Jimmy, Adolph, 56
John, Paul (father), 3, 4, 7, 16, 44, 61, 88, 90,
    92, 93, 94, 104, 129, 131, 145, 146, 148,
    149, 150, 152, 156, 157, 166, 167, 168, 173,
    176, 177, 178, 183, 191, 210, 295, 310, 311,
    362, 366
John, Simeon (son), 16
John, Theresa (daughter), 366
John, Vernon (grandson), 136
Joseph, Camille, 52, 93, 94, 122, 262 n

Kaialuigmiut, 119, 130, 131, 240, 252

Kalukaq (feast), 175. *See also* Ritual: distribution

Kalukaat, 74

Kangaciqaq (ceremonial pole), 287–88, 293. *See also* Bladder Festival; Wild celery

Kangiliryaraq ("to provide with a new beginning"). *See* Naming

Kass'aq (Caucasian), 115, 366

Kassel, Nastasia, 166, 190, 236, 263, 316

Kayak (skin boat), 17, 18, 34, 60, 64, 91, 92, 93, 94, 112; of dead, 218, 220; designs on, 130; launching of, 360; with hunter as bird, 128, 129, 141

Keesing, Roger, 50

Kelek (mask ceremony), 253, 267, 304–23, 345, 362

Kere'tkun Ceremony, 137, 140

Kevgiq (Messenger Feast), 64, 73, 297, 324, 352–53; asking songs during, 326–27; contemporary, 362; functions of, 345–46; origin of, 325–26; presentation of gifts during, 336–48; receiving guests for, 331–36; sending messengers for, 327–31

Kevgiruaq (Pretend Kevgiq), 337, 344–45, 348, 351, 353; contemporary, 362. *See also* Kevgiq

Kilbuck, Edith, 181 n

Kilbuck, John Henry, 33, 111, 177, 271, 281 n, 304, 324

Kinship terminology, 42

Kolmakov, F. L., 134

Kolmakovsky Redoubt, 30

Koranda, Lorraine Donoghue, 279 n, 289

Koryak, 75 n; mourners, 227 n, 229 n

Kungurkaq, Anna, 149, 150, 153, 154, 156, 157, 344

Kuskokwim River, 10, 14, 30, 31, 33, 39, 60, 75

Labrador, 10,

Labrador tea (*ayuq*), 91, 114, 198–200, 207; use in Bladder Festival, 271, 272; use in Elriq, 300

Lamp, seal-oil, 4, 79, 140, 154, 197, 232, 252, 255, 256; in Bladder Festival, 270, 276, 283, 287, 292; beside corpse, 215; soot, 4, 241, 263, 272, 275, 298, 351, 360

Land animals, 113–118, 181; care of bones of, 111; distinct from sea mammals, 117–18; greeting with oil, 116–17; spirit keepers of, 252; spirits of, 259. *See also* "Fishtrap-caught animals"

Land of the dead, 4–5, 8, 210, 211, 215, 238–

43; journey to, 216–17, 220, 228, 234, 264, 269, 278, 279, 303, 304, 305, 315. *See also* Girl who returned from the dead; Pamalirugmiut

Lantis, Margaret, 92 n, 112, 130, 131, 134, 140, 182, 196, 197, 198 n, 201, 202, 204, 215, 227, 231, 239, 258, 259, 260, 267, 268, 279, 284, 289, 291, 310 n, 328, 345

Lee, Sophie, 246

Lincoln, Billy, 4, 8, 56, 67, 92, 97, 103, 113, 128, 131, 137, 146, 148, 155, 214, 218, 220, 222, 230, 236, 240, 241, 243, 245, 255, 268, 270, 271, 275, 278, 280, 283, 289, 293–94, 296–97, 303, 312, 313, 333 n, 338, 355

Lind, Maggie, 120

Llorente, Father Segundo, 55

Loon, 124–25; mating dance of, 138, 174, 281

Lott, James, 77, 79, 117, 120, 158, 167

Luck, 67

McClellan, Catherine, 6

Malaurie, Jean, 367

Mann, Martha, 243

Marriage, 169–78; announcement of, 283; arranged, 345

Martz, Cecelia, 258

Mask, 59, 70, 81, 115, 116, 135, 139, 165, 202, 253, 261, 281; at Bladder Festival, 274, 275, 280, 344, 345–46, 356; at burials, 225; bowl as, 93–94 n; humorous, 351; shamans', 204–205, 206, 304–307, 315–23; story of, 134. *See also* Kelek; Qengarpak

Mather, Elsie, 212, 220, 232, 239, 299, 345, 370

Matthew 6:1–6, 54

Meade, Marie, 364

Men's house. *See* Qasgiq

Menstruation, 287, 356; repelling seals, 98, 141; rules surrounding, 160–69

Meriiq (creature), 85

Merr'aq (Annual Feast for the Dead), 247, 299–300. *See also* Feast for the Dead; Elriq

Messenger Feast, 64, 70, 73, 257. *See also* Kevgiq

Metaphor, 3, 7, 8, 9, 355

Mike, Mary, 191, 242, 243

Miluquyuli (creature), 86

Mind (*umyuaq*), 51, 62, 176, 190, 212; bad, 55, 125; breaking, 178; power of, 52, 53–59, 82, 87, 98, 101, 153, 209; strong, 85

Mining, 31, 33

Missionaries, 30–31, 33, 177, 217 n; suppression by, 202, 213, 362. *See also* Catholic

Mission; Christianity; Moravian mission; Russians: Orthodox church
Mittens, 83, 164, 186, 232, 238, 264, 309, 348; at Bladder Festival, 280; on corpse, 214; thumbless, 160–61, 162
Molly Hotch decision, 39
Moon, 181, 267 n; disease from, 191, 193; personlike, 263–64, 307; shaman's journey to, 310–11, 315–16; as *tuunrat's* home, 252;
Moravian mission, 31
Morrow, Phyllis, 212, 213, 286, 299, 327, 330
Moses, Theresa, 90, 91, 93, 94, 95, 125, 149, 162, 165, 166, 167, 177, 180, 192, 193, 196, 197, 200, 203, 229, 230, 276, 281, 320, 321, 325, 334, 336, 341, 343, 347
Motor boats, 17
Mourning (*kanaranluni*), 76, 214–38
Mouse food, 25, 61; cache of magical worms, 207
Muruayuli (creature), 85
Musk ox, 17, 113, 114

Nakaciruaq (Pretend Bladder Festival), 396–97
Nakaciuq: attention to bladders during, 283–92; ceremonies related to, 267–68; gathering wild celery for, 279–81; *ingulaq* during, 281–83; men's dancing during, 288–89; preliminary activities, 269–79; returning bladders to the sea, 292–96; timing, 268–69
Naknek River, 107
Nalugyaraq ("pulling up"), 278, 292–96. See also Bladder Festival
Name (*ateq*), 51, 59, 213; avoidance of, 245–46. See also Naming
Namesake, 4, 5, 51, 211, 213, 228, 241, 242, 243; gifts honoring, 323; relation with dead, 243–47, 299–304, 355. See also Elriq; Feast for the Dead; Merr'aq
Naming, 42, 160, 243–47. See also Renaming
Napoka, Mary, 55, 65, 117, 119, 158, 161, 165, 179, 194, 203
Nayamin, Ulrick, 364
Nayangaq (men's dancing), 288–89. See also Bladder Festival; *Nakaciuq*
Neck, Herman, 152, 172, 262
Nelson, E. W., 5 n, 8, 59, 75, 76, 111, 130, 131, 134, 138, 139, 140, 167, 191, 193, 208, 213, 215, 228, 239, 240, 247, 258, 259, 262, 267 n, 268, 289, 291, 294, 297, 299, 300, 304, 305, 311, 320, 358, 361, 367
Nelson Island, creation of, 124, 257

Nelson Island Eskimo, 6
Nelson Island Oral History Project, 45
Nepengyat (ghosts), 147, 212 n
Neq'ayarat (stories to remember by), 57, 59, 83–85
Netsilik Eskimos, 248, 360
Nicholas, John, 146
Nightmute, 40, 76, 327, 329, 344; move from Toksook Bay, 337, 339
Niyalruq, 75
Noise: avoidance of, 8, 9, 111, 146–47, 234–38, 248, 252, 270, 284, 286; loud, 208, 252
Nome, 31, 82
Nukalpiaq (good hunter and provider), 36–37, 54, 65, 71, 90, 99, 174
Nunakauyaq, 76
Nunam taqra (land's vein or artery), 72, 263
Nunivak Island, 14, 17, 37, 38, 39, 70; creation of, 257, 258; religion, 202

O'Malley, T. See Winter solstice
Oosten, Jaarich, 248, 283
Oswalt, Wendell H., 196

Pacific coast, 10
Paimiut, 10
Pamalirugmiut, 5, 9, 239, 241, 242. See also Land of the dead
Panruk, Dennis, 103, 146, 185, 192, 268, 289
Parka: birdskin, 132–33; seal gut, 83, 91, 132, 204, 270, 280, 291, 293, 294, 298, 303, 308–309, 312, 360
Pathways: between worlds, 7; blocked, 9, 82, 88, 141, 243, 248; clearing, 7, 9, 53, 87, 140, 155, 228, 236; metaphor, 8, 249; middle, 123; obstructed, 7, 9, 53, 120; preparing, 148–58
Paugvik (village site), 107
Persons: concept of human, 211–13; extraordinary, 62–87, 259; human and nonhuman, 9, 48, 49–52, 57, 61, 62, 87; mutual respect between, 58–59; senses of, 9, 356. See also Qununiq (seal-person); Yuk
Petersen, Robert, 358
Petroff, Ivan, 37
Petugtaq (Asking Festival), 348–54, 362; wand, 262
Phillip, Joshua, 54, 56, 80, 104, 120, 123, 145, 150, 152, 153, 155, 166, 167, 172, 193, 205, 209, 214, 252
Pikmiktalik, 76
Pilot Station, 14

387

Pingayak, John, 82, 83, 258, 267 n, 284, 311, 351
Plants, 14, 18, 25
Platinum, 106
Pleasant, Charlie, 60
Point Hope, 106
Poking (bloodletting), 197
Porter, R. P., 106, 225 n
Postpartum restrictions, 182
Potlatch, 326, 343–45. *See also* Kevgiq
Pregnancy, 53, 55; rules surrounding, 113, 114, 127, 178–81
Prince William Sound, 10
Protestant ethic, 47
Ptarmigan, 17
Puqlii (heat), 212
Purification with smoke. *See* Tarvaryaraq

Qaariitaaq, 270–75, 278–79, 297, 358. *See also* Bladder Festival
Qaluyaarmiut, 28, 29
Qalvinraq, 83
Qamulek (extraordinary person), 82
Qanemciq (narrative), 65, 183, 235–36
Qaneryarat (sayings), 52, 166. *See also* Rules for living
Qasginguaq, 64, 65
Qasgiq (men's house), 34, 36, 37, 39; bladders hosted in, 269–70, 283–92; boys' introduction to, 146; boys' training in, 149–50; model of, 290; names for, 252; refurbishing of, 281; respect for, 147; seals', 3, 36, 61, 62; speaking in, 8, 56, 145–46; spiritual reproduction in, 249; and Yup'ik spatial orientation, 251–57
Qemqeng, 75
Qengarpak, 275, 278, 297. *See also* Bladder Festival
Qinaq, 80
Qissunaq, 132, 133, 138, 167, 237, 238, 308, 310, 321. *See also* Chevak
Qivgayarmiut, 237
Quinhagak, 324
Qukuyarpak, 181
Quliraq (legend), 174
Qungurmiut, 327, 329
Qununiq (male seal-person), 82–83
Quugaarpiit (creatures), 86

Rainey, Froelich, 106
Rain parka. *See* Parka: seal gut
Rasmussen, Knud, 92 n, 333, 360
Raven, 124–25, 126, 130, 141, 142, 257–58,
259, 272; dances imitating, 288; daughter of, 165
Refuse, 120, 149, 150; as a barrier to misfortune, 152–53, 158; care of, 91, 192
Regional confederations, 257
Reincarnation, 211, 213, 243. *See also* Namesake: relation to dead
Reindeer, 75
Relationship: ceremonial reversals of, 266; between host and guest, 5, 88–89, 140, 211; between humans and animals, 5, 6, 49–62, 88–142, 324; between husbands and wives, 159–88; between living and dead, 5, 6, 211–50
Renaming (*kangilirluni*), 203, 244. *See also* Naming
Respect, 168; between humans and animals, 58–59
Ritual, 49; distribution, 34, 37, 62, 184–86; greeting of land animals, 116–17; greeting of seals, 96–98; private, 9
River of tears, 8, 236, 243
Romig, Dr. Joseph, 106, 114
Rules for living, 9, 37, 47, 49, 52–58, 63, 190, 195, 210, 355, 366–67. *See also* Alerquutet; Inerquutet
Russians, 29; Orthodox church, 30–31, 117, 320; Russian American Company, 30; traders, 30

Saiak hunting festival. *See* Siberian Yup'ik Eskimo
St. Lawrence Island, 137, 181, 359, 360
St. Marys Catholic Mission, 39, 258
St. Michael, 30
Saladin d'Anglure, Bernard, 188
Salmon, 23, 25, 62, 120, 122; as people, 123
Scammon Bay, creation of, 257–58
Schneider, David, 48
Sculpin, 17
Seabirds, 17; hunting, 14–17; hunter as, 127–42
Sea lions, 17
Seal party. *See* Uqiquq
Seals, 17, 18, 25, 58; bearded, 3, 14, 17, 25, 61, 83, 98, 103; bladders of, 128, 130, 134, 138, 213; bones, care of, 107–12, 134, 138, 141; distribution of, 98–105, 345; eating restrictions surrounding, 112–13; greeting, 49, 96, 268; heads, care of, 105–107; and humans, 5, 6, 7; hunting, 49, 75, 134, 127–42; *ikuyguuq* (ringed seal), 284; oil from, 18, 25, 197; as people, 60–62, 141; rules surround-

ing treatment of, 89–113; skin, 134; spirit, 139–40; thirst for fresh water, 91; view of humans as birds, 127–42; young boy's first catch, 184–86. *See also* Bladder Festival

Sea mammals, 17, 33, 36, 89, 117. *See also* Seals; Walrus; Whales

Senses, restricted, 9

Serov, Sergie, 75 n, 216 n, 227 n, 229 n

Sexual activity, 248, 285–86; proscribed, 166, 186, 233, 285

Shades. *See* Human shade

Shaman, 3, 5, 9, 30, 94, 115, 130, 142, 183, 243, 294, 328, 356; as healer, 196, 201, 202, 203–10, 360; initiation of, 107; journey of, 167, 181, 256, 260, 262, 264, 289, 291, 292, 308–15; during Kelek, 304–23; rituals, 140; shade of, 247; story, 236–38, 284. *See also* Angalkuq; Kelek

Shares (*nengit*), 103, 186

Sharing, 104–105, 198, 248. *See also* Seals: distribution of

Shellfish, 18, 25

Shrew, 75

Siberia, 10

Siberian Yup'ik Eskimo, 105, 193, 215 n, 225 n, 262 n, 272 n, 359; hunting ceremonies, 128, 137, 360–61; naming, 244

Sickness. *See* Disease

Sight. *See* Vision

Skull, 106, 139, 220. *See also* Head

Skyland, 116, 239, 259, 260, 262, 264, 305, 310, 311, 358

Sleep, 9; avoidance of, 95, 149–50, 175, 191, 192; seals' avoidance of, 94, 128–31

Smith, Helen, 195

Smoke, purification with. *See* Tarvaryaraq

Snowshoe hare. *See* Hare

Socialization. *See* Children: instruction of

Sod house (*ena*), 33, 34, 37, 38, 39; girls' training in, 149; as womb, 180–81, 249, 251; and Yup'ik spatial orientation, 251–57

Solstice. *See* Winter solstice

Songs, 64, 65, 69; asking, 326–27, 336, 345; for bladders, 96, 270, 271, 276, 283–84, 288; bones singing, 107; in healing, 209; of indigestion, 334–36, 347; of shaman, 309, 311; of supplication, 304–305, 320

Soot. *See* Lamp, seal-oil: soot

Soul, 51, 53, 213, 216; loss of, 210; Yup'ik concept of, 243. *See also* Unguva

Spatial orientation, 251–65

Starvation, 183. *See also* Famine

Stealing words, 146

Stebbins elders, 252, 326, 328, 330, 336, 343, 345, 367

Story dances. *See* Yurapiit

Story knife (*yaaruin*), 126

Strathern, Marilyn, 49

Suicide, 40, 42, 239, 362

Sunny, Magdeline, 78, 156

Sweat bath, 36, 138, 252; at Bladder Festival, 273, 280, 285, 296, 297; purification by, 186, 309

Talarun, 202

Taluyaq. *See* Fishing: trap

Tarneq, 210, 212, 213, 217, 227, 228, 239, 243, 244, 249. *See also* Human shade

Tarvaryaraq (purification with smoke), 91–92, 198–200; at Bladder Festival, 277, 286; following a death, 229–30, 233–34

Tears. *See* River of tears

Teasing, 144–45; at Kevgiq, 330, 332, 334–35, 348–54

Teknonomy, 246

Tengesqaukar, 183

Tengmiarpiit (giant birds), 85, 124, 258

Tenguirayulit (extraordinary persons), 79–80, 86

Therchik, Albert, 98, 103

Therchik, Gertrude, 95, 160, 162, 180, 182, 184, 231

Thin earth, 63, 79, 259, 264, 360; origin of, 258

Thunderbirds. *See* Tengmiarpiit

Toksook Bay Elders, 54, 59, 92, 101, 143, 172, 173, 174, 175, 179, 199, 214, 215, 216, 217, 228, 229, 232, 233, 234, 236, 267, 273, 287, 291, 294, 332, 342

Tomcod, 17

Tommy, Elsie, 207, 229, 294

Tony, Agnes, 192

Totem, hunter's, 112

Traders, 32, 33, 257

Trapping, 28, 40

Tumaralria, 75

Tununak, 220–24

Tuunraq (familiar spirit), 181, 208, 212, 252, 284, 312–13, 316, 320, 358

Tyson, William, 177, 183, 229

Ulurrugnaq (creature), 86

Umialik (whaling captain), 37

Umkumiut, 40, 108, 109

Ungalek, 56

Unguva (life, *unguvii* its life), 51, 89, 107, 130, 164, 212, 268
Uqiquq (seal party), 98–101, 103–104, 345
Urine, 149, 197; washing with, 182, 247, 252, 298, 360
Usugan, Frances, 46, 52, 64, 65, 74, 83, 108, 143, 144, 145, 154, 276, 277, 284

Vision: impaired, 94; powerful supernatural, 9, 168, 204–205, 208, 210, 262, 265, 266, 303, 316; restricted, 9, 161, 168, 187, 188, 266; strong, 82, 356
Visor, 130. *See also* Hunting: hats
Voblov, 360, 361

Wagner, Roy, 48, 49, 356
Walrus, 17, 18, 62, 164, 360; bladder, 281, 284; distribution of, 101, 104; mask, 318; skull, 105, 107
Warfare, bow-and-arrow, 29, 183; end of, 325–26; songs of, 283, 340; through dance, 328–29, 340–42
War on Poverty, 39
Waskie, Agnes, 333
Weather, 163, 165; attention to, 150–52; ceremony to influence, 260, 262–63, 359; dangerous conditions of, 161–62, 204
Whales, 18, 360; belukha, 25, 26, 61, 67, 75, 104, 106, 108, 111, 115, 117, 118, 135, 164, 229; bowhead, 30; killer, 74, 75
Whymper, E., 259
Wild celery (*tarvaq*), 18, 91, 198, 202–203; in Bladder Festival, 271, 279–80, 286, 292–93; in Elriq, 300; female flesh of, 184; *kangaciqaq* made from, 287–88

Williams, Jack, 128
Winter solstice, 163, 264, 267, 268, 297
Wolf, 62, 75, 113, 115, 118, 337; *ircenrrat* as, 63, 67–74; whale as, 111
Wolfe, Virginia, 46
Wolverine, 60
Women: bad air of, 9, 166–68, 192, 193, 210; inactivity of, 94–95; odor of, 96, 98; power of, 163–69; types of, 178; work of, 18, 37
Woods, Frank, 19
Worm, Mary, 114, 150, 164, 225, 245

Yaaruin (story knife), 126
Yua (its person; plural, *yuit*), 51, 58, 59, 91, 146, 212, 304; animal's, 88, 118, 140, 173, 239, 256, 310, 316, 319–20, 323; seal's, 6, 98, 107, 187, 211, 213, 278, 280, 286, 298
Yuk (person; plural, *yuut*), 10, 51, 63, 303
Yukon-Kuskokwim Delta, 11; climate, 14, 25, 28; commercial resources, 30, 31–32; economy, 40, 42; fauna, 14–28; flora, 14, 25; history, 29–34, 38–45; population, 28–29, 31, 38, 39–40; prehistory, 10; topography, 10
Yukon River, 10, 14, 25, 31, 39
Yup'ik, 10; cultural identity, 42, 45, 362–70; language, 10, 34, 42, 76–77, 118. *See also* Siberian Yup'ik Eskimo
Yup'ik Eskimo Dictionary, 10 n
Yupiit Nation's Traditional Governance Project, 45
Yurait (verse/chorus dances), 340
Yurapiit (story dances), 340–42
Yuuciq (lifeline), 212